How Might We Live?
Global Ethics in a New Century

CAMBRIDGE
UNIVERSITY PRESS

PUBLISHED BY THE PRESS SYNDICATE OF THE UNIVERSITY OF CAMBRIDGE
The Pitt Building, Trumpington Street, Cambridge, United Kingdom

CAMBRIDGE UNIVERSITY PRESS
The Edinburgh Building, Cambridge CB2 2RU, UK
40 West 20th Street, New York, NY 10011-4211, USA
10 Stamford Road, Oakleigh, Melbourne 3166, Australia
Ruiz de Alarcón 13, 28104 Madrid, Spain

© British International Studies Association 2001

First published 2001

Printed in the United Kingdom by Henry Ling Ltd at the
Dorset Press, Dorchester, Dorset

A catalogue record for this book is available from the British Library

Library of Congress Cataloguing in Publication data
How Might We Live? Global Ethics in a New Century / edited by Ken Booth, Tim Dunne
and Michael Cox.
p. cm.
Includes bibliographical references and index.
1. Ethics. 2. Globalization—Moral and ethical aspects. I. Booth, Ken, 1943— II. Dunne, Timothy,
1965— III. Cox, Michael, 1947—

BJ1031 .H78 2001
172'.4—dc21

2001025800

ISBN 0 521 00520 5 Paperback

How Might We Live? Global Ethics in a New Century

CONTENTS

NOTES ON CONTRIBUTORS

Philip Allott is Professor of International Public Law and Fellow of Trinity College, Cambridge.

Ken Booth is E.H. Carr Professor of International Politics and Head of Department, in the Department of International Politics at the University of Wales, Aberystwyth.

Michael Cox is Professor in the Department of International Politics at the University of Wales, Aberystwyth.

Robert Cox is Professor Emeritus of Political Science at York University, Toronto.

Michael Doyle is Director of the Center for International Studies in the Woodrow Wilson School of Public and International Affairs, Princeton University.

Tim Dunne is Senior Lecturer in the Department of International Politics at the University of Wales, Aberystwyth.

Derek Heater was formerly Dean of Cultural and Social Studies at Brighton Polytechnic.

Richard Higgott is Professor of International Political Economy and Director of the Centre for the Study of Globalisation and Regionalisation, University of Warwick.

Kimberley Hutchings is Senior Lecturer in the Department of Politics, University of Edinburgh.

Peter Jones is Professor of Political Philosophy, University of Newcastle.

Kenan Malik is a writer and journalist.

Mary Midgely, writer and broadcaster, was formerly Senior Lecturer in Philosophy, University of Newcastle.

Terry Nardin is Professor in the Department of Political Science, University of Wisconsin-Milwaukee.

Onora O'Neill is Principal of Newnham College, Cambridge and Honorary Fellow of Somerville College.

ACKNOWLEDGEMENTS

The arrival of most of the essays for this third Special Issue of the *Review of International Studies* saw the ending of Fiona Stephen's time as Editorial Assistant. We want to record our warm thanks for the professionalism, commitment and cheer she has given us over the last three years not only in relation to the Special Issues but also in contributing to making the *Review* the Journal it has become. We wish her well in her new career.

The continued support of BISA is central to the success of the Journal and the Special Issues, and we want to express our appreciation for the advice and backing of the members of both the Editorial Committee and the Executive Committee, and in particular to the outgoing Chair of the Association, Professor Christopher Hill. Thanks are due to Professor Hill for agreeing to write the Foreword to a set of essays which in their nature are challenging and wide-ranging. The direct and indirect backing of the Department of International Politics at the University of Wales, through resources and other types of support, continues to be essential to the operation of the *Review*. On the production side, it is a pleasure to work with such a professional group of people as those in the journal division at Cambridge University Press, and in particular Sue Belo, Michael Cook, Gwenda Edwards, John Haslam, Patrick McCartan and Kate Wain. We would also like to express our gratitude to the anonymous readers whose advice was sought in the production of this volume.

The final pulling together of this third Special Issue, and seeing it through to publication, was undertaken by our new Editorial Assistant, Cindy Germain. We wish to express our thanks to her for hitting the ground running, and we hope she enjoys her time with the *Review*.

Ken Booth, Tim Dunne and Michael Cox

FOREWORD

The British approach to the study of international relations has always been eclectic and interdisciplinary. This has been reflected in the twenty-six years of the British International Studies Association's activities, including particularly its influential Journal, the *Review of International Studies*. The *Review* has accordingly never taken refuge in the safe or the scholastic, and the recent innovation of a Special Issue has permitted attention to be concentrated on the big issues of our time. The first two of these dealt with the state of our discipline and the condition of the contemporary international system respectively. The third, presented to you here in the book form which has become customary so as to reach a wider audience, treats the largest theme imaginable: how human beings can and should live at the start of the third millennium.

The starting-point is that of international relations, yet the ensuing discussion has no limits. This is not a book of moral philosophy, but nor is it a book showing what moral philosophy has to bring to our own profession. Rather, it is a demonstration of how any consideration of ethical issues in our time has to take account of the international dimension. International Studies woke up over twenty years ago to the fact that the normative flame, kept alight by a few determined characters, not least in the United Kingdom, needed carrying to every corner of the subject. Now it can be more self-confident, by showing those in other areas of intellectual and political life that our particular debates are of central relevance to the great dilemmas of the day.

This book demonstrates irresistibly that issues like communitarianism versus cosmopolitanism, the ethical implications of globalization and the degree of priority to give to international laws or norms, are both inherently transdisciplinary and already well-developed within international studies. It also shows how important it is not to divorce reason from history, or theory from practice. Ideas and principles help to shape actions, while changing empirical realities throw up endless new moral choices—or at least, old choices in new forms. *How Might We Live* has assembled a notable array of talent to meet its challenge. Its contributors have provided a wide range of clear and cogent entry-points to the discussion, for the many readers who will be knowledgeable about international relations but not specialists in moral or political philosophy. In bringing them together the Editors have helped us all take an important step forward, by opening out the debate across disciplinary as well as merely territorial frontiers. Whether we end up stressing the virtues of a particular community or of ethical globalism, we can only do so by participating in the rich dialectics on offer here.

Professor Christopher Hill
Chair
British International Studies Association, 1998–2000

How might we live? Global ethics in a new century

Introduction

KEN BOOTH, TIM DUNNE, MICHAEL COX

Choice is at the heart of ethics, but our choices are never entirely free. Human choice is fettered by history, by context, by biology, by expected consequences and by imagination. Every choice has a history, and a price. In world politics, the scope for choice seems particularly fettered. Historical and geographical contextualization, and projected price have meant that politics beyond state borders has traditionally been understood as an arena of necessity, not ethics. Choice may never be entirely free, but neither is it totally determined; to argue it is, as a result of biology, the unconscious, predestination or whatever would be to abolish ethics. This is not our position, or that of the contributors. We do however recognize that the fettering of ethical choice begins at birth.

Humans are nationalized or tribalized once we are born almost as quickly as we are genderized. We learn to live in concentric circles of loyalty, sympathy, duty and conceptions of justice; and for the most part, the tighter the circle, the stronger have been the moral codes shaping behaviour. Even so, the idea that there are natural limits to ethics has not gone uncontested. There has been a long tradition—while still privileging the family bond—which has stressed the need to think ethically from the outside inwards, rather than the opposite. Conceiving ethics from what Henry Sidgwick called 'the point of view of the universe' (an all-embracing perspective which accords strangers no less consideration than one's own kind, however defined)[1] has been a two-thousand year tradition. Politically speaking, though, this tradition has been significantly more marginal than those in-group perspectives which have begun at the hearth and have kept duties and obligations within the boundaries of 'blood and belonging'.[2]

The question *How Might We Live?* in the context of world politics is therefore not simply an invitation to discuss ethical ideas and moral codes—what constitutes a virtuous character and right and wrong behaviour. It is an invitation to do so in the context of boundaries—between peoples and between polities. What are the limits to the 'we' in the question forming the title of this volume? In the eight decades since the academic discipline of International Relations was invented, its students have generally coalesced around a common understanding of the answer. The natural limit to politically relevant ethics has been seen to be a state's boundary. The operational cry has been 'my country right or wrong', even when the country

---

[1] Quoted by Peter Singer, *How Are We to Live? Ethics in an Age of Self-Interest* (Oxford: Oxford University Press, 1997), p. 263.
[2] For an account of a particularly virulent contemporary manifestation of this, see Michael Ignatieff, *Blood and Belonging: Journeys into the New Nationalism* (London: Vintage, 1994).

concerned has been aggressive or oppressive. What has mattered more has been the 'my' not the 'right or wrong'.

This volume examines major questions thrown up by contending traditions about ethics in the global context, at a time when six billion humans look towards the promise and dangers of a new century. How might we live in the face of the dynamics of this first truly global age? In the context of present-day and future global transformations, the contributors below discuss some of the oldest questions about duties and obligations within and beyond humanly constructed boundaries. In so doing, they help us ponder what we consider to be the most profound question in world politics today: who will the twenty-first century be for? This Special Issue is the logical extension of the first two Special Issues of the *Review of International Studies*. *The Eighty Years' Crisis*[3] discussed the development of the academic subject of International Relations from its origins in 1919, while *The Interregnum*[4] examined the major controversies attempting to explain the dynamics of world politics in the decade following the end of the Cold War. The third now asks how might human societies live. In contrast to the orthodoxies of academic Philosophy and International Relations in much of the twentieth-century, which marginalized or rejected the study of ethics, the contributors to this volume assume and assert the belief that politics and ethics are as inseparable as politics and power.

A point of view emphasizing the unity of politics and ethics would have struck many students and practitioners of International Relations over the years as misconceived. Critics of this view would include students of statecraft who have talked of 'balancing' power and morality (how can one balance what cannot be separated?). A recent and high profile illustration of a group of policymakers conceiving power and morality to be distinct were those members of the New Labour Government advocating an 'ethical foreign policy'; this idea wrongly implied the possibility of ethic-free as opposed to differently-ethical foreign policies. Foreign policy is always an-ethics-in-action; one can no more conceive foreign policy quarantined from ethical considerations and implications than one can conceive foreign policy quarantined from power considerations and implications. A point of view rejecting the unity of politics and ethics is itself a particular ethical perspective. The marginalizing of normative thinking in academic International Relations is not a point of view supported by the contributors in this volume.

The 1980s witnessed a growing sense of intellectual inadequacy within many sections of the discipline; the collective failure to foresee the end of the Cold War seemed to be another exposure of the discipline's weaknesses and some vindication of the growing concerns—though the critics did not prove themselves to be any more successful at prediction. This historic turning point confirmed the professional impulse to engage in a season of considerable self-criticism: after the Cold War, the cold shower. But the discipline was never as impoverished—or uniquely blinkered—as was asserted by some of those who attacked it. In this regard, it is important to remember that for a long period what one of us has described as the ethic cleansing of academic International Relations was only a reflection of what was happening in academic Philosophy itself. The latter, from the start of the twentieth century, fell

---

[3] Tim Dunne, Michael Cox, and Ken Booth (eds.), *The Eighty Years' Crisis: International Relations 1919–1999* (Cambridge: Cambridge University Press, 1998).
[4] Michael Cox, Ken Booth, and Tim Dunne (eds.), *The Interregnum: Controversies in World Politics 1989–1999* (Cambridge: Cambridge University Press, 1999).

under the sway of one particular school—that of analytical philosophy—which argued that because ethical claims are beyond proof or testability, deriving as they do from emotions or subjective opinions, that they are not therefore appropriate for philosophical enquiry.[5] Analytical philosophy, which included logical positivism, ruled out speculation about the supernatural ontologies and other beliefs that make up moral philosophy. In their striving for objectivity the logical positivists, for example, rejected philosophizing about the meaning of life—which involves questions about right and wrong—and instead advocated that the philosophical investigation of language was as far as philosophers could go, even though some recognized that this meant they could not go very far. In Britain, modern scepticism about moral philosophy appeared well before the invention of academic International Relations, with G.E. Moore's *Principia Ethica* in 1903; it was then consolidated for a generation with A.J. Ayer's *Language, Truth and Logic*, which appeared in 1936, just at the time the reaction was setting in against what is usually taken to be the initial utopian phase of the new subject of International Relations.[6]

If the continental (mainly Austrian) influence within analytical philosophy at the start of the century in Britain was stronger than has sometimes been credited by British writers—Anglo-Saxon pragmatism has been a more intuitive explanation—there has certainly been no underestimation of continental influence on a later manifestation of moral scepticism in Philosophy, this time in the last third of the century. This later manifestation, post-structuralism, had its mainspring in France, and has been influential in many areas of thought, including academic International Relations. The post-structuralist turn in the history of ideas developed—albeit somewhat ambiguously to some of its 'leading' thinkers[7]—into a confrontation with Enlightenment thinking. This included the latter's concern with ethics based on reason and related ideas of progress and emancipation. The move to deconstruction was in part a move against the established 'foundations' of ethics.

The success of this intellectual movement committed to deconstruction seemed to be confirmed when the term 'post-modernism' entered the mainstream; and by dextrous self-labelling, the post-modernists seemed to have done to so-called modernists what self-labelled realists had earlier done to utopians in the discipline of International Relations. Labelling is one of the tactical moves in all intellectual struggles. The exponents of post-modernism made an exception to their usual critique of progress by at least implying that the signifier 'post' had more than chronological significance; their self-label implied not only that the Enlightenment was dead, but that what had taken its place represented intellectual improvement. This viewpoint, as Martha Nussbaum has gently hinted, has been reinforced in teaching situations by the tendency of its advocates to give post-modernism 'the last word, as though it had eclipsed Enlightenment thinking'.[8] The debate between post-modernists and other schools of thought within both International Relations and

---

[5] A standard work is Michael Dummett, *Origins of Analytical Philosophy* (London: Duckworth, 1993)

[6] E.H. Carr's *Twenty Years' Crisis* is seen as the key work ending the 'idealist'—or as Carr called it, the 'utopian' phase of the discipline. For an account of the ostensible debate between inter-war idealists and realists, see Peter Wilson, 'The Myth of the First Great Debate' in Dunne, Cox and Booth (eds.), *The Eighty Years' Crisis.*

[7] Explored in N. J. Rengger, *Political Theory, Modernity and Postmodernity: Beyond Enlightenment and Critique* (Oxford: Blackwell, 1995).

[8] Martha C. Nussbaum, *Cultivating Humanit:. A Classical Defense of Reform in Liberal Education* (Cambridge MA: Harvard University Press, 1997), p. 77.

Philosophy goes on, though perhaps not as aggressively as a decade ago. Some common ground has been found, with some International Relations scholars engaging with issues relating to language and social construction, while some post-modernists/post-structuralists have shown that their views of the Enlightenment have not always been as extreme as their reputation.[9] A giant among post-modernists, Richard Rorty—albeit in a footnote in his much-cited Oxford Amnesty lecture in 1993—clearly rejected the view that Enlightenment ideas about human freedom were obsolete, and asserted that 'nobody has come up with a better[project].[10]

One important theme in the post-structuralist critique of orthodox International Relations has been to raise awareness about the relationship between power and knowledge. The influence of Michel Foucault has obviously been central in this.[11] But the relationship between power and ideas had already been an important theme in some realist writings in International Relations for some time. In his classic *Twenty Years' Crisis 1919–1939*, Carr had clinically revealed the synergy between international morality and international law and the interests and preferences of the great powers.[12] But earlier than Carr, Gramsci had written about 'hegemony' and 'common sense' in relation to the values and attitudes that served the powerful.[13] Much earlier still, at the very birth of Western philosophy, Plato asked us to think, through the words of Thrasymachus, whether 'the just is nothing other than the advantage of the stronger'. [14]

The relationship between power and ideas is important, and more complex than either realists or post-structuralists usually suggest. Some ideas are backed with more effective power than others; as we said at the start, no choice is entirely free. Our choices are shaped by structures of power. But we also stressed the centrality of choice. The market-places as well as the battle-grounds of ethical contestation have been important sites for shaping the human story. The landscape of all politics, including the world arena, would look markedly different if humans were not what one of the contributors to the volume, Mary Midgley, has called 'ethical primates'.[15] We are as we are on a global scale, in part, because of the contestation of ethics, as well as the contestation of political power, and the two are not simply and directly related. They are importantly interwoven, but they are not synonymous. Christianity and Islam began as the religions of the utterly weak, not religions of state power;

---

[9] Steve Smith, "The Self Images of a Discipline: A Genealogy of International Relations Theory," in Ken Booth and Steve Smith (eds.), *International Relations Theory Today* (Cambridge: Polity Press, 1995), pp. 1–37.

[10] See Richard Rorty, 'Human Rights, Rationality and Sentimentality' in Stephen Shute and Susan Hurley (eds.), *On Human Rights: the Oxford Amnesty Lectures 1993* (New York: Basic Books, 1993), p. 246. For a critical discussion of Rorty's position see Norman Geras, *The Contract of Mutual Indifference: Political Philosophy after the Holocaust* (London: Verso, 1998), pp. 121–4, 130–8.

[11] Michel Foucault, *Power/Knowledge: Selected Interviews and other Writings 1972–1977*, edited by Colin Gordon (Brighton: Harvester, 1980); Michel Foucault, 'Truth and Power', in Paul Rabinow (ed.), *The Foucault Reader* (New York: Pantheon Books, 1984), pp. 51–75. For an overview of Foucault's thinking as it might be relevant to International Relations, see Jenny Edkins, *Post-Structuralism in International Relations* (Boulder, CO: Lynne Rienner, 1999).

[12] Edward Hallett Carr, *The Twenty Years' Crisis 1919–39*, 2nd. edn. (London: Macmillan, 1946).

[13] David Forgacs (ed.), *A Gramsci Reader: Selected Writings 1919–1935* (London: Lawrence and Wishart, 1988). The glossary of entries on 'common sense' (p. 421) and 'hegemony' (pp. 422–4) give detailed references to Gramsci's writings on these themes.

[14] *The Republic of Plato*, trans. with notes by Alan Bloom, 2nd edn. (New York: Basic Books, 1991), pp. 15–34.

[15] Mary Midgley, *The Ethical Primate. Humans, Freedom and Morality* (London: Routledge, 1994).

and democracy and anti-colonial nationalism began as political ideas shared by a few dissidents, not as the dreams of emperors. Power is sometimes in the idea, rather than the idea being in the interests of the contingently powerful.[16]

Despite the emphasis so far on the marginalization of ethics in mainstream thinking about international politics, the discipline conventionally originated and was nourished in the normative commitment of the idealists who helped shape its development in the early inter-war years. But soon an increasingly stubborn resistance developed. Important students of world affairs rejected the idea that ethics belonged in the international arena; this was hardly surprising during what Winston Churchill[17] famously called 'the gathering storm' of international affairs in the 1930s, and then its cataclysmic aftermath in a World War of unparalleled destruction. The academic discipline gathered serious momentum after 1945, and in historic conditions that confirmed rather than undermined realist certainties about the primacy of power and the dangers of dreamers. During the years in which the Cold War intensified, the doctrine of realism seemed to provide a thoroughly plausible rationale for understanding and countering the Soviet threat. But the historical dynamics were always much more complex than the orthodox account propagated— as were the theoretical implications. Realist accounts imply that there is an independent real world that directly generates our explanation of events; we observe, as social scientists, and describe. But this viewpoint does not recognize the extent to which ideas constitute the fabric of the social world. In the Cold War realism provided both a language and a set of policy prescriptions for operating in a world of its own making; its exponents did not see the way in which the theory they claimed was explaining state behaviour was actually helping to constitute that very behaviour. It was self-fulfilling. The almost half-century of bipolarity after 1945, characterized by a sense of constant danger, with the balance of power resting on the threat of Mutual Assured Destruction, was not explained by realism; it was the product of a particularly totalizing form of traditional realist thinking about international politics.

Accounts of how realism came to dominate the study of International Relations have been told many times.[18] It is important to stress here the extent to which a particular form of scientific realism developed in the United States after 1945. The research infrastructure of the major foundations was directed to funding strategic studies and the scientific study of foreign policy. Normative concerns were largely put on hold.[19] That said, there were some notable exceptions. It is important not to exaggerate the extent to which the discipline ignored ethical issues. Peace research was very explicitly value-driven even when it relied on positivist methods.[20] As in the

[16] See Ken Booth, 'Three Tyrannies', in Tim Dunne and Nicholas J. Wheeler (eds.), *Human Rights in Global Politics* (Cambridge: Cambridge University Press, 1999), pp. 53–55.

[17] Winston Churchill, *The Second World War: Volume 1, The Gathering Storm* (London: Cassell, 1964).

[18] Standard accounts include, among others: K. J. Holsti, *The Dividing Discipline: Hegemony and Diversity in International Theory* (Boston, MA: Unwin Hyman, 1995); W. C. Olsen and A. J. R. Groom, *International Relations Then and Now: Origins and Trends in Interpretation* (London: Unwin Hyman, 1991).

[19] This argument is made by Miles Kahler, 'Inventing International Relations Theory after 1945', in Michael Doyle and G. John Ikenberry (eds.), *New Thinking in International Relations Theory* (Boulder, CO: Westview, 1997).

[20] See Peter Lawler, *A Question of Values: Johan Galtung's Peace Research* (Boulder, CO: Lynne Reinner, 1995). This point is also made by Andrew Linklater in his 'General Introduction' to Linklater (ed.), *International Relations: Critical Concepts in Political Science*, vols. I–V (London: Routledge, 2000), pp. 3–4.

inter-war years international law was the point of departure for many normative theorists. This included some notable participants in The World Order Models Project, which was established as an explicitly value-oriented scholarly approach to world politics.[21] Some interest in human rights was evident throughout the era of realist hegemony,[22] and there were analyses of the moral practices of statecraft, particularly in relation to the threat and use of nuclear weapons and the ancient doctrine of Just War. In addition, in Britain a group of scholars set themselves the task of attempting to elucidate the rules, institutions and obligations that distinguished modern international society from earlier states-systems; this was a task that had important ethical as well as historical dimensions.[23] Although the realist domination of the subject was considerable—with its views about the autonomy of the domestic and international realms, and its associated assumptions about domestic politics being an arena of choice while international politics is one of necessity—these examples show that normative traditions never died out in the discipline, even though the agenda was overwhelmingly set by the concerns of the realists. An important and positive turning point in this history of the separation of the ethical and the international came with the publication of Michael Walzer's *Just and Unjust Wars* in 1977.[24] In this volume a distinguished political philosopher turned his attention to the subject matter that had given birth to the academic discipline of International Relations.

Realism and neo-realism continue to hold their sway in important centres where the discipline is professed, especially in the United States. Even so, there are many departments and institutes where academic International Relations is studied, and even some foreign ministries where it is practised, in which it is recognized that we have to understand ethics *in* world politics and not ethics *and* world politics. Ethics are not separate. They cannot be mixed in and stirred; every foreign policy is an ethical one.

The scholarly examination of questions concerning the principles that guide and ought to guide the conduct of world affairs at all levels have become much more respectable in International Relations. To an important degree, the subject has come home to its normative beginnings, though with much greater sophistication than was the case in the 1920s. Important contributions to this development through the 1990s were Chris Brown's *International Theory: New Normative Approaches* and Andrew Linklater's *The Transformation of Political Community*.[25] This momentum helped contribute to a livelier state of thinking about ethics in world politics at the cusp of the new century; however, like realism's rise a half-century earlier, this development has been importantly contextual. The ending of the Cold War seemed

[21] Richard Falk, *A Study of Future Worlds* (New York: Free Press, 1975).
[22] See, for example, Richard Falk's key book, *Human Rights and State Sovereignty* (New York: Holmes and Meier, 1981).
[23] Herbert Butterfield and Martin Wight (eds.), *Diplomatic Investigations: Essays on the Theory of International Politics* (London: Allen and Unwin, 1966); Martin Wight, *Systems of States*, edited by Hedley Bull (Leicester, UK: Leicester University Press, 1978), and Hedley Bull and Adam Watson (eds.), *The Expansion of International Society* (Oxford: Oxford University Press, 1985).
[24] Michael Walzer, *Just and Unjust Wars: A Moral Argument with Historical Illustrations* (New York: Basic Books, 1977). Another key work in the normative turn was Beitz's extension of Rawlsian principles of distributive justice globally; see Charles R. Beitz, *Political Theory and International Relations*, 1st edn. (Princeton, NJ: Princeton University Press, 1979).
[25] Chris Brown, *International Relations Theory: New Normative Approaches* (London: Harvester, 1992); Andrew Linklater, *The Transformation of Political Community* (Cambridge: Polity, 1998).

to open up more space for normative thinking, while the new century focused thinking on the convergence of global problems. This volume attempts to make a small contribution to this body of literature.

In the choice of areas to explore, the editors necessarily had to be selective. Several key areas had to be omitted, for reasons of space or circumstance. The aim was to open up issues rather than attempt to provide policy prescriptions, though the latter is of interest to all students of International Relations, and for the most part why we are interested in theory and ethics: not for their own sake, but for what they can contribute to how people live. If policy prescriptions are not an outcome of this volume, there are some common themes running through the contributions. We do not wish to impose any artificial uniformity on the essays, but would point to several arguments that figure in the contributions to a greater or lesser degree. These are: the value of thinking holistically, though the decks are usually stacked against such an approach; a rejection of determinism in human society, as opposed to an emphasis on human choice, construction, and the opening up of possibility; the inevitability of moral reasoning for the 'ethical primate'; the mutuality of politics and ethics; the tension between moral universalism and political particularism, marked by an ancient debate over the limits of justice in terms of political boundaries and a more recent debate over the referents for justice; the sense that the decades ahead will be particularly significant in human history because of changing material realities—globalization and all its works; the importance of practical reasoning in the context of ethical sophistication; and the false opposition of wholes and parts in world politics—cosmopolitanism and communitarianism, universalism and particularism—and the need to better negotiate the theoretical and practical common ground.

One idea suggested by several contributors later is the view that cosmopolitan writing over time has become more sophisticated. Defenders of such thinking have sometimes had their own work labelled as 'Kantian', which for some critics implies the embracing of an out-of-date package of 'Enlightenment' outlooks (with all this implies for their views about international politics, including an untenable universalism). It is instructive however, to compare the stereotyping of cosmopolitan thinking with the nuance in the actual arguments made by those making the case for thinking universally. Note, for example: Mary Midgley's criticism of the exclusivist humanism and reductive scientific thinking identified with the Enlightenment; the criticism by both Philip Allott and Kimberley Hutchings of the way universalist thinking about human rights can hide particularist interests; Onora O'Neill's clear understanding of the strengths of communitarian ethics; and Michael Doyle's acceptance of the limitations on Kantian thinking about international politics. In the 'cosmopolitan' arguments in this volume there is no agreement about the institutions to deliver it, no facile optimism about the prospects for humanity, and no other-worldliness about the real world of politics.

Taking the point of view of the universe—Henry Sidgwick's phrase mentioned earlier—necessarily involves ethical perspectives that are truly all-embracing, including duties to the non-sentient world, as well as to sentient beings, and this is the approach endorsed in the first essay, by Mary Midgley. It is an approach she emphasizes as being anything but other-worldly: it is, she argues, eminently practical and urgent. Hence, her essay explores ethical questions on the broadest stage of all. The argument is that our duties should not be confined within human or even animal boundaries, but that the condition of global affairs is such that we should think much more seriously—indeed with urgency—about duties to the non-animal world as well.

Despite talk about 'the environment' as a problem in international relations since the 1970s, it is still not treated sufficiently seriously in Midgley's opinion. It is generally seen as an issue at the level of foreign policy rather than being the comprehensive global problem the essay seeks to emphasize. She sees serious thought from this perspective as having been the almost exclusive preserve of global civil society. At the level of states exceptions are rare, and have mostly occurred in the governments of small nations.

The focus of Midgley's essay is the idea of Gaia, and her belief that this is not some New Age fantasy, but a 'really useful idea'. She believes that Gaia—the conception of 'life on earth being a self-sustaining natural system'—is a 'cure' for the problems created by current world-views. Current ways of thinking, she argues, trap us in seventeenth-century images of social life, which she sums up as 'crude and arid', in both their Christian and secular forms; such images have generally been exclusively tailored to cater for human aspirations, and this means that the thought that we might have a duty to something so clearly non-human as the whole natural system of the earth is a difficult one to comprehend. Nevertheless, such would be a more realistic view of the earth, and she believes that this can give us a more realistic view of ourselves.

After explaining Gaian thinking today, Midgley argues that the imaginative vision behind it is very old and is recognizable in many cultures. However, the holistic perspective it represents has been abused by atomistic and reductive explanations in much modern science. She does not underestimate the difficulty of changing our minds, but says the world is simply too rich and complex for reductive strait-jacketing. The latter has been powerful in science and elsewhere, but she sees the growing environmental crisis as a critical factor helping to bring about the needed shift in thinking. She does not offer political solutions in this essay, but rather emphasizes that there is a need for change, and that change is possible. This entails moving from reductivism to holism, from the curiosity of the researcher (though this must be kept) to the imagination of the artist, and from the dualistic notion of ourselves as detached observers separate from the physical world to seeing ourselves as an integral part of it, and it of us. Humans have been urged to wage a war against nature over the centuries, and so we are unable to think of nature as vulnerable, capable of injury and sickness. But the living processes that have kept the natural system working have now been seriously disturbed.

The central message of Midgley's essay is that we—the global we—desperately need to see the problem we face as a whole, and she argues that James Lovelock's metaphor of 'Gaia' is an important way forward. While noting some of the problems in the idea—not least the connotations of the very word 'Gaia' itself—Midgley looks at the positive aspects of conceiving the earth as functioning as an organic whole. She notes the growing scientific acceptability of this outlook, and relates it to a tradition of great scientists who have seen no incompatibility between their scientific research, religious talk, and reverence for the vastness of the issues with which they were grappling.[26]

---

[26] The belief that categories such as wonder and awe are the only possible responses to the natural world in which we find ourselves has long been a theme of Mary Midgley's: see her *Wisdom, Information and Wonder. What is Knowledge For?* (London: Routledge, 1989).

Scientific thinking has not been the only factor inhibiting proper attitudes towards the earth. Midgley identifies others. One has been the humanistic creed which has claimed that only people have value, with the non-human world not mattering except for its relevance for the human. The thought that we might owe a direct duty to the biosphere is therefore seen as puzzling. Another inhibition has been the strength of social contract thinking, which conceptually rules out dealings with anything non-human. So, if duties are conceived as essentially contractual, how can we possibly have duties to the rain forest or Antarctica? Not only is this tradition injurious in terms of dealing with the environmental crisis; according to Midgley, the contract model is notoriously inadequate even within human society.

On a more positive note, she believes that more people—including some scientists—are coming to realize that the human drama is now taking place on the widest stage. She notes: 'The Darwinian perspective on evolution places us firmly in a wider kinship than Descartes or Hobbes ever dreamed of. We know that we belong on this earth.' There is a great deal of 'we' in the essay, but Midgely recognizes that in global terms it does not (yet?) represent most people. Nevertheless, she argues that direct concern about our destruction of nature is a natural, spontaneous feeling and one that we no longer have any good reason to suppress. This sense of shock and outrage is the energy source which makes change possible, but it has not been tapped yet. Only when the threat of a territorial emergency is accepted will there be little doubt about the duty it imposes upon us, and hence will be influential in policy-making. In the meantime, Midgley stresses that selfishness is a surprisingly inefficient guide to policy, and as long as this is dominant, economics will remain a more important science than ecology. In advocating the urgency of transcending the narrow ethos of contract ethics in order to grasp the potentialities of Gaia, Midgley sees the earlier work of John Rawls as having been the definitive statement of contract ethics; but at the same time she believes that it marked the end of the era when such an approach could pass as adequate. This view links directly to an important theme in the following essay, by Onora O'Neill, which discusses one aspect of the work of John Rawls, one of the most prominent political theorists of the past thirty years and one who has extended his earlier theorizing into the international. Aspects of his work are discussed by O'Neill in relation to Kant, the one philosopher from whom nobody can hide when it comes to thinking about ethics in a global context.

The ancient questions O'Neill examines in relation to the work of Rawls and Kant are those relating to the scope of justice. Since earliest times the politically dominating view has held that the context of justice must have boundaries; in parallel with this view has been an alternative perspective arguing that justice by its nature should be cosmopolitan, owed to other humans regardless of contingencies such as location, race or culture. O'Neill considers that framing the ethical debate in terms of cosmopolitanism versus communitarianism is more complex than usually assumed. She argues, for example, that a commitment to cosmopolitan principles does not entail—though it may not rule out—commitment to cosmopolitan political institutions. Accordingly, world government may not necessarily be the most valid institutional expression of universal ethical ideals. In fact, she argues, cosmopolitan justice may be hindered by cosmopolitan institutions, as they risk concentrating global power, with all the problems that raises. Cosmopolitan ideals might well be better served by a separation of powers. Alternatively, bounded institutions may institutionalize justice in ways that exclude some from its benefits and on no better grounds than that some people live on the wrong side of a historically constructed political boundary.

In terms of what she calls 'justice beyond borders', O'Neill begins her comparison by arguing that Kant and Rawls are alert to the claims of both bounded institutions and universal principles. Neither supports the setting up of a world state, but each thinks justice requires more than can be delivered by the internal institutions of states. She offers a strong set of arguments in favour of communitarian thought about justice, but concludes that the 'everyday assumptions' of communitarianism actually undermine its plausibility. Inverting chronology, she first examines the work of Rawls rather than Kant, to see whether he has the answer to the problem of international justice.

In his recent writing, Rawls has explicitly rejected the underlying assumption of the communitarian project. The basis of his argument is that pluralism is the natural outcome of human reason under enduring free institutions. Within each bounded society reasonable persons will not come to complete agreement about ethical matters; they will have different 'conceptions of the good'. As reasonable persons, they may be expected to accept a form of reciprocity. Reasonable persons, committed to a conception of public reason, will attempt to develop workable institutions and justice, despite their irresolvable ethical differences. The key, therefore, is that Rawls's conception of public reason does not assume the shared culture that communitarian reasoning presupposes; it does however presuppose shared political arrangements, including boundaries and (for just societies) liberal democracy and citizenship. The important question O'Neill poses is whether these are state boundaries. The answer offered in *Law of Peoples* by Rawls is that boundaries are important, and prior to justice, but that these boundaries are neither state boundaries nor those set by cultural traditions; what matters for him are liberal peoples. This, for O'Neill, is where his approach becomes problematical for she argues that Rawls's conception of a people, on whom he builds his account of justice beyond borders, is in fact remarkably state-like. She believes that there is little to distinguish liberal peoples from liberal states; and since Rawls holds that peoples can be reasonable whereas states are wedded to rational self-interest, she draws the conclusion that there is a fundamental tension challenging the whole coherence of his argument. She believes that Rawls is anchoring his account of justice in agents who are not well exemplified in the real world, but if they were so exemplified, they would need the (realist state-like) capacities from which he seeks to detach his agents.

Turning to Kant and his account of public reason as freedom without lawlessness, O'Neill discusses his favourite image, that of scholarly communication with the world at large. She expresses her worries about the applicability of this image, and wonders whether a global communication regime could live up to the Kantian ideal of public reason any better than actual communication among scholars. The requirements of reasoned communication themselves need clarifying, and Kant offers some ideas, such as it having to be communicable. Kant of course was addressing his attack against distinct targets in his own time, and O'Neill suggests that Kant's targets today might include post-modernists, new-agers and deconstructionists. The unstructured liberation of thought, Kant believed, would be a disaster and an illusion.

Kant identifies public reason with the requirement of structuring our thought, discourse and action in ways we believe others can follow. He identifies reasoning with the practice of adopting principles of thinking and acting that have a form of law which can be adopted by all. However, he thinks that the implementation of this principle in the actual conditions in which we live is not straightforward. In the actual conditions of world politics—characterized by the competition for scarce resources, the absence of reliable altruism and so on—external freedom will be perpetually insecure without some limited forms of coercion aimed at 'hindering the hindrances of freedom'. In such conditions, the way ahead is through republican states, not anarchy. But for Kant what is of primary importance in this formulation is the republican character of the entities, not their status as states. The latter are not an unconditional requirement for Kant; he fiercely repudiates Hobbes's view that any state is to be preferred to the state of nature. For Kant, state power is not an intrinsic requirement of justice, but rather a historic compromise.

O'Neill then postulates several advantages of an approach to justice across boundaries based on Kant's conception of public reason. She identifies these as follows: it does not presuppose the *status quo*; it does not presuppose any particular institutional structures; it does not ground the account of justice in the realist conception of the state with its ethically disreputable disregard of the moral standing of those beyond one's boundaries; it is not mere abstract cosmopolitanism; it does not contain a puzzling notion of a people as with Rawls; and it is based on a conception of a just world in which cosmopolitan principles of justice are realistically institutionalized in structures which support international justice in the context of legitimate political boundaries. The essay concludes that Kant's strategy may provide a better route for thinking about justice beyond boundaries than the one Rawls offers. Not only is it theoretically deeper, but it is also more realistic and open.

The next two essays exhibit various aspects of Kantian thinking endorsed in principle by O'Neill. They also share her belief that power relations between states are not exempt from considerations of justice, and that the degree of justice available in contemporary world politics is not all that might be achieved.

Philip Allott's contribution is on the theme of self-transformation in the human past, present and future: becoming. Human beings and societies, he argues, are in a constant process of constitution and re-constitution, in which 'the idea of the ideal' has been and remains essential. The ideal is defined as 'the better potentiality of the actual, acting as a moral imperative in the present, with a view to making a better future.' In discussing how the idea of the ideal was made possible, Allott advances a controversial but important argument about the universal power of dialectical thought. He suggests humans may be biologically programmed to think in a binary fashion, a possibility with enormous implications for language, which in turn has given human reality a peculiarly dualistic structure. The dyad of the actual and the ideal has allowed us to make human reality into a moral order.

Allott's perspective is one of social idealism. He argues that the world is made by the human mind, that human reality is constructed collectively, and that we are moral beings; as a result, 'We can make the future but we cannot determine it'. Nowhere is the need for the advancement of social idealism more important for Allott than in international society—which he defines as the society of all–humanity and of all human societies. Allott is scathing about the way in which international society has developed; he describes it as 'the scandal of international unsociety', with its enormous disparities in wealth and life chances. The idea of the ideal is necessary here because the actual self-constituting of international society has historically produced a diseased social reality which threatens the survival of the human species. Despite the inadequacies of the present global situation, Allott intriguingly suggests that there is an unprecedented opportunity for a new human self-enlightening, a New Enlightenment for the new century.

Societies, including international society, constitute themselves in three dimensions: as ideas, as practice, and as law. The latter is Allott's particular concern here, and he proposes that the law is a wonderful creation of the human mind, and the most efficient instrument for the actualizing of the ideal. Thus, to the extent we have justice and liberty in international relations, it is in the form of international law. After explaining the latter's characteristics and functions, he identifies three primary functions of the law which he thinks are especially significant for the actualizing of the legal potentiality of international society: the way in which law makes the economy, makes the public realm, and makes constitutionalism. He sees hope in moving from the real—'the unnatural state of nature'—through globalization from below, involving the propagation of ideas and laws in which humanity repeatedly re-humanizes itself, and thereby conditions the holders of public-realm power.

The second essay with a Kantian inspiration is by Michael Doyle, a writer who has done much to bring Kant into the discourses of contemporary International Relations.[27] His contribution can be seen as a development of some earlier work, but with a more critical edge. He contends that the Kantian peace, for example, 'has significant limitations in the face of increasing globalization'. It also has obvious limits, he believes, in the history of relations between liberal and autocratic states. These are issues that have been sometimes fiercely debated in leading US journals of International Relations.[28]

Doyle then moves to another limitation in Kantian thinking which he thinks has received much less attention. For liberal republics to be self-determining, he argues, the level of interdependence would need to be minimal. This minimal level, according to Doyle, would involve 'some mutual sensitivity, some limited vulnerability, but not enough to challenge the liberal republic's ability to govern itself in the face of social and economic forces outside itself'. This leads Doyle to pose the question: 'can the Kantian liberal peace sustain extensive, "heavy" interdependence?' His answer is complex.

Economic globalization, for Doyle, is eroding the very national accountability that is central to republican states. The norms of non-discrimination advocated by the WTO mean that individual states—or regions—are not able to prevent the import of products they may feel are potentially harmful. Doyle offers the example of the EU's attempt to ban genetically engineered food, a measure that was deemed illegal under international trade law. Globalization is also exacerbating economic inequality as markets concentrate income and wealth in fewer and fewer hands.

[27] Michael Doyle, 'Kant, Liberal Legacies, and Foreign Affairs', *Philosophy and Public Affairs*, 12 (1983), pp. 205–35.

[28] See, among others, Bruce Russett, *Grasping the Democratic Peace* (Princeton, NJ: Princeton University Press, 1993) and the critical response by, among others, Christopher Layne, 'Kant or Cant: The Myth of the Democratic Peace', *International Security* 19: 2 (1994), pp. 87–125. Key articles on the liberal peace are contained in Andrew Linklater (ed.), *International Relations: Critical Concepts in Political Science*, vol. III (London: Routledge, 2000), section 5.

Moreover, the recent history of rapid economic growth in autocratic polities in Asia raises questions about international security and the balance of power beyond the liberal zone. What, then, should our responses be to such challenges? Doyle considers a number of possibilities including 'global democratization'. While he accepts that this is certainly a crucial way of closing the massive legitimacy gap that currently exists in world politics, he is not at all optimistic that the conditions are ripe for such a transformation. He alludes to two structural weaknesses in particular. First, the level of inequality is so great that it will be almost impossible to arrive at consensus on issues concerning trade, development and the environment. Second, the lack of a 'core identity' may also be a significant constraint upon the forging of 'a more perfect union'. Whatever the limitations of the Kantian perspective, and accepting that no single ethical theory can deliver a 'perfect equilibrium', Doyle argues that Kantian liberalism tries to establish 'domestic liberty, republican participation and market democracy' without international anarchy. This appears to be Doyle's version of Kant's historic compromise.

The next essay, by Terry Nardin, takes a distinctive change of direction from those that have preceded it, though it addresses the same central questions. Nardin's contribution contains a defence of pluralism that resonates with some of the arguments advanced by Rawls, who in his *Law of Peoples* argues that pluralism is a 'natural outcome of human reason under enduring free institutions', and who so far in this volume has been on the wrong side of the major arguments. Nardin however identifies with the Rawlsian rather than the Kantian side of the debate discussed by O'Neill, and challenges the sort of universalistic perspective represented by Allott.

Proponents of pluralistic/communitarian/particularistic perspectives on ethics, justice and international politics believe that our obligations to fellow citizens take priority over the lives of strangers belonging to other nations, states, cultures, religions or whatever. 'I am not a citizen of the world', Michael Walzer declared; moreover, 'I am not even aware that there is a world such that one could be a citizen of it'.[29] What matters from this perspective is not some abstract concept of world citizenship but the values and practices—such as language, custom and tradition—that separate 'us' from 'them'. The importance placed upon bounded communities does not mean that there can be no association between the political units to which they belong. To the contrary, it is vital that states agree to respect one another's autonomy so that the pluralist system of states can be maintained. In this respect, an association is formed with the limited aim of facilitating the peaceful coexistence of states. The work of Terry Nardin has long been identified with a normative defence of particularism.[30] He has consistently criticized attempts to turn international society into a community of communities that seeks to arrive at a common morality, and this is the perspective from which Nardin discusses 'International Pluralism and the Rule of Law'.

The problem Nardin focuses upon is that of trying to understand 'the conditions of justice in the emerging, but still pluralist, global order'. He specifically addresses the role of international law in this emerging order—as opposed to 'governance'—and in this shows a similar concern to that of Richard Higgott, in a later essay,

[29] See Michael Walzer, 'Spheres of Affection,' in Martha C. Nussbaum (ed.), *For Love of Country: Debating the Limits of Patriotism* (Boston, MA: Beacon Pess, 1996), pp. 125–7.
[30] Most comprehensively in Terry Nardin, *Law, Morality and the Relations of States* (Princeton, NJ: Princeton University Press, 1983).

which is keen to make distinctions between 'politics' and 'governance'. We see in this contribution Nardin defending a view of international law that is not strictly minimalist (as pluralism is often thought to be); instead he explores a *via media* between positive law and natural law to which he gives the name 'the rule of law'. The aim of his essay is to explore the status of these non-instrumental laws that define and regulate international society. His journey begins with detailed consideration of the two main traditions of thought about the foundations of an international legal order: natural law with its belief that a common moral code can be rationally arrived at, and legal positivism which views international law as a set of customary rules and practices.

The rule of law draws on both of these legal traditions. As is the case with natural law, it invests in law a moral character. In this sense, laws are not commands but rules that constitute the community. Where it departs from natural law is in recognizing that a legal system requires internally coherent procedures for settling conflicts between rules that are valid as law and those that are not. Nardin captures the essence of the rule of law as *via media* in the following sentence: 'The rules of international law should have moral content and they are subject to moral criticism, but their authority as law does not rest on moral criteria'. The rule of law is crucial, he argues, for the functioning of democracy, to guide its discussions and to alter its policies; otherwise democracy is 'discussion unacceptably distorted by unconstrained power.'

Nardin concludes with a forceful plea not to allow the rule of law to become marginal to the theory and practice of international relations. Indeed, he sees the idea of law on the defensive at present both within as well as between states. He senses that the twin challenges of globalization and moral scepticism are beginning to undermine the system of non-instrumental rules that underpin the pluralist society of states. He argues that what is called 'governance' equivocates between collective decisions made in voluntary associations and those made in coercive associations like the state. Conceptions of democratic governance that dispense with the rule of law, in his opinion, 'also dispense with justice.' It is only the rule of law that separates a moral international society from 'a quasi-despotic system of unequal powers'. Allott's essay did not disagree with this, but suggests that the rule of law Nardin discusses is indeed reflective of the rule of a quasi-despotic system of unequal powers. This is not a difference of philosophical perspective, but of empirical judgement. For Allott, true international law is not a *via media* but the foundation of a truly moral international society, instead of the 'international unsociety' we have inherited and mostly replicate.

Following the universalistic perspectives of the earlier essays, Nardin's is a reminder of the continuing power of particularist arguments within the discipline. The three essays that follow Nardin's take a global perspective on ethical issues, but the world they see is not based on the patchwork of sovereign states presented by the traditional realist and pluralist orthodoxy. It is not a territorialist world politics. Instead, the worlds with which the next three chapters engage conceive the critical boundaries separating people(s) to be politically vital, but not vitally defined by traditional political boundaries. These essays engage with the boundaries constructed by the meanings of gender, race and wealth. Each of these essays raises significant issues in terms thinking about the basic question raised in this Introduction: who will the twenty-first century be for?

Academic International Relations experienced the impact of feminist thinking somewhat later than other parts of the social sciences. It occurred only in the late 1980s.[31] If, subsequently, there has been a sense of reduced momentum it is in part because of the extent to which central ideas have been incorporated into the mainstream—at least the mainstream where post-positivist ideas have flourished. One possible avenue of renewed vigour for feminist thinking is in the area of international ethics, as is evident in the contribution by Kimberley Hutchings. The essay emphasizes how there is a powerful normative agenda inherent in any perspective labelled as 'feminist'. In addition, she emphasizes the importance of the empirical in our understanding of normative questions; that is, what is 'seen' or not seen in terms of 'international ethical reality'. Her own essay looks at the gendered character of that 'reality', and this means asking the quintessential Enloesque question: where are the women?[32] Hutchings warns us that much of International Relations in theory and practice is disembodied, and avoids womens' lives.

The starting point of the essay is an assessment of the 'ethics of care' perspective associated with the work of Sarah Ruddick, Fiona Robinson and Margaret Urban-Walker. The point of departure for these writers is to question the assumption of 'impartiality' together with the idea of universal applicability that underpins procedural forms of liberalism. What is important for such writers is uncovering how certain values or practices come to be seen as ethically necessary. Care ethics involve, for Hutchings, a re-thinking of what she terms 'ethical substance' (relations of recognition and responsibility) and a new perspective on ethics (the feminist standpoint) from which certain things can be seen, and on the basis of which ethical judgements can be made.

The 'ethics of care' are seen as bringing four main considerations to the debate about ethics in the global context. First, it is an ethics that takes as its starting point the totality of human relations rather than the more narrowly defined world of mainstream International Relations—the world of diplomatic intercourse and strategic confrontation. Second, it questions the boundaries between private and public/international. Third, the 'domestic' in a literal sense becomes the source of ideas and practices that are applicable to the international. A good example here is that maternal thinking would reject realist theories of militarism as well as liberal notions of a just war, since both 'share a commitment to the expendability of concrete lives in abstract causes to which maternal thinking is inherently opposed'. Finally, Hutchings warns against idealizing moral relations on the basis of pure rationality: instead, we should 'always be sceptical of any kind of moral essentialism or claims to necessity'.

In the latter stages of the essay, Hutchings shows how an 'ethics of care' approach lends itself to thinking about concrete ethical problems such as rape in war, human rights violations, and female genital mutilation. The argument she makes in each case is not to fix where the starting point is, but rather to establish how a certain

---

[31] Key interventions were Jean Bethke Elshtain, *Women and War* (New York: Basic Books, 1987); Cynthia Enloe, *Bananas, Beaches and Bases: Making Feminist Sense of International Relations* (Los Angeles: University of California Press, 1989); and the *Millennium* Special Issue published as Rebecca Grant and Kathleen Newland (eds.), *Gender and International Relations* (Milton Keynes, UK: Open University Press, 1991).
[32] Enloe, *Bananas*, p.7.

practice becomes meaningful in the context of a particular form of life. Human rights, although claimed as universal, have gendered effects; 'torture, rather than female circumcision or domestic violence, tends to be taken as the bedrock example of that which humans have a right not to have to endure'. By incorporating women into a universal category of humanity, she argues that the human rights regime is not able to see the specificity of injustices perpetrated against women and the need for specific measures to secure the basic rights of women. She concludes by arguing that the logic of feminist ethics is to move international ethics away from the 'idealisations' inherent in the dominant ethical traditions towards a position she believes is best characterized by the term 'ethical realism'.

An ethics of care is directly relevant to what many today, and in the past, believe to be the most lasting boundary of all between people, that between the haves and the have-nots. Globalization, which poses new normative challenges across this critical borderline, is the focus of Richard Higgott's essay. He begins by being mindful of old (Adam Smith's) and contemporary warnings that an economic system in which great numbers live in poverty, and is seen as unjust, will not flourish. At the start of this new century, the question this raises is whether the neo-liberal version of globalization contains the seeds of its own demise. The general aim of the chapter is to ask a series of questions about the nature of contemporary global governance. It assumes a need for greater distributive justice at the global level for the world's poor, but focuses not on the philosophical grounds for this assumption, but rather the related 'governance questions', for without the institutions capable of addressing the ethical challenges, justice is unlikely to prevail however defined.

Higgott's contribution charts some of the growing resistance to globalization, notably in the aftermath of the financial crises of the late 1990s. This is no longer a marginal opinion, it is suggested, but one that exists across the political spectrum. A widespread view is that there is a correlation between globalization and poverty, and that this generates a variety of combative politics as the gap between the victims and beneficiaries of globalization has become more apparent. There is a recognition even among its supporters that globalization cannot simply be driven by the neo-liberal agenda. Instead, globalization has to be politically legitimized, democratized and socialized if the gains of economic liberalism are not to be lost to its major beneficiaries.

There is then an examination of the current policy debate on global governance, to see what changes, if any, are in train. Of particular importance, for Higgott, is the shift from the Washington Consensus ('liberalisation, deregulation and privatisation') that shaped the 1980s and 1990s to what he calls the 'Post-Washington Consensus' ('civil society, social capital, capacity building, governance, transparency, a new international economic architecture, institution building and safety nets'). In the market-dominated consensus, there was no conception of governance, but the Post-Washington Consensus represented a minimum response to the increasing hostility towards the liberalization and deregulation processes that had been at the heart of globalization; a limited understanding of governance developed, Higgott argues, but it has been one of 'governance without politics'. There has been a 'mood swing' on globalization, the outcome of which has been a greater concentration in the international policy community on the 'governance' of or 'management' of globalization than was apparent in the last two decades, with their 'fundamentalist free market' ideas. A constant theme of the chapter is the need to understand the difference between 'governance' and 'politics'. It is argued that much of the global governance agenda is under-developed, because of the limited conception of politics in the minds of its proponents; that is, politics is conceived as the pursuit of effective and efficient government, and not—as Higgott claims circumstances demand—a normative, 'indeed explicitly ethical', approach to the advancement of a more just agenda of global economic management.

The chapter gives illustrations of the 'genuine recognition' in some quarters of the importance of tackling ethical questions in relation to the global economy, and points to some positive changes that have taken place, notably a greater sensitivity to gender empowerment and the promotion of democracy. The unequal distribution of wealth is higher on the agenda than in the 1990s, but it is not at the top. For the most part the Post-Washington Consensus has largely removed questions of 'power, domination, resistance and accountability' from the debate. For many key players, therefore, global governance is not about politics. There is only a limited notion of the public good, and the serious redistribution of wealth towards the world's poorest is not considered a public good. There is therefore a need to think beyond the Post-Washington Consensus.

In its broadest implications, the chapter finally invites us to consider how we might conceptualize a 'global polity', or an international system with polity-like symptoms. This is against the background of a twentieth century which was characterized by the growth of multilateral and regional institutions, and alongside the growing interest in the idea of global governance in recent decades—what one writer calls the evolving 'constitutionalization' of world order. Higgott sees a longer term historical development of emerging international norms and regimes, both public and private, that create a rudimentary framework of 'governance without government'. There is also, today, a dominant if contested global ideology and the beginnings of a debate about the prospects for transnational democracy. Throughout the discussion, the chapter's call is to bring politics back into the management of the global economic order—with all this implies. One academic implication would be an invigorated normative scholarship of international political economy—one that would go 'beyond economics'

The last of the three chapters dealing with life-shaping boundaries between peoples, but not those boundaries created by sovereignty, deals with the meaning of 'race'. The inverted commas are there to signify that questions about race are as contested as any answers. The only thing certain is that race has been as politically significant a concept as it now appears to be scientifically untenable (though this has never stopped racially-minded scientists from trying to legitimize it). Given this significance it is somewhat uncomfortable to realize that race attracted little discussion in academic International Relations, although it was an immensely powerful feature of so much that defined world politics in the twentieth century, including the rise and fall of imperialism, the philosophy of Nazi Germany, the Holocaust, apartheid and the ethnic rivalries that have led to the collapse of states in the past decade.

In his essay 'Universalism and Difference in Discourses of Race', Kenan Malik argues that race is a cultural and historical phenomenon more than it is a biological fact. In adopting this stance he rejects the view of Benjamin Disraeli, and others like him, who more or less loudly, and more or less violently, in all areas of human interaction, have agreed that 'All is race. There is no other truth.'[33] Malik enters this controversial landscape of race through a skirmish across some of the hardest terrain of cultural politics in the past few decades. In particular, his essay challenges the implications for the meanings and politics of race of the world-view of post-colonial and post-structuralist writers. According to Malik, important ideas that these writers have propagated over recent decades feed into a discourse of race that has helped recast social differences as natural ones, eternalizing what he wants to argue were historically contingent differences. The theme of his essay is that the 'framework' of thinking developed by the schools of thought just mentioned have nurtured binaries such as 'the West and its Others' and the 'West and the Rest' which are unhelpful in understanding the concept of race. Writers such as Stuart Hall and Edward Said, while claiming to be doing the opposite, have engaged in what Malik considers to be essentializing exercises. Their arguments erroneously essentialize the 'West', while at the same time comprise ahistorical representations of the West's Other, which take little account of the specificities of time and place. In both cases historical, social and geographical differences are 'steamrollered' into a single discourse of West/Others, West/Rest, and so on, which unhelpfully contributes to the naturalizing of a discourse of race—a discourse which has led to and/or legitimized all the horrors of racist politics in modern history.

Malik's essay begins by discussing the distinction between the West and the Other which for so many contemporary cultural theorists is implicit in the categories of Enlightenment universalism, and which for Malik has been so central to contemporary theories of the meaning of race. The cause of particular concern to Malik is Edward Said's assertion of 'a fundamental ontological distinction' between the West and the rest of the world, a boundary Said says we may consider 'absolute'. For Malik this is a 'transhistorical, ontological distinction that collapses the subtleties of two millennia of history'. Instead, he emphasizes the importance of contextualization, and brings on Othello to argue that the meaning of black skin has not always been the same, just as concepts of self and of difference have changed over time. This leads to a discussion of the 'confusions and contradictions' in Said's idea of 'Orientalism', which Malik argues reflect broader problems with post-structuralist theories of difference. While for Said the discourse of Orientalism establishes a dualism between the West and the Orient which empowers the former while imprisoning the latter, Malik argues that there is a 'total lack of precision' in the concept, and major weaknesses in the conception of its historic and epistemic boundaries. He finds the concept of Orientalism 'meaningless' and the argument ahistorical, resulting in a view of 'Western thought' as essentially unchanged since its creation, paralleling the myth of 'Western civilisation' propagated by such advocates of Western superiority as Gobineau and Goebbels. Unlike the latter, Malik suggests, Said actually extends his argument to say that *every* European must necessarily be racist, 'in what he could say about the Orient'.

Malik sees in Michel Foucault's discussion of 'power' an equivalent vagueness to that which he sees in Said's notion of Orientalism. But whereas the dualism of Said's world-view leads to a clear conception of oppressors and victims, Malik argues that Foucault's ideas about the arbitrary nature of power and truth leads to an extreme

[33] Kenan Malik, *The Meaning of Race: Race, History and Culture in Western Society* (London: Macmillan, 1996), p. 1.

relativism. If discourse makes its own truth, and discourse is validated by power, how are we to distinguish between different discourses, and pass the value judgements necessary for politics? Developing this line of thought into a critique of 'theoreticians of difference' such as Levinas, Young and Spivak, Malik argues that 'difference becomes resolved into *indifference*'. And in what he calls the indifference of post-modernism, Malik argues that the politics of difference mirrors the arguments of racial thinking. In short, 'the advocates of racial thinking and the theorists of difference seem equally indifferent to our common humanity'.

Associated with anti-universalist thinking has been an 'unremitting hostility' to a humanist approach. This anti-humanistic thinking developed, Malik argues, largely in opposition to the idea of 'rational human emancipation'. Such anti-humanism is regressive in Malik's view because 'no emancipatory philosophy is possible without a humanistic perspective'—which in turn requires a belief in human rationality and a capacity for social progress. Identifying strands of anti-humanism over the past two centuries in versions of conservatism, in nihilist thinking and in Nazism, he argues that anti-humanism developed as a central component of elite theories 'and hence of racial theories'.

Important for Malik in explaining the relationship between theories of race and the contemporary discourse of difference has been the radical anti-racist, anti-imperialist ideas of such critics of Western society as Frantz Fanon, Jean-Paul Sartre, Michel Foucault, Jacques Derrida and Louis Althusser. This diverse group were involved politically in anti-colonial struggles and the campaigns of 'new social movements'. Their anti-humanism took on a different form to that of the earlier reactionary tradition: this group began to interrogate racist and imperialistic discourses, not celebrate them. Among the (mainly French) anti-colonial writers, humanism was seen as part of a Western ideology to legitimize aggression against the rest of the world (though Third World radicals held on to at least a 'residual support' for a humanistic outlook in their continued engagement in the 'project of liberation'). Other thinkers, however, increasingly rejected humanism 'not simply in its guise as a cover for racism and colonialism, but in its entirety'. One of the main themes of this critique was summed up by the words of Theodor Adorno and Max Horkheimer of the Frankfurt School: 'Enlightenment is totalitarian'. Such ideas fed into the post-structuralist thesis that the Holocaust—the deepest pit yet of the convergence of racism and statism—was not the result of the 'failure' of modernity, but was its 'product'. Malik argues that the beliefs of those holding such views about the relationship between the Enlightenment and racial theories (such as Zygmunt Bauman and Richard Rubinstein) are as badly flawed as those of the cultural theorists he had criticized earlier for their over-simplifications about the West and the rest. He criticizes the former, for example, for conflating arguments about the post-Enlightenment discourse with a supposed tradition that has existed from the beginnings of Western/Judeo-Christian history, and at the same time conflating two different meanings of 'modernity' (the 'Enlightenment project' on the one hand and 'capitalism' on the other). The result of these conflations propagates poor history, weak arguments and unprogressive politics.

The fight against racism, Malik concludes, requires the recentring of universalism. We must once again learn to proclaim 'the right to be the same', rather than 'the right to be different' advanced by many post-colonial theorists. We must not be satisfied with a political struggle that remains—even celebrates—living on the margins. In an uncompromising fashion, Malik argues that 'the philosophy of difference is the politics of defeat, born out of defeat'.

Malik does not here discuss the applied ethics of his argument, though the political drums of humanism, universalism, and emancipation ring clear. What his argument does reveal in a distinct fashion is the meaning of Steve Smith's cogent defence of taking epistemology seriously—'because much more than epistemology is at stake'.[34] Epistemological arguments have ontological and political assumptions, and the aim of Malik's contribution is to show how schools of thought associated with radical and anti-racist thinking, as a result of flawed historical understandings and related argumentation, feed into a regressive discourse of race.

A recent book by Paul Gilroy, *Between Camps: Nations, Cultures and the Allure of Race*, develops Malik's thesis to a degree which might surprise many people at the start of this new century, in which we are told that difference, including racial difference, is the fundamental feature of peoples from local communities to world politics.[35] Against conventional opinion, Gilroy argues that race is on the way to extinction, being of declining conceptual relevance and political purchase. Like Malik, he sees race as a cultural invention, not a scientific category: human difference is shaped more by the happenings and prejudices of history—paradoxically legitimized by contemporary preoccupations with the theory and practice of identity—than by genetic determination. Some scientists, notably Charles Murray, still use biology to explain destiny, as in his attempt to account for the large number of African-Americans living on welfare.[36] Other scientists support Gilroy's view that the biological differences between people are trivial but they can be deadly when inflated, and sometimes inflamed, by their labelling with the powerful word 'race'. The foreseeable erosion of this powerful boundary–maker between people(s) is surely not as likely as Gilroy seems to imply, however desirable it may be. Look around. The record of race in the past century suggests that its erosion will require heroic levels of ethical commitment and political agency. In Malik's words: 'To transcend the concept of race we require not just an intellectual revolution, but a social one too'.

The next two contributions, by Derek Heater and Peter Jones, return to more traditional International Relations territory, including the familiar distinction between cosmopolitan and communitarian perspectives. Both essays, on the basis of examining different issue-areas, seek to argue that cosmopolitanism and communitarianism should not be interpreted as exclusive concepts; we should not conceive them as binary oppositions, as an either/or choice. Rather, we should think of cosmopolitanism and communitarianism as a both/and relationship.

Heater begins by discussing four connected issues: first, whether state citizenship might be paralleled by a notion of world citizenship invested with comparable content; second, the likely implications for an individual's moral and political behaviour to facilitate the sort of cosmopolitan behaviour envisaged, and the appropriate institutional contexts; third, the ways in which the novice world citizen

---

[34] Steve Smith, 'Positivism and Beyond', p. 38 in Steve Smith, Ken Booth and Marysia Zalewski (eds.), *International Theory: Positivism and Beyond* (Cambridge: Cambridge University Press, 1996).

[35] Paul Gilroy, *Between Camps. Nations, Cultures and the Allure of Race* (London: Allen Lane, The Penguin Press, 2000).

[36] Richard J. Hernstein and Charles Murray, *Bell Curve: Intelligence and Class Structure in American Life* (London: Simon and Schuster, 1996).

might be educated into this role; and finally and more generally, the essay discusses whether cosmopolitan thinking has a future. Heater addresses these issues in an intellectual climate in which he describes the case for cosmopolitanism as having been under sustained attack from a variety of sources. These include post-modern sceptics like R.B.J. Walker who accuse cosmopolitans of ignoring the centrality of the particular, political philosophers like Michael Walzer who insist that world citizenship is a contradiction in terms, communitarian International Relations ethicists such as Chris Brown, and mainstream conservatives such as Gertrude Himmelfarb who attack the notion for its lack of realism and for failing to recognize the simple but irrefutable fact that there is no such entity as 'the world' in the abstract but only a world of nations, peoples and specific concrete polities.

Heater accepts the force of these arguments but seeks to refute each in turn. Thus the oft-repeated charge that cosmopolitanism does not reflect something called reality is patently false, he argues. Instead, he argues that a powerful case could be made in favour of a morality and identity above and beyond the demands of the state or the existence of communities. If nothing else, the very dynamics of globalization are increasingly rendering the local and the specific less important while forcing those who look forward—rather than backwards—to rethink the notion of citizenship in a rapidly changing world. In particular, he wants us to accept a more flexible notion of the concept of 'citizenship' than communitarians would allow. With a broader concept, there is also no necessary conflict of interest in Heater's view between citizenship within a nation and what he wants to consider to be world citizenship. He argues that this duality was not the case before 1800 and need not be so at the start of this new century either. Indeed, in an age where the most pressing problems facing the individual arise from sources that are global rather than local, there is a pressing urgency for a sense of cosmopolitan responsibility and a consciousness that will move our thinking beyond the level of the nation state. Whether or not this consciousness will overcome the legacy of the past remains uncertain in Heater's view. To this extent, the world of international politics remains finely balanced between a new world that beckons and an old one that continues to exert its influence.

Students of International Relations in recent times have been invited to consider a variety of 'Back to the Future' scenarios, the most prominent being the image of a return to the balance of power inter-state system that characterized the years up to the First World War or a return to a neo-Medieval system. Heater offers another alternative: 'the new classicism'. It is a view, he believes, that is well-grounded historically, from ancient Greece to Enlightenment Europe. He explains how a 'peaceful co-existence' existed between conceptions of state citizenship, nationhood and the idea of being a citizen of the world. What mattered was the 'relatively weak political contents' of the idea of nationhood and world citizenship, so that each could be held in 'mutually compatible, parallel spheres of life'. Like Hutchings in an earlier essay, Heater is arguing for those who study ethics on a global scale to recognize that different ethical claims (to those that have dominated the discipline) actually rest on empirical realities, though realities that have generally not been seen.

One section of Heater's essay, discussing the education of potential world citizens, will be of particular interest to those engaged in any form of pedagogy. He traces the interesting history of education for world citizenship, which includes some of the early luminaries in academic International Relations, such as Charles Webster. The account is carried through to more recent and heated debates, such as that over World Studies or Peace Studies in the Thatcherite hot-house of the 1980s. The history of such education raises critical questions for teachers of International Relations and Politics in general—not to mention Literature—at a time when 'identity politics' are so prominent. Nussbaum is one who has warned that the goal of producing world citizens is profoundly opposed to the spirit of identity politics, which question the very possibility of common understandings, sympathy and even dialogue across cultures.[37] As an exemplar of the sort of education Heater discusses, Nussbaum advocates the importance of opening up moral imaginations across cultures, a process that has an important empirical as well as theoretical dimension. Heater gives hope to those sympathetic to such perspectives by arguing that cosmopolitan thinking today is of a much higher standard than in the past.

In parallel with Heater's contribution, but with a narrower focus, Peter Jones also raises important questions about conceiving the particular and the universal in exclusivist terms. Equally, his essay shares the outlook of several others in rejecting the idea that cosmopolitan sensibilities (in Jones's case relating to human rights) means buying into a particular conception of cosmopolitan institutions. Here again, in a different form, is the issue posed by O'Neill in her discussion of Rawls and Kant about the practicalities of furthering international justice in a multi-cultural and inter-state world.

The two global norms that are most widely recognized in our world, according to Peter Jones, are human rights and the principle of national self-determination. However, the two principles elicit very different responses from politicians, scholars and the great mass of humanity. Thus while the idea of self-determination remains virtually unchallenged in law and in practice—in spite of the many problems associated with it—the doctrine of human rights is not one that commands universal support around the world. The aim of the essay is to explore why many people have reservations about the 'global pretensions' that accompany the doctrine of human rights, and to examine how far these reservations 'should really make us hesitate' about giving the idea of human rights a 'truly universal status'.

Jones provides a many-sided answer to the central question he poses in his essay. He focuses initially on the critique of a universal notion of human rights advanced by cultural relativists and moral sceptics—both of whom deny either the possibility or applicability of human rights to all situations. But such critics cannot sustain the case against the notion of human rights, he believes; the more powerful case is made (in his view) by those who assert that proponents of human rights deny the most basic right of all: the right of the members of any society to determine for themselves how they shall live and how they shall organize their own affairs. Jones explores this issue in detail before going on to examine the often complex relationship between human rights and political democracy, individual rights and group rights.

He concludes with three key propositions: the doctrine of human rights does not necessarily devalue the communal aspects of people's lives as claimed by some; the potential rivalry between the right of self-determination and human rights does not of necessity have to translate into irreconcilable opposition; and that human rights thinking can fully recognize the communal dimensions of people's lives and can

[37] Nussbaum, *Cultivating Humanity*, p. 109.

provide for those dimensions through collective as well as individual rights. Put another way, Jones stresses that it is simple nonsense—'nonsense upon stilts'—to suppose that if we treat individual persons as the ultimate units of moral concern, that must prevent us from taking full account of the communal dimensions of their lives.

The final essay, by Robert W. Cox, forms an appropriate book-end to match Midgley's first essay, in that it refers on several occasions to the theme she emphasized regarding the unity of humanity and nature. Cox's aim in the essay is to suggest some political realities shaping the ethical dimensions of the century ahead, but it emphasizes that such realities are importantly material, and that the environment is a critical aspect of those realities.

The essay begins by noting the recent revival of the usage of the word 'civilization', and notes how its meanings have altered with historical context. Cox presents a situation in which the issue for the future structure of world order is one of universal globalization (a Western form of universalization with the United States at its core) versus alternative paths of economic social and cultural development; in short, one all-embracing civilization versus a coexistence of several. Cox's own definition of 'civilization' eschews the idea of a 'feeling of belonging' and instead emphasizes 'the almost unconscious, taken for granted, common sense that expresses a people's shared idea of reality'. This includes a normative guide to action as well as a perception of 'objectivity'. A civilization is a 'fit between material conditions of existence and inter-subjective meanings'. Cox rejects a 'vulgar Marxist' position, seeing the material base as determining the inter-subjective superstructure; instead, his position is akin to Weber's 'elective affinity', which allows the possibility of different sets of inter-subjective meanings to fit similar material circumstances. Change is the essence of this idea of civilization, and Cox proposes that change comes about from internal contradictions and from encounters with other civilizations.

After discussing the three dimensions of thought that help distinguish between civilizations (time/space, individual/community, humanity/cosmos) the essay distinguishes the notion of civilization from those of culture and identity. Culture involves the idea of equilibrium, and Cox sees this as being alien to the idea of civilization. Identity for Cox refers to self-consciousness, whereas civilization lies at a deeper level, in which ideas about common sense and reality are sustained. The essay then looks at present day issues in the development of civilizations in the light of the contradictions within contemporary civilizations that pose choices among visions of the future, and the external influences that have an impact on those choices. It concludes that the challenge to established ways of understanding the world—dominated by Western globalizers—is everywhere rather weak compared with the form of 'common sense' propagated by the global media; nevertheless, popular movements, stimulated by material inequities and grievances, have articulated alternative albeit still very diverse projects (as indicated by the 'battle in Seattle').

In his discussion of civilizations and world order for the coming century, Cox parallels two themes in Allott's essay, namely the importance of the historical dialectic and the importance of collective choice about the future of societies. Cox predicts that there will be several, rather than one, collective visions of world order in future, and considers that the role played by NATO in the war in Yugoslavia underlined the choice between a single concept of civilization and a recognition of a plurality. The common understanding of the nature of the world and a vision of the future of society held by civil society is what Cox means by 'collective choice', and he believes that a major factor in the dominance of globalization ideology and the one-civilizational perspective has been the weakness of civil society in both the West and non-West. But he does see signs of a renaissance of civil society out of 'people's alienation from formal politics and economic power'. However, this renaissance lacks a coherent doctrine and institutional support. The United Nations does not provide a framework for a multi-civilizational perspective because it is a hostage to the power of the United States.

Cox ends his essay by touching upon some of the historical precedents for a future world order mentioned by Heater, characterized by a weak centre embodying certain accepted common principles in a world fragmented among peoples guided by different sets of social practices and goals. He identifies his own position with that of a multi-civilizational world, as opposed to the belief that there is no alternative to the 'one final civilization of globalization'. How might this position gain greater political strength? Here he returns to his two elements that bring about civilizational change. One is a changed sense of the global situation—the threats to the biosphere, the danger of social polarization, the spread of weapons of mass destruction and so on. The other is the strengthening of civil societies, and in particular the need to encourage the formation of 'organic intellectuals'. Here he is hopeful, believing that in today's world many more people than in the past have the experience and knowledge to help in this task. He is cautious about the prospect of such a movement emerging strongly through existing institutions, provoked by an aversion to the results of globalization; instead he leaves us with the thought that it might need some more 'dramatic catalyst', such as a global catastrophe, to bring about the normative changes he endorses.

If these summaries of the essays describe an opening up of issues rather than the laying down of policy prescriptions, this is as it was meant to be. Books on ethics, even books on ethics in the practical business of world politics, primarily exist to help us think about how we ought to behave, as opposed to being step-by-step guides to policy. Nutritionists do not necessarily make the best cooks. It is the same in politics, with moral philosophers and decision-makers. Aristotle illustrated the gap between the practical world and the exponent of ideal theory in Philosophy in the person of Thales, the scientist-philosopher who always fell into wells. And which one of us would have wanted a moral philosopher as US President in the Cuban Missile Crisis, or any of our academic colleagues in International Relations looking out at the weather over the Channel at the start of June 1944 and having to decide whether to launch Operation Overlord? Nobody should expect too much from philosophers in the practice of international politics—or from Professors of International Relations for that matter. Professor/Secretary of State Henry Kissinger, according to his many critics, is the paradigm illustration of the tragedy of a theorist of statecraft becoming the real thing.[38] Ethical deliberation is one thing, and difficult enough, but knowing about the technicalities and psychology of nuclear deterrence, naval strategy, orders-of-battle and the rest is another, especially in the context of multiple players, compressed time and the very highest of stakes.

We stressed at the outset that the world of politics is an ethical arena, but here we are suggesting that thinking is not the same as doing; they are different activities and

---

[38] See, for example, Hedley Bull, 'The Primacy of Geopolitics,' *International Affairs*, 56 (1980), pp. 484–7.

require different skills to be performed well. Few individuals have them both in equal abundance. Be that as it may, we believe that politics and policies should be done better if their executors know why: their grounds, causes, reasons, authorities, assumptions, and methodology. Philosopher-kings and kingly-philosophers are welcome, but are truly rare. In the arena of world politics this is in part because the international is a dimension of ethical deliberation that has often been overlooked by moral philosophers—and indeed others in the humanities and social sciences. This point helps put into some perspective the criticism sometimes levelled against academic International Relations on the ground that it has ignored moral philosophy, social theory and the rest. But equally, other disciplines have ignored the hardest case: the global. To give one example. There has been a revival of interest in virtue ethics since the 1980s, but it has been in the domestic rather than the international arena.[39] To attempt, in any circumstances, to behave virtuously is akin to trying to swim in a straight line in a fast-flowing river; when that river opens into international space, the sea, even more powerful currents, tides and eddies sweep in. This creates a radically more difficult environment in which to keep afloat 'responsibly', let alone swim 'virtuously'.

Despite these caveats, we are convinced that in this first truly global age, ethical enquiry in the global perspective is both desirable and urgent. Ethical enquiry is desirable from many points of view, and in a recent book Norman Geras has given us one very compelling reason why.[40] The alternative is indifference, the human costs of which were only too apparent in many places in the twentieth century, both distant and close by. Ethical enquiry is also urgent from many points of view, and in a recent book Eugene Linden has given us nine compelling reasons why.[41] The alternative is social, political and environmental disasters, the potential human and non-human costs of which in the twenty-first century we are only just beginning to comprehend. The essays in this volume refer many times to ancient questions and long-dead philosophers—and implicitly and explicitly to their relevance; but it would be wrong to conclude from this that when it comes to ethics in the context of world politics there is nothing new under the sun. In some quarters at least there is a strong sense, at the start of the twenty-first century, that we face radical ethical challenges. The concatenation and pace of change in global material circumstances is reconfiguring traditional questions about the limits of duty, the bounds of obligation and the referents for justice. To adapt an old Leninist adage for this predictably overloaded new century: quantity will have an ethical quality all of its own.

While there are pressing political—'applied'—issues in terms of *How we might live?* there are also profound questions relating to ethics and morality in terms of the nature of the choice we have as humans. The tradition of Enlightenment thinking, and even that of a century or so earlier, has been to think of morality in terms of the opening up of choice through the exercise of reason, with individuals escaping from the religious and other strictures and structures of the medieval world.[42] The

---

[39] For example, Alasdair MacIntyre, *After Virtue* (London: Duckworth, 1981).
[40] Geras, *Contract of Mutual Indifference*, pp. 19–24.
[41] Eugene Linden, *The Future in Plain Sight: Nine Clues to the Coming Instability* (New York: Simon & Schuster, 1998).
[42] Stuart Hall, 'The Question of Cultural Identity' in Stuart Hall, David Held and Anthony McGrew (eds.), *Modernity and its Futures* (Cambridge: Polity Press, 1992), pp. 281–5.

idea of these fixed—'centred'—persons capable of autonomous moral reasoning has been challenged by a variety of other analyses, including the idea of the 'sociological self' of symbolic interactionism and the decentred 'post-modern self', constructed by history, not biology.[43] But biology has certainly not given up the struggle in the debate about ethics, and the growing prominence of neo-Darwinian thinking in many branches of the study of human society through the 1990s was a testimony to this; and it did so in a way that sought to bring together the historical (in the longest evolutionary perspective) and the biological. In the field of ethics, Matt Ridley's *The Origins of Virtue* seeks to overturn the image of the state of nature as one of naked conflict. The book argues that 'Society was not invented by reasoning men. It evolved as part of our nature. It is as much a product of our genes as our bodies are.'[44] Put simply, humans do not in effect have much choice; morality—reciprocal altruism—is genetically programmed. These views are very controversial, of course, and have attracted considerable criticism. The latter has ranged from ideological opponents who do not want to be challenged by knowing anything about biology or evolution, to (a significant group of) philosophically-minded scientists who come to different conclusions. Steven Rose's book *Lifelines: Biology, Freedom, Determinism*, for example, emphasizes the poverty of all reductionist thinking about biology (such as the 'selfish gene') and the importance of complexity in the human story. He emphasizes the radical unpredictability of human choice, and so of both ethics and of the human future. For Rose, 'it is therefore our biology that makes us free'.[45]

One branch of thinking about human society since the 1970s that has fiercely debated this terrain of nature/nurture and history/biology has been feminism. A central work here—with significant implications for ideas about moral choice—has been Carol Gilligan's *In A Different Voice*. The book, published first in 1982, challenged the psychologist Lawrence Kohlberg's research on the stages of moral reasoning as children grow up, and in particular what she saw as its masculinist bias. Gilligan's counter-claim was that the socialization of boys emphasized autonomy, whereas that of girls emphasized interdependence; in consequence, the moral thinking of men leads them to emphasize rights and rules, whereas the moral thinking of women leads them to emphasize responsibility and relationships. The moral reasoning of men and women, and so their capacity for choice, therefore comes 'in a different voice'.[46] Such arguments—again the subject of considerable dispute—continue to challenge the idea of an ethical domain as the highest achievement of reason, somehow disembodied from biology, society and history—not to mention from class, geography and all the other explanations that flesh is heir to. These controversies point yet again to the need to explore the workings of the mind, for some time touted as the key research area for the century ahead. In this regard, Emilia Steuerman has recently intervened in the debate between 'modernity' and 'postmodernity' to try and show how the psychoanalytic theory and practice of Melanie Klein can expose the limits of both 'rationalist and irrationalist' positions. In her view the 'ethical turn' in contemporary philosophy can learn a great deal from

---

43 Hall, 'The Question', pp. 274–9.
44 Matt Ridley, *The Origins of Virtue* (London: Viking, 1996), pp. 6–7.
45 Steven Rose, *Lifelines. Biology, Freedom, Determinism* (London: Allan Lane, 1997) passim, quotation at p. 309.
46 Carol Gilligan, *In a Different Voice: Psychological Theory and Women's Development* (Cambridge, MA: Harvard University Press, 1982).

psychoanalysis, and in particular, 'the recognition of the intersubjectivity of reason . . . [which] leads to an immediate concern with . . . intersubjective community, without which no idea of rational truth or freedom could be maintained'.[47] The argument is that Kleinian psychoanalysis can contribute to ethical discussion by showing that even in our most 'inner' core, 'even as pre-verbal infants, we are already part of an emotional and cognitive web of interrelations'. Steuerman draws the conclusion, again with profound implications, that 'the more traditional ethical idea of freedom as autonomy has to be articulated with the concern for others, that is, through the idea of solidarity'. Solidarity with others, it appears, is less of a choice than some have thought; and is not separate from an inner self. The purpose of drawing attention to these debates is to emphasize that students of International Relations these days must not only engage with the problem of choice, in terms of the familiar decision-making dilemmas for governments, but also in relation to the most profound questions about humans and their very capacity, in the first place, to choose.

If those views stressing the inevitability of ethics are persuasive, then serious questions are raised for students and researchers in International Relations, in terms of what and how we teach and research. There is no space—nor would it be appropriate in a volume such as this—for the editors to lay out their own pedagogic prescriptions. What we do end in asserting, though, is the potential value of the synergy between scholars in International Relations and moral philosophers. We said earlier that there could be no expectation of step-by-step guides to policy-making from moral philosophers, but there is a tradition going back to Socrates of 'applied' philosophy, and scholars in International Relations should welcome and encourage excursions into our field by its exponents. This means that we need to make space for moral philosophers to help us think about the normative assumptions of our positions in a more critical fashion.

The history of this coming century, now so uncertain, will in part be shaped by the decisions we—as individuals, collectives and the collective of collectives—take in terms of who we think global politics is for. We have just lived through the end of a century in which, in the words of Susan Buck-Morss, 'The construction of mass utopia was the dream'.[48] The dream—in which she argues the socialist imaginary failed because it mirrored the dreamworlds of capitalism too faithfully—is being left behind, and the question is what will take its place. As long as old structures of power remain intact, Buck-Morss argues that the space that global changes have opened up for 'new imaginings' will only produce dreamworlds. To be a real cause for hope, the new imaginings need to create new identities, rather than shoring up existing ones.[49] This is one set of choices for the new century—'as radical as reality itself' to quote Lenin. Another set of choices involves exploring the implications of particularism in a globalizing context. In explicating the grounds and justifications for whatever choices we might make about world politics, moral philosophers have a significant role; in explicating the opportunities and constraints that surround those choices, International Relations scholars have a significant role. Students of

[47] Emilia Steuerman, *The Bounds of Reason: Habermas, Lyotard and Melanie Klein on Rationality* (London: Routledge, 2000), p. xv.

[48] Susan Buck-Morss, *Dreamworld and Catastrophe: The Passing of Mass Utopia in East and West* (Cambridge, MA: The MIT Press, 2000), pp. ix–x.

[49] Buck Morss, *Dreamworld*, pp. 277–8.

International Relations over the past decade or more have been more than ready to criticize our own failure to bring Philosophy into the international, but we have not been sufficiently assertive in arguing the importance and need to bring the international into philosophy—not to mention Sociology and Political Science. There is a need for transcending traditional boundaries here as in so many other aspects of life.

Together, moral philosophers and International Relations specialists can make a contribution to helping those with power, those wanting power, and those who care, to think in more sophisticated ways about the good and the possible in the context of world politics. This context always exists at the interface of the good, the bad and the possible: the traditional 'dirty hands' problem.[50] Doing is not the same as thinking, and doing good is always more difficult than thinking good, in a multi-cultural and inter-state world, characterized as it is by divisions between haves and have-nots, between people of different race, between different genders, and the rest. At whatever level of human society we might want to consider, from the hearth to the grandest stage of all, global politics, Tolstoy was surely not far from the mark when he warned that it was easier to write volumes of philosophy than 'put a single precept into practice'. Even if we—whoever we are—can agree upon the global good, bringing it about will never be guaranteed. Our discipline, sadly, still has a long future.

---

[50] See Michael Walzer, 'Political Action: The Problem of Dirty Hands', *Philosophy and Public Affairs*, 2:2, 1973.

Individualism and the concept of Gaia

MARY MIDGLEY*

Introduction: why Gaian thinking is not a luxury

The idea of Gaia—of life on earth as a self-sustaining natural system—is not a gratuitous, semi-mystical fantasy. It is a really useful idea, a cure for distortions that spoil our current world-view. Its most obvious use is, of course, in suggesting practical solutions to environmental problems. But, more widely, it also attacks deeper tangles which now block our thinking. Some of these are puzzles about the reasons why the fate of our planet should concern us. We are bewildered by the thought that we might have a duty to something so clearly non-human. But more centrally, too, we are puzzled about how we should view ourselves. Current ways of thought still tend to trap us in the narrow, atomistic, seventeenth-century image of social life which grounds today's crude and arid individualism, though there are currently signs that we are beginning to move away from it. A more realistic view of the earth can give us a more realistic view of ourselves as its inhabitants.

What is the theory?

The current Gaian thinking that I believe can help here is a new scientific development of an old concept. The imaginative vision behind it the idea of our planet as in some sense a single organism, is very old. Plato called the earth 'a single great living creature' and this is language that people in many cultures would find natural.[1] Our own culture, however, shut out this notion for a long time from serious thought. Orthodox Christian doctrine damned it as involving pagan nature-worship. And modern scientists, for their part, were for a long time so exclusively devoted to atomistic and reductive explanations that they too rejected this reference to a wider whole. Indeed, during much of the twentieth century the very word 'holistic' has served in some scientific circles simply as a term of abuse.

Recently, however, scientists have been becoming somewhat less wedded to this odd one-sided reductive ideology—less sure that nothing is really science except physics. The environmental crisis has helped this shift by making clear the indisputable importance of ecology, which always refers outwards from particulars to

---

* A fuller version of this article is forthcoming as a DEMOS pamphlet, and a still longer, rather different one will form the conclusion of my book *Science and Poetry*, to be published by Routledge. Both of these will appear in 2001.
[1] Plato, *Timaeus*, § 33.

larger wholes. In that changed context, solid scientific reasons have emerged for thinking that the notion of our biosphere as a self-maintaining system—analogous in some sense to individual organisms—is not just a useful idea but actually a scientifically necessary one. Science, after all, is not just an inert store of neutral facts. It always organizes them according to patterns which are drawn from ordinary thinking in the first place (where else, after all, could they come from?) and which often rebound in a changed form to affect that thinking profoundly in their turn. These strong pieces of imaginative equipment need to be understood and criticized in both their aspects. We shouldn't slide into accepting their apparent moral implications merely because they are presented as part of science.

The two-way influence of imagery is shown impressively by the powerful Machine Image which was central both to the Newtonian view of the cosmos and to the Enlightenment's notion of determinism. As Karl Popper put it, 'Physical determinism … was a daydream of omniscience which seemed to become more real with every advance of physics until it became an apparently inescapable nightmare'.[2] The machine-imagery had taken charge of the thought. And another striking example today is the neo-Darwinist picture—still extremely influential, though its absurdities have been often noted—of evolution as essentially a simple projection of the money-market. Here the noisy rhetoric of selfishness, spite, exploitation, manipulation, investment, insurance and war-games easily persuades people that this new form of Victorian social-atomist ideology must be true because it has the support of science. By using a different imagery and a different basic pattern, Gaian thinking tends to correct this outdated bias. It does not reject the central scientific message of neo-Darwinism. It simply points out that it is not the whole story. Doing this is, indeed, one of its more obvious advantages.

Planetary considerations

I have been suggesting that this way of thinking has implications far beyond science. But the scientific case for it must, I think, be sketched first, however inadequately, so as to make clear what the term 'Gaia' actually means today.

The idea first arose out of considerations about the difference between the earth and its siblings. James Lovelock was employed by NASA in the early 1960s, designing sensitive instruments that would analyse the surfaces and atmospheres of other planets. But Lovelock was a chemist who had previously worked in biophysics and medicine, and it seemed to him that the experiments proposed for detecting life on other planets were too closely bound to expecting particular features similar to life on earth. A wider strategy occurred to him. Perhaps, he thought,

the most certain way to detect life on planets was to analyse their atmospheres … life on a planet would be obliged to use the atmosphere and oceans as conveyors of raw materials and depositories for the products of its metabolism. This would change the chemical composition of the atmosphere so as to render it recognisably different from the atmosphere of a lifeless planet.[3]

[2] Karl Popper, 'Of Clouds And Clocks', in *Objective Knowledge; An Evolutionary Approach* (Oxford University Press, 1972), p. 222.
[3] James Lovelock, *The Ages of Gaia* (Oxford University Press, 1988), p. 5.

He therefore compared the atmospheres of Mars and Venus with that of the earth and found indeed a startling difference. By this test Mars and Venus appeared, in a simple sense, static and dead. They had

atmospheres close to equilibrium, like exhaust gases, and both were dominated by the generally unreactive gas carbon dioxide. [By contrast] the earth, the only planet that we know to bear life, is in a deep state of disequilibrium ... Earth's atmosphere is like a dilute form of the energy-rich mixture that enters the intake manifold of a car before combustion; hydrocarbons and oxygen mixed. ... An awesome thought came to me. The earth's atmosphere was an extraordinary and unstable mixture of gases, yet I knew that it was constant in composition over long periods of time. *Could it be that life on earth not only made the atmosphere but also regulated it*—keeping it at a constant composition and at a level favourable for organisms?[4]

Checking what might follow from this, Lovelock found that there is indeed a whole range of mechanisms by which the presence of life seems, from its first appearance on the earth, to have deeply influenced the atmosphere in a way that made its own continuance possible when it otherwise would not have been.

The scale on which this happens is hard to grasp. I will mention here only one simple and dramatic element in it—the Carbon Cycle. The carbon which living things use to form their bodies mostly comes, directly or indirectly, from carbon dioxide—the somewhat inert gas which, on the other planets, acts as a full-stop to atmospheric reactions. Life is therefore always withdrawing this gas from the atmosphere and two statistics may convey something of the scale on which it does it. First, if you stand on the cliffs of Dover, you have beneath you *hundreds of metres of chalk*—tiny shells left by the creatures of an ancient ocean. These shells are made of calcium carbonate, using carbon that mostly came from the air via the weathering of rocks—the reaction of carbon dioxide with basaltic rock dissolved by rain.

This process of rock-weathering can itself take place without life. But when life is present—when organisms are working on the rock and the earth that surrounds it—it takes place one thousand times faster than it would on sterile rock.[5] Coal and oil, similarly, are storehouses of carbon withdrawn from the air. All this carbon will go back into circulation one day, but meanwhile it is locked away, leaving the breathable air that we know, air that makes possible the manifold operations of life. Similar life-driven cycles can be traced for other essential elements such as oxygen, nitrogen, sulphur and that more familiar priceless thing, water.

There is also the matter of warmth. In the time that life has existed on earth, the sun has become 25 per cent hotter, yet the mean temperature at the earth's surface has always remained fairly constant. Unlike Venus, which simply went on heating up till it reached temperatures far above what makes life possible, the earth gradually consumed much of the blanket of greenhouse gas—mostly carbon dioxide—which had originally warmed it. Feedback from living organisms seems to have played a crucial part in this steadying process and to have ensured, too, that it did not go too far. In this way the atmosphere remained substantial enough to avoid the fate of Mars, whose water and gases largely streamed away very early, leaving it unprotected

---

[4] Lovelock, *Gaia: The Practical Science of Planetary Medicine* (London, Gaia Books, 1991), pp. 21–2. Emphasis mine.
[5] Ibid., p. 111.

against the deadly cold of space. Here again, conditions on earth stabilized in a most remarkable way within the quite narrow range which made continued life possible.

Lastly, there is the soil. We think of the stuff we walk on as earth. the natural material of our planet, and so it is. But it was not there at the start. Mars and Venus and the Moon have nothing like it. On them there is only what is called *regolith*, naked broken stone and dust. By contrast our soil, as Lynn Margulis points out, is a museum of past life:

Soil is not unalive. It is a mixture of broken rock, pollen, fungal filaments, ciliate cysts, bacterial spores, nematodes and other microscopic animals and their parts. *'Nature' Aristotle observed, 'proceeds little by little from things lifeless to animal life in such a way that it is impossible to determine the exact line of demarcation'. Independence is a political, not a scientific term.*[6]

In short, if all this is right, living things—including ourselves—and the planet that has produced them form a continuous system and act as such. Life, then, has not been just a casual passenger of the earth's development. It has always been and remains a crucial agent in determining its course.

Putting life together

I cannot discuss the scientific details further here. Orthodox scientists, though they were at first sceptical about it, now accept this general approach as one which can be used and debated within science.[7] Their debates about these aspects of it will of course go on. But, as I have suggested, the importance of the concept is by no means confined to science. It concerns the general framework of our thought. It supplies an approach which, once fully grasped, makes a profound difference, not just to how we see the earth but to how we understand life and ourselves. The new scientific arguments bring back into focus the traditional imaginative vision of a living earth which I mentioned at the start—a vision which is already returning but needs to be made much clearer—and show how much we need it in our social and personal thinking.

As Lewis Thomas has pointed out, this vision already took on a new meaning for many of us when we first saw the pictures of earth sent back by the astronauts:

Viewed from the distance of the moon, the astonishing thing about the earth, catching the breath, is that it is alive. The photographs show the dry, pounded surface of the moon in the foreground, dead as an old bone. Aloft, floating free beneath the moist, gleaming membrane of bright blue sky, is the rising earth, the only exuberant thing in this part of the cosmos. If you could look long enough, you would see the swirling of the great drift of white cloud, covering and uncovering the half-hidden masses of land. If you had been looking a very long, geologic time, you could have seen the continents themselves in motion, drifting apart on their crustal plates, held aloft by the fire beneath. It has the organised, self-contained look of a live creature, full of information, marvellously skilled in handling the sun.[8]

[6] Lynn Margulis and Dorion Sagan, *What is Life?* (London: Weidenfeld, 1995), p. 26. Emphasis mine.
[7] For a review of recent discussions see Timothy M. Lenton, 'Gaia And Natural Selection', in *Nature*, 394, 30 July 1998.
[8] Lewis Thomas, *The Lives Of A Cell* (London: Futura, 1976), p. 170.

No other planet, incidentally, has continental drift and there is some reason to think that the presence of living things may have contributed to making that mechanism possible by changing the composition of the crustal rocks. Again, it's a question of the carbon cycle. Early organisms may have deposited calcium carbonate on a scale that changed the composition of the ocean floor. As Lovelock explains, 'the formation of limestone deposits by organisms may have been important in triggering the change of composition of lithospheric rocks—a change that allowed plate formation and motion'.[9]

One aquarium, many windows

The scientific details that now articulate this picture of the living earth give it a new kind of standing because of the special importance that scientific thought has for us today. They make us bring our official scientific beliefs together with our imaginative life. That rapprochement is surely welcome. But it is not easy for us. Many dualisms in recent thought have urged us to keep these matters apart. We are used to hearing of a stark war between the two cultures and of a total separation between facts and values. In our universities, the Arts Block and the Science Block tend to be well separated. But we will never make much sense of life if we do not somehow keep our various faculties on speaking terms with one another.

Much of the difficulty about grasping the concept of Gaia is not scientific but comes from this fragmented general framework of our thought. It arises—for scientists as well as for the rest of us—from these artificial fences that we have raised across the scene and centrally from Descartes' original fence between mind and body. Our moral, psychological and political ideas have all been armed against holism. They are both too specialized and too atomistic. As many people are pointing out today, that slant is giving us trouble in plenty of other places as well as over Gaia. Yet we find it very hard to change it.

This difficulty in changing concepts is, of course, a common one. We are always in trouble when we are asked to think about the world in a new way. It is as if we had been looking into a vast, rather ill-lit aquarium through a single window and are suddenly told that things look different from the other side.

We cannot have a single comprehensive view of the whole aquarium—a single, all-purpose, philosophic Theory of Everything. Many prophets, from the seventeenth century to the nineteenth, from Leibniz to Hegel and Marx, have tried to give us such a view. But their efforts have proved misguided. The world is simply too rich for such reductive strait-jacketing. There is not—as Leibniz thought—a single underlying quasi-mathematical language into which the views from all aspects can be translated.

This does not mean that no understanding is possible. We can relate these various aspects rationally because they all occur within the framework of our lives. We can walk round and look at other windows and can discuss them with each other. But we cannot eliminate any of them. We have to combine a number of different ways of thinking—the views through several windows, historical, biological, mathematical,

[9] Lovelock, *Gaia: The Practical Science of Planetary Medicine*, p. 131.

everyday and the rest—and somehow fit them together. When Galileo first expressed his views about the world, not only the Pope but the scientists of his day found them largely incomprehensible. Yet those ideas, when developed by Descartes, Newton, Laplace and the rest, shaped the set of windows through which the whole Enlightenment looked into the vast aquarium which is our world. That is the set through which many in our own age still want to see everything. This set is now called 'modern' by those who want to use that word as a term of abuse for past errors, contrasting it with various 'postmodern' sets which may be expected to replace it. Though I don't myself find this vague time-snobbery very helpful, there is no doubt that the Cartesian vision needs radical revision.

The age of alienation

As many people have pointed out,[10] the central trouble is the dualism of mind and body. The notion of our selves—our minds—as detached observers or colonists, separate from the physical world and therefore from each other, watching and exploiting a lifeless mechanism, has been with us since the dawn of modern science (and of the Industrial Revolution). Descartes taught us to think of matter essentially as our resource—a jumble of material blindly interacting. Animals and plants were machines and were provided for us to build into more machines.

It is this vision that still makes it so hard for us to take seriously the disasters that now infest our environment. Such a lifeless jumble would be no more capable of being injured than an avalanche would. Indeed, until quite lately our sages have repeatedly urged us to carry on a 'war against Nature'.[11] We did not expect the earth to be vulnerable, capable of health or sickness, wholeness or injury. But it turns out that we were wrong; the earth is now unmistakably sick. The living processes (or, as we say, 'mechanisms') that have so far kept the system working are disturbed, as is shown, for instance, by the surge of extinctions.

Descartes' world-view did, of course, produce many triumphs. But it produced them largely by dividing things—mind from body, reason from feeling, and the human race from the rest of the physical universe. It produced a huge harvest of local knowledge about many of the provinces. But it has made it very hard for people even to contemplate putting the parts together.

For a long time now our culture tolerated this deprivation. But it has become a serious nuisance in many areas of knowledge. The rise of systems theory and complexity theory are thriving attempts to break its restraints. Another such place is the lively debate now going on about problems of Consciousness—a topic once systematically tabooed by academics, but now agreed to constitute one of their most potentially interesting areas of study.[12] This change has been an intriguing showcase for the workings of intellectual fashion and it has interesting implications for discussions of Gaia. It is clear by now that many of us want to see our aquarium—our

[10] See, for instance, Keith Devlin in *Goodbye Descartes; The End of Logic and the Search for a New Cosmology of the Mind* (New York, John Wiley & Sons, 1997) and the entire works of Richard Rorty.
[11] For examples, see John Passmore, *Man's Responsibility For Nature* (London: Duckworth, 1974), ch. 1.
[12] There is now a thriving *Journal of Consciousness Studies*—something that would have been inconceivable twenty years ago.

world, including ourselves—more as a whole, indeed, that we desperately need to do this. To do so, we must attend to aspects of it which Enlightenment dualism cannot reach, aspects which simply do not appear at our traditional window.

Why 'Gaia'?

One of these areas that has been made artificially difficult—the connection between scientific thought and the rest of life—comes out quaintly in the sharp debate about the implications of the name Gaia itself. That name arose when Lovelock told his friend, the novelist William Golding, that people found it hard to grasp his idea, and Golding promptly replied 'Why don't you call it Gaia?' which is the name of the Greek earth-goddess, mother of gods and men. That name, when he used it, did indeed rouse much more interest in the theory. Many people who had not previously understood it now grasped it and thought it useful. Others, however, particularly in the scientific establishment, now rejected it so violently that they refused to attend to the details of it altogether.

In our culture at present, people find it somewhat surprising that an idea can be large enough to have both a scientific and a religious aspect. This is because, during the last century, our ideas of religion, of science and indeed of life have all become narrowed in a way that makes it difficult to get these topics into the same perspective. (Here our window has become a good deal narrower than it was when Galileo and Newton and Faraday used it. They never doubted that these things belonged together).[13] To get round this difficulty, Lovelock used a different image. He launched the medical model of Gaia—the idea of the damaged earth as a patient for whom we humans are the only available doctor, even though (as he points out) we lack the long experience of other sick planets which a doctor attending such a case really ought to have. So he invented the name *geophysiology* to cover the skills needed by such a physician.[14]

This medical imagery at once made it much easier for scientists to accept the notion of Gaia. When the point is put in medical terms, they begin to find it plausible that the earth does indeed in some way function as an organic whole, that its climate and oceans work together with living things to maintain a normal balance, and that what gravely upsets any part of the system is liable to upset others. They can see that, for such a whole, the notion of health is really quite suitable. And of course they find the patient Gaia, lying in bed and politely awaiting their attention, much less threatening than that scandalous pagan goddess.

Gods, goddesses and scientific status

Lovelock, accordingly, came under great pressure to calm the scientists by withdrawing the goddess and for a while he seriously considered doing so. Eventually,

---

[13] On the radical interdependence between their religious and scientific thinking see Margaret Wertheim, *Pythagoras' Trousers, God, Physics and the Gender Wars* (London: Fourth Estate, 1997), chs. 5 and 6.
[14] This is the topic of his book *Gaia, The Practical Science of Planetary Medicine.*

however, he decided that the whole idea had to be kept together because the complexity was real. As Fred Pearce put it in an impressive article in *New Scientist*:

Gaia as metaphor; Gaia as a catalyst for scientific enquiry; Gaia as literal truth; Gaia as Earth Goddess. Whoever she is, let's keep her. If science cannot find room for the grand vision, if Gaia dare not speak her name in Nature, then shame on science. To recant now would be a terrible thing, Jim. Don't do it.[15]

Lovelock didn't recant. He does indeed constantly emphasize the scientific status of the concept:

I am not thinking in an animistic way of a planet with sentience ... I often describe the planetary ecosystem, Gaia, as alive because it behaves like a living organism to the extent that temperature and chemical composition are actively kept constant in the face of perturbations ... I am well aware that the term itself is metaphorical and that the earth is not alive in the same way as you or me or even a bacterium.[16]

But he still writes, with equal firmness, 'For me, Gaia is a religious as well as a scientific concept, and in both spheres it is manageable ... God and Gaia, theology and science, even physics and biology are not separate but a single way of thought'.[17]

This raises the question; is religious talk actually incompatible with science? It is interesting to note that in one area of science—an area which is often viewed as the archetype of all science—such talk is readily accepted. That area is theoretical physics. As Margaret Wertheim has pointed out, most of the great physicists of the past, from Copernicus to Clerk Maxwell, insisted that their work was primarily and essentially religious. Most remarkably, too, their modern successors still make the claim:

In spite of the officially secular climate of modern science, physicists have continued to retain a quasi-religious attitude to their work. They have continued to comport themselves as a scientific priesthood, and to present themselves to the public in that light. To quote Einstein, 'A contemporary has said, not unjustly, that *in this materialistic age of ours the serious scientific workers are the only truly religious people*'.[18]

Einstein himself showed how sincerely he meant this by constantly referring to God in explaining his own reasoning ('God does not play dice ...'. 'The lord is subtle but not malicious' and so forth). And he explicitly said that this attitude was serious;

Science can only be created by those who are thoroughly imbued with the aspiration towards truth and understanding. The source of this feeling, however, springs from the sphere of religion.[19]

Later physicists have not dismissed this approach as a mere personal quirk of Einstein's. Instead, they have developed it in many best-selling books with titles such as *God And The New Physics*,[20] *The Mind Of God*,[21] *The God Particle*,[22] *The Physics*

[15] Fred Pearce, 'Gaia, Gaia, Don't Go Away', in *New Scientist*, 28 May 1994.
[16] Lovelock, *Gaia: The Practical Science of Planetary Medicine*, pp. 6, 11, 31.
[17] Lovelock, *The Ages Of Gaia*, pp. 206 and 212.
[18] Margaret Wertheim, *Pythagoras' Trousers* (London: Fourth Estate 1997), p. 12.
[19] Einstein, 'Science and Religion', *Nature*, 146:65 (1940), p. 605.
[20] By Paul Davies (New York: Simon and Schuster, 1984).
[21] By Paul Davies (New York: Simon and Schuster,1992)
[22] By Leon Lederman and Dick Teresi (Boston, MA: Houghton Miflin, 1993).

of Immortality; Modern Cosmology, God and the Resurrection of the Dead,[23] and many more.

Is there perhaps some special reason why religious talk of this kind can count as a proper language for physics, but becomes inappropriate and scandalous when the chemical and biological concerns of Gaian thinking are in question? Or is it not so much the subject-matter as the sex of the deity that makes the scandal? Is it perhaps held to be scientifically proper to speak of a male power in the cosmos but not of a female one? There is a powerful tradition which might make this odd view look plausible. As Wertheim shows, throughout the history of physics, a strong and somewhat fantastic element of misogyny has indeed accompanied the sense of sacredness that always distinguished this study. The physical priesthood was a male one guarding a male god. It went to great lengths to protect its secrets from intruding females:

Walter Charleton, another founding member of the Royal Society, summed up many of his colleagues' antipathy towards women when he wrote, 'you are the true Hienas that allure us with the fairness of your skins ... You are the traitors to wisdom, the impediments to industry... the clogs to virtue and the goads that drive us all to Vice, Impiety and Ruin'. Henry Oldenburg, the Society's first secretary, declared that its express purpose was 'to raise a Masculine philosophy' ... This bastion of British science did not admit a woman as a full member until 1945.[24]

This talk of a masculine philosophy echoes, of course, Francis Bacon's clarion-call for the new science to produce 'a Masculine birth of time' where men could turn their 'united forces against the nature of things, to storm and occupy her castle and strongholds'.[25]

Of course the personifications in thinking of this kind should not be taken literally. Yet the reverent, awe-struck attitude that lies behind those personifications is surely a suitable one both for science and for our general relation to the cosmos. Einstein was not being silly. Anyone who tries to contemplate these vast questions without any sense of reverence for their vastness simply shows ignorance of what they entail. And of course, if the system of life itself is taken to have participated in the history of evolution in the sort of way that Gaian thinking suggests, then a substantial part of this reverence is surely due to that system. If it has indeed played a crucial part in stabilizing conditions on earth through billions of years to the point where we ourselves are now here and able to profit from them—if it has managed the remarkable feat of preserving the atmosphere and controlling the temperature, thus saving the earth from becoming a dead planet like Mars and Venus and turning it instead into the cherished blue-green sphere whose picture we all welcomed—if it has done all this for us, then the only possible response to that feat is surely wonder, awe and gratitude.

That sense of wonder and gratitude is clearly what the Greeks had in mind when they named the earth Gaia, the divine mother of gods and men. They never developed that naming into a full humanization. They never brought Gaia into the

---

[23] By Frank J. Tipler (New York: Doubleday, 1994).
[24] *Pythagoras' Trousers*, p. 100. For more about this amazing but highly influential sexual chauvinism see Brian Easlea, *Science And Sexual Oppression* (London: Weidenfeld and Nicolson, 1981).
[25] Farrington, *Philosophy of Francis Bacon*, pp. 62, 92, 93; Spedding, *Works of Francis Bacon*, 4, pp. 42, 373.

scandalous human stories that they told about other gods—stories which, in the end, made it impossible to take those gods seriously at all. But the name still expressed their awe and gratitude at being part of that great whole.

And today there is evidently more, not less, reason to feel that awe and gratitude, because we have learnt something of the scope of the achievement. The sense of life itself as active and effective throughout this vast development has been made far stronger, not weaker, by our understanding of our evolutionary history. This is the sense that Darwin expressed when he wrote, at the end of the *Origin*, 'There is grandeur in this view of life'.

Intrinsic value and the social contract

It does not seem to me to matter much whether one calls this wonder and reverence religious or not except to people who have declared a tribal war about the use of that word. It is of course an element that lies at the root of all religions. In the great religions with which we are familiar, it always plays its part and is subsumed within a wider whole. Reverence for the creation can there quite properly inspire and enrich the reverence that is due to its creator.

But such wonder and reverence are equally essential to belief-systems that reject religion. All such systems involve some order of values, some pyramid of priorities which has to end somewhere. In order to make sense of our lives, we have to see some things as mattering in themselves, not merely as a means to something else. Some things have to have what the theorists call intrinsic value. Secular thought in the West has not dropped that notion. Instead, during the last century, it has simply decreed that human individuality itself is the only thing that has this status. Today it uses words such as sacred and sanctity readily to describe human life, but becomes embarrassed if they are used for anything else. People with this approach tend to be alarmed by the direct reverence for the non-human world that was expressed by people like Wordsworth and Rousseau and to treat it as something not quite serious.

Here we come back to the question that I mentioned at the outset about the possible reasons why the fate of the earth should concern us. The early twentieth century's humanistic creed that only people have value—that non-human affairs do not matter except for their effect on people—means that there cannot be any such reason. This is the unspoken creed that leaves us—or at least leaves the professional moralists among us—so puzzled by the environmental crisis—by the thought that we might actually owe some direct duty to the biosphere.[26]

Our individualism has accustomed us to using a minimalist moral approach which gives us no clue to such matters. But that minimal approach has, of course, already created a difficulty in explaining why each of us should be concerned about any other individual besides our own self in the first place; why our value-system should ever go beyond simple egoism. It answers this question in terms of the social contract which is supposed to make it worthwhile for each of us to secure the interests of fellow-citizens. The answer to the question 'Why should I bother about

---

[26] John Passmore laid out this problem admirably in *Man's Responsibility for Nature* (London: Duckworth, 1974), and it has continued to occupy environmental philosophers ever since.

this?' is then always 'Because of the contract which gives you your entrance-ticket to society'.

This contract model excludes dealings with anything non-human. It works quite well for political life—for which, of course, it was originally invented. But even within human existence it is notoriously inadequate. Even within our own lives, we know that we cannot think of rights and duties as optional contracts set up between essentially separate individuals. Relations between parents and children are not like this (and each of us, after all, started life as a non-contracting baby). Nor indeed are most of our personal relations. But we have not yet grasped how much worse this misfit becomes when we have to deal with the rest of the world.

Even over animals, the legalistic notion of contractual rights works badly. And when we come to such chronic non-litigants as the rain-forest and the Antarctic it fails us completely. Entities like these are not fellow-citizens. They never signed a contract. They know nothing of us. How, then, if duties are essentially contractual, can we possibly have duties to them? John Rawls raised this question rather suddenly as an afterthought at the very end of his famous book *A Theory of Justice* and could only say that it was one which lay outside his contractual theory.[27] He added that it ought to be investigated some day. But, as often in such cases, the real response has to be 'you shouldn't have started from here'. Rawls's book was the definitive statement of contract ethics and it marked the end of the era when they could pass as adequate.

Individualism is bankrupt of suggestions for dealing with these non-human entities. Yet we now have to deal with them, and promptly. They can no longer be ignored. Clearly, too, most of us do now think of the human drama as taking place within this larger theatre, not on a private stage of its own. The Darwinian perspective on evolution places us firmly in a wider kinship than Descartes or Hobbes ever dreamed of. We know that we belong on this earth. We are not machines or alien beings or disembodied spirits but primates—animals as naturally and incurably dependent on the earthly biosphere as each one of us is dependent on human society. We know we are members of it and that our technology already commits us to acting in it. By our pollution and our forest-clearances we are already doing so.

What element, then, does the concept of Gaia add to this dawning awareness? It is something beyond the fact of human sociability, which has already been stated, for instance by communitarians. It is not just the mutual dependence of organisms around us, which is already to some extent being brought home to us by ecology. It goes beyond thinking of these organisms as originally separate units that have somehow been forced to cooperate—as basically independent entities which drive bargains for social contracts with each other ('reciprocal altruism') because they just happen to need each other to survive. The metaphysical idea that only individuals are real entities is still present in this picture and it is misleading. Wholes and parts are equally real.

Recent habits make it hard for us to take this in. As science fiction makes clear, we are still amazingly ready to think of our species as a mere casual visitor on this

---

[27] John Rawls, *A Theory of Justice* (Cambridge, MA: Harvard University Press, 1971), p. 512, cf. p. 17. I have discussed this remarkable move in *Animals And Why they Matter* (University of Georgia Press, 1984), pp. 49–50.

planet, as something too special to have developed here. Of course it is true that we are a somewhat special kind of primate, one that is particularly adaptable through culture and gifted with singular talents. But those gifts and talents still come to us from the earth out of which we grow and to which we shall return. The top of our tree still grows from that root as much as the lower branches. We cannot live elsewhere. Our fantasies of moving to outer space mean no more than the magic tales with which other cultures have often consoled themselves for their mortality. Even people who still expect that move in the long term are beginning to see that it cannot be expected to arrive in time to relieve our present emergency. Since the end of the Cold War, NASA has found it increasingly hard to raise funds to keep space programmes going. And environmental disasters are likely to make that process harder, not easier.

All this means that, in spite of recent influences, direct concern about destruction of the natural world is still a natural, spontaneous feeling in us and one that we no longer have any good reason to suppress. Most people, hearing about the wanton destruction of forests and oceans find it shocking and—as has become clear in the last few decades—many of them are prepared to take a good deal of trouble to prevent it. This feeling of shock and outrage is the energy-source which makes change possible.

It has not, of course, been properly tapped yet. As happened over nuclear power, it takes a disaster to bring such needs home to people. Yet the feeling is there and it is surely already becoming stronger and more vocal. It is, of course, what leads people to subscribe to organizations trying to protect the environment. Though we have been educated to detach ourselves from the physical matter of our planet as something alien to us, this detachment is still not a natural or necessary attitude to us. Since we now know that we have evolved from a whole continuum of other life-forms and are closely akin to them—a point which nobody ever explained to Descartes—it is not at all clear why we should separate ourselves from them in this way. On this point, of course, the findings of modern science agree much better with the attitude of those supposedly more primitive cultures where people see themselves as part of the whole spectrum of life around them than they do with the exclusive humanism of the Enlightenment. They also agree better with most of our everyday thought. The element in that thought which is now beginning to look arbitrary and unreal is its exclusive humanism.

Indignant concern on behalf of the environment does, then, already exist. Our difficulty is that we cannot see how to fit it into our traditional morality which—both in its Christian and its secular forms—has in general been carefully tailored to fit only the human scene. How should we deal with this conceptual emergency? I do not think that it is very helpful to proceed as some moralists have done by promoting various selected outside entities such as 'wildernesses' to the status of honorary members of human society. If we claim (for instance) that a wilderness such as the Antarctic has intrinsic value because it has independent moral status, meaning by this that we have decided to grant it the privilege of treating it like an extra fellow-citizen, we shall sound rather inadequate. These larger wholes are independent of us in a quite different sense from that in which extra humans—or even animals—who were candidates for citizenship might be so. Our relation to them is of a totally different kind from the one which links us to our fellow-citizens.

There is, indeed, something unreal about the whole way of thinking which speaks of these places as though they were distinct individual 'wildernesses', units which are applying separately for admission to our value-spectrum. Though we divide them for our thought, they function as parts of the whole. At present, indeed, the Arctic and the Antarctic are letting us know this because their ice, melted by global warming, is affecting the entire state of the oceans. That process is already producing widespread floods which threaten the destruction of places such as Bangladesh and Mauritius and widespread damage elsewhere. Nearer home, it also looks liable to upset the Gulf Stream in a way that may drastically chill the climate of Europe. Without that convenient warming system, we in Britain would find ourselves ten degrees colder, sharing the climate of Labrador, which is on much the same latitude. And if that change happens it could apparently happen quite quickly. Globalization is not just an option offered to our culture. It is a fact that is here already.

The surprising inefficiency of selfishness

This is, of course, a prudential consideration. It may suggest that rational self-interest alone will be enough to guide us here—as Hobbes supposed it always would be. And of course it is true that self-interest should indeed drive us this way. The odd thing is that it does not.[28] The human imagination does not work that way. When things go well, we simply don't believe in disasters. Long-term prudence, reaching beyond the accepted, routine precautions of everyday life, is therefore an extraordinarily feeble motive. Its weakness has lately appeared sharply in the failure of the electronic industry to provide in advance against the Millennium Bug. If humans are naturally rational and prudent—at least in their business hours—it should surely surprise us that for fifty years all these highly-qualified, intelligent and well-funded people have apparently been assuming that the twentieth century would never come to an end.

This example is interesting because—as in the case of our own death—that particular outcome was not in doubt. Prudence, however, is supposed to operate on probabilities as well as on certainties. And the increasing probability of environmental disaster has been well-attested for at least the last thirty years. During all that while, each time that the travellers in steerage pointed out that the ship was sinking the first-class passengers have continued to reply placidly, 'Not at our end'. Only very gradually and shakily is this prospect beginning to be admitted as an influence on policy—a topic that should be allowed now and then to compete for the attention of decision-makers, alongside football and teenage sex and the Dow-Jones Index and European Monetary Union. Only gradually is it beginning to be seen that ecology is actually a more important science than economics—that the profitable exchange of goods within the ship is a less urgent matter than how to keep the whole ship above water. When the story of our age comes to be written, this perspective may surely seem surprising.

---

[28] I have discussed this fascinating point more fully in *Beast and Man* (London: Routledge revised paperback edition, 1995), ch. 6.

Our imaginations, however, are not ruled by our reason. We do not easily expect the unfamiliar, and major disasters are always unfamiliar. When we are trying to be prudent, our thoughts turn to well-known and immediate dangers, nervously avoiding a wider scene. That is why self-interest alone cannot be trusted to answer our question about why the earth should concern us. Of course prudence must come in, but unless other reasons are already recognized prudence usually manages to evade the larger topic. That is why we need to think about those other reasons—about the ways in which the terrestrial whole, of which we are a part, directly concerns us, and would still do so even if we could get away with abusing it. As I am suggesting, we shall never grasp the nature of that kind of concern so long as we try to model it on the civic concern that links fellow-citizens. *Duties to wholes, of which one is a part, naturally differ in form from duties to other individuals.*

Since the Enlightenment, our culture has made huge efforts to exclude outward-looking duties altogether from Western morality. Pronouncements such as 'there is no such thing as society' and 'the state is only a logical construction out of its members' are only recent shots in this long individualist campaign. But the natural strength of outward-looking concern can be seen from the way in which many such duties are still accepted. For instance, the idea of *duty to one's country* still persists and it certainly does not just mean duty to obey the government. Again, even in our society, where the idea of *duty to a family, clan, locality or racial group* has been deliberately played down, those ideas still have great force whenever a particular group feels threatened by outside oppression. The current revival of nationalism among various groups, especially in the United States, and the emphasis laid on sisterhood by feminists, all testify to this force. In other cultures, where no attempt has been made to undermine it, its strength is unmistakable.

Another corporate claim which can operate powerfully is the idea of a *duty to posterity*. This is not just the idea of a string of separate duties to particular future individuals. It is rather the sense of being part of a great historical stream of effort within which we live and to which we owe loyalty. That identification with the stream explains the sense in which we can—rather surprisingly—owe duties to the dead and also to a great range of anonymous future people, two things which have baffled individualistic thinkers. Even when there is no conscious talk of duty, people who work in any cooperative enterprise—school, firm, shop, orchestra, theatrical company, teenage gang, political party, football team—find it thoroughly natural to act as if they had a duty to that enclosing whole if it is in some way threatened.

And this, it seems to me, is what is now beginning to happen about the earth itself, as the threat to it begins to be grasped. When an enclosing whole which has been taken for granted is suddenly seen as really endangered, all at once its hidden claims become visible. It would be good if we could accept the overwhelming existing evidence of a terrestrial emergency without needing to be hit by a disaster. But whatever causes that belief to be accepted, once it becomes so there is surely little doubt about the duty it lays upon us.

Our mainstream tradition has played down this corporate element in morals and that is not surprising. Political theorists such as Hobbes and Rousseau—and their contemporaries in active politics—wanted above all, to stop certain dominant groups, notably the Church, exploiting this loyalty for their own ends. They succeeded to an extent which would surely have astonished them if they could have foreseen it, and which Rousseau at least would have found alarming. Between them, they managed to swing the balance of moral thinking right over to its individualistic pole.

As we have seen, they did not manage to destroy the idea of corporate duty entirely. *Fraternity* was supposed to be among the ideals of the French Revolution, though in practice it was usually thrust aside by Equality and Freedom. Rousseau himself did try to balance the individualism of his contract theory by introducing the idea of the General Will, a corporate will in the nation distinct from the mere summing of separate decisions—something to be relied on more deeply, something which individuals should seek out and follow. This and similar hints were developed by Hegel into a fully fledged Organic Theory of the State, by which individuals are always incomplete entities, more or less comparable with cells in a plant or animal, needing to find their place in a wider whole for full realization.

Up to a point this suggestion clearly has to be true. Most of us, if we can act freely at all, want to place ourselves within such larger groupings—families, clubs, friendships, orchestras, gangs, political movements. But it is a sort of doctrine which sounds very different according to which kind of larger group we have in mind. By bad luck, Hegel centred his theory on the nation-state and in particular on his own state of Prussia, which was then (in the early nineteenth century) preparing to dominate the rest of Germany and thereby the rest of Europe. Marx, following Hegel's organic approach, also expected his precepts to be taken up in Germany and, though he envisaged a distant time when nation-states would not be needed, he expected them to be the main social unit for the foreseeable future. As the eventual adoption of Marxism in Russia did not produce any sort of Utopia, it is not surprising that these two unattractive examples have put people off organic theories of society, or that many of them end up saying, with Nietzsche's Zarathustra: 'The State lieth in all the languages of good and evil; whatsoever it saith, it lieth; whatsoever it hath, it hath stolen'.[29]

Thus, through most of the twentieth century, many prophets in the West have preached a kind of narrow and romantic individualism, a moral outlook which simply assumes that individual freedom is the only unquestionable value. This is a doctrine held in common by J.-P. Sartre and Ayn Rand. Despite the difference of style, the European and the American forms of it share a central message: social atomism. Both conceive the individual's freedom as negative—a matter of avoiding interference. Politically, however, there is rather an important difference because of the kind of entity that counts as an individual is different in the two versions.

The European version still speaks of individual people and therefore stays close to real anarchism. The American one, however, expands to include 'commercial freedom'. And commercial freedom, in its modern form, is a different thing and a very strange one. The entities which it conceives as free are no longer individuals but corporations, often very big and impersonal ones. The rhetoric of 'free trade', in fact, does not now refer to individual freedom at all. The old romantic vision of commercial freedom which (as we shall see in a moment) Herbert Spencer presented in the 1880s—a vision of heroic individual tycoons carving out the course of evolution with their bare hands—does not fit today's conditions at all, whatever may be thought of its exactness in his own day.

---

[29] Friedrich Nietzsche, *Thus Spake Zarathustra*, part 1, section 'Of The New Idol'.

There has, in fact, been an extraordinary shift here in the central tenet of individualism. The metaphysical belief in human individuals as the true atoms of social life—the only properly real and sacred kind of unit—has given way. At the moment, the focus has shifted to another kind of entity, the big corporation. But since that kind of entity, in its turn, is now beginning to look rather less than ultimate—since the Internet is threatening its supremacy by building a more diffused way of doing business, while individual speculators infest it from within and shake its control—this does not seem likely to be the end of the story. These corporations may prove to be dinosaurs, entities remembered only as we remember medieval guilds. What surely emerges is that the whole idea of a single favoured, exclusively real unit was mistaken in the first place. *Life goes on on various scales, each of which is real and has to be thought of in its own terms.*

This shift of emphasis to a kind of corporate freedom is, however, just one more indication of how—as communitarians have recently been pointing out—individualist propaganda cannot destroy the corporate element in morals. Of course we still value our personal freedom very highly. Psychologically, our emphasis on it may perhaps be largely produced by overcrowding, by the sheer increase in human numbers and in social mobility during the last century. We all see far more people, especially far more strangers, in our daily lives than our ancestors did, which certainly imposes stress and social exhaustion.

Yet humans—even modern, civilized humans—are still social animals to whom, on average, the desolation of loneliness is a much worse threat than the interference of their fellows. On the positive side, too, we have talents and capacities which absolutely require generous, outgoing cooperation for their fulfilment—a point which Hegel got right. Paradoxically, there are many things which a free, solitary individualist is not free to do. He cannot be a parent, a quartet-player, a tragic actor, a teacher, a social reformer or even a revolutionary. Even Nietzsche's Zarathustra noticed this difficulty:

A light hath dawned on me. I need companions ... living companions which follow me because they desire to follow themselves—and to go to that place whither I wish to go.[30]

In fact (as Butler pointed out against Hobbes), apart from certain narrow political contexts human beings are not in the least like the pure, consistent, prudent egoists that social contract thinking requires. And today people are coming to see this.

Of course it is true that we need to stop the powerful oppressing the weak, so we must have political institutions to prevent the exploitation of these corporate loyalties. That is why we need a free press to answer the propaganda of governments. And since the press itself comes under commercial pressure, that pressure, working through the labour market, through advertisements and through countless other channels, is, on the whole, much more alarming today than the power of religion. But the need to ward off these dangers cannot mean that we can do without corporate loyalties altogether. The outgoing, social side of human life vitally needs them.

[30] Nietzsche, *Thus Spake Zarathustra*, Introductory Discourse, § 9.

Bounded and cosmopolitan justice

ONORA O'NEILL[1]

1. The scope of justice

Since antiquity justice has been thought of as a political or civic virtue, more recently as belonging in a 'bounded society',[2] or as a primary task of states.[3] All such views assume that the context of justice has boundaries, which demarcate those who are to render and to receive justice from one another from others who are to be excluded. Yet the view that justice is intrinsically bounded sits ill with the many claims that it is cosmopolitan, owed to all regardless of location or origin, race or gender, class or citizenship. The tension between moral cosmopolitanism and institutional anti-cosmopolitanism has been widely discussed over the last twenty years, but there is still a lot of disagreement about its proper resolution.[4]

Take, for example, the specific version of this thought that views justice as wholly internal to states. If we start with cosmopolitan principles, the justice of states will suffice for justice only if we can show that any system of just states will itself be just.

---

[1] An earlier rather different version of this article appeared under the title 'Civic and Cosmopolitan Justice' as the Lindley Lecture for 2000, published by the Philosophy Department of the University of Kansas.

[2] John Rawls relies on the idea of a *bounded society* throughout his work. References to Rawls's writings cited here may be abbreviated in subsequent footnotes: *A Theory of Justice* (Cambridge, MA: Harvard University Press, 1971); 'Themes in Kant's Moral Philosophy' (1989), in *Collected Papers*, Samuel Freeman (ed.), (Cambridge, MA: Harvard University Press, 1999), pp. 497–528; *Political Liberalism* (New York: Columbia University Press, 1993); *The Law of Peoples* (Cambridge, MA: Harvard University Press, 1999).

[3] This view evidently underlies the UN *Universal Declaration of Human Rights* of 1948; the text uses a varied range of seemingly nonequivalent terms, including *member states*, *peoples*, *nations* and *countries*; a coherent reading of the document requires us to take all of these as referring to states.

[4] A selection from this literature might begin by noting Charles Beitz, *Political Theory and International Relations* (Princeton, NJ: Princeton University Press, 1979), 'Cosmopolitan Ideals and National Sentiment', *Journal of Philosophy*, 80 (1983), pp. 591–600 and 'Cosmopolitan Liberalism and the State System', in Chris Brown (ed.) *Political Restructuring in Europe: Ethical Perspectives*, (London: Routledge, 1994); Simon Caney, 'Global Equality of Opportunity and the Sovereignty of States', in *International Justice*, ed. Anthony Coates (Aldershot: Ashgate, 2000), and 'Cosmopolitan Justice and Equalizing Opportunities', forthcoming in *Metaphilosophy*; Joseph Carens, 'Aliens and Citizens: The Case for Open Borders', *Review of Politics*, 49 (1987), pp. 251–73; Charles Jones, *Global Justice: Defending Cosmopolitanism* (Oxford: Oxford University Press, 1999); David Miller, 'The Nation State: A Modest Defence', in *Political Restructuring in Europe*, Chris Brown (ed.), pp. 137–62 and 'The Limits of Cosmopolitan Justice' in *International Society: Diverse Ethical Perspectives*, David R. Mapel and Terry Nardin (eds.) (Princeton, NJ: Princeton University Press), Thomas Pogge, 'Cosmopolitanism and Sovereignty' in *Political Restructuring in Europe*, Chris Brown (ed.), pp. 89–122 and 'An Egalitarian Law of Peoples', *Philosophy and Public Affairs*, 23 (1994), pp. 195–224; Onora O'Neill, 'Justice and Boundaries', in *Political Restructuring in Europe*, Chris Brown (ed.), pp. 69–88 and *Bounds of Justice* (Cambridge: Cambridge University Press, 2000), Henry Shue, *Basic Rights: Subsistence, Affluence and US Foreign Policy*, 2nd edn. (Princeton, NJ: Princeton University Press, 1996).

But this claim is implausible. We can certainly imagine a system of states that would be just provided that each state was just. For example, a set of just states without mutual influence or effects (imagine that they are located on different continents in a premodern world, or on different planets today) could be just provided that each state was just. But the system of states in the various forms in which it has existed in recent centuries is not at all like this. The prospects and powers of states, and the structures they can establish internally, are always shaped by the relations of domination and subordination between them, and the exclusions which state boundaries create may themselves be sources of injustice. The same line of thought suggests that it is equally implausible to think that bounded societies, or cities, or communities, or other bounded entities, provide the sole contexts of justice. Boundaries of whatever sort are not unquestionable presuppositions of thinking about justice, but rather institutions whose structure raises questions of justice.

Equally, commitment to cosmopolitan principles does not entail—although it also may not rule out—commitment to cosmopolitan political institutions, such as a world state, or a world federation. Principles are intrinsically indeterminate, and may be institutionalized in many distinct ways.[5] In some circumstances the best way of institutionalizing a commitment to cosmopolitan justice might be to abolish certain sorts of boundaries, and in others it might not. The risk of cosmopolitan institutions is that they concentrate power, and that we have very good reasons for ensuring that power is not concentrated at a global level, just as the political philosophers of the seventeenth and eighteenth century had very good reasons for insisting on the separation of powers within states. On the other hand, the risk of anti-cosmopolitan institutions is that they may institutionalize justice in ways that groundlessly exclude some from its benefits—and its burdens.

In this article I shall contrast two views of justice beyond borders; both of them are supposedly alert to the claims both of bounded institutions and of universal principles. The two positions are those proposed by Immanuel Kant in a number of works, but in particular in his political writings of the 1780s and 1790s, and by John Rawls in *Political Liberalism* (1993) and in *The Law of Peoples* (1999). Rawlsian and Kantian views of justice are often thought of as quite similar: Rawls speaks of his own work as 'Kantian', and follows Kant in building his account of justice on a conception of 'public reason' which has certain affinities with Kant's conception of public reason. More specifically, both Rawls and Kant advance what may be loosely called a semi-cosmopolitan view of just institutions: neither endorses a world state, but each thinks that justice requires more than can be delivered by the internal institutions of states. I shall not, however, say very much about the specific institutional proposals for international justice that Rawls and Kant put forward, and will concentrate mainly on their respective starting points rather than their policy recommendations.

There are two reasons for choosing this focus. The first is that comparisons between proposals that address such different worlds may mislead. Kant's proposals were in their day a remarkable blend of political realism and radical thinking.

---

[5] Alan Gewirth, 'Ethical Universalism and Particularism', *Journal of Philosophy*, 85 (1988), pp. 283–302; Onora O'Neill, *Towards Justice and Virtue* (Cambridge: Cambridge University Press, 1996), and 'Principles, Practical Judgement and Institutions', in *Bounds of Justice* (Cambridge: Cambridge University Press, 2000), pp. 50–64.

Writing at a time when there were few republican states and no full democracies, he proposes a league of republican states that acknowledge certain obligations not only to their own citizens but also to the citizens of other (republican) states. By contrast, Rawls's proposals for justice across boundaries are quite conservative for our day. Writing at a time in which the United Nations and its organizations, the World Bank and various international courts have all existed for some time, he suggests simply that international justice will require some institutions of roughly these sorts.[6] My second reason for saying rather little about the specific institutions of justice across borders to which Kant and Rawls point is that much has already been said by many others.[7] But in my view too little has been said about the respective starting points of their thought about justice beyond borders; so it is to these that I shall turn. For reasons that will become clear, I shall discuss Rawls before Kant rather than sticking to the historical order.

2. Communitarians and justice beyond boundaries

Before turning to Rawls, it is useful to call to mind the communitarian views he opposes, in which the very principles of justice and the reasoning that is to support them are viewed as bounded. A merit of communitarian thought is that it incorporates a strong view of the basis of practical reasoning, which it views as legitimately formed and bounded by the categories, norms and practices of actual communities and their cultures. Although this move may seem arbitrary from the point of view of outsiders, it is anchored in a conception of human identity as shaped by the constitutive norms and practices of the communities and traditions of which a given individual is part, and so offers substantial premises for working out an account of justice and other normative issues appropriate to that community. These norms and practices are, to use a useful Hegelian phrase, seen as *nicht hintergehbar*: there is no going behind them. Since they are constitutive of the identity of the community or tradition, and so of its members, there is no deeper range of premises that could provide a basis for challenging these norms.

Communitarians are not unaware of the possibility that the constitutive norms of communities and traditions may change, indeed be changed by those within a community. They see the categories and values of communities as open to revision in the light of its internal conceptual resources. Hence it would be a mistake to think that communitarian reasoning is inevitably *conservative*. However, I believe that it would

---

[6] By contrast many of his critics have argued that Rawlsian conceptions of domestic justice should be applied globally, for example that the difference principle should be applied to global distributive justice, or that fair equality of opportunity should be extended globally. See especially the works by Beitz, Caney and Pogge cited in fn. 4.

[7] See in particular the papers in James Bohman and Matthias Lutz-Bachmann (eds.), *Perpetual Peace: Essays on Kant's Cosmopolitan Ideal* (Cambridge, MA: MIT Press, 1997), especially Jürgen Habermas, 'Kant's Idea of Perpetual Peace, with the Benefit of Two Hundred Years' Hindsight', pp. 113–53, and on Rawls, see Charles Beitz, *Political Theory and International Relations*; Andrew Kuper, 'Rawlsian Global Justice: Beyond *The Law of Peoples* to a Cosmopolitan Law of Persons', *Political Theory*, forthcoming; Thomas Pogge, *Realizing Rawls* (Ithaca, NY: Cornell University Press, 1989), esp. part III, and 'An Egalitarian Law of Peoples', as well as papers in the forthcoming issue of *Metaphilosophy* on the theme of Global Justice, edited by Thomas Pogge.

not be mistaken to think that reasoning which proceeds within the constraints set by the categories, norms and other resources of a community or tradition must inevitably be *ethnocentric*. Communitarian reasoning is inevitably insiders' reasoning, and takes no account of the categories, the concerns or the views of outsiders. This does not, of course, mean that communitarians can have no view of the proper treatment of outsiders: they might be convinced of the merits of exclusion or of integration, of neglect or of assimilation, or perhaps (more worryingly) of marginalization, colonization or extermination.[8] However, they do not think that there could be reasoned dialogue with unassimilated outsiders, with whom neither categories nor norms, nor therefore the means of reasoning, are shared.

Although communitarians take a realistic view of the possibilities for change within any given tradition, I believe that they take an unrealistic view of the boundaries between traditions and communities. Political boundaries form highly variable filters; the cultural boundaries with which communitarian reasoning is chiefly concerned are yet more diverse and malleable. Many people are conversant with the categories and norms of a number of traditions; those who are not initially familiar with the thought of some community can often grasp a good deal about others' categories and norms, and therefore about their reasoning.[9] (For contemporary evidence, consider the amazing spread of the rhetoric of rights.) Sense of identity is not invariably anchored in the actual norms and categories of a single community; even where it is, the ways of thought and life of that community may allow understanding of and by a fair range of outsiders. Like the rest of us, communitarians in fact hold that foreigners and other cultural outsiders are persons with whom we can communicate, if not perfectly, still a great deal, and that trade and translation, travel and collaboration are real possibilities. In my view these everyday assumptions undermine the plausibility of any communitarian conception of practical reason and show that it offers no convincing basis for reasoning either about domestic justice or about justice beyond boundaries.

However, reasoning that does not draw on culturally specific categories and norms will be considerably impoverished. It is not obvious what alternative premises for practical reasoning will be available. Once we allow that not all reasoning about justice can be based on the rich conceptual resources of a tradition or community, we must look for an alternative account of practical reason. One promising direction in which to look is to John Rawls's work, and in particular to his later work, in which he both advances and deploys a conception of practical reason as 'public' reason to address questions of justice.

3. Rawls on public reason

In *Political Liberalism* and in *The Law of Peoples*, which is published together with a further separate essay on 'The Idea of Public Reason', John Rawls explicitly rejects

---

[8] Communitarian reasoning has often been put forward by writers whose substantive political commitments are more or less liberal—but its potential is not adequately assessed unless account is taken of the fact that communitarianism is equally hospitable to substantive norms that are anti-liberal, excluding, separatist or even imperial.

[9] See the papers in Onora O'Neill, *Bounds of Justice*, part II.

the underlying assumption of the communitarian project: 'pluralism is not seen as a disaster but rather as the natural outcome of human reason under enduring free institutions'.[10] If this is the case, it will not always be possible to identify constitutive categories and norms for the very units for which Rawls thinks questions of justice primarily arise. Justice, as he sees it, has its context in a *bounded society*, a per-petually continuing scheme of cooperation that persons enter only by birth and leave only by death, and which is self-sufficient.[11] Within each bounded society, reasonable persons will not come to complete agreement about ethical matters and may be expected to form differing 'conceptions of the good'. However, as reasonable, they may be expected to accept a form of reciprocity, namely to be 'ready to propose principles and standards as fair terms of co-operation and to abide by them willingly, given the assurance that others will likewise do so'.[12] Reasonable persons are committed to a conception of public reason, and prepared to work out the framework for the public social world they share and to construct the principles of justice by which they will live together, despite their irresolvable ethical disagree-ments. Public reason, as Rawls construes it, is "citizens' reasoning in the public forum about constitutional essentials and basic questions of justice".[13] Evidently this conception of public reason as reciprocity between fellow-citizens presupposes the constitutive institutions that define not just *citizenship* but *fellow-citizenship*: the bounded society and the constitutional basis of citizenship (including liberal rights and democracy in just societies, on Rawls's account). This essentially civic con-ception of public reason is coupled with what we might view as an associative conception of practical reasoning for narrower spheres (Rawls calls this 'non-public reason'; his thought is close to Kant's writing on 'private uses of reason').[14]

In short, although Rawls's conception of public reason in *Political Liberalism* does not assume the shared culture that communitarian reasoning presupposes, it does presuppose shared political arrangements, including boundaries, and (for just societies) liberal democracy and citizenship. It is a nice question whether the boundaries that are presupposed are—contrary to Rawls's intentions—in fact state boundaries. On the one hand he claims only to presuppose a 'bounded society', on the other hand the assumption that nobody enters except by birth or leaves except by death suggests that Rawlsian bounded societies are well policed, that within their territories legitimate force is exercised, so presumably monopolized. And this is the Weberian definition of a state.

These issues are discussed in more detail in Rawls's *The Law of Peoples*. Here he argues that issues of justice beyond boundaries are to be approached by considering public reasoning as conducted by *peoples*. He rejects both the communitarian thought that the basis of reasoning is to be culturally defined (a community, a tradition), and the thought that the parties who consider justice beyond boundaries

---

[10] John Rawls, *Political Liberalism* (New York: Columbia University Press, 1993), xxiv; cf. pp. 47, 55. 3; *Law of Peoples*, pp. 31–2. 'The Idea of Public Reason' (included in *Law of Peoples*), p. 131.

[11] This formulation is to be found throughout Rawls, *A Theory of Justice*; in later works the emphasis on bounded societies continues, but their liberal democracy and the citizenship of their members are increasingly emphasized; these shifts are corollaries of Rawls's shift to a 'political' conception of justification.

[12] Rawls, *Political Liberalism*, p. 49 including the note.

[13] Ibid., p. 10; cf. pp. 212 ff. and *Law of Peoples*, pp. 132–3.

[14] For Rawls's views on non-public reasoning see *Political Liberalism*, pp. 213 ff., esp. pp. 220–2 and *Law of Peoples*, p. 134; for Kant's views on public and private reason, see sections 4 to 6 below.

are to be thought of either as individuals or as states.[15] Liberal peoples are thought of as inhabiting their own territories, and as negotiating standards of international justice with other liberal peoples, as well as with those non-liberal peoples who have what Rawls calls a 'decent hierarchical society'. Rawls believes that the principles that would be mutually accepted will include those of non-aggression, non-intervention except in self-defence (and sparingly to end grave violations of human rights in other societies).[16] He also thinks that reasonable peoples are likely to agree on some version of the UN organizations, some form of World Bank and some form of global trade agreement.[17] Reasonable peoples also, he thinks, have some duty of assistance to help heavily burdened societies to progress towards justice; but the difference principle is not to be extended to global economic institutions.[18] Since the procedures of Rawlsian public reasoning are specified only in very general terms, it is reasonable to ask whether there would be mutual agreement on these specific arrangements. Rawls's claims that the 'Law of Peoples' will take this limited view of transnational economic justice depends crucially on his assumption that boundaries—but not state boundaries—are prior to justice. Otherwise it would be obscure why reasonable peoples would not agree to a more extended view of the duties of richer towards poorer societies.

The conception of the state that Rawls rejects in *The Law of Peoples* is in my view indeed a pretty unpromising basis for any account of justice beyond boundaries. What he rejects is the realist conception of states as 'anxiously concerned with their power—their capacity (military, economic, diplomatic)—to influence others and always guided by their basic interests'.[19] However, this has always been an idealized, indeed ideologized, conception of the state; it is certainly not the only option. Others have thought that states themselves are capable of action that is not self-interested, and that they can and should be bound to justice in their dealings with other states.

Curiously, the conception of a 'people' on which Rawls builds his account of justice beyond boundaries is in fact remarkably state-like, since it views peoples too as preoccupied by protection of territory and self-interest:

Liberal peoples do, however, have their fundamental interests as permitted by their conceptions of right and justice. They seek to protect their territory, to ensure the security and safety of their citizens, and to preserve their free political institutions and the liberties and free culture of their civil society.[20]

Evidently Rawls conceives of peoples as territorially bounded and politically organized, and as able to appoint representatives[21] through whom they are to reason with other peoples about justice beyond boundaries. In short, peoples are conceived

---

[15] Rawls, *Political Liberalism*, p. 18; *Law of Peoples*, pp. 23–30.
[16] Rawls, *Law of Peoples*, p. 35.
[17] Ibid., p. 38.
[18] Ibid., pp. 115–19; for contrary views see Charles Beitz, *Political Theory and International Relations* and Thomas Pogge, *Realizing Rawls*, 'Towards an Egalitarian Law of Peoples' and more recently 'On Global Economic Justice', *Metaphilosophy*, forthcoming.
[19] Rawls, *Law of Peoples*, p. 28.
[20] Ibid., p. 29. Note also the following: 'The point of the institution of property is that, unless a definite agent is given responsibility for maintaining an asset … that asset tends to deteriorate. In this case the asset is the people's territory and its capacity to support them in perpetuity; and the agent is the people themselves as politically organized', *Law of Peoples*, p. 39.
[21] Ibid., pp. 32, 34.

as having all the powers, capacities and features of states, and in addition the concern 'to preserve their free political institutions and the liberties and free culture of their civil society'. There is little here that distinguishes liberal peoples from liberal states. Rawls, however, holds that

What distinguishes peoples from states—and this is crucial—is that just peoples are fully prepared to grant the very same proper respect and recognition to other peoples as equal.[22]

In Rawls's view, peoples can be reasonable, but states are wedded—or condemned—to rational self-interest.

Rawls's choice of *peoples* rather than *states* as the agents whose deliberations are basic to justice beyond boundaries is, I think, motivated in large part by the inaccurate assumption that states must be ideal typical structures that fit the realist paradigm. Yet states, *as we have actually known them* do not fit that paradigm.[23] The view that states and governments have limited powers, yet can adhere to fundamental principles by which they modify the pursuit of rational self-interest, is central to the liberal tradition of political philosophy and to contemporary international politics. States *as they have really existed and exist* never had and never have unlimited sovereignty, internal or external—although various theorists of sovereignty, proponents of strategic reasoning, hawks in powerful states, and romantic nationalists without powerful states have made grandiose claims. States *as they currently exist* are committed by numerous treaty obligations to a limited conception of sovereignty and a degree of respect for human rights; and there is nothing contradictory about these commitments, although like other commitments they are sometimes not honoured. Peoples as *they may once have existed* independently of state structures, lack bounded territories; peoples who negotiate with other peoples, who keep outsiders out and make agreements achieve this by building on state and governmental structures.

It is not hard to see what leads Rawls to his distinctive view of the basis for thinking about international justice. Since he has proposed an account of public reason that focuses on the notion of reciprocity among agents, he has to determine who the relevant agents shall be, among whom reciprocity is to be achieved—or not achieved. Since he assumes that the realist conception of the state, according to which states must act solely from self-interest and will not be capable of reciprocity, is canonical it follows that states cannot be agents of justice who rely on Rawlsian public reason. By default, the reasonable agents who are to carry the burden of international negotiation and justice across boundaries are then identified as *peoples*. Yet in reality the only peoples who have well defined and controlled boundaries and capacities to negotiate with outsiders on a sustained and potentially reasonable basis are peoples with states. There is something laborious about anchoring an account of reasoning in a conception of territorial agents not well exemplified in our world, who (if they were exemplified) would acquire the political capacities Rawls imputes to them only by developing the very state and governmental structures from which he tries to detach his argument.

---

[22] Ibid., p. 35.

[23] Theorists of international relations acknowledge that many of the states we see around us fall far short of the realist paradigm of statehood: they speak of quasi-states and dependent states; Rawls acknowledges that realism about state action is false—yet leaves realists in possession of conceptions of the state, see *Law of Peoples*, p. 46.

4. Kant: public reason as non-derivative

Rawls views his philosophy as in many ways Kantian, and makes frequent references to Kant in his writing on justice across boundaries. However, he also, and in my view rightly, distances his work from Kant's. In *The Law of Peoples* he writes:

> Since my presentation of the Law of Peoples is greatly indebted to Kant's idea of *foedus pacificum* and to so much in his thought, I should say the following: at no point are we deducing the principles of right and justice, or decency, or the principles of rationality, from a conception of practical reason in the background. Rather, we are giving content to an idea of practical reason and three of its component parts, the ideas of reasonableness, decency and rationality. The criteria for these three normative ideas are not deduced, but enumerated and characterized in each case. Practical reasoning as such is simply reasoning about what to do, or reasoning about what institutions and policies are reasonable, decent, or rational and why. There is no list of necessary or sufficient conditions for each of these three ideas ...[24]

As Rawls sees it, Kant's reliance on an account of practical reason has unacceptable metaphysical presuppositions.[25] Kant, by contrast, does seek to derive his account of justice from an account of practical reason. However, it is not obvious that Kant's conceptions of practical reason, of ethics, of justice or specifically of international justice *must* be derived from transcendental idealism under a strongly metaphysical interpretation. In particular, Kant's distinctive non-Rawlsian understanding of public reason provides relatively accessible arguments, which do not draw on metaphysical assumptions, yet aim to vindicate a specific conception of practical reason: they can be given, indeed they invite, an anti-metaphysical reading.[26]

The central thought of Kant's account of public reason is that the standards of reason cannot be derivative. Any appeal to other, external authorities to buttress our reasoning must fail. Just as a learner cyclist who clutches at passing objects and leans on them to balance thereby fails to balance at all, so a would-be reasoner who leans on some socially or civilly constituted power or authority which lacks reasoned vindication fails to reason.

This view is explicit in the quite distinctive way in which Kant characterizes the difference between his conceptions of *public* and *private* uses of reason in various

---

[24] Rawls, *Law of Peoples*, pp. 86–7; see also John Rawls, 'Themes in Kant's Moral Philosophy' for further elaboration of ways in which Rawls views his position on reason as differing from Kant's.

[25] For a discussion of some of Rawls's reasons for distancing himself from Kant, and some of the ways in which he arrives at a very weak conception of public reason, see Thomas McCarthy, 'A Reasonable Law of Peoples', in James Bohman and Matthias Lutz-Bachmann, *Perpetual Peace: Essays on Kant's Cosmopolitan Ideal* (Cambridge, MA: MIT Press, 1997), pp. 201–17. For further suggestions for an anti-foundationalist reading of Kant's vindication of reason see Onora O'Neill, *Constructions of Reason: Explorations of Kant's Practical Philosophy* (Cambridge: Cambridge University Press, 1989), especially the first two papers, and 'Vindicating Reason' in Paul Guyer (ed.), *The Cambridge Companion to Kant* (Cambridge: Cambridge University Press, 1992), pp. 280–308 and 'Kant's Conception of Public Reason', Proceedings of The VIIIth Kant Kongress, Berlin 2000 (Berlin: de Grunter), forthcoming.

[26] Kant offers other non-metaphysical arguments for his account of reason, which do not make explicit use of the conception of *public reason*. In various texts he leans more heavily on terms such as *negative self-discipline*, *authentic interpretation* and *autonomy*.

works of the 1780's and 1790's.[27] Here I shall refer only to two short essays of the 1780's, neglecting Kant's other extended discussions of public and private reason and of related notions.[28] In these essays Kant characterizes uses of reason that appeal to rationally ungrounded assumptions, such as the civilly constituted authority of Church or state, not as public but as private. In *What is Enlightenment?* he speaks of the reasoning of military officers, of pastors of the established Church and of civil servants in carrying out their roles as *private*: these functionaries derive their authority from their civil offices. Their official communications assume *without argument* the authority of the civil power that establishes the office and its constitutive powers and rules. Kant states explicitly that 'the private use of reason is that which one may make of it in a certain *civil* post or office with which he is entrusted'.[29] It follows that the sorts of reasoning exhibited in democratic political debate and in communitarian thought, as well as in the civic reasoning Rawls commends, are all in Kant's view *private*, because each presupposes the authority of civilly and socially constituted roles, institutions and practices. Rawlsian peoples are not identifiable independently of their bounded territories and the constitutive institutional structures that secure these territories, distinguish citizen from non-citizen, and provide the contexts for their (democratic) government, including that part of (democratic) government which counts as foreign policy: hence Kant would see their reasoning as private.

Kant himself offers a quite different view of (fully) public reason as *intrinsically* non-derivative. He contrasts all 'private' uses of reason with 'the public use of one's own reason ... which someone makes of it *as a scholar* before the entire public of the *world of readers*',[30] a scholar 'who by his writings speaks to the public in the strict sense, that is, the world'.[31]

In these and other passages Kant sets out a dilemma. If we appeal to any civilly or socially constituted powers or authorities, let alone to mere brute force—if we try to constrain or control attempts to reason—we lose the very justifications we seek. Discourse that defers to authorities that lack reasoned vindication achieves at best restricted scope and authority, and those who buttress their conclusions by appealing to authorities they do not vindicate end up relying on the dubious merits of an argument from authority.

---

[27] All references to Kant's works and all quotations are taken from the *Cambridge Edition of the Works of Immanuel Kant*, Paul Guyer and Allen J. Wood (eds.) (Cambridge: Cambridge University Press). The relevant volumes are *Practical Philosophy*, Mary J. Gregor (trans.), 1996 and *Religion and Rational Theology*, trans. Allen J. Wood and George Givoanni (Cambridge, 1996). The volume and page references are to the Prussian Academy edition; they are included in the margins of the Cambridge edition. The following titles cited here may be abbreviated in subsequent footnotes: *What is Enlightenment?* (1784); *Groundwork of the Metaphysic of Morals* (1785); *What Does it Mean to Orient Oneself in Thinking?* (1786); *The Metaphysic of Morals* (1797); *Toward Perpetual Peace* (1795); *On the Common Saying: That May be Correct in Theory, but Is of No Use in Practice* (1793); *Religion Within the Boundaries of Mere Reason* (1793); *The Conflict of the Faculties* (1798). Only the latter two are in the *Religion and Rational Theology* volume.

[28] In particular, I shall say nothing about Kant's discussion of public and private uses of reason in the interpretation of Scripture, which is a major theme of *Conflict of the Faculties*, and discussed using the closely related conception of *authentic interpretation* in *Religion Within the Boundaries*.

[29] Kant, *What is Enlightenment?*, 8, p. 37.

[30] Ibid., 8, p. 37.

[31] Ibid., 8, p. 38.

5. Kant: public reason as freedom without lawlessness

Kant's criticism of *private* uses of reason is both convincing and problematic. It is convincing because it is clear enough what any appeal to contingently available authorities amounts to—the introduction of some arbitrary premise asserting the claims of that authority; and clear enough what it costs—the relativization of conclusions to that arbitrary premise. It is easy to agree that reasoning is limited as soon as it takes for granted some civilly constituted authority, indeed any contingent 'authority' for which no justification is provided, and that this independence is the condition of reaching audiences of wider scope. It is easy to see how this Kantian criticism of 'private' reason can be extended to undermine attempts to develop *democratic, communitarian* and even Rawlsian—in short, *civic*—conceptions of public reason.

However, it is less easy to understand what we are going to be left with when all appeal to 'alien' authorities is set aside. Kant's favoured image of public reason is scholarly communication with the world at large. It has evident limitations. Perhaps Kant could find no better image of non-derivative reasoning than this; but we are more suspicious, and in my view rightly suspicious, about the relations between power and knowledge. Practices of scholarly communication include and exclude, highlight and suppress. Can we seriously expect to find, or to live by, communicative practices which do not introduce unargued assumptions—even if these assumptions change through history? (I personally doubt whether the much heralded emerging global communication regime, which some see as the basis for a deeper democratization of political life, lives up the Kantian ideal of public reason any better than the communication among scholars to which Kant points.)

Can we expect to say *anything* about the requirements of reasoned communication, other than making the negative point that it fails wherever it merely defers to the edicts and assumptions of civil or other powers or authorities? Reasoning surely cannot be merely a matter of discourse that does not defer—for if this were the case, every sort of gibberish and incoherence would count as reasoned, provided only that it does not draw on the authority or edicts of whatever powers there be.

Clearly Kant thinks that we can say more about the demands of public reason. He never maintains that reasoning has *merely* to be free and non-deferential. He sets out the other requirements of reasoning quite clearly in *What Does it Mean to Orient Oneself in Thinking?*, which was published soon after *What is Enlightenment?*. In the second essay he argues that nothing could deserve to be called reason if it was wholly without structure and discipline, because a minimal condition for any discourse to count as reasoned is that it be *communicable*, that it be *followable* by all whom it is to reach. And without a structure that can be followed there will be no communication, *a fortiori* no reasoning. Reasons are the sorts of things that we can give to others, receive or refuse to receive from others. Since Kant rejects the idea that reasons could be devised by the arbitrary fiat of individual reasoners, he rejects the thought that reasoning can be wholly unfollowable:

... how much and how correctly would we think if we did not *think* as it were in community with others to whom we *communicate* our thoughts, and who communicate theirs with us! [32]

---

[32] Kant, *What Does it Mean to Orient Oneself in Thinking?*, 8, p. 144.

The standards of reason cannot be found in solitary thinking: on the contrary those who seek to reason *must* structure their thought, speech and communication in ways that others *can* follow. This double modal constraint is fundamental to the positive aspect of Kant's account of public reason, and a crucial part of his entire vindication of reason.

At times Kant uses a fiercely sarcastic rhetoric[33] to chastise those who try to purvey the illusion that reasoning could be without all structure or discipline and delude themselves that this 'lawless' freedom will be liberating, and that freedom is all there is to reasoning. He had clear targets in mind, including the fans of religious enthusiasm (Schwärmerei) and of exaggerated views of the powers of genius; today his targets might include a fair range of postmodernists, new-agers and deconstructionists. In each case he believes that the opponents of reason fail to see that *by itself* the unstructured liberation of thought and discourse that they crave will be a disaster, and an illusion:

… if reason will not subject itself to the laws it gives itself, it has to bow under the yoke of laws given by another; for without law, nothing—not even nonsense—can play its game for long. Thus the unavoidable consequence of *declared* lawlessness in thinking (of liberation from the limitations of reason) is that the freedom to think will ultimately be forfeited …[34]

The illusions of 'lawless' thinking end, Kant thinks, not merely in intellectual confusion, but in lack of defence against the very sorts of deference and subordination which enthusiasts for 'lawless' thinking wish to escape. Because anarchic, 'lawless' thinking is no more than babble, it is defenceless in the face of the claims of superstition, of enthusiasm and of the rules extolled by those who peddle religious and political dogmas.

6. Kant: public reason as law-like

If 'lawless' thinking ends not in freedom of thought and communication, but in gibberish and isolation, even in superstition and cognitive disorientation, whose political consequences include vulnerability to tyrants and demagogues, then any activity in human life that can count as reasoned must be structured. This structure must enable us to distinguish good reasons from poor reasons, to distinguish claims we ought to accept from those we ought to reject. Reasoning—whether theoretical or practical—will lack authority and normative force if it has no structure by which this distinction can be made. So if anything is to count as more than 'private' reason, in Kant's sense of the term, if there is to be anything that is to count as fully public reason, then its structure cannot be derived from existing institutions and practices. What then can provide the internal, non-derivative discipline or structure of fully public reasoning? Kant's answer is straightforward:

Freedom in thinking signifies the subjection of reason to no laws except *those, which it gives itself*; and its opposite is the maxim of a *lawless* use of reason …[35]

---

[33] As those who seek to reason with postmodernists often discover, rhetoric is the only remaining way to engage with those who purport to dispense with reason and deny its authority.

[34] Kant, *What Does it Mean to Orient Oneself in Thinking?*, 8, p. 145.

[35] Ibid., 8, p. 145.

Public uses of reason must have *law-like* rather than *lawless* structure, but since they are not to derive their law-likeness from any external sources, it will have to be freely chosen: the discipline of reason is that of *self-legislation* or *autonomy*.

Kant's identification of reason with autonomy is initially startling, despite the fact that familiar passages in the *Groundwork of the Metaphysic of Morals* make it plain that he identifies *practical* reason with autonomy.[36] The reason that it is startling is, I believe, that the contemporary conception of autonomy identifies it with independence rather than with reason. But Kant distinguishes autonomy sharply from mere freedom or independence.[37] Unlike most recent 'Kantian' writers (and many of their critics), he views autonomy or self-legislation as emphasizing not *some* (*rather amazing sort of*) *self that does the legislating*, but rather *legislation that is not borrowed from unvindicated sources, that is not derivative, that is both freely chosen and has the form of law*. Non-derivative 'legislation' cannot require us to adopt the actual laws or rules of some institution or authority; it can therefore only require that any principle we use to structure thought or action be law-like, that it have 'the form of law'. Only those who freely choose principles that have the 'form of law' meet the demands of Kantian autonomy; only they show commitment to the Kantian conception of public reason: indeed this is all that there is to his conception of practical reason, which explains why he can write:

Now the power to judge autonomously—that is, freely (according to principles of thought in general)—is called reason.[38]

Another way of formulating the same point is to note that Kant identifies public reason with a double modal criterion: with the *requirement* of structuring our thought, discourse and action in ways in which (we believe) others *can* follow. A general statement of this criterion can be found at the end of *What Does it Mean to Orient Oneself in Thinking?* where Kant identifies reasoning with the practice of adopting principles of thinking and acting that have the form of law, which can be adopted by all:

To make use of one's own reason means no more than to ask oneself, whenever one is supposed to assume something, whether one could find it feasible to make the ground or the rule on which one assumes it into a universal principle for the use of reason.[39]

We are most of us more familiar with a restricted version of this principle, formulated specifically for the domain of action, which Kant rather pompously calls 'the supreme principle of practical reason' or 'the Categorical Imperative'. The best known of these more restricted formulations is the Formula of Universal Law version of the Categorical Imperative, whose double modal structure is particularly plain: '*act only in accordance with that maxim through which you can at the same time will that it become a universal law*'.[40]

---

[36] See esp. Kant, *Groundwork of the Metaphysic of Morals*, 4, p. 440.

[37] Kant holds that various *specific* forms of independence (Selbständigkeit, sibisufficientia) are important—but they are quite different from Kantian autonomy. A just, republican state is one where independence of action is safeguarded by the fact that nobody is either outside or above the law; active citizens need a degree of economic independence. Kant, *On the Common Saying*, 8. pp. 294–6; *The Metaphysic of Morals*, 6, pp. 314–5.

[38] Kant, *Conflict of the Faculties*, 7, p. 27: the important phrase here is the one in parentheses!

[39] Kant, *What Does it Mean to Orient Oneself in Thinking?*, 8, p. 146n.

[40] Kant, *Groundwork of the Metaphysic of Morals*, 4, p. 421.

7. Kant and domestic justice

Where does this account of the vindication of practical reason take Kant's account of justice, and specifically of justice beyond boundaries? I shall first comment briefly on Kant's account of domestic or 'internal' justice. His justification of political institutions does not appeal simply to a version of social contract[41] or contractarian thought but to a more abstract 'Universal Principle of Justice'. A particularly clear formulation of this principle is given early in the *Doctrine of Right* (the first part of the *Metaphysics of Morals*). It runs:

Any action is *right* if it can coexist with everyone's freedom in accordance with a universal law, or if on its maxim the freedom of choice of each can coexist with everyone's freedom in accordance with a universal law.[42]

The Universal Principle of Justice makes no explicit reference to consent. Its justification lies rather in its relationship to the formulae of the Categorical Imperative, and so to Kant's vindication of practical reason as grounded in the necessary conditions for any possible fully public reasoning. Kant's argument for justice begins simply from the requirement that reasoned thought and action adhere to principles that could be fully public, in the sense that it never invokes arbitrary authority, but rather can be followed in thought or adopted in action by all, without presupposing any pre-established agreement, shared ideology or religion or other given (and unvindicated) source of coordination.

The most familiar statement of this requirement for the domain of practical reason is the Formula of Universal Law version of the Categorical Imperative. This principle covers maxims—practical principles—for all sorts of action, inward and outward, personal and public. By contrast the Universal Principle of Justice is restricted in two ways. First, it is concerned only with maxims for outward action, that is with the aspects of action, which could be enforced (so not, for example, with maxims for virtue or with moral worth). Second, it is concerned only with maxims for structuring the domain of external freedom, that is the public domain, so not with maxims for all outward aspects of personal conduct. The Universal Principle of Justice therefore requires the rejection of those basic maxims for structuring the domain of the external use of freedom that could not be adopted by all.

Kant thinks that the implementation of this principle in the actual conditions in which we live is not straightforward. We find ourselves living on a spherical and finite globe that brings us into contact with others with whom we compete for scarce

---

[41] For Kant the term 'social contract' refers not to the fundamental principle of political justification, but to a specific step in the derivation of an account of just institutions from the Universal Principle of Justice. Unlike that principle, the idea of the social contract takes cognizance of historically specific conditions, for example of the fact that we live with moderate scarcity and limited altruism, yet in mutual proximity. Hence in our world the social contract has to accept state coercion, but can require state structures to take a republican form. See Onora O'Neill, 'Kant and the Social Contract Tradition', in F. Duscheneau, Y. LaFrance and Claude Piché (eds.), *Kant Actuel: Hommage à Pierre Laberge* (Paris: Vrin, 2000), pp. 185–200.

[42] Kant, *The Metaphysic of Morals*, 6, p. 230.

resources; and we are not reliably altruistic.[43] In our world, external freedom will be perpetually insecure without at least limited forms of coercion, aimed at 'hindering the hindrances of freedom'. In these conditions the Universal Principle of Justice can, as Kant sees it, best be implemented not by unlimited freedom—anarchy—but by establishing states with republican constitutions, which guarantee freedom within the law at least within bounded territories. Although such states will coerce, and although their boundaries create unjust exclusions, they provide a better realization of justice than any universal state of nature: the first requirement of justice is therefore to leave the state of nature.[44] However, this requirement is not unconditional. Kant fiercely repudiates the Hobbesian view that any state is to be preferred to the state of nature: tyranny can be worse than insecurity, and legitimate state power is always not absolute but limited. On Kant's view, state power is not an intrinsic requirement of justice, but the compromise which we have to make under actual conditions.

Kant's statement of the elements of this compromise is succinctly formulated in his statement of the requirements of a republican *constitution* in *Perpetual Peace*:

A constitution established, first on principles of the *freedom* of the member of a society ... second on principles of the *dependence* of all upon a single common legislation ... third, on the law of their *equality (as citizens of a state)*—the sole constitution ... on which all rightful legislation of a people must be based—is a *republican* constitution.[45]

Republican justice is evidently not democratic justice, but I do not think it is trivial. Consider how much it rules out. Societies or states that do not secure the rule of law (anarchic or despotic societies) undermine or jeopardize external freedom for some or for all, so base their constitutions on principles that cannot be principles for all; they are unjust. Societies or states which leave some persons above or outside the law (monarchies, dictatorships, states within states, slave states) undermine or jeopardize external freedom for some or for all, so base their constitutions on principles that cannot be principles for all; they are unjust. Societies or states which do not secure equality of status for all citizens under law (feudalism, caste societies) undermine or jeopardize external freedom for some or for all, so base their constitutions on principles that cannot be principles for all; they are unjust. It is plausible to think that Kant's account of domestic justice could be extended to show that patriarchal and undemocratic states, which undermine or jeopardize external freedom for many, so also base their constitutions on principles that cannot be principles for all, are also unjust.

---

[43] For Kant then, it might be said, boundaries are still basic to justice, although he considers what is enclosed within the bounded globe rather than within bounded societies. The analogy fails because for Kant the boundary of the globe is significant not because it excludes non-earthlings, but because it requires us to share the earth with all others with whom we have even remote connection. If human life were to spread beyond the planet, the boundaries of Kantian justice would spread with it. Kant's recognition that the globe is bounded does not mean that his thinking on justice ceases to be cosmopolitan.

[44] Kant, *On the Common Saying*, 8, p. 302.

[45] Kant, *Toward Perpetual Peace*, 8, p. 350; cf. *The Metaphysic of Morals*, 6, p. 340.

8. Kant on justice beyond boundaries

I want now to indicate quite briefly some advantages of an approach to justice across boundaries based on Kant's conception of public reason. The first advantage is that his conception of public reason does not presuppose the *status quo*; it merely insists on the modal conditions that all discourse must meet if it is to be capable of being fully public, hence fully reasoned. If anything can count as a vindication of reason, as opposed to the mere assertion that something is reasonable because it is liked, or accepted, even liked or accepted by lots of people, or even by lots of peoples, this seems to me the most promising strategy.

The second advantage is a corollary of the first. Because he has offered a distinctive, modal vindication of reason, Kant need not presuppose any institutional structures in arguing for the basic principles of justice: he can address the agenda of seeing which principles would and which would not be reasonable without begging questions. In Kant's thought human rights, democracy, state power *and boundaries* are all of them institutions whose justice is to be established rather than presupposed.

The approach has several further advantages. Kant does not ground his account of justice in the realist conception of the state, with its ethically disreputable disregard of the moral standing of others on the far side of borders whose lives are in fact whom economic and foreign policies affect, and to whose suffering such policies may contribute. Nor does he argue for a merely abstract cosmopolitanism. Nor does he anchor justice in the puzzling conception of a territorial people who lack a state but police their boundaries tightly.

For Kant a just world is one in which cosmopolitan principles of justice are realistically institutionalized, and this will be a world in which boundaries are not absent, but also one in which there are further institutional structures which support international justice between states and cosmopolitan justice for people when they interact across borders. In such a world, he argues, the justice of republican states would be complemented by structures that secure international justice and cosmopolitan right, including a league of states.[46]

Kant's entire account of just republican states, of international justice and of cosmopolitan right—is grounded in his account of the reasons we have for rejecting principles unless they can be adopted by all. The Universal Principle of Justice formulates this requirement specifically for the public domain—the domain in which conflict is least avoidable—and suggests why in human conditions universal principles of justice may nevertheless be best instituted through a plurality of bounded republican states, linked by commitments to international justice and cosmopolitan right. Since there are no *a priori* reasons for thinking that states must be anything like those about which realists fantasize, the way is left open for considering which sorts of interaction between all agents, including states, are compatible with justice and which are not.

In my view this strategy may provide a better route for thinking about justice beyond boundaries than the one Rawls offers, not only because the Kant's strategy of vindication aims deeper, but because it is *more realistic* and *more open*. The

---

[46] Kant, *Toward Perpetual Peace*, 8, pp. 357–60, 367, 385; *The Metaphysic of Morals*, 6, pp. 311, 352–7.

greater *realism* lies in Kant's clear acknowledgment that republican states are not ideally just: they are a compromise we have to make in order to start securing freedom under real world conditions. By the same token the boundaries of these states are not invariably just: the particular filters they institutionalize, the inclusions and the exclusions, the domination and the subordination which they secure, may constitute unjust action towards outsiders. If boundaries are a requirement of realism, their construction and adjustment and the sorts of filters that they institutionalize raises questions of justice. Kant's views on justice are also *more open* in that they do not preclude the possibility that institutions other than states may contribute towards the institutionalizations of justice. States may usually be the primary agents of justice, but where they are either unjust or weak other institutions—including Churches, nongovernmental organizations and transnational corporations—can also contribute to justice (and by the same token often contribute to injustice).[47]

In the world as we now know it, state boundaries are porous not in all but in many ways: they are for the most part highly porous to transfers of goods and capital, communications, and technologies, but rather less so to ideas, cultures and religions. The respects in which they are least porous are to flows of people and of public finance.[48] However, for Kant the *status quo* is not the end of the story. If we can find more just ways in which to structure boundaries in the world as it actually is, or can construct institutions which are able to secure improvements of justice within and between just states, they these may form part of a better implementation of the Universal Principle of Justice. In the meantime we deceive ourselves if we imagine that power relations between states are exempt from considerations of justice, or that the degree of international and cosmopolitan justice established at the start of the twenty-first century is all that might be achieved.

---

[47] Thomas Risse-Kappen (ed.), *Bringing Transnational Relations Back in: Non-State Actors, Domestic Structures and International Institutions* (Cambridge: Cambridge University Press, 1995); Onora O'Neill, 'Agents of Justice', *Metaphilosophy*, forthcoming.

[48] Brian Barry and Robert E. Goodin, *Free Movement: Ethical Issues in the Transnational Migration of People and Money*, (PA: Pennsylvania State University Press) for comparisons of ways in which boundaries are porous for different purposes.

Globalization from above: actualizing the ideal through law

PHILIP ALLOTT

Becoming

We, human beings and human societies, are processes of becoming. We are what we have been and what we will be. What we have been, what we call our *past*, exists nowhere else than as an idea in our minds. What we will be, what we call our *future*, exists nowhere else than as an idea in our minds. What we call the *present* is the vanishing-point between the past and the future, a mere idea within our minds of the relationship between what we have been and what we will be. In the continuous present of our idea of our becoming, we present the past and the future to ourselves as a contrast between an actuality and a potentiality.

In the continuous present of our idea of our becoming, we can constantly re-imagine the actuality of our past, through the mental processes which we call personal *memory* and social *history*, but that is the limit of the potentiality-for-us of the past. Otherwise the past is beyond our power. And we can imagine, and constantly re-imagine, the potentiality-for-us of the future, imagining what we could become, what we will be. But, in the case of the future, the human mind understands its relationship to the future in the form of a strange paradox, a strange feature of the way in which the human mind seems to have evolved within the evolution of all living things, within the development of the universe of all-that-is. We can make the future but we cannot determine it. What will be will be what we do, but not only what we do. The future will also be made by the willing and acting of other human beings and other human societies, and by all other organic and inorganic processes of becoming, as they actualize themselves within the becoming of the universe of all-that-is.

So it is that the strange paradox of our relationship to the future is also a strange fate. We can imagine the future; we can choose to actualize this potentiality rather than that; and we can will and act to actualize our chosen potentiality. But we cannot be certain that our chosen future will become an actuality, a presence within our past. We may be able only to console ourselves by imagining what might have been, or by re-imagining and re-evaluating, through personal memory and social history, what has been, making it conform, so far as we are able, to the potentiality which we chose or might have chosen—the road we might have taken, the words we might have spoken, the unintended effects of wanted and unwanted events, the war we won by losing it or which we lost by winning it, the revolution which created new possibilities by destroying old potentialities, the suffering which made us better. The future of the human species is within the power, and beyond the power, of the human species.

The strangest feature of our paradoxical relationship to the future, the central fact of our evolved destiny, lies in the fact that the vanishing-point which we call the *present* is filled with the idea of *responsibility,* the permanent and inescapable burden of choosing the future, of choosing what to do next. Our life, as it presents itself to our minds, as human individuals and as human societies, is a process of becoming, but, above all, it is a process of choosing to become. The human species is a species of *moral* beings, because we cannot avoid the burden of choosing, of willing with a view to acting. Moral freedom is moral duty.[1]

The way in which we understand the past affects the future because it affects the way in which we understand the potentialities of the future, and hence the way in which we understand our moral responsibility in relation to the future. In this sense, the past is always an active presence in the present, in the place where we are doomed to play our part in making the future. The moral burden of choosing the future includes the moral burden of choosing our idea of the past, of forming our idea of what we were, as individuals and as societies. We are what we have been, whether we remember it or not. But what we remember, and the way in which we choose to remember it, are added to what we have been in making what we will be. Memory and history shape the process of our becoming, up to and including the becoming of all-humanity.[2]

Minds

International society is a society like any other human society, except that it is the society of the whole human race, the society of all societies.[3] A society is a socializing of the human mind. From the society of the family, through the society of a nation or state, to the international society of the whole human race, a society is a form of functioning of the human mind. The mind of a society—social consciousness or the *public mind*, as we may call it—functions in ways which are characteristic of the functioning of the *private mind* of the human individual and in ways which are particular to the public mind of society. The role played by the mind in the *becoming* of a society is accordingly concordant with, and distinct from, the role of mind in the becoming of the human individual.

As human individuals, we have four minds. We have the *personal consciousness* by which we constitute our self within our ultimate solitude. We have the *interpersonal*

---

[1] 'We human beings do not possess freedom; ... freedom possesses [*besitzt*] us.' M. Heidegger, *Wegmarken* (Frankfurt am Main: Vittorio Klostermann, 1967), p. 85 (present author's translation). Heidegger's discussion of 'the nature of freedom' formed part of a lecture (on the nature of truth) first given in 1930 and included in this volume in a revised version first published in 1943.

[2] On the nature and social function of *history*, see Philip Allott, 'International Law and the Idea of History', *Journal of the History of International Law* (1999), pp. 1–21.

[3] For an exposition of this conception of international society, see Philip Allott, *Eunomia—New Order for a New World* (Oxford: Oxford University Press, 1990). Since the Reformation of the sixteenth century no single reified unifying conception of the social aspect of human existence has established itself, leaving the speculative field open to competing ideas: a universal society of human beings or of states or nations, an international society of states, the international community, an anarchical society of states, the international system, world order, and so on. Greek and Roman thought, and pre-Reformation Christian thought, had produced many such ideas: *homonoia, kosmopolis, humanitas, civitas maxima, concordia, the earthly kingdom, the City of Man, Christendom.*

consciousness by which we constitute our self in contact with the minds of others. We mutually construct each other. We have the *social consciousness* by which our mind participates in the public minds of societies, and by which the public minds of societies enter into our personal and interpersonal consciousness. We have the *spiritual consciousness* which integrates and transcends all the other forms of consciousness and which manifests itself in, but not only in, religious belief and practice.

The public mind of a society is also a multiple mind. Human societies have a *personal consciousness* by which a society constitutes its self in communion with itself, through its own social processes, including the private minds of society-members and the public minds of the subordinate societies which it contains. A society also has an *interpersonal consciousness* through which it constitutes itself in contact with the public minds of other societies—for example, a nation or state in its relations with other nations and states. Societies mutually construct each other. A society also has a *social consciousness* formed as the society participates in the public minds of the superordinate societies to which it belongs—including, for example, intergovernmental organizations—up to and including the international society of all-humanity, the society of all societies. Finally, a society shares in the integrating power of *spiritual consciousness*, not least, but not only, because of the extreme socializing of religion in human practice.

All human consciousness, individual and social, is thus both an aspect of the *phylogeny* of the human species, our shared evolutionary inheritance, and an aspect of the *ontogeny* of each individual organic system, human being or human society, the product of its own life-history.

Realities

The reality of reality has for ever been the central question of philosophy, that is to say, the central question raised by the self-contemplating of the human mind. All cultures—and, especially, all religions—have sought to find a satisfactory way of resolving the question. In the Western philosophical tradition, originating in the philosophy of ancient Greece, it was very soon accepted that there could be no one answer, let alone one final answer. On the contrary, the clash of opposing solutions to the problem itself became the means of powerfully enriching the substance of human self-contemplating, especially the philosophy of being (metaphysics—what is it to use the word *is*?) and the philosophy of knowing (epistemology—what is it to say that I *know* that something is or is-so?).[4] The

---

[4] 'One party is trying to drag everything down to earth out of heaven and the unseen ... and strenuously affirm that real existence belongs only to that which can be handled and offers resistance to the touch. They define reality as the same thing as body, and as soon as one of the opposite party asserts that anything without a body is real, they are utterly contemptuous and will not listen to another word ... and accordingly their adversaries are very wary in defending their position somewhere in the heights of the unseen, maintaining with all their force that true reality consists in certain intelligible and bodiless forms ... and what those others allege to be true reality they call, not real being but a sort of moving process of becoming. On this issue an interminable battle is always going on between the two camps.' Plato, *Sophist* (trans. F. M. Cornford), 246b–c, in E. Hamilton and H. Cairns (eds.), *The Collected Dialogues of Plato* (Princeton, NJ: Princeton University Press, 1961), p. 990.

dialectic of idealism and realism, and of the countless intermediate positions, continues to the present day.[5]

The problem of the reality of reality presents itself in a quite special way in relation to the reality which the human mind has itself made. Human beings inhabit a *human world*, entirely made by the human mind, a world parallel to the natural world, a self-made second human habitat, a human mind-world with its own *human reality*. Human reality is one reality and countless realities. On the one hand, human reality is constructed collectively through the interaction of consciousness in the activity of what have been referred to above as our interpersonal, social, human, and spiritual minds. The becoming of international society—the society of all-humanity and of all human societies—contains the actuality and the potentiality of a universal human reality. But, on the other hand, the human world also contains countless particular human realities. Every person's idea of human reality is 'my reality' or a 'reality-for-me'. Like a Leibnizian monad, every human being and every human society has its own unique point of view from which the human world is seen, a perspective which contains the whole human world seen from that point of view.[6]

Over the course of the last three centuries, significant intellectual attention has been devoted (if not always *eo nomine*) to the problem of *human reality*, and we may regard ourselves as now being exceptionally well placed to offer a fruitful response to that problem. That we are able to do so may be seen as a side-effect or after-effect of what might crudely be called a Kantian revolution, a revolution which, as is the way with revolutions in general, was a restoration and a recapitulation rather than a new beginning, a provocation rather than a programme.[7] We have come to understand much more clearly the way in which human reality—including, of course, the reality of international society—is constructed. In particular, we are able to identify more clearly the existence and the interaction of four *vectors* of human reality-making—the rational, the social, the unconscious, and the linguistic.

[5] The negating of idealism has been called, at different times: sophism, pyrrhonism, scepticism, empiricism, nominalism, materialism, relativism, nihilism, positivism, naturalism, realism, pragmatism, logical positivism, phenomenology, neopragmatism, postmodernism. For contemporary examples of characteristically American fundamentalist anti-idealism, see: J. B. Watson, *Behaviorism*, 2nd edn. (London: Kegan Paul, 1931); H. S. Sullivan, *The Interpersonal Theory of Psychiatry* (New York: Norton, 1953); H. J. Morgenthau, *Politics among Nations: the Struggle for Power and Peace*, 6th edn. (New York: McGraw-Hill, 1985); R. Rorty, *Philosophy and the Mirror of Nature* (Princeton, NJ: Princeton University Press, 1969); E. O. Wilson, *Sociobiology* (Cambridge, MA: Harvard University Press, 1975); R. A. Posner, *Economic Analysis of Law* (Boston, MA: Little, Brown, c. 1986); D. Dennett, *Consciousness Explained* (London: Allen Lane, 1992).

[6] 'And so, since what acts upon me is for me and for no one else, I, and no one else, am actually perceiving it … Then my perception is true for me, for its object at any moment is my reality, and I am, as Protagoras says, a judge of what is for me, and of what is not, that it is not.' Plato, *Theaetetus* (trans. F. M. Cornford), 160c, *Collected Dialogues*, p. 866. Plato's Socrates is here speaking about a subjectivist conception of the reality of reality (that is, of universal reality, not merely of what we are here calling human reality). G.W. Leibniz (1646–1716) conceived of the universe as being formed from ultimate indivisible 'monads' each of which contains the whole order of the universe organized around its unique 'point of view' [*point de vue*], so that each 'simple substance' is 'a perpetual living mirror of the universe'. *The Monadology*, §§56, 57, in his *Philosophical Papers and Letters* (ed. and trans. L. E. Loemker, 2nd edn. (Dordrecht: D. Reidel, 1969), p. 648.

[7] Kant compared his own work to the Copernican revolution, resituating the human observer in relation to universal reality by making the human mind an integral part of the constructing of the reality of the universe. I. Kant, *Critique of Pure Reason* (1781–87), 2nd edn., trans. N. Kemp-Smith (London: Macmillan, 1929), pp. 22, 25. 'What a Copernicus or a Darwin really achieved was not the discovery of a true theory but of a fertile new point of view [*eines fruchtbaren neuen Aspekts*].' L. Wittgenstein, *Culture and Value* (trans. P. Winch, ed. G. H.von Wright) (Oxford: Blackwell, 1980), p.18e.

(1) It is possible to accept the idea that there is a *rational* component within human reality without taking any fundamental metaphysical or epistemological position relating to reality in general. The idea merely acknowledges that the human mind constructs relatively stable representations of reality, natural and human, which are communicable from mind to mind and which are thus able to have effect in all aspects of human consciousness from the personal to the spiritual, including social consciousness.[8] In social consciousness, such *models* of reality acquire world-changing power, equivalent not only to the most effective hypotheses of the natural sciences but even to the natural forces which those hypotheses rationalize. It is to such creative rationalizing that we owe all the flora and fauna of the human mind-world—*state, nation, people, law, treaty, rule, war, peace, sovereignty, money, power, interest,* and so on and on.

(2) The *social* component in the making of human reality means that a given society—from the family to the international society of all-humanity—constructs a mental universe, a social world-view, which has the extraordinary characteristic that, although it is necessarily the product of particular human minds at particular moments in time, it somehow takes on a transcendental life of its own, in isolation from any particular minds and persisting through time, as society-members are born and die, join and leave the society. It is the mental atmosphere of the society within which the society forms itself and which forms the minds of society-members, that is, the public minds of subordinate societies and the private minds of individual human beings. It is retained in countless substantial forms—buildings, institutions, customs and rituals and conventions, the law, literature, the fine arts, historiography, cultural artefacts of every kind. It contains a network of aspirations and con-straints—moral, legal, political, and cultural—which are internalized by society-members and take effect in their everyday willing and acting.[9]

(3) Whatever theory of the structure and functioning of the human mind we may accept, if any, it is difficult now not to acknowledge a powerful *unconscious* com-ponent in the formation of human reality, The mind finds within itself a *self-consciousness*, in which it seems to be aware of itself, the master of its own reality, the writer, the director, and the actor in its own drama. And, in each of our minds, there is an area which surpasses and eludes us, off-stage, out-of-sight—the *unconscious mind*, as it has come to be called—the area behind and beneath and

---

[8] In the philosophy of the natural sciences, the Kantian point of view was reflected in the influential ideas of Ernst Mach (1838–1916) for whom science is a product of biological evolution which enables us to create 'economical' (simple, coherent, efficient) representations (primarily mathematical) of the universe, the 'necessity' of the universe being logical rather than physical. See R. Haller, 'Poetic Imagination and Economy: Ernst Mach as Theorist of Science', in J. Blackmore (ed.), *Ernst Mach: A Deeper Look. Documents and New Perspectives* (Dordrecht: Kluwer Academic Publishers, 1992), pp. 215–28. For an exposition of the analogous role of *models* in the social sciences, see P. Winch, *The Idea of a Social Science and its Relation to Philosophy* (London: Routledge & Kegan Paul, 1958/90).

[9] 'The phantoms formed in the human brain are also, necessarily, sublimates of [active man's] life-process, which is empirically verifiable and bound to material premises. Morality, religion, metaphysics, all the rest of ideology and their corresponding forms of consciousness, thus no longer retain their independence.' 'Consciousness is, therefore, from the very beginning a social product, and remains so as long as men exist at all'. K. Marx and F. Engels, *The German Ideology: Part One*, 1845–46 (trans. W. Lough, ed. C. J. Arthur) (London: Lawrence & Wishart, 1977), pp. 47, 51.

beyond self-consciousness.[10] And we have reason to believe that there is the same duality in the minds of those we meet in interpersonal consciousness, in the public mind of society, and in the spiritual mind, the mind of all minds. It means that psychic reality is analogous to the putative real reality of the physical universe (the *noumena*, to recall the Kantian term),[11] in that the ultimate contents of our minds are unknowable. Our self-consciousness is placed between two unknowable realities.[12] We live our lives with an unknowable world within us, a social order which we make but which is both within us and beyond us, and a natural universe of which we form part but which we cannot know except as we represent it to ourselves in our minds. The power of the unconscious mind is nowhere more apparent than in social reality, including the reality of international society, as feeling and imagination lend to rationally formed ideas the social power of life and death, and socialized forms of the psychopathology of the individual mind inflict suffering of every kind and degree on individual human beings.

(4) Although the role of *language* in the formation of human reality was an obsessive subject of study in the twentieth century, the general problem of the nature and origin of language is as old as philosophy, and as crucial as ever in humanity's never-ending search for self-awareness. We may usefully distinguish between language as a biological phenomenon present in many species of animal, language as a specific system within human consciousness, and language as a necessary component of social reality.[13] Biological evolution has conferred certain species-characteristics on human language, and the socializing of human language has transformed it into the means of expressing a specific form of human reality. Connecting the personal mind, where we speak to ourselves in isolation, to the interpersonal and social minds, and by integrating the personal and social minds with the spiritual mind, language has made the human species what it is for-itself and what the universe of all-that-is is for us human beings.

For those who have lived in the long twentieth century (from 1870), amazing and terrible as it was, the world-making and world-changing power of words is a lived and vivid experience. The human world is a world of words. Nouns and names rule our minds. We live and die for words. They give form to our feelings, determine our willing and acting, define our possibilities, as individuals and societies. The long history of the philosophy of language—mind contemplating the possibility of the

---

[10] 'I received the profoundest impression of the possibility that there could be powerful mental processes which nevertheless remained hidden from the consciousness of men.' 'But the study of pathogenic repression and other phenomena which have still to be mentioned compelled psycho-analysis to take the concept of the "unconscious" seriously. Psycho-analysis regarded everything mental as being in the first instance unconscious; the further quality of "consciousness" might also be present, or again it might be absent.' S. Freud, *An Autobiographical Study* (1925), in *Standard Edition of the Complete Psychological Works*, vol. XX, trans. and ed. J. Strachey (London: Hogarth Press, n.d.; revised version of translation published separately in 1935), pp. 17, 31. In the first sentence quoted, Freud is recalling the effect of his observation in 1889 of the effects of hypnosis.

[11] For Kant, the *noumena* (plural of *noumenon*) are conceived by the mind (*nous*) as that of which the *phenomena* are the appearances available to us.

[12] 'The unconscious is the true psychical reality; *in its innermost nature it is as much unknown to us as the reality of the external world, and it is as incompletely presented to us by the data of consciousness as is the external world by the communications of our sense organs.*' S. Freud, *The Interpretation of Dreams* (1900), in *Standard Edition*, vol. V (1953), p. 613 (emphasis in original).

[13] Saussure proposed analogous distinctions (*langage, langue, parole*) which have been influential in the modern study of language. F. de Saussure, *Course in General Linguistics* (1915, posthumous), trans. W. Baskin, eds. C. Bally and A. Sechehaye (New York: Philosophical Library, 1959).

public mind—now offers to the public mind of the twenty-first century a powerful collection of ideas on the nature and origin of language, an unprecedented opportunity for a new human self-enlightening, a New Enlightenment.[14]

The metaphor of enlightenment has been a dominant archetype of many religions and philosophies across the world. It affirms the possibility that the human mind can raise itself by its own effort, can speak to itself, and about itself, in qualitatively new ways, and hence that humanity can repeatedly re-humanize itself.[15]

Constitutions

A society does not have a constitution. A society is a constituting, an unceasing process of self-creating. A society constitutes itself simultaneously in three dimensions—as ideas, as practice, and as law. Each society, including the international society of all-humanity, the society of all societies, is a unique but ever-changing product of its threefold self-constituting. In its *ideal* constitution, a society presents its becoming to itself as actuality and potentiality, forming a *reality-for-itself* which includes its *history,* its self-explanatory *theories*, and its *ideals*. In its *real* constitution, the willing and acting of individual human beings is socialized as they exercise *social power* in the course of their own personal self-constituting. In its *legal* constitution, social power is given the form of *legal power*, so that the willing and acting of individual human beings may serve the *common interest* of society in its self-constituting.[16]

Since a society is a socializing of the human mind, there is a direct and necessary concordance between the self-constituting of a society and the self-constituting of an individual human being. The constitution of a society is its personality. The

[14] The history of ideas about language is a striking instance of what Augustine and other optimists have called 'the education of the human race'. (1) In an exceptionally inconclusive dialogue worthy of the later Wittgenstein, Plato's Socrates says: 'How real existence is to be studied or discovered is, I suspect, beyond you and me. But we admit so much, that the knowledge of things is not to be derived from names. No, they must be studied and investigated in themselves'. Plato, *Cratylus* (trans. B. Jowett), 439b, *Collected Dialogues*, p. 473. (2) Aristotle proposed a conventionalist view of language. 'A noun is a sound having meaning established by convention alone ... No sound is by nature a noun; it becomes one, becoming a symbol.' *On Interpretation*, II (trans. H. P. Cooke; Loeb Classical Library), p. 117. (3) A naturalist view of language was proposed by Lucretius. 'But the various sounds of the tongue nature drove them to utter, and convenience (*utilitas*) moulded the names for things.' *On the Nature of Things*, V, 1028–29 (trans. W. H. D. Rouse and M. F. Smith; Loeb Classical Library), p. 459. For the view that the way in which language expresses meaning has an evolutionary origin, see R. M. Allott, *The Motor Theory of Language Origin* (Lewes: Book Guild, 1989). (4) For the view that it is possible to establish the logically necessary *substantive universals* of language, see N. Chomsky, *Language and Mind* (New York: Harcourt Brace Jovanovich, 1968/*c*.1972). (5) For the view that language, as social reality, is a set of languages, connected by 'family resemblances', see L. Wittgenstein, *Philosophical Investigations*, trans. G. E. M. Anscombe (Oxford: Basil Blackwell, 1974).

[15] In the cultural history of western Europe, five enlightenments, at intervals of three centuries, have been identified since the end of the Roman Empire in the West: western monasticism (6th century: the Rule of St. Benedict); the Carolingian renaissance (9th century: centred on the court of Charlemagne); the 12th century renaissance (centred on the University of Paris); the 15th century renaissance (centred on Italy); the 18th century Enlightenment. For the idea of a 21st-century enlightenment, see Philip Allott, *Eutopia—New Mind for a New Humanity* (forthcoming).

[16] For further discussion of the three dimensions of a society's self-constituting, see Philip Allott, *Eunomia*, ch. 9.

personality of human beings is their constitution. My personality, which includes my reality-for-myself, is also a unique and ever-changing product of my ideas, my practice, and my law-for-myself, that is, my moral order. Like my reality-for-myself, society's reality-for-itself contains social poetry as well as social prose, the contribution of the imagination and the unconscious to the work of rationality.[17] Social practice is a product of ideas and law. Law is a product of ideas and practice. The ideas which take the form of *theories* within a society's ideal self-constituting and which help to form its reality-for-itself are that society's explanation of itself to itself, a society's philosophy-for-itself, one part of the totality of the self-contemplating of the human mind. As *practical* theory, they express themselves in the course of social practice, the programme of actual willing and acting. As *pure theory*, they act as the theory of practical theory, the programme of society's programmes.[18] As *transcendental theory*, they act as the theory of theory, a society's epistemology.

The present essay is proposed as a contribution to the self-explaining of international society at the level of transcendental theory and pure theory, with a view to modifying the practical theory of international society, and thereby the willing and acting of all who participate in its real and legal self-constituting. The history of human societies contains many examples of revolutionary change not only in the real constitutions of societies but also in their ideal self-constituting, revolutions in the mind. Such events are moments of human self-enlightenment which transform the potentiality and the actuality of those societies. There is no reason why international society should be incapable of such self-enlightening, and every reason, derived from the lamentable history of its own self-constituting, why it should find a new potentiality for human self-creating at the level of all-humanity, the self-evolving of the human species, a revolution in the human species-mind.

The ideal

The potentiality of human self-creating takes the particular form of the *ideal* when the mind *conceives* of the present in the light of a *better* future, when the mind *judges* the actual by reference to a *better* potentiality, when the mind dedicates its moral freedom to the *purpose* of actualizing that *better* potentiality. The ideal is the

---

[17] The term 'social poetry' is particularly associated with the names of Giambattista Vico (1668–1744), for whom historiography is the social reconstructing of the story of the social self-constructing of human consciousness, and Georges Sorel (1847–1922), for whom social consciousness is both a weapon and the target of revolutionary social change. '[As] force is always on the side of the governed, the governors have nothing to support them but opinion. It is therefore, on opinion only that government is founded.' D. Hume, 'Of the first principles of government', in *Essays Moral, Political, and Literary*, I. IV, eds. T. H. Green and T. H. Grose (London: Longmans, Green, 1907), p. 110. 'For a society is not made up merely of the mass of individuals who compose it, the ground which they occupy, the things which they use and the movements which they perform, but above all is the idea which it forms of itself.' E. Durkheim, *The Elementary Forms of Religious Life* (1912), trans. J. W. Swain (London: George Allen & Unwin, 1915/76), p. 422.

[18] This distinction between pure theory and practical theory is analogous to Aristotle's distinction between speculative reason and practical reason (*Politics*, VII.14) or, as he expresses it in the *Nicomachean Ethics* (I.vii), the difference between the thinking of the geometer and the thinking of the carpenter. For further discussion, see *Eunomia*, §§2.52ff.

better potentiality of the actual, acting as a moral imperative in the present, with a view to making a better future.

The idea of the ideal was made possible by three developments in the self-knowing of the human mind.

(1) It was first necessary for philosophy to produce the idea of *rationalized abstraction*. Reflecting upon the thesis of Heraclitus that all reality is *change*, Greek metaphysics and epistemology identified a capacity of the human mind to postulate the unchanging in the midst of change, that to which the process of becoming applies. It did so by postulating the universal aspect of every particular process of becoming—from the becoming of material objects (whose formal substance remains) to the becoming of living things (whose integrating form remains) to language itself (whose structure of rationality remains beneath the infinite diversity of actual communication). In this way, every single particular element in the universe could be seen as an instance of something more general, up to and including the universality of the universe itself (*kosmos* or *god*).

It became possible to see a particular collection of human beings living together as a particular instance of a universal idea of *society* (*koinōnia*) and, perhaps, of a *constituted society* under *law* (*polis*). It thereupon became possible to compare particular instances by reference to a universal model—Athens and Sparta, Greek and Egyptian, the governors and the governed, monarchy and oligarchy, oligarchy and democracy. It became possible to objectify and even to personalize particular cases of the generic universal (this state, that nation, all-humanity). It became possible to universalize and substantiate standards of comparison (values)—freedom, tyranny, justice, the rule of law, well-being. It even became possible to universalize the standards behind the standards of comparison, the value of values—the good, the true, the beautiful, virtue, happiness.

(2) Reflecting on another insight of Heraclitus, that change is the product of negation, the human mind became conscious of another remarkable feature of its functioning, namely, its propensity to present ideas to itself in the form of *duality*. It seems likely that we are biologically programmed—perhaps literally so, in some binary process within the systematic functioning of the brain—to construct reality by integrating opposing ideas (1 | 1 = 1). Philosophy very soon identified and appropriated this mental process as the amazing universal power of *dialectical thought*.[19] What may be an aspect of the physiology of the human brain, which has determined the functioning of the human mind, and which has been reproduced in the structure of human language through the long process of socializing, has given to human reality a peculiarly *dualistic* structure—life and death, being and nothing, appearance and reality, essence and existence, mind and matter, good and evil, pleasure and pain, true and false, the past and the future, the actual and the potential.

The dyad of *appearance and reality* has allowed us to make a human reality which is a mental reconstruction of a reality which we suppose to be not mind-made, enabling us to take power not only over the physical world (through the mental reconstruction effected by the natural sciences) but also over the human world

---

[19] The idea of the dialectic, made explicit in Plato's dialogues, retained its extraordinary power within pure theories of society up to and including the work of Hegel and Marx in the 19th century, and has continually haunted practical theories of society, up to and including the power-legitimating political parties and elections of democracy and the value-determining competitive struggle of capitalism.

(through the power of thought communicated through language). The dyad of *the actual and the ideal* has allowed us to make human reality into a moral order in which the actual can pass judgement upon itself by reference to its better potentiality, which is the ideal.

(3) Reflecting on human practice, especially social practice, philosophy was able, finally, to see that the power of the ideal stems from the fact that the idea of the better contains both the idea of the possible and the idea of the desirable. It generates a powerful attractive force inclining us to seek to actualize it. It engages, in our spiritual mind, something which is akin to physical love in our interpersonal mind. As evolutionary biology has used the power of physical love to negate physical separation with a view to the creation of new life, so it has made possible the power of spiritual love to negate the opposition between the present and the future with a view to the creation of better life, including better life in society. From the spiritual mind, energized by the idea of the ideal, come our most passionate moral feelings—of anger (for example, in the face of injustice and oppression), of hope (for example, for freedom and self-fulfilment), of joy (for example, in the face of the good and the beautiful)—feelings capable of inspiring limitless self-surpassing and self-sacrifice. Moral freedom is moral desire.[20]

These developments have given a particular form to *human reality*, the world made by the human mind. It is a form which we so much take for granted that it is difficult to see that it might have been otherwise—and that, at different times and in different places, it has been otherwise. Humanity discovered within itself a self-transcending power of self-conceiving, self-evaluating, and self-making, an inexhaustible source of human progress, of the self-evolving of the species. The idea of the ideal is the permanent possibility of the moral transformation of human beings and human societies, the permanent possibility of revolutionary human self-perfecting. We would not be as we are without the idea of the ideal. We will not be what we could be without the idea of the ideal.

The legal

The idea of the ideal has entered into the *ideal* self-constituting, and the revolutionary transformation, of countless societies. It has had a particularly powerful effect in the *legal* self-constituting of societies. It is present, if at all, only embryonically and immanently, in the *legal* self-constituting of international society, the society of all societies.

The law is another of the wonderful creations of the human mind. It enables a society to carry its structures and systems from the past through the present into the future. It enables a society to choose particular social futures from among the

---

[20] '[Love] is the ancient source of our highest good ... For neither family, nor privilege, nor wealth, nor anything but Love can light that beacon which a man must steer by when he sets out to live the better life. How shall I describe it—as that contempt for the vile, and emulation of the good, without which neither cities nor citizens are capable of any great or noble work.' Plato, *Symposium* (trans. M. Joyce), 178 c–d , *Collected Dialogues*, p. 533. 'We live by Admiration, Hope and Love; / And, even as these are well and wisely fixed, / In dignity of being we ascend.' W. Wordsworth, *The Excursion* (1814), IV, lines 763–6.

infinite range of possible futures. Above all, it enables society to insert the *common interest* of society into the willing and acting of every society-member, human individuals and subordinate societies, so that the energy and the ambition, the self-interest of each of them may serve the common interest of them all. Law is the most efficient instrument for the actualizing of the ideal, universalizing the particular in law-making, particularizing the universal in law-application, a primary source of a society's survival and prospering within the self-perfecting of all-humanity.[21]

It is possible to identify rather precisely the way in which law achieves its wonder-working. Within general human reality, and within the social reality of a particular society, there is a *legal reality* in which everything without exception—every person, every thing, every event—has legal significance. Legal reality is created by means very similar to the way, discussed above, in which the human mind constructs human reality generally—that is to say, by representing to itself in the form of ideas what it conceives as being the 'real' world. Legal reality is a language-reality, made from words. Law is a language-world, in which special words, and words from other language-worlds, have their own self-contained life-process. Law shares in general ideas of human psychology, but has its own methods of explaining behaviour and attributing responsibility. Law shares in general rationality, but has its own methods of analysis, argument, and proof. In particular, legal relations are a special application of the capacity of the human mind for abstract generalizing, followed by the substantializing and even personalizing of abstract ideas.

Legal significance is given to that idealized reality in the form of what are called *legal relations*—that is, rights, duties, freedoms, powers, liabilities, immunities, disabilities—conferred on legal persons (human beings or legally recognized social forms). Legal reality is a network of infinite density and complexity in which everything, without exception, is the subject of countless legal relations.

My *freedom* to conclude a contract engages with your *freedom* to conclude a contract, and the resulting contract creates *rights* and *duties* upon each of us; gives me the *power* to invoke the protection of a court of law, if you fail to carry out a *duty* under the contract (unless you have an *immunity* from legal proceedings); gives to the court the *power* to make orders which alter the *rights* and *duties* of the parties to the contract, including, perhaps, the imposing on you of a *duty* to pay damages; thus giving a *power,* and imposing a *duty,* on a court official to enforce the court orders; all because a legislator exercised a *power* to enact a law about contracts and a law about courts; and because someone exercised a *power* to appoint judges and court officials under legislation on those matters—and so on, *ad infinitum.*

A legal relation is an abstracted pattern of potentiality into which actual persons and things and situations may be fitted. It is a *matrix* which identifies persons and

---

[21] 'How can it be that all should obey, yet nobody take upon him to command, and that all should serve, and yet have no masters, but be more free, as, in apparent subjection, each loses no part of his liberty but what might be hurtful to that of another? These wonders are the work of law. It is to law alone that men owe justice and liberty. It is this salutary organ of the will of all which establishes, in civil right, the natural equality between men. It is this celestial voice which dictates to each citizen the precepts of public reason, and teaches him to act according to the rules of his own judgment, and not to behave inconsistently with himself. It is with this voice alone that political rulers should speak when they command; for no sooner does one man, setting aside the law, claim to subject another to his private will, than he departs from the state of civil society, and confronts him face to face in the pure state of nature, in which obedience is prescribed solely by necessity.' J-J. Rousseau, *A Discourse on Political Economy* (1755), in *The Social Contract and Discourses*, trans. G. D. H. Cole (London: J. M. Dent, Everyman's Library, 1913), p. 124.

things and situations in an abstract form distinct from their status in general reality (person, corporation, state, contract, treaty, judge, plaintiff, government, parliament, property, territory, money). It is an *heuristic* which connects aspects of those persons and things and situations to each other in a particular way (contracting parties, shareholders in a corporation, parties to legal proceedings, sovereign of territory, government of a state, voter in an election). It is an *algorithm*, a mini-programme of action, which triggers a succession of consequences (especially the application of other legal relations) when actual persons, things, and situations fit into the pattern of potentiality (you step onto a pedestrian crossing, you ratify a treaty, you speak falsely about another person, you put money into a slot-machine). When the legal relation is applied, social reality is modified accordingly, by the conforming behaviour of actual human beings, actualizing a possible future which had been selected by society in the common interest. From the selection-by-election of the members of a parliament, through the way in which the accounts of a commercial corporation are presented, to where you park your car, every aspect of human behaviour may be modified by law in the common interest.

It is the function of the *legislative process* to insert the common interest into legal relations, by resolving conflicting conceptions of the common interest into a single conception reflected in the substance of the law. It is the function of the *judicial process* to interpret the common interest when the abstracted patterns of the law are applied to particular situations. It is the function of *politics*, in the most general sense, to provide the forum in which conflicting conceptions of the common interest are brought into the dialectical competition of the *real constitution*. It is the *ideal constitution* of the society, its total self-constituting in the form of ideas, which generates the values and purposes which are the raw material of politics and which may ultimately be reflected in the law.

There are three primary functions of the law which are especially significant for the actualizing of the legal potentiality of international society.

(1) Law makes the economy. Whatever the naturalist fantasies of the pure theories of an economy, not least theories of free-market capitalism, the economy is a legal structure, that is to say, an artificial structure, made possible by the creation by the law of all the paraphernalia of the economy, from property and money to the corporation. The common interest which is supposed to guide the invisible hand of the market must first make itself visible in the superstructure of the law. Crucial question for the future of international society—what is the legal basis of the global economy?

(2) Law makes the public realm. The public realm consists of legal powers which are to be exercised *in the public interest*. A legal power generally gives to the power-holder a choice of possible decisions within the limits of the power, which may include decisions which are chosen to serve whatever interest the power-holder chooses to serve (to vote or not to vote; to vote for this candidate or that). A *public-realm legal power* limits the choice of possible decisions to those which serve the public interest, as determined explicitly or implicitly by the terms of the power itself or by the status of the power-holder.[22] If we take seriously capitalism's own story

---

[22] Locke similarly defined *political power* as the right to make and execute the laws and defend the commonwealth from foreign injury, 'and all this only for the Publick Good'. J. Locke, *Two Treatises of Government* (1690), II.§3, ed. P. Laslett (Cambridge: Cambridge University Press, 1960), p. 286.

about itself, namely, that private wealth-seeking is justified because it is public wealth-creating, then we should regard economic power as a form of public-realm power, to be exercised in the common interest. Crucial question for the future of international society—in whose interest are the international powers attributed to states and other international actors to be exercised?

(3) Law makes constitutionalism. In countless societies, throughout the course of human history, social theory has been able to generate ideas whose common feature is that they place the ultimate source of the authority of law in something other than the will of the person or persons currently making or enforcing the law.[23] All law, and especially public-realm power, is essentially a delegation of power. Crucial question for the future of international society—what is the ultimate source of the authority of law at the global level?

The real

Who or what has caused the scandal of international unsociety, the unsociety of all-humanity, an inhuman human reality of everyday social evil and social injustice, of cynical parodies of law and social order, an unnatural state of nature in which social predators oppress, abuse, and kill human beings in their millions, a world seething with fraudulent democracies and criminal presidential monarchies, a social reality in which some human beings worry about the colour of the bed-linen for their holiday-home in Provence, while other human beings worry about their next meal or the leaking tin-roof of the shack which is their only home?

In a society's *real constitution*, a society creates itself through the actual day-to-day practice of actual human beings, including, above all, the decisions of the holders of public-realm powers, their behaviour being conditioned by every aspect of social reality, as society also creates itself, as ideas and as law, in its ideal and legal constitutions.[24] The real self-constituting of international society has produced a

---

[23] The 'higher' source of everyday law has been identified, at different times and in different places, as divine order, the sovereignty of law, natural cosmic order, and natural social order—with the last idea being used in the pure theory of liberal democracy (social contract) and in the practical theory of many national constitutions. See Philip Allott, 'Intergovernmental Societies and the Idea of Constitutionalism,' in V. Heiskanen and J.-M. Coicaud (eds.), *The Legitimacy of International Organisations* (Tokyo: UN University Press, 2000).

[24] 'The laws reach but a very little way. Constitute Government how you please, infinitely the greater part of it must depend upon the exercise of powers which are left at large to the prudence and uprightness of Ministers of State ... Without them, your Commonwealth is no better than a scheme on paper, and not a living, active, effective constitution.' E. Burke, *Thoughts on the Cause of our Present Discontents* (1770), in P. Langford (ed.), *The Writings and Speeches of Edmund Burke*, vol. II (Oxford: Clarendon Press, 1981), pp. 251–322, at p. 277. '... the real constitution (*wirkliche Verfassung*) of a country exists only in the true actual power-relations which are present in the country; written constitutions thus only have worth and durability if they are an exact expression of the real power-relations of society.' F. Lassalle, 'Über Verfassungswesen' (On the Nature of the Constitution) (1863), in *Gesammelte Reden und Schriften*, vol. II (E. Bernstein (ed.) (Berlin: P. Cassirer, 1919), at p. 60 (present author's translation). Lassalle, a follower of Hegel and, less faithfully, of Marx, and the founder of the General Union of German Workers (the first political party of the working-class), contrasted the real constitution with the written (or legal) constitution, the former but not the latter (in the Germany of the 1860s) being the expression of the real power of the nobles, great landowners, industrialists, bankers, and major capitalists.

diseased social reality, a psychopathic condition which threatens the survival of the human species.

Given the relative simplicity and transparency of international society, it is relatively easy to explain the present tragic state of international society. The root cause has been the emergence, in the period since the end of the fifteenth century, of a discontinuity in human reality, a duality in the social self-constituting of the human species—a duality reflected in *practice*, especially in the practice of war and diplomacy, as international society was isolated and insulated from the amazing development of national social systems; in *ideas*, especially through the conceiving of separate national and international human realities; and, not least, in *law*, as the development of international law was isolated and insulated from the amazing development of national legal systems.

(1) The universal and perennial dialectic of the duality of the One and the Many has shaped the constituting of human societies throughout human history. The development of the modern (European) idea of the 'state' is a world-transforming product of that dialectic. The post-medieval (Renaissance and Reformation) individualizing of the human being was accompanied by an equal and opposite individualizing of society, so that the historical development of particular societies would be an endless succession of particular resolutions of the forces of individualism and collectivism, and the historical development of international society came to be a mere side-effect of that process.[25]

(2) The One of the Leviathan state was then personalized through the operation of the universal and perennial dialectic of the Self and the Other which has shaped the self-constituting of societies throughout human history.[26] The holders of public-realm power, kings and public officials, could identify their self-interest with the public interest of the One they so nobly served, and could, by force or by mind-manipulation, induce the people to suppose that it was their patriotic and moral duty to kill and be killed by their neighbours on behalf of their own so-called commonwealths.[27] Again and again, the agonistic relationship has produced a third thing (1 + 1 = 3), a fantasy construct within the interpersonal consciousness of each

---

[25] The leading role in Act One of the drama was taken by Thomas Hobbes (1588–1679), who managed to proceed from an heuristic model of the personality of the individual human being to the total socializing of the individual person in the individualizing and substantializing and personalizing of the 'commonwealth' that is to say, 'the Multitude so united in one Person'. The 'sovereign', to whom they have transferred their powers, 'may use the strength and means of them all, as he [or it, in the case of a collective sovereign] shall think expedient, for their Peace and Common Defence'. (*Leviathan*, ch. xvii).

[26] The word 'state' acquired two senses, referring to an aspect of a society's internal constitution and, externally, referring to a society's participation in international relations. But the semantics of the word soon took on a great weight of additional semiotic significance. After 1789, the word 'nation (*Volk*)' also took on great semiotic power, referring to a society in its genetic individuality and subjectivity. See Philip Allott, 'The nation as mind politic', *Journal of International Law and Politics*, 24 (1992), pp. 1361–98.

[27] 'The wonder of this infernal enterprise is that each leader of the murderers has his standards blessed and solemnly invokes God before setting out to exterminate his neighbour.' Voltaire, *Dictonnaire philosophique* (1764–5), article on *War* (Paris, GF-Flammarion; 1964), p. 218. The heroes of Act Two of the drama were the masterful makers of the modern states: kings and courtiers and politicians and their obsequious acolytes. See Philip Allott, 'International Law and the International *Hofmafia*. Towards a Sociology of Diplomacy', in W. Benedek, et al. (eds.), *Development and Developing International and European Law. Essays in Honour of Konrad Ginther* (Frankfurt am Main: Peter Lang, 1999), pp. 3–19.

society, a *folie à deux* which reached a sublime level of insanity in the so-called Cold War of the later twentieth century.

(3) The third Act was an act of omission. Social philosophers, despite their achievements in the revolutionary reconceiving of national society, mysteriously failed to extend their vision to encompass the condition of humanity as a whole. Philosophy is surely universal or it is not philosophy. Moral philosophy is surely universal or it is not moral philosophy. The moral order does not contain political frontiers.[28]

(4) Pure and practical theories of international law filled the vacuum left by social philosophy, dissolving the perennial and universal dilemma of justice and social justice into a vapid simulacrum of law. Spawning an exiguous vocabulary of concepts, adding fashionably 'democratic' overtones to their medieval feudal land-holding, a new international language-world re-empowered the powerful in their relations with each other, using the language of the law to dignify, as right and duty, the self-seeking of those who could continue to behave externally as if they were *ancien régime* monarchs, more or less free from the tiresome requirements of political or moral accountability, free from the burden of any form of self-justification beyond the anti-morality of *reason of state*.[29]

(5) The becoming of international society came to be practised as a permanent game of social Darwinism, in which the national game of politics extruded a misbegotten form known as 'foreign policy' pursued through the rituals of diplomacy and war. In the nineteenth century, the game took on a substantial economic aspect, as industrial capitalism became a central feature of the national struggle to survive, a determining factor in the causes and the conduct of war.[30] The condition of all-humanity came to be a random by-product of the national struggle to survive. Social Darwinism is not merely an anti-idealism. It is an anti-philosophy, a pragmatic default-theory. Democracy-capitalism is the institutionalizing of social Darwinism, with democratic *public opinion* and the capitalist *market* acting as dynamic myth-forms within a mental absolutism whose high-values (*consent* and *efficiency*) are functional rather than transcendental.

(6) In the twentieth century, the volume of the internationally abnormal came vastly to exceed the volume of what was supposed to be the normal. The externalizing and the interpenetration of economic systems, and of the national legal systems which subtend the economic systems, were anomalous in relation to the continuing isolation of the national political systems. The assertion of high-level principles for controlling the exercise of public-realm power (human rights), and the naïve or cynical extrapolation of internal constitutional forms (courts, assemblies), were anomalous in relation to the continuing isolation of national constitutional

---

[28] The most striking failures of vision were those of Locke, Rousseau, and Hegel.

[29] The benign *maître à penser* of the new world order was Emmerich de Vattel (1714–67) whose simplistic ideas were both comprehensible and delightful for the holders of public power. Nations or states, he said, may be regarded as so many free persons living together in a state of nature. They are free, independent, equal, and sovereign. Their duties to themselves clearly prevail over their duties to others. The law of nations consists of various constraints which they choose to impose upon themselves. War remained, in the formula cherished by Louis XIV of France, the 'ultimate reason of kings' (*ultima ratio regum*).

[30] Herbert Spencer (1820–1903), anguished apostle of 19th-century optimism, believed that human progress is a form of biological evolution, including a Lamarckian inheritance of acquired mental characteristics. Competitive industrial capitalism could be seen as the continuation of war by other (better) means.

systems. The development of conceptions of international public order was anomalous in relation to the continuing 'territorial integrity' of states. The development of complex systems of international government was anomalous in relation to the 'political independence' of states, and the emerging hegemonic international public realm was anomalous in relation to 'sovereign' national public realms. The bureaucratized international redistribution of wealth was anomalous in relation to the institutionalized *laissez faire, laissez aller* of the global economy. The formulation of masses of international legislation, in the form of treaties and decisions of international institutions, was anomalous in relation to a conception of international law as setting the minimum conditions of the coexistence of neighbouring feudal land-owners. Above all, a gathering global revolution of rising expectations as to human flourishing, a moral revolution in people's ideas about the good life in society, was anomalous in relation to the structural inequality and injustice and atavism of the international system.

(7) In the twentieth century also, we experienced extremes of the pathology of human socializing, as evil minds corrupted the minds of millions, as episodes of insanity possessed the public minds of whole societies, and whole nations paid the price in suffering. The growing complexity of law and government, at every social level, revealed itself, as it has throughout human history, as the growing sophistication of structures of social inequality. So-called 'human rights' in legalistic formulations, and technocratic programmes of 'good governance', revealed themselves as new forms of the age-old mask which conceals the exploitation and the oppression of the many by the few. The twentieth century taught us once more a lesson which is as old as human society. The only constant in human social history is the ruthless self-protecting of social privilege. The only human right which is universally enforced is the right of the rich to get richer.[31]

Globalization from below

The problem of social evil is as old as human socializing. Social evil is humanity's self-wounding and self-destroying through the operation of social processes, from

---

[31] 'Consequently, when I consider and turn over in my mind the state of all commonwealths flourishing anywhere today, so help me God, I can see nothing else than a kind of conspiracy of the rich, who are aiming at their own interests under the name and title of the commonwealth. They invent and devise all ways and means by which, first, they may keep without fear of loss all that they have amassed by evil practices and, secondly, they may then purchase as cheaply as possible and abuse the toil and labour of all the poor. These devices become law as soon as the rich have once decreed their observance in the name of the public—that is, of the poor also! ... What is worse, the rich every day extort [*abradunt*] a part of their daily allowance from the poor not only by private fraud but by public law ... and finally, by making laws, have palmed it off as justice.' Thomas More, *Utopia* (1516), in E. Surtz and J. H. Hexter (eds.), *The Complete Works of St Thomas More*, vol. 4 (New Haven, CT & London: Yale University Press, 1965), p. 421. 'Laws and government may be considered ... as a combination of the rich to oppress the poor, and preserve to themselves the inequality of goods which would otherwise be destroyed by the attacks of the poor ... The government and laws ... tell them they must either continue poor or acquire wealth in the same manner as they have done.' Adam Smith, *Lectures on Jurisprudence* (lecture of 22 Feb. 1763), eds. R. L. Meek, D. D. Raphael and P. G. Stein (Oxford: Clarendon Press, 1978), pp. 208–9. '... the art of becoming "rich", in the common sense, is not absolutely nor finally the act of accumulating much money for ourselves, but also of contriving that our neighbours shall have less.' J. Ruskin, *Unto This Last. Four Essays on the First Principles of Political Economy* (1860) (London: George Allen & Sons, 1862/1910), pp. 45–6.

war and genocide to social oppression and social injustice of every kind. Humanity in the twenty-first century has inherited from the self-inflicted suffering of the turbid twentieth century an unprecedented and unbearable legacy of world-wide social evil.

Social evil is a systematic product of social systems, caused by human beings acting in their official capacity in the public interest, alienated from their moral responsibility as individual human beings, or caused by social systems so complex that their products can be attributed to no human beings in particular. Social systems and their products escape moral judgement. They are beyond good and evil. But the wages of social evil are paid in *suffering*, the suffering of actual human beings, of whole peoples, of all humanity. The price is paid in *corruption*, the corrupting of all human values, down to and including the values of the most intimate interpersonal consciousness of individual human beings. And the price is paid in *destruction*, the relentless degradation of the natural habitat of the human species.

It so happens that we have also inherited from the twentieth century an unprecedented degree of human socialization, unprecedented possibilities of the good that social systems can do, unprecedented possibilities of social evil. What is called 'globalization' is seen, like the political and economic imperialism of the nineteenth century, as an extrapolating of the national realm into the international realm. The risk now facing humanity is the globalizing of all-powerful, all-consuming social systems, without the moral, legal, political and cultural aspirations and constraints, such as they are, which moderate social action at the national level.[32]

In particular, and above all, international society now contains the potentiality of a human future in which the globalizing of economic and governmental social systems will be merged with a rudimentary international social system inherited from the past, a system which has been the cause of so much social evil, local and global. It is a social system in which the highest value continues to be the maximizing of the advantage of the particular social formations known as 'states', and in which the maximizing of the survival and prospering of each human individual and of all-humanity is conceptually secondary, in practice and in theory. It is an international system which, with the overwhelming political and economic energies generated by globalization, is perfectly designed to maximize the risk of every form of international social evil.

Globalization from above

So it is that international society now contains the potentiality of a human future determined by the unrelenting force of the social actual, unmoved by the self-surpassing power of the social ideal. It is a burden made almost unbearable by crude historicism, by self-disempowering in the face of the human future, by the belief that humanity is beyond self-redeeming, and that social evil is an unalterable fact of

[32] In the parable of the Grand Inquisitor (*The Brothers Karamazov*, bk. 5), Dostoevsky expressed, with passionate intensity, what he saw as the paradox of Roman Christianity, that a liberating human enlightenment had become an absolutist social system. We need a Dostoevsky to express the paradox of democracy-capitalism, that a system dedicated to 'freedom' has produced social systems of totalitarian social power, systems that are now being globalized.

social life. The idea of the end of history is a vision of the end of humanity. The idea of the clash of civilizations is a vision of the end of civilization. Social evil, and our despair in the face of social evil, are the symptoms of a diseased human reality. The great task of the twenty-first century is to install the idea of the ideal in dialectical opposition to the fact of the actual as a creative force in the making of the human future. International social idealism is the dialectical negation of international social Darwinism.

To redeem international society requires a fundamental reconceiving of our inherited international world-view, a psychological and philosophical reconstituting, a revolution-from-above in the public mind of all-humanity. It is possible already to diagnose the symptoms of diseased international social reality and so to prescribe a cure, identifying the guiding principles of a new international reality, a new ideal self-constituting of a true international society, a charter of international social idealism, a New Enlightenment.

- A social reality (international society or the international system) which is commonly supposed to be merely the interaction of instances of a certain kind of reified concept (states)[33] is a dehumanized social reality.
- A social reality in which social consciousness is formed, not by the interacting of the private minds of all human beings and the public minds of subordinate societies, but primarily through the systematic interacting of agents of sub-ordinate societies (governments), can never be a fully human social reality.
- A social reality conceived as the actualizing through foreign policy, diplomacy, and war of a pragmatic highest value (the prospering of each particular state) is a demoralized social reality.
- A social reality in which war and the use of force are seen as the ultimate instruments of social cohesion is an anti-social social reality.
- A social reality in which law is seen, not as the source, the limit, and the judge of social power but as merely an incidental by-product of social power, is an illegitimate social reality.

Globalization from above means the application of every self-creating potentiality of human consciousness to the self-constituting of international society. It is to set the human-world-transforming attraction of the ideal in dialectical opposition to the human-world-affirming force of the actual, the universal in dialectical opposition to the particular.

- There is only one human world, one human reality, one moral order, and one social order extending from the family and the village up to the international society of the whole human race.
- Our culturally diverse ideals of human existence, our ideas of the good life as individuals and as societies, are, for each human being, one and indivisible. And those ideals include not only our ideas of justice and injustice, good and evil, but

[33] A 'state', on this traditional view, is a generic society whose public realm is under the authority of a 'government' and which is recognized as a state by other governments. A 'state' is then treated as being an entity and a legal person, with some of the characteristics of a natural person (will, purposes, interests, and so on). The primary social process of the international society or system so formed is supposed to consist of intergovernmental behaviour, especially through the practices known as 'foreign policy' and 'diplomacy'.

also our transcendental ideas of the particularity of human existence within the order of the universe of all-that-is.

- The rule of law is one and indivisible. All public power is derived from law, and is subject to the law, at the global level as at the level of individual societies. International law will be the true law of an international society truly conceived.[34]
- All legal power exists to serve the common interest. International law exists to serve the common interest of all humanity and of all subordinate societies.
- The common interest of international society is the survival and prospering of all human beings within a natural habitat shared by all.

Our capacity to form the idea of the ideal allows us to undertake our moral self-transforming, to actualize our revolutionary self-recreating. Our spiritual consciousness allows us to desire human self-perfecting. Our moral freedom allows us to recognize a moral duty to make a better human future. We are what we think. We will be what we think. We must make a revolution-from-above in the name of the ideal, a revolution in the private mind of every human being, in the public minds of all societies, and, eventually and at last, in the public mind of the society of all-humanity.

How beauteous mankind is! O brave new world,
That has such people in 't!
W. Shakespeare, *The Tempest*, Act V, sc.1.

---

[34] For the blueprint of a true international law of a true international society, see Philip Allott, 'The Concept of International Law', in *European Journal of International Law*, 10 (1999), pp. 31–50, and in M. Byers (ed.), *The Role of Law in International Politics. Essays in International Relations and International Law* (Oxford: Oxford University Press, 2000), pp. 69–89.

A more perfect union? The liberal peace and the challenge of globalization

MICHAEL W. DOYLE[1]

Global democratization rose to the international agenda in the past year as the three peak global economic associations all came under attack. In Seattle, at the meeting of the new World Trade Organization, and in Washington at the meetings of the World Bank and the International Monetary Fund, a diverse collection of labour unions and environmentalists from the industrial North and trade and finance ministers from the developing countries of the South each launched sharply critical barbs. The critics successfully disrupted the WTO meeting that had been designed to launch (and celebrate) a 'Millennium Round' of further reductions of barriers to global trade. The aims of the critics were very different, but together they derailed the entire proceedings and exposed important differences in priority among the developed states, and particularly the US and Europe. Charlene Barshefsky, the US Trade Representative and the meeting's chair, later conceded, 'We needed a process which had a greater degree of internal transparency and inclusion to accommodate a larger and more diverse membership'.[2] This highly-regarded trade-o-crat had come to recognize that the eminently oligarchic WTO needed some democratization (as yet undefined).

Joe Stiglitz, until recently the chief economist of the World Bank, offered a still broader criticism of the Bank's sister institution, the International Monetary Fund. The IMF was designed to rescue countries in temporary balance of payments difficulties. It actually operates, Stiglitz charges, more like a bureaucratic cabal than an international rescue team:

The IMF likes to go about its business without outsiders asking too many questions. In theory, the fund supports democratic institutions in the nations it assists. In practice, it undermines the democratic process by imposing policies. Officially, of course, the IMF doesn't 'impose' anything. It 'negotiates' the conditions for receiving aid. But all the power in the negotiations is on one side—the IMF's—and the fund rarely allows sufficient time for broad consensus-building or even widespread consultations with either parliaments or civil society. Sometimes the IMF dispenses with the pretense of openness altogether and negotiates secret covenants.[3]

[1] A version of this article was delivered as 'The 2000 Welling Lecture' at George Washington University, on 9 March, 2000. I thank Monique Ramgoolie and Daniel H. Else for assistance. I am grateful for comments and discussion at a Millennium Seminar of GWU on 10 March, organized by Harry Harding, and for comments from William Antholis and Sophie Meunier.
[2] Quoted from Martin Khor, 'Take Care, the WTO Majority is Tired of Being Manipulated', *International Herald Tribune*, 21 December, 1999.
[3] Joseph Stiglitz, 'What I Learned at the World Economic Crisis', *The New Republic*, 17 April, 2000.

Two themes resonate through the denunciations: global governance and global (or international) democratization. The key question is how they relate to each other. Three issues connect them. The first is the broad ethical question of how could and should the world be organized politically?[4] I present the claims for the leading organizational political framework today, one designed to bring world order while recognizing the reality of sovereign independence, which is the Kantian idea of a pacific union of free republics, or the liberal democratic peace. More controversially, I then argue that however good the Kantian peace has been and could be, it has significant limitations that have been exposed by increasing globalization. Globalization both sustains elements of the Kantian peace and also undermines it, making it less sustainable and indeed vitiating some of the democracy on which it is founded. And third, I discuss a range of possible responses to the challenges that globalization poses for the existing international order, and conclude with a comment on why global democratic sovereignty is not yet viable while global norms—more democratically derived—seem needed to promote a more perfect a union of order and democracy.

Global political theory

How could and should the world be politically organized? That is, how should one assess various forms of political organization of world politics with respect to their ability to fulfil a set of human values that would be very widely shared—even if not exactly in the same way—around the world? Take, for example, these values: peace; prosperity; national independence, cultural identity or pluralism (so that people can express their identities in some public form); and individual human rights (including democracy, participation, equality and self-determination).

How well do various schemes of international order fulfil these basic human values at the global scale? Political philosophers have told us that the international system is a mix of hard choices among values. The political theorist Michael Walzer has reformulated those choices well in an essay that explores the range of values from little to much international governance, that is from national autonomy (and international anarchy) to a global, hierarchical, centralized government over all individuals.[5] There is no single arrangement that obtains everything—one that procures international peace, domestic peace, liberty, democracy, prosperity, and pluralistic identity. Instead, while the virtues of the nation state are domestic peace and perhaps national identity and national democracy, those same virtues are the foundations of international anarchy, geopolitical insecurity and international economic rivalry. Global government can be a foundation for global peace and a single efficient world market, and maybe even a global democratic polity, but it could also be the institution that represses national particularity, the global 'soul-less

---

[4] A similar debate engages the European Union. See, for example, Wayne Sandholtz and Alec Stone (eds.), *European Integration and Supranational Governance* (Oxford: Oxford University Press, 1998); Jack Hayward (ed.), *The Crisis of Representation in Europe* (Ilford, UK: Frank Cass, 1995); and Robert Keohane and Stanley Hoffmann (eds.), *The New European Community* (Boulder, CO: Westview, 1991).
[5] Michael Walzer's essay is forthcoming in *Dissent* (Fall, 2000).

despotism' against which the eighteenth century German philosopher, Immanuel Kant, eloquently warned the liberals of his day. In between global authority and national independence, one can imagine confederal arrangements that allowed room for a diversity of civil societies, but again only at the cost of both national autonomy and international insecurity. The message of Michael Walzer's spectrum of global governance is hard choices: there is no perfect equilibrium.

Although there is no perfect solution to the problem of implementing human values on a global scale, the Kantian liberal peace lays claim to being the optimal combination, the one that gets us the most peace and global prosperity at the least cost in liberty, independence, and the least trampling on national identities. Immanuel Kant's essay, *Perpetual Peace*, published in 1795, was a direct response and alternative to both the autarkic nation state and a sovereign world government.

The key to the liberal argument is the claim that by establishing domestic liberty, political participation, and market exchange one can have the international payoff of peace as well.[6] Kant described a decentralized, self-enforcing peace achieved without the world government that the global governance claim posits as necessary. This is a claim that has resonated in the modern literature on the 'democratic peace'. It draws on the ideas of American presidents as diverse as Woodrow Wilson, Ronald Reagan and Bill Clinton and British prime ministers from Gladstone to Blair. Promoting freedom and 'enlarging' the zone of democratic rule were the doctrinal centrepieces of their foreign policies. Advocates of the 'democratic peace' have claimed that over time, country by democratizing country, a peace would spread to cover the entire world, building one world order—democratic, free, prosperous, and peaceful.

Kant's argument was much more complicated, presented in three necessary conditions, each an 'article' in a hypothetical peace 'treaty' he asks sovereigns to sign. First, states should adopt a liberal constitutional, representative, republican form of government which would constrain the state such that the sovereign would, on average, usually follow the interest of most of the people, or the majority. Second, the citizens of this liberal, constitutional, representative republic must affirm a commitment to human rights, one holding that all human beings are morally equal. Then states that represent liberal democratic majorities in their own countries will regard with respect other states that also represent free and equal citizens. Tolerance for various national liberal cultures and trust emerges, as does nonaggression and peace among fellow liberal republics. Third, given trust, states then lower the barriers that would have been raised to protect the state from invasion or exploitation in the competition of the balance of power. Trade, tourism and other forms of transnational contact grow which lead to prosperity, reinforcing mutual understanding with many opportunities for profitable exchange, and producing contacts that offset in their multiplicity the occasional sources of conflict.

For many, this seems the optimal equilibrium given both the world as it is and a commitment to the values of peace, liberty, prosperity, national identity and democratic participation. Does that mean that there are no tradeoffs? No. There is no such thing as a perfect political equilibrium. There are two major limitations. One is

---

[6] I contributed a two-part essay to the elaboration of Kant's proposition ('Kant, Liberal Legacies and Foreign Affairs', in *Philosophy and Public Affairs* (Summer and Fall, 1983). The extensive debate is well presented in *Debating the Democratic Peace*, ed. M. E. Brown et al. (Cambridge, MA: MIT Press, 1996).

that this peace is limited only to other liberal republics. International respect is only extended to other, similarly republican liberal states. The very same principle of trust that operates among liberal republics tends to corrode attempts at cooperation between liberal republics and autocratic states, whether modern dictatorships or traditional monarchies. The liberal warns: 'If the autocrat is so ruthless that he is unwilling to trust his own citizens to participate in the polity and control his behavior, just think what he will do to us'. Liberals then raise trade and other barriers, ensuring that conflicts are not dampened. The prejudice may be true. Many dictators—think of Napoleon or Hitler—have been aggressive. Many dictators, however, are also quite shy and cautious. They like the benefits of being absolute ruler and may fear overburdening the quiescence of their subjects with costly foreign adventures. The distrust and hostility are probably thus a joint product. The autocrats do like to gain the profits and glory of expansion and the citizens—cannon fodder and taxpayers—have no constitutional right to stop them. At the same time, the liberals are prejudiced against the autocratic regime and do not extend to those regimes the normal trust in international exchanges or negotiations and may, indeed, launch 'freedom fighters' against them. Although the record of wars between liberals and non-liberals and the history of liberal imperialism testify to the depth of this tension, it can be overcome by autocratic prudence and liberal statesmanship.

The second limitation is associated with the assumption of minimal inter-dependence. In order for liberal republics to remain effectively sovereign and self-determining, allowing free citizens to govern themselves, material ties to other liberal republics would need be limited. Kant assumed that those ties were limited to nonaggression, collective security and hospitality (free trade and mutual transit privileges). This is 'light' interdependence[7]—some mutual sensitivity, some limited vulnerability, but not enough to challenge the liberal republic's ability to govern itself in the face of social and economic forces outside itself. Kantianism presumes marginal trade, marginal investment, marginal tourism; not extensive interdependence. This second limitation is increasingly unrealistic today.

Does modern interdependence challenge the Kantian liberal peace? Can the liberal peace sustain extensive, 'heavy' interdependence? That is the question to which I turn next.

Challenges of globalization

The first challenge of global interdependence is to the sustainability of the liberal peace. Can it operate in a much more intensive environment of social and economic exchange? And the second is to the legitimacy of the liberal democratic system. Can the people truly govern themselves when much of their social and economic inter-action is with other societies outside their borders and outside the reach of their representative government? Two major challenges, indeed.

---

[7] For a discussion of the features of interdependence see Robert Keohane and Joseph Nye, *Power and Interdependence* (Boston, MA: Little, Brown, 1977).

Globalization I

The first challenge to liberal sustainability was articulated in one of the great books of the twentieth century, Karl Polanyi's *The Great Transformation*.[8] His book is a profound study of the effects of the market economy both domestically and internationally. Polanyi's argument, in summary, holds that marketization makes peace unsustainable. Kantian liberals hoped that over time, with some ups and downs, international markets would tend to liberalize non-liberal societies leading to more and more liberal republics, which would eventually cover the whole world and thus create global peace. Polanyi says it cannot work that way: there are built-in sources of corrosion produced by economic interdependence that make liberal politics and the liberal peace unsustainable.

He acknowledges that, indeed, the combination of the domestic market economy, political representation, the gold standard and the international balance of power did create a sustaining circle of mutually reinforcing economic contacts that helped produce the peace of the nineteenth century—the Long Peace of 1815 to 1914. But, he warns us, contrary to Immanuel Kant, trade is not just an exchange of commodities at arms length or at the border. Trade is a revolutionary form of exchange. Exchanging commodities changes the value in relative and absolute terms of the factors that go into producing the commodities that are exchanged. As was later elaborated in a set of theorems concerning factor price equalization, trade in commodities has potentially revolutionary effects in changing the returns to various factors—land, labour, and capital—that go into the production of these commodities. Countries tend to export commodities that intensively use the factors with which they are most endowed and import commodities that embody scarce domestic factors. Trade thus increases demand and price, and eventually factor return for relatively abundant factors as it shrinks demand, price and return for scarce domestic factors. Together this tends toward global 'factor price equalization' (in theory, with many assumptions, and thus real-world qualifications).[9] In 1795, however, Kant seemed to assume that trade was arms length commodity exchange. He neglected the potential effects of commodity trade on the factors that go into the production of the commodities exchanged (land, labour, and capital).

Why is this important? Trade, whether national or international, destabilizes the social relations among land, labour, and capital, disrupting relations that had become embedded in social hierarchies and in political power. Treating land, labour and capital as commodities dislocates established communities, village life, regional life, the relations among classes, industries and sectors and eventually changes the international balance of power. Trade therefore produces a reaction. Farmers do not like to have the prices of their farm products drop to the prices set by more competitive rivals. Consumers might prefer the lower prices, but the usually better organized producers resist. Labourers and manufacturers do not want to compete with labour that makes one tenth of their income or with firms that have costs a

---

[8] Karl Polanyi, *The Great Transformation: The Political and Economic Origins of Our Time* (New York: Beacon Press, 1980). Originally published in 1944.
[9] The key theoretical contributions were made by Heckscher, Ohlin, Rybczynski, Stolper and Samuleson. For a non-technical survey, see John Williamson, *The Open Economy and the World Economy* (New York: Basic Books, 1983), ch. 3.

fraction of their own, whether in a newly integrated national or international market. When peoples livelihoods are marginalized, they tend to react.

Polanyi recounts that, at the end of the nineteenth century, the reaction to the market took the form of either social democracy on the left or fascism on the right. National economies attempted to protect themselves from the swings of the global economy by raising tariffs in order to protect national consumption or by launching imperial conquests to expand national resources. The resulting rivalry produced, Polanyi continues, World War I, the Great Depression and its competitive devaluations, and eventually World War II. Liberal peace, prosperity, democracy collapsed under the weight of heavy interdependence.

Globalization II

Following World War II, the allied leaders successfully rebuilt liberal interdependence, constructing a new way to mix together democracy and social stability. They developed a series of safety nets that would make people less vulnerable to the vagaries of the market both domestically and internationally. Rather than adjusting to an autarkic world of intense national competition (as in the 1930's) or letting trade and finance flow freely in response to market incentives (the nineteenth century); the capitalist democracies in the postwar period constructed the IMF, the GATT, and the World Bank to help regulate and consciously politically manage the shape of the world market economy. Trade was opened on a regulated basis, currencies were made convertible when economies could sustain the convertibility and cushioned with financing to help maintain parities. Long term financing, a form of global Keynesianism, was provided first to Europe and then (in lesser amounts) to the developing countries in order to spread opportunity and reduce the conflicts between haves and have nots that had wracked the interwar period. All this helped promote stability, cooperation, and solidarity in the Cold War struggle against the Soviet Union. Thus with a set of political-economic policies that have been called 'embedded liberalism', the postwar leaders of the West found a way to manage the tensions that Polanyi had described, the dangers of marketization.[10]

It was good while it lasted, but by the 1980s, frustration with over-regulation, falling productivity and the oil shock, together with a demand for ever more profit and cheap goods produced a move back to marketization, the Thatcher–Reagan 'magic of the marketplace'. Reacting to the welfare state's restrictions on consumption and profit and seeking a more dynamic spur to industrial reallocation and profits, many of the protections embedded in the postwar political economy were relaxed. Increasing trade, floating exchange rates, and opening financial markets became the 'Washington Consensus', the watchword of international economic orthodoxy and the standard prescription of the IMF.

As the barriers to global marketization fell, the forces that propelled ever closer interdependence accelerated. One force accelerating the effects of global marketiz-

---

[10] See John Ruggie's 'International Regimes, Transactions and Change: Embedded Liberalism in the Postwar Economic Order', *International Organization*, 36 (Spring, 1982), pp. 379–415.

ation was advances in communication and transportation technology. The costs of transportation and communication began to fall radically in the postwar period. In 1930, the cost of a telephone call between New York and London was (in 1990 dollars) $245 for three minutes. By 1998, the same call cost 35¢: a vast reduction in the cost of communications. That and the related explosion of the Internet are what makes much of global banking and all of global academia possible. If we were still paying $245 for three minutes across the Atlantic, there would be less that we could afford to say.

The second force was trade. There has been a near revolution in the amount of trade tying the countries of the world together. Let me inflict a few figures on you. Even the US, which because of its continental scale is one of the less interdependent economies, has experienced a large change in the impact of trade. In 1910 (that is, during Globalization I), 11 per cent of US gross domestic product (GDP) was in trade (exports and imports). By 1950, this fell to 9 per cent. That is what the Globalization I crisis—the Great Depression and the two world wars—was all about. But by 1995, trade had risen to 24 per cent. This is more than double the extent of interdependence in the previous era of globalization. In the Germany of 1910, 38 per cent of its GDP was in trade exports and imports. By 1950, this fell to 27 per cent; by 1995, up to 46 per cent. The UK, the leader of the first wave of globalization and the most globalized economy at the time, in 1910 had 44 per cent of its GDP in trade. In 1950, this dropped to 30 per cent. By 1995, 57 per cent was in exchangeables. Among the highly developed industrial economies, only Japan is less dependent upon trade and investment income than it was in 1910. It is the only major industrialized economy that is less globalized now than it was in 1910.

And if you think trade is globalizing the world, you should examine foreign direct investment (FDI) and portfolio flows of finance. Between 1980 and 1994, trade doubled; but in that same period, foreign direct investment grew six times, and portfolio flows of finance grew by nine times.

As in the earlier age of globalization, these flows of trade and finance are beginning to change the operation of the world's political economy—altering what is profitable, what is politically sustainable, and what is not. Perhaps most strikingly from an economic point of view, the world now increasingly appears as one large market, a single division of labour. From the standpoint of the multinational company, production strategies are genuinely global, as parts of the production process are allocated to subsidiaries and contractors in countries or regions around the world where they are most cost-effective, forming a global process of production and marketing that is a highly interdependent whole at the global level. In the old global interdependence, cars and shoes were traded among many countries or even made in many countries by one company; now one company makes cars or shoes globally with component factories spread around the world.[11]

---

[11] Peter Drucker, 'The Global Economy and the Nation State', *Foreign Affairs* (Sep/Oct, 1997) calls this 'transnational strategy', p. 168. Marina Whitman, *New World, New Rules: The Changing Role of the American Corporation* (Cambridge, MA: Harvard Business School, 1999) explores how American companies that were once stable, lumbering, globe-striding giants with paternalistic ties to their home communities have become lean, mean and footloose.

Challenges to liberal democratic peace

The new market interdependence poses three challenges to the liberal scheme of global democratic peace.

Commodification

The World Trade Organization meeting, and demonstrations in Seattle against it, demonstrate the first tradeoff, the tradeoff between globally regulated market prosperity and democracy. The tradeoffs are becoming more politically costly as interdependence increases. Politically, the democratic challenge was well put recently by Ed Mortimer (then *Financial Times* foreign editor) when he said that too much democracy kills the market (that's Polanyi's account of national and social democracy in reaction to Globalization I) and, on the other hand, too much market kills democracy (this is the threat some see posed by Globalization II). Commodities seem to rule citizens.

US environmentalists struggled for years in order to lobby for a US Endangered Species Act that protects turtles inadvertently caught in the course of the fishing for shrimp. It requires that shrimp nets be designed in a way that permits turtles to escape. The environmentalists struggled long and hard in order to pass the Bill, but they forgot that a new arena of interdependence had engendered a new arena of regulation. When the US government attempted to reduce the impact of the Bill on favoured allies, the WTO not surprisingly declared the effort discriminatory, and therefore illegal under international trade law.

In the European Union, many of its consumer advocates struggled for a campaign to protect European consumers from genetically engineered food—so called 'Frankenfood'. The WTO has yet to rule on this issue that pits American corporations against European food activists. Signs of more sympathy toward health regulation are recently in evidence in WTO decisions. But the WTO earlier ruled that bans against hormone treated food were a form of trade discrimination and illegal under international trade law.[12]

In a wider challenge, the developing countries have insisted upon the right not to be bound by the standards of labour safety, child labour prohibitions, and the minimum wages that hold within the industrialized world. They believe that it is only by taking advantage of their large supplies of talented, hard-working inexpensive labour that they will be able to develop their countries. But the US, responding to pressure from labour unions and human rights advocates, argued at Seattle that the US-level standards on labour rights and environmental protection be applied to all traded goods. This the developing countries see as a denial of their ability to choose their own development path. At the WTO in Seattle, moreover, the developing countries were outraged with the prevalence of so-called 'green room' procedures under which the wealthy industrial countries caucus and decide how to manage the WTO. The developing country majority of the membership want much

---

[12] Sophie Meunier, 'Globalization and the French Exception', *Foreign Affairs*, 79:4 (July/August, 2000).

broader participation in order to avoid having rules imposed upon them that favour the industrialized market economies. National policymakers in the developing world thank the World Bank and IMF for the doors to development they open and for not as yet succumbing to the demands for increased global regulation made by the environmentalist protesters at Seattle and Washington.[13]

In each of these cases, globally regulated norms of non-discrimination—however efficient and fair from a global point of view—are eroding democratic, or at least national, accountability.

Inequality

The second challenge to democratization concerns both intra-national and international equality. Globalization allows for those who are most efficient to earn the most. That is what markets usually do. And as the barriers fall to global sales, production, and investment, inequality also tends to rise.

Let me give you some figures. Domestically in the US, beginning about 1975, the economic fates of the top 5 per cent and bottom 20 per cent of the US population substantially diverged. By 1995, the real family income of the top 5 per cent stood at 130 per cent of the 1973 level, but over the same period, the real family income of the bottom 20 per cent stayed at the 1973 level.[14] Internationally, let us compare the OECD (the rich industrial economies) to the rest of the world and compare the 1970s to 1995. In 1970, the OECD enjoyed 66 per cent of global GDP. By 1978, its share was up to 68 per cent; in 1989, to 71 per cent; and in 1995, to 78 per cent. The rest of the entire world lived on the complement to that: their figures go from 34 per cent in 1970, sinking to 22 per cent in 1995. Increasing global inequality is associated with global marketization. The most productive are winning, accumulating wealth in their own hands. The consequences of globalization appear to be relatively depriving some in favour of others—the rising tide is not lifting all the boats at the same rate. Not surprisingly, demands for accountable control rise.

Security

The third challenge is security. Kantian liberalism produces security and peace (among the liberal republics). But globalization challenges the stability of liberal geopolitics in two ways. On the one hand, what Americans call *globalization* is what many others call *Americanization*. That is, the US leading role within the world economy, which to Americans appears as an economic issue of dollars and cents, is to other countries a power issue, one fraught with control and guns. The other hand

---

[13] Ambassador Francisco Aguirre-Sacassa, 'A Debt of Thanks to the World Bank', *Financial Times*, 4 May, 2000.

[14] Robert Gilpin, *The Challenge of Global Capitalism* (Princeton, NJ: Princeton University Press, 2000), p. 307. For global GDP comparisons, see Tahir Beg, 'Globalization, Development and Debt-Management', *The Balance* (Spring 2000), table 2, http://balanced-development.org/articles/globalization.html.

is that global rules for trade and investment have allowed China to benefit from its high savings rate and labour productivity, becoming one of the fastest growing economies in the world. If you add rapid growth to a large population (and if the World Bank projections are correct and if China continues to grow at recent past rates) then by the year 2020, China will have a GDP that is not only larger than that of the United States or Europe, but as big as them both together. From an economic point of view, the prospect of many more Chinese consumers and producers should make everyone content. But from a geopolitical point of view, China's growth entails a massive shift of world political power eastward. That makes the statesmen of the US and Europe nervous, especially if, referring again to the Kantian liberal argument, China has not democratized.

Responses

Those are some of the challenges. There have been a variety of responses of widely varying purpose and consequence. The key question that faces us today is whether and how the liberal equilibrium can be renovated, reincorporating a combined prospect of peace, prosperity and self-government.

Protectionism

Polanyi called this the 'Crustacean' strategy—one that reinforced the hard shell of the nation state. It focuses on each nation protecting itself from globalization. This is familiar to us. In the US, Ross Perot and Pat Buchanan made these kind of arguments; in France, Jose Bove (the anti-McDonald impresario); in Austria, Jorg Haider. Their themes are simple: 'globalization is a threat to the cultural integrity and prosperity of many of us who are vulnerable, it is a threat to democracy, to our way of life. Let us build a thick shell'.

   In a much more sophisticated version, this is the heart of claims made by the organizers at Seattle. Lori Wallach, the chief organizer of the wide coalition that disrupted the WTO meeting, described her alternative to current globalization in this way: 'There would be a global regime of rules that more than anything create the political space for the kinds of value decisions that mechanisms like the WTO now make, at a level where people living with the results can hold decision makers accountable'.[15] Interdependence would then be made subject to reach of democratic accountability at the local level. This could lead to effective global rules for interdependence, but it is more likely to build national 'shells'. Apart from national non-discrimination (national treatment) provisions, each country would make its own rules for environmental standards, intellectual property, child labour, wages and have a right to bar any import that did not reflect those standards.

   These movements may create democratic control and they may be good for national solidarity, but they could be very bad for overall national prosperity, as

---

[15] FP Interview, 'Lori's War', *Foreign Policy*, 118, Spring 2000, p. 34.

nation retaliates against nation for each restriction it finds unjustifiable. A recent study by a group of economists who are associated with the European Union estimates the possible benefits from the next Millennium Round of the WTO at $400 bn per year.[16] For many, whether rich or poor, that is too much extra world income to forego. If they are correct, there is a great deal to be lost if global trade suddenly starts closing down, or global investments start being drawn back.

National champions

A second strategy is also attractive to some. If protectionism is a 'crustacean' strategy, we can extend Polanyi's aquatic metaphor, bringing into view 'sea slug' strategies. The sea slug, a voracious and non-discriminating eater, consumes anything that is smaller than itself. This is the strategy of *national champions*. The nation state supports its own firms in order to compete to win more global sales and seeks to lure foreign firms, increasing shares of inward FDI for the national economy. The Clinton administration was very successful in persuading Saudi Arabia to buy just American aircraft, built by McDonnell/Boeing, headquartered in Seattle. The large sale included both F-15s and passenger airliners. It was very popular in the American Northwest. Not so popular in France (which also engages in the same practice) where Airbus was seen to be just as good a plane. Why did the Europeans not get the sale to Saudi Arabia? Many speculate that the US security relationship with the Gulf, and particularly the protection offered against the ambitions of Saddam Hussein, had much to do with the business deal. But, that does not make the French or other Europeans happy. Nor were Americans pleased when Quaddafi gave the contract to build the Mediterranean pipeline from Libya solely to a European consortium.

To the extent that states try to foster national champions or subsidize inward FDI to attract capital and jobs, they produce similar behaviour by other countries. This may benefit international consumers. It may also lead to a 'race to the bottom' with fewer and fewer environmental and labour standards, or increased international conflicts, as short-term prosperity is again pitted against long-run democratic autonomy.

Democratic solidarity

Let us turn to a third strategy, 'democratic solidarity'. Here statesmen seek to extend the liberal *political* peace into an economic arrangement. Forget about the rest of the world, let us build a stronger WTO for the democracies, a democratic WTO. (Bill Antholis, recently of National Security Council's economic staff, is writing a fascinating book on this topic.) Why not have a *democratic* WTO where we will solve our problems more easily than we would in a *global* WTO? If you look at the recent US trade bill extending 'most favored nation' status to China and exempting it from

---

[16] http://www.europa.eu.int/commm/trade/2000_round/ecowtomr.htm

annual reviews, one of the things that made it more difficult for the Administration to mobilize a Congressional majority is that China is regularly vulnerable to charges that it is threatening Taiwan with invasion and abusing its own nationals' human rights. If democracies limited their most extensive trade privileges to the area of fellow democracies, they would find progress toward further integration easier, or at least free from the baggage of political strife over human rights and security concerns. The problem, of course, is that such a 'democratic WTO' leaves China and other rapidly developing countries out. Excluding the potentially biggest, fastest growing economy in the world is not good for prosperity or for global cooperation on other issues. If you will pardon me for paraphrasing President Lyndon Johnson's apt reference to the higher logic of cooperating with an opponent, recall his words: 'Do you want him inside the tent pissing out, or outside the tent pissing in?' That is the China problem. If China is not part of the WTO, it is very likely to cause an immense amount of strife in the world political economy and be absent from important efforts to curb pollution or stabilize East Asian rivalry.

Disaggregated cooperation

The fourth response is the most pragmatic of the hopeful responses. It is 'dis-aggregated cooperation'. Proponents urge us to break down the problem. Let's let the multinational corporations (MNCs) deal with other MNCs and markets solve as many of the problems as they can. State bureaucracies will scramble to keep up, doing less than may be ideal but enough to avoid catastrophe. Genetically engineered food may be sold with less controversy if the United States labels organic food and then lets consumers buy it or not as they wish. US organic food exports, having been certified, could be sold in Europe. Consumers, not governments, will decide; hopefully, depoliticizing the issue. Furthermore, courts will deal with courts, bureaucrats with bureaucrats, experts with experts. Take it out of politics and solve the problems pragmatically.[17]

Unfortunately, there are some problems that just are not pragmatic. For the environmental organization that worked so hard to reform the Endangered Species Act in order to protect turtles, a turtle was not a technical question that they were willing to see negotiated away. It became a part of their own sense of identity, their own sense of moral worth, their sense of responsibility to the globe—not something that they would let the bureaucrats decide. And second, when things get tougher, that is when the world economy moves into the next recession, it will be more difficult to delegate to careful bureaucrats and their allegedly objective global criteria.

Global democratization

Responding to the concerns noted above, some have begun to wonder, 'Don't we need some increased accountability, increased legitimacy, to contain and govern the

---

[17] See Wolfgang Reinicke, *Global Public Policy: Governing Without Government* (Washington, DC: Brookings, 1998) and Anne-Marie Slaughter, 'The Real New World Order', *Foreign Affairs*, 76:5 (September/October, 1997), pp. 183–97.

practical negotiations among the experts? Don't we need to have norms that are more broadly shared, or even decisions that are legitimate because people across borders have participated in outlining their direction?'[18] We want expert pilots to fly the planes we ride in, but do we want them to choose our destinations?[19] We are thus concerned about the dangers of increasingly non-democratic control of key financial decisions.[20] For some it is now time for a global parliament or civic assembly, structured on the model of the European parliament in Strasbourg. That pillar of the burgeoning EU represents voters across Europe and operates through cross-national parties, not national delegations. Others hoped that the recent Millennium Assembly of the United Nations which provided a forum for non-governmental organizations from around the world, would take a first step in this direction.

Realistically, however, no strong version of global democracy is viable at the present time. We will not soon see global legislation deciding new regulatory standards for the global economy. Why not? Because global democracy is not about being willing to *win* democratically, it is about being willing to *lose* democratically. None of the popular advocates of increased democratization, whether in Seattle or Strasbourg or New Delhi, are willing to lose an issue and accept it because it went through a democratic process. The world is simply too unequal and too diverse. To give an example, the top one-fifth of the countries have 74 times the income of the bottom one-fifth of the countries, and it is getting worse. That is more than double the greatest degree of inequality within the most unequal domestic economy, the Brazilian economy, where the ratio between the top fifth and the bottom fifth is 32 to 1. More than double the Brazilian ratio, and yet Brazil itself has found its democratic processes repeatedly subject to extra-constitutional pressures.

With respect to culture, moreover, the globe falls far short of the preconditions of ordinary democracy. India, the largest and one of the most linguistically diverse democracies, has 81 per cent of its population describing itself as Hindu and an elite all of whom are fluent in English. That is a huge core of common identity that helps sustain the Indian democracy despite all of its diversity and internal dissention. There is no such core identity in the globe today. There is no single such identity (other than the thin identity of basic human dignity) to which 81 per cent of the world will subscribe.

Our primitive political global condition is reflected in disputes about the very meaning of global democracy. Is the world more democratic when the majority of nations decide, when the most populous nations decide, when only democratic nations participate, or when the majority of the world's people decide? Unfortunately, there is as yet no agreed meaning of 'global democratization'.

Therefore, I suggest that we must be more moderate in our democratizing ambitions. The role of global democratization should be limited to helping to develop norms. Not legislation, but deliberation over norms will make the process of cooperation among the bureaucrats easier, more readily achievable, more legitimate,

---

[18] A good introduction to this issue is in Daniele Archibugi and David Held, *Cosmopolitan Democracy* (Cambridge: Polity, 1995). For further discussion of cosmopolitan individual rights and democratic governance, see Thomas Pogge, 'Creating Supra-National Institutions Democratically', *Journal of Political Philosophy*, 5:2 (June 1997), pp. 163–82, and Dennis Thompson, 'Democratic Theory and Global Society', *Journal of Political Philosophy*, 7:2 (June 1999), pp. 1–15.

[19] Robert Dahl, *Democracy and Its Critics* (New Haven, CT: Yale University Press, 1989), ch. 5.

[20] Sheri Berman and Kate McNamara, 'Bank on Democracy', *Foreign Affairs*, 78:2 (March/April, 1999), pp. 2–8.

less contested. We must be very modest because norms do not do that much work, usually. What they do, however, is make it easier for national politicians and international bureaucrats to cut pragmatic deals. Therefore, global democratization should be limited to endorsing measures such as those advocated in the Carlsson-Ramphal Commission, the *Global Neighborhood* report.[21] In addition to sending diplomats to the annual meetings of the United Nations General Assembly, we should also send legislators. Every country can put five members in the General Assembly. At least two of them should be elected from the legislatures of their home countries. Bringing in the other branches of government, those somewhat more tied to the people, may help to begin to create a transmission belt between home and globe, fostering a more legitimate articulation of global standards at the international level. The hope is that these elected legislators will take the role seriously and participate actively in the annual general debate in the fall of each year and interject a sense of democratic legitimacy and accountability.

The second way to enhance global normative articulation is to bring in civil society. In 1955 there were fewer than 2,000 international non-governmental organizations; today there are more than 20,000.[22] None of them are genuinely democratic; their virtue is that they are voluntary and broad-based. But it is worth establishing an annual global forum that brings together representatives of global civil society, meeting the week before the General Assembly meets each year. Non-governmental organizations (NGOs) would be invited from all over the world to discuss and issue recommendations about global standards for the environment, humanitarian intervention, international economic assistance and reforms of international institutions such as the IMF or the World Bank, or the United Nations itself.

Conclusion

These recommendations constitute far from a cure-all. Electing legislators from non-democratic legislatures to the UN does not enhance global democracy strikingly. Others will ask who elected the NGOs, for whom there is no internal process of democratic accountability to their members or to those whom their policies affect. But, merely that act of debating in a global forum about who is there legitimately and who is not—all in the same room, talking about global problems—will itself be a process which helps build global norms and gives more voice to those who will bear the consequences of globalization. This is far short of democratic legitimation. In terms of democratic evolution, this represents much less than a modern equivalent of the meeting of the English barons at Runnymede in 1215, a cautious consultation far short of accountability. There will be mounting tension among prosperity, stability and accountability. Global interdependence will subject the liberal peace to increasing stress. But it can be the preliminary to increasingly responsible deliberation. And that may well be the best we can do in the world as it is today.

[21] Ingvar Carlsson and Shridath Ramphal, *Our Global Neighborhood: The Report of the Commission on Global Governance* (Geneva: The Commission on Global Governance, 1995) [as seen at World Wide Web address http://www.cgg.ch/contents.htm]

[22] Kofi Annan, *We the Peoples: The Role of the United Nations in the 21st Century* (New York: UN, 2000), Figure 13, p. 70.

International pluralism and the rule of law

TERRY NARDIN

Does international law have a place in a world being reshaped by globalization? Sceptics argue that international law belongs to a world order, based on relations among sovereign states, that is rapidly receding into history. But such a claim itself invites scepticism. Globalization is a journalist's term—a rough tool for making sense of what appears to be a trend toward a more integrated international economy and its attendant cultural homogenization.[1] Academics who use the term link it to the proliferation of intergovernmental organizations and transnational interest groups concerned with human rights, the environment, or economic issues, and to the emergence of a new normative framework, distinct from classical ('Westphalian') international law, for 'global civil society' and 'cosmopolitan democracy'.[2] Whether these trends will continue and how they might affect familiar political arrangements is not yet clear. It is possible that international law will disappear along with the pluralist system of sovereign states that the new global order is said to be replacing. It is more likely, however, that the old system will continue in a new form, and that there will be a place for international law in the new order. In this article, I discuss the character of law in the international system, on the assumption that globalization will not destroy that system. But even if international law does vanish, perhaps to be replaced by a different system of world law, the issues I consider here will remain relevant because they are inherent in the idea of law itself.

Democracy, if it is to be more than a tyranny of the many, requires a specific kind of legal order. It presupposes an order governed by the rule of law—one that limits as well as empowers collective decision-making.[3] Because 'the rule of law' is more often invoked than understood, the meaning of that expression cannot be taken for granted. Accordingly, those who are concerned with shaping the emerging global order could profit from a careful effort to reconstruct that idea. I hope the reader will bear this in mind in working through the argument of this article.

We can begin by distinguishing two modes of human association, the first a relationship based on laws governing the transactions of independent, formally

---

[1] It is common to identify globalization with cultural uniformity and to contrast it with difference. See, for example, Benjamin R. Barber, *Jihad vs. McWorld: How Globalism and Tribalism are Reshaping the World* (New York: Ballantine Books, 1996), and Thomas L. Friedman, *The Lexus and the Olive Tree: Understanding Globalization*, expanded paperback edn. (New York: Anchor Books, 2000).

[2] See, for example, Michael Walzer (ed.), *Toward a Global Civil Society* (Oxford: Berghahn Books, 1995) and Daniele Archibugi, David Held, and Martin Köhler (eds.), *Re-imagining Political Community: Studies in Cosmopolitan Democracy* (Oxford: Polity Press, 1998).

[3] A constitution can serve both these purposes, but constitutional government is not identical with the rule of law. A constitution can be the enemy of the rule of law and the rule of law can be realized without a constitution.

equal legal persons, the second a relationship based on force in which 'the powerful do what they can and the weak suffer what they must'.[4] These modes are not particular, historical realities; they are abstract alternatives, both of which are realized to some degree in any actual association. They reflect the fundamental categories, law and force, in terms of which politics has been theorized for as long as there have been political theorists. The contrast between law and violence, between civility and barbarism, is a recurring theme in Thucydides' history. Aristotle distinguishes the *polis* from despotic regimes in similar terms: a polis is a legal association of citizens, 'fellow subjects' of its laws, despotism a coercive association between master and slaves.[5] But because the rules by which masters coerce slaves are sometimes called 'laws', we have somehow to resolve the ambiguity that arises when the word 'law' is used comprehensively for the rules characteristic of both modes of association. One way that theorists have attempted to resolve this ambiguity is through the idea of the rule of law. When they want to distinguish what I am calling a relationship based on laws, a relationship of fellow subjects, from a despotic relationship, a relationship in which the strong use the weak and in which law is merely their instrument, they sometimes speak not of 'law', which refers ambiguously to both, but 'the rule of law'.

How does the rule of law apply to international relations? International law is not a single, coherent practice or institution. Like other kinds of law, it is a miscellaneous aggregate of rules, principles, procedures, decisions, orders, policies, precedents, and other normative elements. The international legal system, as it exists, serves different ends and reflects different conceptions of international order. For these reasons, the idea of international law is ill-defined and ambiguous. As with law generally, the chief ambiguity here is between international law as a tool used by the powerful to coerce the weak, and international law as a body of rules constituting an 'international society' whose members, states, are fellow subjects of its laws. (To keep things simple, we can ignore the fact that persons, corporations, and other entities are sometimes treated as subjects of international law.) Something important is lost when we fail to distinguish relations between states as members of an international society, possessing rights and duties under its rules, from relations between states as 'powers' coercing or being coerced by one another according to their relative power. Both kinds of relationship exist in any actual international system, but this does not mean that they cannot be distinguished analytically. And it is important to distinguish them because law is understood differently in each mode. Where the rule of law is the mode of association, states recognize and respect one another as independent agents. What this means, fundamentally, is that a state is barred from coercively using other states for its own ends, though it may use coercion, within limits, to defend itself or others against those who violate this principle of respect.

One way of distinguishing these two modes of interpersonal and international association is to identify the kind of relationship defined and regulated by non-instrumental rules as a 'moral' relationship and to identify the law that governs this relationship as a kind of 'morality'. In a moral relationship, those related recognize one another as 'persons' pursuing ends of their own, and entitled to pursue those

---

[4] In the words of the Athenian generals at Melos, according to Thucydides, *The Peloponnesian War*, trans. Richard Crawley (New York: McGraw Hill, 1989), book 5, ch. 89.
[5] *Politics*, book 1.

ends without hindrance and therefore without hindering one another. (A moral relationship can exist between collective or artificial persons, like corporations or states, as well as between natural persons.) What is essential in a moral relationship is that persons treat one another as ends and not merely as a resource for satisfying their own desires.[6] Whatever the difficulties of this conception, it expresses how moral relationships are best distinguished, within the tradition of 'natural law', from power-based relationships.

Natural law theory is conventionally understood as an alternative to 'legal positivism', which can be defined in this context as the view that laws, properly speaking, are rules laid down ('posited') by a ruling authority and backed by effective enforcement, and that any authoritative and effective system of rules must be counted as law, no matter what its moral qualities. The idea of 'the rule of law' allows us, however, to distinguish law and force as modes of association without relying on this conventional understanding of the distinction between natural and positive law. To put it differently, the idea of the rule of law allows us to distinguish these modes of relationship within legal positivism as well as within natural law, for the laws that are enacted to govern a particular human community can be *either* non-instrumental ('moral') constraints on the conduct of its members *or* instrumental rules used by of those members to coercively impose their purposes on others. The idea of the rule of law serves to emphasize that rules of the latter kind are mere instruments of force, rules that lack the moral qualities we usually associate with lawfulness or legality. If this is correct, the debate between natural law and legal positivism over the definition of law, as that debate is usually understood, is misconceived. True law, natural *or* positive, belongs to a mode of association constituted by rules of a certain kind, non-instrumental rules that govern transactions between independent agents who understand themselves to be fellow subjects of a common law.[7] In the circumstances of international relations, then, the rule of law identifies a kind of relationship that exists in so far as states observe the non-instrumental laws that define and regulate international society. Such a mode, which excludes relations based solely on power, is (to repeat) a *possible* mode of relationship that is only partly actualized in any historic international order. International law as it exists includes instrumental rules that have permitted governments to unjustly coerce other governments, or to oppress their own subjects, but such rules do not express, and are in fact antithetical to, the rule of law.

To make these conclusions about the international rule of law intelligible, never mind plausible, is not an easy task. I will begin by reconsidering the debate between natural law and legal positivism, focusing on how law is understood within each of these traditions. With this as a foundation, I will explain how the rule of law in any legal order, including the international legal system, can be defined and defended in a way that draws upon both traditions. Finally, I will consider the implications of this explanation for an international order that is being reshaped by globalization.

---

[6] This is how morality is understood by Kant, whose 'principle of respect' is one version of the fundamental principle of morality. Immanuel Kant, *Foundations of the Metaphysics of Morals*, trans. Lewis White Beck (Indianapolis: Bobbs-Merrill, 1959), pp. 66–7.

[7] Richard Friedman, 'Some Thoughts on Natural Law and International Order', in David R. Mapel and Terry Nardin (eds.), *International Society: Diverse Ethical Perspectives* (Princeton, NJ: Princeton University Press, 1998).

Natural law

The modern idea of natural law can be traced back to Stoicism, a school of thought that emerged in Greece after the Macedonian conquest in response to the disappearance of the polis. As interpreted by Cicero and other Romans (most of the original Greek texts having been lost), Stoic ideas became part of the intellectual inheritance of modern Europe.

Central to Stoicism is the idea of an eternal and immutable law governing all motion and change in the universe (the 'cosmos'). This law establishes a rational order that can, in principle, be understood by human intelligence. Human beings are themselves part of this rationally ordered universe and their conduct is governed by its law, 'natural law'. But because they can choose to disobey it, natural law does no more than set a standard for guiding and judging conduct. And because of their shared character as rational beings—beings whose potential, and therefore essence, is to be rational—all human beings are citizens of a single, ideal community: a universal community or 'cosmopolis' whose law is this rationally-knowable natural law. The Stoics did not deny that every person is also a citizen or subject of some particular state with rights and duties under the laws of that state. Their point is that human beings have rights and duties as members of this rational cosmopolis that are distinct from those they enjoy as citizens of a polis, and that they have a law to guide them, even if they are not citizens of any polis.

For the Stoics, the cosmopolis is an ideal model for all man-made political communities, whether cities, kingdoms, or empires. Such communities may be considered 'just' in so far as they are true copies of the cosmopolis (the argument here draws on Plato). Natural law, which is the law of this ideal cosmopolis, provides a universal criterion by which to determine the justice or injustice of local human laws and institutions. It is the standard for measuring the moral rightness of positive law. In the tradition that springs from these Stoic ideas, morality is not a system of laws or customs, actual or possible, that is practiced by some community of human beings. It is a standard according to which all such systems are to be judged and according to which every human being should live, regardless of the laws and customs of his community.

The Stoics understood this morality to be 'the true and divine law', a law willed by the gods as well as required by reason. But the idea of divine will is in fact incidental to morality understood as natural law. The Stoics argued that the content of natural law, though divine, can be discovered by reason without directly invoking the will of the gods. Adopting this Stoic principle, Christianity came to distinguish between a divine law that is binding on all human beings as rational agents and divine commands addressed to the members of particular communities, for example, to Christians or Jews. A problem in Christian ethics is therefore to distinguish the commandments obligating only believers from those obligating all human beings. When Grotius set out in 1603 to consider whether the Dutch had a right to make war on their rivals in the East Indies, he wanted a universal answer, one based on principles applicable to any state. He therefore did not look either to the Bible or to Dutch law. Scripture does not contain universal law—divine commands to be obeyed as law by all human beings. The law revealed to the Hebrews is law only for them, and Christian doctrine is not law but divine advice about how to be a good

Christian.[8] According to this view, observance of many of the precepts that Jews and Christians assert to be 'moral' is required only of those who wish to live a full Jewish or Christian life. It is not required by morality understood, as it is within the tradition of natural law, to be a set of precepts binding on all human beings as rational creatures—precepts that can in principle be known, not because they have been specially revealed, but through the use of reason.

In the later Stoic tradition, 'nature' came to mean reason and nothing more. The law of nature applies to human beings because of their nature as rational beings, not because what it forbids is 'against nature'.[9] The expression 'natural law' is unfortunate because it invites this misunderstanding, and also because the word 'nature' obscures a categorical gap between the realm of intelligent thought and that of not-intelligent processes, between the intentional world of human action and the extensional world of natural processes. Morality belongs to the former realm, so it is confusing to identify it by a name that evokes the latter. But no name can forestall misunderstanding. Seeking to avoid the connotations that have accrued to the expression 'natural law', the philosopher Alan Donagan has revived the Stoic expression *koinos nomos*, which he translates as 'common morality'. The problem with this expression is that it is easily misconstrued as a name for moral precepts recognized in (and therefore common to) many different societies, although Donagan is concerned only with precepts that can in principle be understood by human beings and are binding on all. The failure to distinguish widely recognized principles (*ius gentium*) from universally binding principles (*ius naturae*) has led to recurrent confusion.

One important strand of natural law thinking runs from Aquinas through the Spanish neo-scholastics of the sixteenth and seventeenth centuries. It is a strand picked up again in our own time by John Finnis and other theorists of 'the new natural law'.[10] Another and equally important strand of natural law thinking can be found in the works of Grotius, Hobbes, Pufendorf, Locke, and the eighteenth-century Scottish moral philosophers.[11] In each of these traditions, the law of nature is more than a set of precepts; it is a system and much effort has gone into analysing its systematic character. Aquinas, for example, can be understood as systematizing the insights of his predecessors. Grotius, in his unpublished manuscript on the law of prize, derives a system of natural law from a set of primitive assumptions. This system, parts of which Grotius borrowed from Suarez and other neo-scholastics, defines the school of natural law in the seventeenth and eighteenth centuries. Pufendorf worked out an especially systematic and, for a time, influential version of

---

[8] Hugo Grotius, *Commentary on the Law of Prize and Booty*, trans. Gladys L. Williams (Oxford: Oxford University Press, 1950), pp. 10–11.

[9] Alan Donagan, *The Theory of Morality* (Chicago, IL: University of Chicago Press, 1977), p. 6.

[10] John Finnis, *Natural Rights and Natural Law* (Oxford: Clarendon Press, 1980) and 'The Ethics of War and Peace in the Catholic Natural Law Tradition', in Terry Nardin (ed.), *The Ethics of War and Peace: Religious and Secular Perspectives* (Princeton, NJ: Princeton University Press, 1996); Joseph Boyle, 'Natural Law and International Ethics', in Terry Nardin and David R. Mapel (eds.), *Traditions of International Ethics* (Cambridge: Cambridge University Press, 1992).

[11] Knud Haakonssen, *Natural Law and Moral Philosophy: From Grotius to the Scottish Enlightenment* (Cambridge: Cambridge University Press, 1996).

it, giving careful attention to its implications for international relations. But the most powerful theoretical reconstruction of natural law is Kant's.[12]

According to Kant, what unites the precepts of common morality into a coherent system is a single fundamental principle: act always so that you respect every human being, yourself or another, as being a rational creature.[13] In other words: it is impermissible not to recognize and treat every human being as a thinking, choosing agent. This principle, an improvement on 'the Golden Rule' as the fundamental principle of morality, supports a body of precepts that are 'categorical', that is, independent of contingencies. They are not 'hypothetical' precepts like 'if you want to be healthy, get some exercise regularly'.

The natural law tradition attaches special importance to the distinction between precepts forbidding actions that violate the principle of respect and those requiring us to bring about good outcomes, if we can—that is, between absolute ('perfect') and contingent ('imperfect') duties. Moral conduct means acting within a constraining framework of principles that are independent of consequential considerations. This does not mean that agents have no duty to bring about good consequences. But doing so is not the ultimate criterion of right and wrong in conduct. We can seek to bring about good outcomes for ourselves and others, but only by morally permissible actions. It is this priority of principles forbidding wrong over injunctions to produce good ends that distinguishes common morality as a moral system. Unlike consequentialist systems, which appeal to good outcomes to justify particular acts or practices, an appeal that can lead to the violation of moral prohibitions, common morality must give priority to its prohibitions. Because its fundamental principle categorically forbids violating the respect owed to human beings as rational, common morality must condemn any action or practice that violates that respect.[14] This reasoning is sometimes distilled into a formula like 'the end does not justify the means' or 'evil is not to be done that good may come'. However one puts it, the prohibitory precepts of common morality are absolute; they may not be violated for the sake of promoting the good of one's own self or of others.

Natural law thinking has many implications for international affairs. If what is right and wrong is independent of the moral beliefs and practices of this or that community, for example, there is a direct challenge to cultural relativism. Acts that violate common morality cannot be justified on the grounds that morality is culturally specific. Natural law therefore provides a way of arguing for human rights against the practices of particular communities where the two are in tension, and for action to protect those rights when they are violated. Communal autonomy must be respected, but it does not authorize a state to violate the moral rights of other states or of its own inhabitants. It follows that there is a moral foundation both for the

---

[12] I disagree with readers who take his criticism of the natural law theories of his day as proving that Kant cannot be considered a natural law thinker. By arguing that true morality springs from personal autonomy, not the authority of a superior, Kant can be seen as putting natural law on a more secure foundation. The meaning of 'natural law' is not determined by what it meant in the seventeenth and eighteenth centuries. For another view, see J. B. Schneewind, *The Invention of Autonomy: A History of Modern Moral Philosophy* (Cambridge: Cambridge University Press, 1998).

[13] Immanuel Kant, *Foundations of the Metaphysics of Morals*, trans. Lewis White Beck (Indianapolis: Bobbs-Merrill, 1959), pp. 66–7.

[14] Donagan, *Theory of Morality*, p. 154. I recognize that interpreters of Kant differ on the implications of the principle of respect, but the issue is not one I can consider in this article.

non-intervention principle and for exceptions to that principle, including coercive action by those outside the community in response to gross violations of human rights. In the natural law tradition, what we have come to call 'humanitarian intervention' is derived from the duty to protect the innocent from violence, which is in turn derived from a duty of beneficence that requires us to assist others when we can, provided we can do so at reasonable cost and without violating anyone's basic moral rights.[15] International law has in the past not required such assistance and in some cases even forbidden it, but this does not mean that this law cannot be altered to accommodate a concern for human rights or an ethic of beneficence.

The word 'law' has acquired different meanings in the course of its long career. It can mean principles of natural order, like those of Aristotelian teleology or the causal laws of modern physics. It can mean principles of human conduct, rules to be obeyed or disobeyed as a matter of conscious or intelligent choice by human agents. And it can mean rules deliberately enacted within particular human communities: laws made and applied by human beings that reflect not universal reason but contingent will. The expression 'natural law' today is best understood, in other than historical contexts, as a synonym for 'common morality'. The systematic structure of common morality, as theorized in the natural law tradition, can help us clarify the purpose of law in human society and distinguish the rule of law from other modes of relationship identified by the name 'law'.

Legal positivism

To understand the idea of positive international law, it is helpful to consider the contexts in which the expressions 'positive law' and 'legal positivism' are normally used. Given my aims in this article, an appropriate place to start is with the context provided by early modern discussions of how common morality might be actualized both within and between states, for this is the period during which the modern European international system and the modern idea of international law emerged.

The ancient conception of law as a body of rules enacted by a superior, human or divine, acquired new significance in debates about the locus of supreme legal authority ('sovereignty') in the emerging territorial states of early modern Europe. The modern view that law 'properly so called' is positive law springs from the judgment, widely understood since the sixteenth century, that because religious disagreements were unlikely ever to be decisively resolved, theologically or philosophically, a way had to be found to prevent these disagreements from escalating into civil war. And this view, cogently articulated by Hobbes, was that an authoritative and effective power was required to manage the consequences of religious disagreement. Where there are differences over the interpretation of law, there can only be law where there exists an authoritative procedure for choosing among interpretations. A legal order implies a single agreed system of law, a body of 'common law' within which persons holding different religious beliefs, and believing themselves to be guided by different divine laws, can coexist.

---

[15] I consider these natural law arguments historically and philosophically in 'The Moral Basis of Humanitarian Intervention', a working paper distributed by the Center for Global Peace and Conflict Studies, University of California, Irvine, 2000.

At the core of 'legal positivism', then, is the view that laws are rules enacted and enforced by a superior but this-worldly authority, a sovereign ruler. Since reason and revelation generate a diversity of competing 'laws', a choice among them must be made by some person or assembly (the 'sovereign') authorized to make this choice. True law, positive law, results when a sovereign declares a putative obligation to be law. Law, in other words, is created by an authoritative act of will. In time it came to be understood that sovereignty could be an attribute not only of a person or an assembly but of the larger community from whose will a monarch or legislature derived its authority ('popular sovereignty'), or even of the procedures by which lawmakers were chosen and laws were validated. From the theory that law is the command of the sovereign, legal positivism evolved into the theory that law is a particular kind of social practice, one that is distinct from other practices (like morality, religion, etiquette, games, and so on) in which conduct-governing rules are discerned and used. Twentieth-century legal positivism distinguishes law from morality by the presence of authoritative procedures for recognizing and applying rules, as in H. L. A. Hart's theory of law as a 'union of primary and secondary rules'.[16]

Clearly, defining law as the command of a sovereign creates a problem for international law. Hobbes, for example, concludes that legal order is possible only within a state and that relations between states are relations of force, not law. For if by 'law' we mean enacted law, international law, which is not in any straightforward sense enacted, fails to meet the criterion. For positivists, international law is not really law but 'positive morality'.[17] One response to such doubts is to argue that there is a sense, intelligible though hardly straightforward, in which international law *is* enacted. It is enacted by an imaginary collective sovereign that comes into being when the actual sovereigns of the world are in agreement. This is Wolff's theory of the supreme state (*civitas maximus*), according to which all states taken together must be imagined to hold a kind of sovereignty over each individual state.[18] Wolff offers a version of what international lawyers later called the 'consent theory', according to which international law is composed of rules to which states have given their consent. Because no sovereign can submit to the commands of another, international law is binding only by consent. Civil law is a sovereign's will expressed internally in legislation, international law the joint will of several sovereigns expressed either in treaties (which make their agreement explicit) or custom (which expresses their tacit agreement).

Most positivist theorizing today rejects the view that international law is binding on a state only by its own consent, and rightly so, since one must postulate antecedently-authoritative rules of international law to explain how the consent of states can come to be binding. Applied to international relations, the broader conception of legal positivism (that law is a social practice distinct from morality, religion, and other practices) yields the view that international law rests on the customary practice of states and on their agreements with one another. As an autonomous normative system, its rules are determined by examining evidence drawn from practice and not by reasoning directly from moral principles. The law of

---

[16] H. L. A. Hart, *The Concept of Law* (Oxford: Clarendon Press, 1961).

[17] John Austin, *The Province of Jurisprudence Determined* (London: Weidenfeld and Nicolson, 1955).

[18] Christian von Wolff, *The Law of Nations Treated according to the Scientific Method*, trans. Joseph D. Drake (Oxford: Oxford University Press, 1934), Prolegomena, §§ 7–21.

nations cannot be regarded simply as natural law applied to the relations of states. This new view of international law, which can be found in a handful of seventeenth-century works, had by the end of the eighteenth century become the standard view of international lawyers. Because it rests on concrete state practice, not abstract reason, international law must be distinguished from natural law.

There is disagreement, then, within the positivist tradition about the moral character of international law as well as about whether it is really law. Some argue that international law is deficient because there is no legislative body to enact laws, no judges to apply them in particular disputes, and no power to compel obedience. The institutions for authoritatively declaring and applying rules are so rudimentary as to preclude the possibility of an international legal order. Foreign policy, for these sceptical realists, takes place in a realm of power, not law, and must be guided by prudence, not principle. Other legal positivists believe that legal order can exist without such institutions. For them, the criterion of law lies in the reasonably consistent, reliable, and impartial application of common rules, not in the particular institutions by which this is accomplished. And they argue that the rules of international society are applied in ways that meet the criterion.

The positivist tradition is agreed, however, that the validity and obligatory character of legal rules is determined according to procedures that are internal to the legal system. Positive law is a set of rules distinguishable from common morality as well as from revealed divine law and the accepted moral beliefs and practices of a given society. A legal system may exemplify or explicitly incorporate moral principles, but whether a rule is valid as law does not depend on its satisfying a moral criterion. Nor does it depend, as utilitarians, realists, and other instrumentalists sometimes argue, on its consequential desirability. As John Austin famously put it, 'the existence of law is one thing; its merit or demerit another'.[19] To take this position is not to deny that international law departs in significant ways from common morality, but to recognize that all positive law, because of its procedural character, must develop in ways that separate it to some degree from morality. Law is in this respect like democracy: each is premised on a moral conception, but neither can preserve the purity of that conception against the contingencies of practice. Critics of modern international law who forget this are rightly accused of utopianism.

A recurring objection to legal positivism is that in emphasizing that law is an autonomous normative system, it begs the question that a legal theory is supposed to answer, which is how human beings can coexist justly with one together. Those who see natural law not only as a source of moral guidance but a source of law sometimes argue that positive laws that deviate from natural law are not really law: 'That which is not just seems to be no law at all', says Augustine, and Aquinas adds: 'Consequently, every human law has just so much of the nature of law as it is derived from the law of nature'.[20] What is being claimed here is not necessarily that the moral character of a given rule straightforwardly determines whether or not it counts as law, but rather that law as a mode of relationship would appear to have moral qualities that distinguish its rules from the edicts of a despot. To deal adequately with this objection, legal positivism must distinguish positive law from

---

[19] Austin, *Province*, p. 184.
[20] Thomas Aquinas, *Summary of Theology* I–II, q. 95, a. 2.

the mere exercise of power. What positivism needs, to meet the natural lawyer's objection, is not merely a definition of law but a conception of legality that is distinct from effective power. The idea of the rule of law can be seen as a proposed solution to this problem within the limits of positivist legal theory.

The rule of law

Because the rule of law is itself a contested concept, it cannot without further clarification be used to resolve disputes about the meaning of law. The concept is often presented as a list of criteria for evaluating a legal order: there should be no secret or retrospective laws, no obligations other than those imposed by law, no arbitrary exemptions or private laws, and so on.[21] But such a list is of little value, theoretically speaking, unless it rests on a coherent account of the place of law in a social order. The rule of law, as an analytical concept, belongs to the effort to distinguish one particular kind of social order from the diversity of orders to which the name 'law' might be applied. In the tradition of theorizing that is concerned with this project, the rule of law is viewed as a moral practice distilled into a system of non-instrumental rules and augmented by institutions for identifying and applying these rules. Understood in this way, the rule of law can be seen as reflecting the concerns of both natural law theory and legal positivism.

From the perspective of natural law, the rationale of a legal system is that it offers a way to realize the ideal of a moral relationship among human beings in the contingent circumstances of actual communities. Furthermore, if the purpose of law is to get people to behave morally, moral limits must be imposed on the conduct of public officials as well as on that of ordinary citizens. And this means imposing constraints on ordinary lawmaking as well as on the arbitrary, extra-legal use of political power. For the natural law tradition, the rule of law expresses the inherently moral character of true law and the superiority of common morality to mere positive law.

From the standpoint of legal positivism, however, it seems clear that a legal system can serve the purpose of institutionalizing common morality only if the obligations it imposes are determined by its own internal criteria of validity. Law is as an invention designed to remedy the inability of morality to settle disputes about the interpretation of rules by providing agreed procedures for determining their meaning, and thereby distinguishing rules that are valid as law from those that are not. Such procedures make it possible to establish the validity of a disputed rule in a given system in the face of disagreements regarding its moral rightness or consequential desirability. Whether a rule is morally justified may remain in dispute, but

---

[21] Lon L. Fuller, *The Morality of Law*, revised edn. (New Haven, CT: Yale University Press, 1969), p. 39. See also Lawrence B. Solum, 'Equity and the Rule of Law', in Ian Shapiro (ed.), *The Rule of Law* (New York: New York University Press, 1994), pp. 121–2, and András Sajó, *Limiting Government: An Introduction to Constitutionalism* (Budapest: Central European University Press, 1999), pp. 205–23.

the moral question has been separated from the question of legal validity.[22] For the legal positivist, then, natural law is deficient as a theory of law because it cannot distinguish the legal validity of a rule from its moral rightness. In transforming a body of moral rules into a system of effective law, the first problem is to know what the rules are, that is, to establish which rules are to be recognized as authoritative and therefore as law.

In an association governed by the rule of law, laws retain their moral quality as rules regulating the coexistence of individual or collective persons, each pursuing its own self-chosen goals, by prescribing obligations to be observed in that pursuit. Like the categorical precepts of common morality, the laws of a community governed by the rule of law are rules, not commands. And the most fundamental of these are non-instrumental rules that constitute the community and regulate the transactions of its members, not instrumental devices for securing the satisfaction of particular, substantive desires. A legal system may include instrumental rules but these must be compatible with the non-instrumental rules on which the system rests, and which may be found in its written or unwritten constitution. Non-instrumental rules are concerned with the propriety of actions, not their usefulness in achieving particular outcomes. The authority of such rules rests on their character as law, as determined by whatever procedures a legal system has for determining this character, not on their instrumental value. That is why an association whose government is conceived as an instrument for achieving collective goals by issuing orders cannot be said to be an association governed according to the rule of law. The rule of law thus provides an alternative, within positivism, to the view that any expression of sovereign will counts as law.

Emphasizing the non-instrumental character of law does not entirely resolve the problem of the relationship between morality and law, however. Because conduct can be judged both morally and legally, it is not clear what justice requires where moral and legal considerations are in tension with one another.

Some in the positivist tradition, following Hobbes, have argued that the justice of a law is nothing other than its validity as law. But because it makes law the sole standard of justice, this argument leaves little room for moral criticism: whatever is legally valid is also just. But we don't have to accept Hobbes's conclusion on this point. We can, along with Hart and many other legal positivists, regard the justice, the moral rightness, of a law as distinct from its validity as law.[23] By doing so we make room for the moral criticism of law. But we also keep moral criticism separate from legal interpretation. On this view, the justice of a law is unrelated to the procedure by which it was made. A just law, here, is not one that has been properly enacted but one that is proper to have been enacted.

To avoid subverting the rule of law, moral criticism of a legal system must draw upon principles of justice that are already recognized, at least in part, within that

---

[22] A legal system can include moral considerations among the criteria used to determine the validity of legal rules, but in that case such considerations have been incorporated into the law and are no longer external. On this point, see Jules L. Coleman and Brian Leiter, 'Legal Positivism', in Dennis Patterson (ed.), *A Companion to Law and Legal Philosophy* (Oxford: Blackwell, 1996), p. 243, and the literature cited therein.

[23] H. L. A. Hart, 'Positivism and the Separation of Law and Morals', in *Essays in Jurisprudence and Philosophy* (Oxford: Clarendon Press, 1983), and Michael Oakeshott, 'The Rule of Law', in *On History and Other Essays* (Oxford: Blackwell, 1983).

system. If we identify justice with universal moral standards that are entirely independent of the legal culture of a community, as some moral theories do, justice becomes an alternative to law. The effect of this identification is to subvert the rule of law because it results in two distinct standards of conduct, positive law and abstract justice. A legal order can avoid being forced to choose between law and justice only if it already embodies the moral standards that are used to criticize it. An appropriate standard by which to evaluate the justice of a particular legal rule is therefore one that is already implicit in the system to which that rule belongs. Such a standard, which reflects concern for the integrity of a legal system, rules out, as a practical criterion for determining the justice or injustice of particular laws, the requirement that they should conform to extra-systemic moral principles. The frequent invocation of such principles—under the name of God's will, natural law, human rights, utility, or social justice—as an alternative to law is a sign not of the flourishing of the rule of law but of its decay.[24]

This understanding of the rule of law is easily extended to the international level. The rule of law, as a mode of association between states, cannot be identified with international law as it exists. International law is a mixture of instrumental and non-instrumental rules. Like any other body of law, it contains agreements, decisions, policy goals, administrative orders, and other devices designed to further particular goals and confer benefits on particular recipients. But these instrumental devices often represent an obtrusion of interests and power upon the rule of law. Though international law can without injustice be used to achieve substantive purposes, to be concerned with the rule of law in international relations is to be concerned with ensuring that the members of international society treat one another justly, not with producing or distributing particular substantive benefits. This is not, of course, as political realists concerned with security or idealists concerned with global distributive justice or sustainable development remind us, the only concern states might have with respect to one another, but where the rule of law prevails it is one that constrains the pursuit of other concerns.

Furthermore, if the rule of law is to be the basis of international relations, the moral considerations used in the criticism of international law must be restricted to those inferred from the customs and usages of international society. Utopian conceptions of international justice have little to contribute to the practical reform of international law. Criticism of the international order that reflects a concern for sustaining the rule of law must draw on principles that are sensitive to the kinds of obligations that are appropriately imposed by international law, given its particular character as a system of law—that lawmaking and adjudication are decentralized, for example. Such criticism will avoid the temptation to import, into discussions of what international law is or should be, abstract conceptions of justice that are incompatible with, and therefore subversive of, the basic principles of international society.

The idea of the rule of law is a delicate construction designed to avoid the extremes of legal positivism, which makes conformity to law the criterion of justice, and natural law, which makes justice into a criterion of legality. Against positivism, it denies that scepticism regarding moral claims must end in the conclusion that justice can have no meaning apart from law. Against natural law, it reminds us that

---

[24] Oakeshott, 'Rule of Law', pp. 140–4.

legal order is grounded on recognition of the authority of laws, not on abstract moral judgments of their justice or injustice. Law can supply a community's need for common rules only where the authority of particular rules as law is established according to antecedently-authoritative legal procedures rather than by direct appeal to their consequential desirability or moral rightness. The rules of international law should have moral content and they are subject to moral criticism, but their authority as law does not rest on moral criteria.

Preserving international pluralism

Pluralism, in the globalization literature, is usually identified with cultural particularism: with the 'tribalism' represented by religious or ethnic attachments. But the kind of pluralism sustained by the modern international system is different, for that system is composed of states, not religious or ethnic communities. States often privilege particular religious faiths or ethnic cultures, but the state itself is a legal construct. It is an association of persons organized by a common body of laws. In the modern period, the state has been the primary locus of lawmaking. The transformation of sovereignty in response to economic and social changes in an emerging confederation like the European Union does not disprove this observation: if sovereignty were to be decisively transferred from France, Germany, and so on to the Union, it would have been acquired by an entity that had, as a consequence of this transfer, become a state. A super-state, whether small (like the Swiss confederation) or large (like the United States), is itself a state. The character of the states system is not altered by unions of this kind. And it must not be forgotten that states can also disintegrate—sometimes unexpectedly, as in the case of the Soviet Union or Yugoslavia. It is ironic that the Soviet Union was originally imagined as the beginning of a transnational socialist society and that political theorists not long ago celebrated Yugoslavia as a model of trans-ethnic civil society and participatory democracy. The making and unmaking of states is a persistent, but nevertheless incidental, feature of the pluralist international system.

Is globalism generating forms of human association that will ultimately replace the modern state and system of states? Many globalists argue that the international system is giving way to a world order in which states are replaced by other, non-legal, forms of human community, and that this change is desirable and should be encouraged. Their arguments, which resemble those once made by Marxists, anarchists, libertarians, and other antinomian visionaries, take a variety of forms.

According to one such argument, globalization is producing a world order regulated not by government but by the market.[25] In this new order, the territorial state is an anachronism. Today, a government's constituents are not only its subjects, who live in its territory, but its bondholders, who might live anywhere. The market is both more rational and more powerful than government, which has become a reactionary force by defending functions that are often better performed by private enterprise. But far from replacing law, global governance via the market presupposes it. The

---

[25] Friedman, *Lexus and Olive Tree*, reporting (and, in ch. 9, criticizing) a view common among economists and members of the business community.

global market, especially, demands undistorted information and financial predict-
ability, and this means that communities that do not wish to be excluded from this
market must have laws that guarantee professional accounting standards, a free
press, a judicial system capable of controlling corruption, and other institutions that
depend upon the rule of law.

A second antinomian argument holds that democracy is possible without the state
because modern communication technologies, including the Internet, are providing
people with new ways to interact with one another. It is suggested, for example, that
unlike traditional democracy, which is linked to decision-making within a territorial
state, 'discursive democracy' is possible in many different kinds of community. A
'discursive community' is a network of individuals united to achieve a common goal.
A transnational advocacy organization like that devoted to banning land mines is an
example of such a non-governmental, non-territorial network.[26] Critics of the states
system argue that such non-territorial communities can substitute for the political
communities of the past: that 'civil society' is possible without the state and that
'governance' is possible without government. But, we must ask, what are the rules by
which this governance will proceed? How will rights be preserved and unjust
coercion limited?

Such antinomian arguments fail to appreciate the place of law in providing a
framework for deliberation. They ignore what Habermas calls the 'internal relation'
between democracy and the rule of law, a relation I would formulate as the
proposition that democracy presupposes laws that define the community whose
members are to make decisions and upon whom these collective decisions are
binding.[27] The idea of 'governance' equivocates between collective decisions made in
voluntary associations and those made in coercive associations like the state.
Conceptions of democratic governance that dispense with the rule of law also
dispense with justice. An interest group can without injustice pursue purposes shared
by its members, but it cannot without injustice impose those purposes on persons
who do not share them. Such conceptions are frightening because they point toward
a world in which power is everything and law nothing. Democracy, strictly speaking,
is a way of deliberating about rules that the members of a community are justly
compelled to observe. The idea of discursive democracy without law misunderstands
the point of democracy because the discourse it postulates is disconnected from
decision-making. Democracy, properly speaking, is a method of rule, a way of
making enforceable decisions in a community. Democracy is not necessarily linked
to a defined territory but it *is* linked to defined membership: it presupposes rules that
distinguish citizens from non-citizens, and thereby identify those on whom
democratically-reached decisions are binding.[28] If deliberation does not result in
binding rules ('laws'), democracy is not a form of government but only a metaphor.

---

[26] J. S. Dryzek, 'Transnational Democracy', *Journal of Political Philosophy*, 7 (1999), p. 44, and Richard
Price, 'Reversing the Gun Sights: Transnational Civil Society Targets Land Mines', *International
Organization*, 52 (1998), p. 615.

[27] Jürgen Habermas, 'On the Internal Relation between the Rule of Law and Democracy', in *The
Inclusion of the Other: Studies in Political Theory* (Cambridge, MA: MIT Press, 1998), p. 261. Writers
on global, cosmopolitan, or transnational democracy—the vocabulary of this discourse has not yet
stabilized—often assume a relationship between law and democratic politics without specifying the
character of that relationship. Barber, *Jihad vs. McWorld*, ch. 19, is illustrative.

[28] Robert A. Dahl, 'Procedural Democracy', in Peter Laslett and James A. Fishkin (eds.), *Philosophy,
Politics and Society*, 5th series (New Haven, CT: Yale University Press, 1979).

Democracy without law means discussion but no framework of laws to guide that discussion or to be altered by it.[29] And democracy without the rule of law means a discussion unacceptably distorted by unconstrained power.

There is a vision of globalization that does preserve the rule of law, but it is also one that is compatible with the continued existence of a pluralist international system. Thinkers since the time of Gibbon and Kant have understood the states system, with all its imperfection, to be the guarantor of communal freedom (political independence) and therefore, indirectly, of individual freedom. The problem that Kant tackles in 'Perpetual Peace' is how to diminish this imperfection by actualizing the rule of law not only within states but universally. His well-known solution is to imagine an arrangement in which rule-of-law states ('republics') unite to form a federation, itself governed by the rule of law, in which they retain their independence. The rule of law will become universal when all states have become republics and then members of this federation.[30] Although it includes no very clear conception of the rule of law, John Rawls's recently proposed 'law of peoples' essentially reiterates this Kantian conception of a pluralist international order. For Rawls, law governs conduct within and between 'well-ordered states' (states whose governments respect basic human rights and are democratically elected or at least consult in some manner with the people they govern). States that are not well-ordered are regulated by coercion, not law, and because such states do not respect international law, they are 'outlaws' against whom other states are entitled to use force.[31] For both Kant and Rawls, then, justice at the global level presupposes the continued existence of a plurality of independent political communities and of an international law to regulate their coexistence and cooperation.

Despite arguments like these, the idea of law is on the defensive within as well as between states. All law is being eroded by distrust of law and scepticism about the foundations, religious or rational, of moral knowledge. Contemporary thought does not leave much room for belief in law as an authoritative constraint on human activity. It sees law as an instrument of human purposes, a set of tools for getting things done. This is not law as it was once understood: a constraint on the pursuit of all human purposes. Scepticism regarding this understanding of law goes beyond the man-made laws of the modern state, positive law. It also undermines the idea of morality as a body of higher law, natural law. The attack on the state, and therefore on a global order organized through states, is only one manifestation of these doubts about law. International law is in trouble not because of its alleged defects as law but because it has come, like other kinds of law, to be regarded as an instrument of human purposes rather than as a constraint on their pursuit. The idea of the rule of law can therefore be seen, in the context of the globalization debate, as a way of

---

[29] Similar criticisms can be made of the related literature on global civil society as an alternative to the states system. In this literature, 'civil society' is not, as it was before Hegel, a synonym for the state, but for the sphere of private relationships: a 'space of uncoerced human association', as Michael Walzer puts it. But this space, between as well as within states, is defined by laws, and only where the rule of law is respected will it be significant. Terry Nardin, 'Private and Public Roles in Civil Society', in Walzer (ed.), *Toward a Global Civil Society*, pp. 29–34. Chris Brown sceptically examines the global civil society literature in 'Cosmopolitanism, World Citizenship and Global Civil Society', *Critical Review of International Social and Political Philosophy*, 3 (2000).

[30] Immanuel Kant, 'Perpetual Peace', in Hans Reiss (ed.), *Political Writings*, 2nd edn. (Cambridge: Cambridge University Press, 1991).

[31] John Rawls, *The Law of Peoples* (Cambridge, MA: Harvard University Press, 1999).

restating, in a modern idiom, the proposition that it is government within a framework of non-instrumental rules of coexistence, not instrumental rules of cooperation on the basis of relative power, that distinguishes a just society from a despotism and a moral international society from a quasi-despotic system of unequal powers. Of course, the rule of law may be even further from being realized between states than within them. Even so, it remains relevant as a tool for helping us to understand the conditions of justice in the emerging, but still pluralist, global order.[32]

---

[32] This article was originally written for a conference on international norms organized in 1997 by the Leonard Davis Institute of International Relations at the Hebrew University of Jerusalem. It was subsequently circulated as a working paper of the international legal theory group of the American Society of International Law. In revising the article for publication I have benefited from criticism by members of the theory group, the editors of the *Review*, and Pablo De Grieff.

Towards a feminist international ethics

KIMBERLY HUTCHINGS*

Introduction

The title of this article brings together two terms, the latter, 'international ethics', is instantly recognizable as referring to a distinct aspect of the academic study of international relations with its own canonic tradition and debates. The former term, 'feminist', is much less familiar, and for many normative theorists in international relations refers to a political movement and set of ideological positions whose relevance to international ethics is far from clear. It is therefore necessary to engage in some preliminary explanation of the term 'feminism' and how it has come to be linked to 'international ethics' in recent scholarship in order to set out the argument of this article. It is only in the last fifteen years that theoretical perspectives under the label of feminism have come to be applied to international relations, although they have a rather longer history within other social sciences and, significantly, within ethical theory. Feminism as a political movement comes in a variety of ideological forms and the same is true of feminism within the academy. The common theme which connects diverse theoretical positions under the label of 'feminism' is the claim that paying attention to the ways in which social reality is 'gendered' has a productive impact on how it is to be understood, judged and may be changed. What counts as 'productive' is related not simply to the goal of enriching understanding and judgment as such (by drawing attention to its gendered dimension), but to the explicitly political goal of exposing and addressing the multiple ways in which both women and men are oppressed by gendered relations of power. It is clear, from the first, therefore, that there is a powerfully normative agenda inherent in any perspective labelled as 'feminist'.

However, as any scholar of the feminist movement inside or outside the academy knows, the normative agenda of feminism is itself a matter of political contestation amongst feminists. Different schools of feminism differ about the meaning of the term 'gender', about the roots of gendered relations of power and about the most effective means for combating oppression based on gendered relations of power. Within the confines of a single article, it is impossible to do justice to the variety and complexity of feminist politics and feminist theory.[1] Nevertheless, from my own

* With thanks to the anonymous reviewer and the editors of the Special Issue for their helpful comments

[1] A useful overview of this variety and complexity can be found in I. Whelehan, *Modern Feminist Thought* (Edinburgh: Edinburgh University Press, 1995). For an overview of feminist contributions to international relations, see J. Steans, *Gender and International Relations: An Introduction* (Cambridge: Polity Press, 1998), pp. 10–37.

point of view it is central to the richness of the contributions made by feminist scholarship within the academy (including the study of international relations) that they are always involved in an ongoing process of feminist debate. That is, debate which persistently drags feminist work back to the questions: How is gender possible? Why is gender entwined with power? How can oppression on the basis of gender be resisted? Any self-consciously feminist intervention into the realm of ethical theory has to be engaged in examining, defending and reassessing its claims in the light of ongoing arguments in feminist politics. It is therefore not possible for feminist ethics to detach itself from feminist politics, not simply because political implications may flow from any particular feminist analysis but because feminism knows itself to be always already political. In this respect, feminist theory shares a great deal with Marxist approaches to normative understanding and judgment but is radically different from the mainstream perspectives on international ethics, within which a clear line is drawn between the domains of morality and politics.[2] In what follows, I will suggest that precisely because of the ongoing political contestation characteristic of the feminist movement (within and outside of the academy) feminist insights transform not only the understanding of social reality but also the nature and scope of normative theorizing itself. This is work which acts as a challenge to the meta-ethical assumptions underpinning mainstream debates between deontologists and consequentialists, cosmopolitans and communitarians in international ethics.

This article's aim is to offer an assessment of the contribution to international ethics which is made by feminist perspectives and, more particularly, to offer my own analysis of the most fruitful directions in which this work might develop. As is evident from the discussion in the previous paragraph, feminist ethical theory is not a monolithic project, and I am therefore going to be highly selective in relation to the 'feminist perspectives' upon which I choose to concentrate. There are two principles underlying this selection. First, it seems to me to be potentially most enlightening in examining the contribution of feminist ethics to begin by focusing on that ethical perspective which is most clearly a product of feminist inquiry, that is to say, the ethic of care.[3] Secondly, part of my argument here is not simply about the substantive strengths and weaknesses of particular theories but about the political dynamic within feminist theoretical debate, and few feminist normative theories have been quite so productive of feminist critique and engagement than those utilizing an ethic of care approach. I will begin my account of feminist ethics therefore by examining the influential contribution of Sarah Ruddick, a pioneering feminist moral theorist whose work is linked explicitly to international ethical issues. Having examined the implications of this approach in Ruddick's work, I will go on in the

---

[2] See K. Hutchings, 'The Possibility of Judgment: Moralizing and Theorizing in International Relations', *Review of International Studies*, 18:1 (1992), pp. 51–62.

[3] I do not mean by this that there is a necessary connection between feminism and the ethic of care. Rather, my point is that the ethic of care is the most significant ethical theory which has emerged as a product of specifically feminist analysis. Many feminists argue that feminism fits better with alternative ethical traditions, from deontology to pragmatism—but these traditions are not specifically feminist in origin. Throughout this article I will use the term 'feminist ethics' as a shorthand for the particular trajectory of feminist thinking with which I am concerned. A broader sense of the scope of feminist ethics as such can be found in: E.Browning Cole and S. Coultrap-McQuin (eds.), *Explorations in Feminist Ethics* (Bloomington and Indianapolis: Indiana University Press, 1992); E. Frazer, J. Hornsby and S. Lovibond, *A Reader in Feminist Ethics* (Oxford: Blackwell, 1992).

second part of the article to look critically at the strengths and weaknesses of that work as they have been identified by other feminists and at the recent development of a 'critical' international ethics of care in the work of Fiona Robinson. Both the exposition and critique of care approaches will be oriented in relation to the following three questions:

- From a feminist perspective, how are the nature and conditions of ethical judgement within the international arena to be understood?
- From a feminist perspective, what is ethically significant within the realm of international politics?
- What are the prescriptive consequences of taking a feminist turn in international ethics?

I will argue that the critical engagement in both theory and practice of feminists with care ethics offers important lessons for how a feminist international ethics should proceed in relation to these three key questions. Drawing upon the work of Margaret Urban-Walker, in the third part of the article I will argue that the key feature of feminist international ethics is that it necessarily brings politics back into the heart of moral judgment and prescription. This has profound consequences for answers to the above three questions, suggesting a different way of thinking about normative theory as well as having important implications for considering substantive fields of ethical concern within international ethics, such as just war and human rights. Following on from the discussion of these substantive areas of concern, I will conclude that the logic of feminist ethics is to move international ethics away from the idealizations inherent in the dominant ethical traditions towards a position best characterized as ethical realism.

An ethic of care in international politics

Women's moral judgment is more contextual, more immersed in the detail of relationships and narratives. It shows a greater propensity to take the standpoint of the 'particular other', and women appear more adept at revealing feelings of empathy and sympathy required by this.[4]

The quotation above sums up the research findings of the social psychologist Carol Gilligan in her now famous book *In A Different Voice*.[5] In this book, Gilligan not only reported on empirical evidence for the gendered nature of patterns of moral reasoning, but used this as a basis for challenging accepted assumptions about the meaning of moral maturity. Traditionally, following Kohlberg's model of the hierarchy of moral growth and learning, the highest level of moral maturity had been associated with the capacity to utilize impartial universalist principles in making ethical judgments. Gilligan challenged this, arguing that the contextual,

---

[4] S. Benhabib, *Situating the Self: Gender, Community and Postmodernism in Contemporary Ethics* (Cambridge: Polity Press, 1992), p. 270.
[5] C. Gilligan, *In a Different Voice: Psychological Theory and Women's Development* (Cambridge MA: Harvard University Press, 1982).

relational and empathetic features of moral reasoning, more often displayed by adult women than the impartial, universalist approaches more typical of adult men, were equally sophisticated and valuable. Since the impartial universalist account of moral maturity dovetails with the dominant deontological and consequentialist paradigms in ethical theory, it is unsurprising that Gilligan's debate with Kohlberg inspired a more general debate about the nature of ethical judgment within ethical and political theory. This has become known as the debate between an 'ethic of justice' (impartial universalism) and 'ethic of care' (contextual particularism) in moral thinking.[6]

In her book, *Maternal Thinking: Towards a Politics of Peace*, Ruddick draws on Gilligan's idea of an ethic of care as a central part of her argument for a feminist moral orientation in the context of international politics.[7] Ruddick is aware of the problems of simply taking and applying the regulative ideals of care-giving practices to the realm of international politics, but nevertheless, she extrapolates criteria of ethical judgment from caregiving practice which she argues do have implications for what should or should not be permissible within the international realm. She does this by invoking the idea of a 'feminist standpoint' in terms of 'maternal thinking'.[8] 'Maternal thinking', according to Ruddick, 'is a discipline in attentive love', a discipline which is rooted in the demands of a particular relation of care, that between mother and child, and which reflects a particular range of attitudes to others, cognitive capacities and virtues.[9] Ruddick is fully aware that not all mothers exemplify the regulative ideal of maternal thinking, she also makes clear that there is no reason why mothers cannot be men. This is not an argument about biological essentialism or female ethical superiority. Rather, it is an argument that the practice of rearing children embodies certain virtues and attitudes which provide a standpoint from which other kinds of practices may be judged.

When maternal thinking takes upon itself the critical perspective of a feminist standpoint, it reveals a contradiction between mothering and war. Mothering begins in birth and promises life; military thinking justifies organized, deliberate deaths. A mother preserves the bodies, nurtures the psychic growth, and disciplines the conscience of children; although the military trains its soldiers to survive the situations it puts them in, it also deliberately endangers their bodies, minds and consciences in the name of victory and abstract causes.[10]

There are several different implications of Ruddick's argument in relation to the three questions raised in the Introduction above about ethical judgment, ethical significance and prescription. For Ruddick, the appropriate way of thinking of the

[6] D. Bubeck, 'Ethic of Care and Feminist Ethics', *Women's Philosophy Review*, 18 (1998), pp. 22–50.

[7] S. Ruddick, *Maternal Thinking: Towards a Politics of Peace* (London: Women's Press, 1990).

[8] The idea of a feminist standpoint derives from Hartsock's appropriation of Marx's analysis of capitalism as being based on the standpoint (serving the objective interests) of the oppressed class. According to Hartsock, the exploitative character of capitalist relations of production becomes clear when understood from the vantage point of the proletariat. Similarly, the patriarchal character of relations of reproduction as well as production under capitalism is revealed from the standpoint of the women who bear the brunt of those relations (N. Hartsock, 'The Feminist Standpoint: Developing the Ground for a Specifically Feminist Historical Materialism' in S. Harding (ed.), *Feminism and Methodology* (Milton Keynes: Open University Press, 1987), pp. 157–80. Ruddick argues that maternal thinking, located as it is in the marginalized and denigrated sphere of caring labour, provides a standpoint from which the absurdity of both strategic military and just-war thinking becomes evident.

[9] Ruddick, *Maternal Thinking*, p. 123.

[10] Ibid., p. 135.

nature and conditions of ethical judgment puts emphasis on particularity, connectedness and context. From the standpoint of maternal thinking, the best stance to take in ethical judgment is to attempt to build on particular experiences of the practice of care to help to identify with and take responsibility for the needs and suffering of others. Ruddick frequently cites the example of the Argentinian mothers of the disappeared, whose movement gradually grew to embrace concerns with children across the world who had suffered harm: 'This is not transcendent impartiality but a sympathetic apprehension of another grounded in one's own particular suffering'.[11] This is not just a matter of 'feeling for' another's pain, but assuming an attitude of responsibility for it and therefore trying to do something about it. In addition, however, maternal thinking is sensitive to the specific contexts in which ethical dilemmas are embedded and the importance of appreciating the ethical weight of the perspectives of all parties to any dispute or conflict. For Ruddick, ethical judgment has to be on a case by case basis, but without ready made principles of adjudication. Although the idea of maternal thinking is in principle non-violent and therefore rules out certain types of action, it also makes clear that there are no universally applicable algorithms that can be applied to any given situation to render definitive answers to ethical questions. The judgment of the maternal thinker is oriented by the ideals implicit in care, but these are regulative rather than determining in their effects.

The orientation of judgment in terms of care has implications for what assumes ethical significance within the field of judgment of the moral agent. In traditional normative international relations theory, ethical significance inheres in states and/or individuals. In communitarian traditions the state is given ethical primacy on the basis of its identification with the 'community' which has its own inherent value; in the utilitarian tradition ethical significance is located in the individual; in other traditions (contractualist, Kantian), both individuals and states have ethical significance but the ethical significance of states is parasitic on the ethical significance of individuals. Ruddick places all of these ethical traditions firmly in the realm of 'masculinist' theory and practice. Although it is clear that Ruddick does put an ethical value on humans, this is based not on a notion of inherent individual right or interest, but on relation—value inheres in relations to others, in particular in the recognition of responsibility for others. For Ruddick then, the realm of international politics is primarily a realm of human relations, not of human, nation or state rights/interests or an international state system. In a very basic sense, this alteration of focus changes what is 'seen' by the ethical theorist of international politics. The boundary between state and interstate relations is dissolved and attention shifts from collective or individual rights and interests to focus on questions of relations of recognition and responsibility. More importantly still, the private sphere (normally doubly excluded from consideration in international contexts) is made visible in two senses: first as itself a part of the international realm; secondly as a source of lessons for both domestic and international politics.

Although Ruddick presents an understanding of the international realm very different from mainstream ethical theories, nevertheless, as with those theories, it is clear that for her the articulation of the standpoint of maternal thinking is tied up

---

[11] S. Ruddick, 'Notes Toward a Feminist Peace Politics', in M. Cooke and A. Woollacott (eds.), *Gendering War Talk* (Princeton, NJ: Princeton University Press, 1993), p. 123.

with a prescriptive agenda. For Ruddick, both militarism and just war theory share a commitment to the expendability of concrete lives in abstract causes to which maternal thinking is inherently opposed. Ruddick claims that this means that the implication of maternal thinking is not just the rejection of war but the active embracing of peace politics, a fight against war which draws on the acknowledgement of responsibility and relationship and the specificity of need and obligations which are inherent in a proper understanding of the labour of caring.[12]

One of the tasks of peace making is to transform this ordinary peacefulness that surrounds us into a public commitment to, and capacity for, making peace.[13]

Towards a critical ethics of care

Ruddick's account of maternal thinking, along with Gilligan's identification of the 'different voice' of care, has been a crucial reference point for later feminist ethicists, both critical and sympathetic.[14] Critical engagement typically comes from two different directions: there is the 'justice' critique which identifies problems for feminism with the abandonment of reliance on universal principle; then there is the 'difference' critique which argues, contrary to the justice critics, that the ethic of care remains too close to the logic of traditional ethical paradigms in the context of international politics. The former critique is troubled by the particularism and implicit relativism of care ethics. It argues that feminist goals are better served by attributing fundamental ethical significance to the category of 'humanity' and aspiring towards universal principles of justice. The 'difference' critique is more sympathetic to the particularism and contextualism of care ethics, but argues that this very particularism and contextualism is threatened by the idealization of the perspective of care which care ethics involves. Neither critique is solely concerned with the meta-ethical issues raised by care ethics, they are both bound up with worries about the incapacity of care ethics to further the goals of feminism, goals broadly conceived as those of redressing gendered inequalities of power across the international arena.

Feminist justice critics are concerned about care ethics' accounts of the scope and the ground of ethical judgment. How can a moral orientation which relies on actual embedded relations of care and is always relative to context be generalizable to strangers? If ethical judgment is always grounded in actual conditions of relationship (rather than in rationally derived values or rules which are in principle accessible to anyone and therefore capable of underpinning universally compelling obligations) then how can a feminist commitment to global goals such as the equality of women be justified? And how can one formulate arguments against those defending practices oppressive to women on grounds of local practices of care? In addition, justice critics draw attention to the dangers of reinforcing the legitimacy of

---

[12] Ruddick, *Maternal Thinking*, pp. 141–59.
[13] Ruddick, 'Notes Towards a Feminist Peace Politics', p. 118.
[14] For examples of a 'sympathetic' response, a 'justice' critique and a 'difference' critique respectively see the essays by R. Manning ('Just Caring'), P. Ward Scaltsas ('Do Feminist Ethics Counter Feminist Aims?') and C. Bunch ('A Global Perspective on Feminist Ethics and Diversity') in Browning Cole and Coultrap-McQuin (eds.), *Explorations in Feminist Ethics*, pp. 45–54; 15–26; 176–85.

existing gendered relations of power by making existing patterns of care and responsibility for women morally paradigmatic. The main charges made by justice critics against care ethics, therefore, are moral relativism (parochialism) and that care ethics idealizes and thereby implicitly endorses ethical relations which are premised on a gendered division of labour and of the private from the public sphere, ethical relations which feminism should actually be concerned to challenge and change. In both cases the charges derive from the assumption that both moral critique and political improvement require judgment and action which are based on abstractly derived and generalizable principles.

At the heart of the 'difference' criticism of care ethics is a perceived tension between the idea of grounding ethical theory in a relational ontology and in specific contexts of responsibility and action on the one hand, and the notion of a 'feminist standpoint' for ethical judgment and prescription on the other.[15] There is an ongoing concern within feminist theory about theoretical positions which rest on ideas of a 'feminist standpoint' which suggest a fixed account (not necessarily biologically based) of the meaning of sexual difference. Over the past twenty years feminists, both within multicultural states and internationally, have been arguing that the predominant political campaigns and accounts of women's oppression within the feminist movement have reflected the position (and served the interests) of white, middle class, northern women rather than those of the majority of women. What has emerged from this debate has been a growing dissatisfaction with any feminist account which relies on a generalizable notion of a feminist perspective. It is argued that the inclusive ambition of such theories is in practice exclusive, since no single understanding of the feminist standpoint can possibly reflect the multiple and often contradictory positions in which different feminists stand.[16] In addition, as with justice critics, difference critics are also concerned at the apparent neglect by ethicists of care of the power relations at work within caring practices such as mothering and at the way those practices are embedded in broader gendered relations of power. In spite of some apparent overlap, the responses of justice and difference critics to the account of ethical judgment in care ethics are distinct. Each perspective sees problems with the idea of a feminist standpoint for moral judgment, but in the former case this is because such a standpoint is seen to be relative to context, and in the latter, because the standpoint is seen to be over-readily generalized. Each perspective sees problems in relation to the neglect of power in care ethics, but whereas justice critics theorize on the basis of an ideal ground of judgment beyond power and politics, difference critics raise the question of whether ethics and power, morality and politics can ever be clearly distinguished in either moral judgment or action.

To date there is only one major example of a feminist ethicist who explicitly takes up the challenge to develop a feminist international ethics based on central insights of care ethics, but is alert to the kinds of criticisms made by both justice and difference critics referred to above. In her book, *Globalizing Care: Ethics, Feminist*

---

[15] S. Hekman, *Moral Voices/Moral Selves: Carol Gilligan and Feminist Moral Theory* (Cambridge: Polity Press, 1995); see also Hekman, 'Truth and Method: Feminist Standpoint Theory Revisited', *Signs*, 22:2 (1997), pp. 341–65.

[16] See the debates in L. Nicholson (ed.), *Feminism/Postmodernism* (London: Routledge, 1990); C. Mohanty, A. Russo and L. Torres (eds.), *Third World Women and the Politics of Feminism* (Bloomington and Indianapolis: Indiana University Press, 1991); M. H. Marchand and J. L. Parpart (eds.), *Feminism, Postmodernism, Development* (London: Routledge, 1995).

Theory and International Relations, Robinson argues for the superiority of what she terms a 'critical' care approach over traditional paradigms in international ethics in relation not only to issues of political violence but also to questions about international human rights and global distributive justice.[17] The breadth of Robinson's focus is matched by the breadth of the feminist theoretical literature on which her own defence of care ethics as a global ethics rests. Ruddick is only one of the feminist theorists upon whom Robinson draws and her analysis is informed by the ongoing arguments which successive waves of feminist critics have had with the ethic of care as originally developed in the work of theorists such as Gilligan and Ruddick. Robinson's argument is concerned to demonstrate the far reaching implications of taking an ethic of care as the starting point for international ethics, but also to strengthen and substantiate care ethics in response to feminist (and other) critics. Unlike Ruddick, Robinson does not rely on a concept of 'maternal thinking', but more generally on the idea of care as an everyday practice and moral orientation, embedded in a number of actual contexts. Moreover, Robinson places more emphasis than Ruddick on the significance for care ethics of the broader political, social and economic context of the international sphere and the ways in which particular patterns of advantage and disadvantage, power and oppression, sameness and difference are institutionalized within it. Nevertheless, although Robinson's work is broader in focus and elaborates a more flexible account and defence of care ethics than Ruddick, there are strong similarities in the way in which Robinson presents an ethic of care as an orientation for moral judgment and as a distinctive moral ontology. What is less clear in Robinson's account are the specific prescriptive consequences of her argument.

As with Ruddick, Robinson rejects an understanding of the nature and conditions of moral judgment in terms of abstractly derived principles and values. Morality is not a matter of reason or will but of modes of responsiveness to others which are embedded in actual relationships. This means that ethical judgment is always relational and contextual and, as with Ruddick's maternal thinking, there are no principles which can determine in advance the rights and wrongs even of similar situations.[18] At the same time, however, the contextual judgments which are both necessary and difficult are oriented in relation to the mode of responsiveness to others which is defined as 'caring', something which Robinson defines broadly as a mode of responding to others which recognizes others as 'real' human beings.[19] That is to say, as beings embedded in their own complex modes of responsiveness to others, with vulnerabilities, capacities, needs and values which matter. Above all the orientation of judgment in terms of care necessitates avoiding a rush to judgment and paying attention to the actual situations from which moral dilemmas and questions emerge.

This is not an abstract ethics about the application of rules, but a phenomenology of moral life which recognizes that addressing moral problems involves first, an understanding of identities, relationships, and contexts, and second, a degree of social coordination and cooperation in order to try to answer questions and disputes about who cares for whom, and

[17] F. Robinson, *Globalizing Care: Ethics, Feminist Theory and International Relations* (Boulder, CO: Westview Press, 1999).
[18] Robinson, *Globalizing Care*, p. 41.
[19] Ibid., p. 46.

about how responsibilities will be discharged. The ethics of care focuses not on the moment of rational moral judgment or of pure moral will, but on the permanent background to decision-making, which may often be characterized by apparent inaction—waiting, listening, focusing attention.[20]

As with Ruddick, again, Robinson's view of what is ethically significant in the international realm moves away from the focus of mainstream ethics on the abstractions of individuals, states or nations to concentrate instead on the examination of relations of recognition and responsibility wherever they occur. In Robinson's case, however, this focus explicitly draws attention to international structures and institutions and, most importantly, power relations within the inter- national arena. Ruddick's emphasis is on using the positive relationality of maternal thinking to criticize the instrumental rationality of the institutions which enable the prosecution of war. The disposability of real people's lives in war is condemned as antithetical to the morality of care but the reasons why this attitude is possible in the first place are not a primary focus of concern. Robinson, however, insists that care ethics must go further and reflect critically upon the institutional and structural underpinnings of global violence and inequality, not simply by asserting them to be wrong but by understanding how it is that their wrongness is possible. 'Wrongness', however, is defined similarly to Ruddick as that which serves 'to undermine the ability of moral agents to identify and understand others as 'real' individuals—with real, special, unique lives'.[21]

An ethics of care is not about the application of a universal principle ('We all must care about all others') nor is it about a sentimental ideal ('A more caring world will be a better world'). Rather it is a starting point for transforming the values and practices of international society; thus it requires an examination of the contexts in which caring does or does not take place, and a commitment to the creation of more humanly responsive institutions which can be shaped to embody expressive and communicative possibilities between actors on a global scale.[22]

Robinson does not pursue an explicit prescriptive agenda in relation to war as Ruddick does, and the prescriptive implications following from her elaborated global ethic of care are less clearly defined. The purpose of taking an ethic of care approach is to contribute to the transformation of the contemporary international system into one in which caring is enabled, sustained and protected. But what does this mean? It is at this point that a certain ambiguity in Robinson's account of her own ethical theory becomes apparent. On the one hand, Robinson is deeply com- mitted to the idea of a critical ethic of care as a transformative project, a starting point for changing the world in the light of the regulative ideal of care understood broadly as relating to others as 'real' individuals. The idea of care, as in Ruddick's notion of maternal thinking, provides the critical perspective from which the injustices of the world become apparent and may be judged. In this sense, care emerges as distinct from international politics as usual. The valorization of relations of care becomes the goal of the generalization of these relations to a broader context. On the other hand, Robinson's insistence of the importance of power relations, complexity and context sits uneasily with any notion of the moral high

---

[20] Ibid., p. 31.
[21] Ibid., p. 47.
[22] Ibid., pp. 47–8.

ground. Her argument slips between an idealization of care and an anxiety to be both realistic (in the sense of political realism) and contextually sensitive in her analysis. The latter tendency is one which undercuts the former and makes the task of prescription impossible outside of specific cases. When Robinson introduces her version of the ethics of care as critical, she is intending to emphasize that care ethics does not straightforwardly valorize virtues specific to the private sphere and that it can become a critical tool within ethical analysis in the broadest of contexts. In my view, however, the critical contribution made by her version of care ethics is that it raises very powerfully the question of the possibility of critique as it is traditionally understood to operate in ethical theory. It is this insight which most thoroughly informs my own view of the best way to take forward the project of a feminist international ethics.

Feminist international ethics without a standpoint

We *can* be better or worse justified in our own moral beliefs, and we *can* make justified judgments on others' moral practices and beliefs. What we *can't* do is assume that our judgments ought to have *authority* for them, much less that it is a test of our or anybody else's moral beliefs that they achieve *universal* authority.[23]

One of the key references in Robinson's work is the feminist moral theory of Margaret Urban Walker. In her book *Moral Understandings: A Feminist Study in Ethics*, Urban Walker suggests answers to our three questions about ethical judgment, significance and prescription which pick up on problems which the difference critics of an international ethic of care have pointed out and which Robinson's work attempts to counter. Urban Walker is writing at the level of philosophical meta-ethics, but her analysis offers clear guidance as to how feminist ethics might move forward in the wake of rejecting a feminist standpoint as such.

Care ethics involves a rethinking of what might be termed 'ethical substance' (in terms of a moral ontology of relations of recognition and responsibility) along with bringing in a new perspective on ethics (the feminist standpoint), from which certain things can be 'seen' and on the basis of which ethical judgments can be made. Problems arise because the characterization of ethical substance and of the feminist standpoint are both highly idealized, posing difficulties for recent feminist thinking which has been forged in political contestation between different women, both within states and in the international realm. Although theorists such as Ruddick take issue with traditional ethical paradigms, they do not challenge the understanding that the fundamental characteristic of ethics is that it provides the vantage point from which all else can be evaluated and judged—specifically it provides a vantage point beyond politics/power. And I have suggested that Robinson's work remains torn between setting up care as the orientation for ethical judgment and prescription, and an abandonment of the possibility of ethical theory of this kind. Urban Walker's argument, however, follows through the logic of the particularism and contextualism inherent in care approaches consistently, without re-establishing

---

[23] M. Urban Walker, *Moral Understandings: A Feminist Study in Ethics* (London: Routledge, 1998), p. 208.

the moral high ground in the notion of a feminist standpoint. The result is a rather different account of the nature and scope of ethical theory.

When it comes to the nature and conditions of ethical judgment, as noted in the quotation at the beginning of this section, Urban Walker's understanding of ethical substance (her moral ontology) entails the abandonment of strong 'authority'. Instead, ethical judgment is either already authoritative within existing forms of moral life—and therefore in effect, if not immediately self-evident, certainly potentially evident to reflective participants—or it has to be built collaboratively. Crucial to Urban Walker's account, as with the ethics of care, is the reliance of the authority and credibility of ethical claims on their meaningfulness within specific contexts. That meaning is not carried transcendentally, it is this-worldly and where it does not exist, ethical judgment is not authoritative but coercive. Like Ruddick and Robinson, Urban Walker locates ethical significance in relationality and in responsibilities which follow from relationship. Her emphasis, however, is not on a particular ideal-type of relation (as exemplified by maternal thinking or particular relations of care), but on the complex and constructed character of ethical substance and the ways in which particular patterns of responsibility and dependence inhere within it. These are patterns which have a history. They involve assumptions about moral identity and value, and the question of their necessity is crucial to debates about the legitimacy or otherwise of the obligations and practices with which they are bound up. In assessing ethical significance, traditionally the ethical theorist has been concerned to discriminate between necessary and contingent identities and values in order to work out what carries moral weight. In the case of Ruddick, as we have seen, moral weight is carried by the practices inherent in maternal thinking but not by the practices of just war. Urban Walker changes the debate by starting from the premise of contingency and asking that the crucial question not be how we know what is ethically necessary, but how certain values or practices come to be seen as ethically necessary.

I suggest we have an urgent need for *geographies of responsibility*, mapping the structure of standing assumptions that guides the distribution of responsibilities—how they are assigned, negotiated, deflected—in particular forms of moral life.[24]

The point is not to establish in advance the relative ethical weight to be carried by communities as opposed to individuals, or by the private as opposed to the public sphere, but to gain a deeper knowledge of the 'forms of moral life'. This deeper knowledge does not take any manifestation of moral values and relations as simply given, but looks at how it has come to be and, crucially, at how interests are constructed and served by the 'bedrock' character of any particular moral practice. In Ruddick's work, what is 'seen' is seen from a perspective which is taken to be the moral bedrock. For Urban Walker, the 'seeing' of the ethical theorist necessarily involves accepting the contingency of ones own 'bedrock' as well as that of others. It is a 'seeing' which involves both moral phenomenology and genealogy.[25] On this view, moral values and practices are inseparable from the broader social and political context within which they operate, and ethics is never entirely divorced from

---

[24] Urban Walker, *Moral Understandings*, p. 99.
[25] For a discussion of phenomenology and genealogy as approaches to normative theory, see
K. Hutchings, *International Political Theory: Rethinking Ethics in a Global Era* (London: Sage, 1999), pp. 143–52.

power. Urban Walker's account of ethical significance and ethical judgment would seem to imply that ethical prescription is no longer the concern of the moral theorist. However, this is not her conclusion. She suggests instead that the work of the moral theorist is prescriptive generally insofar as it challenges any claim that certain moral values or practices are inherently unquestionable. More specifically, she argues for the reflective articulation of ethical prescriptions which acknowledge the condition of their own meaningfulness and therefore are more likely to become intelligible and persuasive to others.

On the basis of the above discussion, following through the lessons from critical engagement with an ethic of care, I want to conclude by putting forward a sketch of a feminist international ethical theory in terms of a series of answers to the questions about ethical judgment, significance and prescription which have been raised above. In doing this it should become clear that there is no question that feminist ethical theory puts forward an 'ethics for women' or an ethics for the private sphere alone, this is not a partial ethics but a generalizable account for how ethics 'should be done' in the contemporary international context. Paradoxically, however, it is grounded on the assumption of the inevitability of partiality and the status of particular partialities as contingent aspects of complex forms of ethical life. It is an ethics which draws on both the insights of the ethic of care and those of care's difference critics. I will focus first on offering a generic analysis of the answers to our three questions. I will then go on to put some flesh on these theoretical bones by illustrating how the feminist approach affects consideration of substantive areas of concern in international ethics, to do with war and human rights.

According to feminist ethics the nature and conditions of ethical judgment are inseparable from the moral forms of life within which they are embedded. This has specific consequences for the authority carried by such judgments which draw attention to the crucial importance of conditions of intelligibility within the sphere of ethics. Moral judgments make sense within contexts, the intelligibility of those judgments is straightforward when a context is shared but becomes a challenge when contexts are not shared or are partially shared. The guarantees of the meaningfulness of moral claims are not to be found in reason in abstraction from ethical life. This means that persuasion of others rests not on rational argument as such, but on putting the conditions in place within which arguments will be understood as rational. In order for this to be possible without coercion, work has to be put in to deconstruct the conditions of possibility of judgment in order to identify possibilities of shared meaning. This implies that the work of the ethical theorist has to have a strong phenomenological dimension, there are no easy knock-down arguments which rest on essential truths. Alongside moral phenomenology, however, goes genealogy; it is equally the responsibility of the ethical theorist to investigate how it comes about that any particular judgment is understood as embodying ethical necessity, and what is the pattern of benefits and costs associated with that judgment. For the feminist ethical theorist, it is, in particular, the role of gender in the construction and maintenance of particular patterns of benefits and costs which will be the focus of concern.

Feminist ethics' most well known contribution to international ethics is to bring in the values and practices of the private sphere to the realm of what is counted as ethically significant. As we have seen, this move is an ambiguous one in the ethics of Ruddick or of Robinson, in that it can become a claim as to the essential value, and therefore ethical primacy, of the values and practices of the private sphere as well as the much more modest claim that the moral ontology of relations of recognition and responsibility which is identified within the private sphere is the key to understanding 'moral substance' as such. It is the latter version of the claim which seems to me to emerge most powerfully from feminist ethics. It is essentially a claim about the nature of the world we inhabit rather than a claim about what ought to be the case. Whereas traditional cosmopolitan and communitarian paradigms, simply by virtue of their identification of ethical significance with states and/or individuals, always already bring in a normative agenda into international ethics (the fundamental importance of respect for state/human rights/interests), the feminist starting point of relational ontology simply draws attention to the always already normatively inflected nature of the world we inhabit. The ontological claims of feminist ethics, however, go deeper than the already strong (if prescriptively neutral) claim that moral reality is embedded in relations/practices of responsibility and recognition. They also assert that such reality is constructed not given, and that gendered relations of power form a significant part of it. By doing this they institutionalize a orientation of 'suspicion' towards any moral values and practices which present themselves as given because tied to some kind of essential identity, including gendered identities. More than anything else, feminist ethicists find ethical significance in those gendered aspects of international ethical reality which, in being presented as necessary, are either not 'seen' at all or are seen as unquestionable. In itself however, this keeps the category of ethical significance wide open. Within a feminist international ethics, it is possible for anything to be ethically significant.

The prescriptions following from feminist ethics will vary depending on the context within which particular feminists are making ethical judgments. This means that even if a first world and a third world feminist share a conception of moral ontology they may have very different prescriptive attitudes. In so far as they articulate ethical prescriptions, theorists must take responsibility for also articulating the conditions within which those prescriptions are meaningful and therefore the kind of world which they imply. Responsibility for the persuasiveness and strength of ethical prescriptions cannot be sloughed onto a first best world of idealized moral relations and agents, or of pure rationality. There is, however, one prescription which has to be common to the practice of feminist ethics of the kind which I have been discussing: always be sceptical of any kind of moral essentialism or claims to ethical necessity. It is not possible to spell out all the ways in which a feminist international ethics of the kind proposed above would affect ethical debate about war or human rights; however, some of the implications can be illustrated by looking briefly at each of these examples in turn.

In the case of war, traditional just war theory has focused on the tension between the value to be given to communities or states as opposed to individuals and the limits which should rightfully be placed on any actual exercise of political violence. In working on these problems, reliance has been placed on deontological, utilitarian and communitarian modes of moral thinking. On the account given above, I would argue that feminist ethics is able to extend the concerns and the conceptual vocabulary of traditional just war theory, but also that it may provide a more radical challenge to the notion of a just war as it is commonly understood. An example of the former, more modest contribution to be made by feminist ethics may be furnished by considering how traditional understandings of the concepts of 'peace' and 'security' have focused on the absence of inter-state political violence as a crucial condition. Once the realm of ethical significance is understood in terms of the full range of relations of recognition and responsibility, the ethical implications of both violent and non-violent international interventions become much more readily apparent and the meanings of both peace and security are altered. A small example of this can be found in current feminist work which has focused attention on the gendered effects of economic sanctions or on the gendered effects of displacement of populations through war in the treatment of refugees. The responsibility for the caring work within the family makes women more vulnerable to the effects of sanctions, because they feed and care for their husbands and children before they feed and care for themselves. Female refugees have also been shown to be peculiarly vulnerable to ill-treatment because of assumptions about their status as women.[26] By bringing the private sphere into the sphere of ethical significance within international politics, feminist ethics alters the ethical assessment of the consequences of non-violent and violent international intervention. More generally it calls into question the assumed boundaries between violence and non-violence, peace and war, security and insecurity.[27] The ethical consideration of war is enriched by a more detailed and complex understanding of the moral ontology of actual human relations. In this respect, the contribution of feminist ethics is as much about enhancing ethical sensitivity and perception as about offering definitive answers to the question of the rights and wrongs of war.

Nevertheless, feminist ethics does present more fundamental challenges to just war thinking in that it puts into question the ethical necessity seen to reside in either individual or community, according to the mainstream ethical paradigms. Feminist ethics as I have outlined it has to be inherently opposed to any justification of political violence which is presented as necessary. The first move of a feminist ethics would not be to establish the justice of the cause or the proportionality of the means, but to put into question the kind of ethical life which generates the tragic dilemma of weighing up individual lives against each other or against collective interests or abstract norms. Once this is essayed, a whole host of cultural, social, economic and political relations come under scrutiny, including the ways that gendered relations of power operate to confirm and perpetuate the legitimacy of war. The question of whether a war is just or could be just is the tip of an ethical iceberg. Feminist ethics, in 'deconstructing' the iceberg, forces acknowledgement that the idea of war as a 'last resort' covers the endorsement of a way of life in which it can be a last resort—it is not an unfortunate necessity but an implication of the world human beings have made, which is attributed necessity in order for that world to be maintained. Once the assumption of ethical necessity is challenged, it becomes possible to think about the conditions of possibility for other kinds of worlds and how they might be built.

The above account, however, needs to be distinguished from the argument (made by Ruddick amongst others) that there is a necessary connection between feminism and a commitment to non-violence. This latter argument has been essential to a distinctively feminist anti-nuclear peace politics which came to prominence in several

---

[26] See G. Ashworth, 'The Silencing of Women', in T. Dunne and N. Wheeler (eds.), *Human Rights in Global Politics* (Cambridge: Cambridge University Press, 1999), p. 269; fn 25, p. 276.

[27] For a more extensive discussion of how feminist analysis shifts the understanding of security in international ethics, see J. Steans, *Gender and International Relations*, pp. 110–29.

Western European countries as well as the USA and Australia during the 1980s. Although clearly sharing much ground with other anti-war and pacifist movements, this feminist peace politics was premised on the idea of a special link between women and peace.[28] One of the interesting things about it was its use of the technique of relying on certain traditional stereotypes of womanhood as the basis for an evaluation of strategic and just war thinking. Essentially, these feminist peace activists reversed the dominant hierarchy of evaluation of masculine civic virtue and feminine private virtue in which the former takes priority over the latter and the latter is essentially supposed to sustain the former. Instead feminine private virtue was taken into the public realm and held up as the (subversive) yardstick of ethical conduct within that realm. The tactics employed at peace camps such as Greenham Common were imbued by the idea of the ethical superiority of the notions of care, connection and responsibility embedded in women's work within the family, over the strategic and just war thinking which could even contemplate the destruction of large swathes of the human race in the pursuit of some greater goal.

For many Western feminists, the work of the womens' peace camps exemplifies the prescriptive implications of a feminist international ethics and clearly follows from the kind of ethic of care exemplified in Ruddick's work. However, according to my account of feminist ethics, which emerges from a critical engagement with care ethics, the positing of an essential link between women and/or feminism and peace is based on mistakes which are evident both in Ruddick's work and in the critical questioning of non-violence within the feminist movement world-wide, particularly in the light of the participation of women in revolutionary or national liberation struggles. Although I have argued that feminist ethics will be unable to work with just war discourse, this is not a position which rests on the elevation of an alternative ideal for moral judgment and action which inherently forbids the use of violence. What is forbidden is the assumption of the necessity of violence; this then enables the opening up of the question of what is sustained by and sustains the presumption of that necessity as the starting point for assessing questions about judgment and action. My suspicion is that on most occasions where issues of the justification of political violence inter- or intra-state arise in the current world order, feminist ethics will be unlikely to offer arguments legitimating violence. But this follows not from a necessary connection, but from the contingent fact that few instances of the use of violence do anything but sustain, or at the very least leave unaltered, gendered relations of power in the world as it is. Aside from some exceptional ideological positions in which violence is seen as inherently a good, most ethical perspectives would claim peace as a goal and deplore the use of violence. Feminists, along with other ethicists of a liberal or communitarian persuasion, live in a world in which violence is possible. It is never a world in which violence is necessary in the sense of there being no other way in which the world could be or any particular agent could act. Feminists, therefore, like all others, cannot avoid the difficulties of weighing up the means by which the world might be transformed and the way in which they, as a specific individual, should act. The decision not to use violence, like the decision to use violence, is one for which agents in the world take

---

[28] A. Harris and Y. King, *Rocking the Ship of State: Towards a Feminist Peace Politics* (Boulder, CO: Westview Press, 1989); K. Warren and D. Cady (eds.), *Hypatia Special Issue: Feminism and Peace*, 9:2 (1994).

responsibility; it is not a responsibility which can be sloughed off onto a categorical obligation always to act in any particular way. The argument remains open as to the possibility of justifying the use of political violence on a contingent basis—this is an argument which may never be persuasive, but its legitimacy cannot simply be ruled out in advance by an appeal to a necessary standpoint for judgment.

The contribution that can be made by feminist ethics to thinking about international human rights, as with the rights and wrongs of war, is one which may both enrich and challenge this ethical discourse. It has been evident to feminist critics for some time that the concept of universal human rights, as exemplified by the UDHR, is gendered in so far as it reflects, without acknowledging, assumptions about gendered identities. This is exemplified by instances standardly pointed out by feminist critics of the UDHR, such as the identification of human with head of household, property owner, wage earner or independent discrete individual (that is, not pregnant).[29] Those humans who don't fit into this mould fall outside of the realm of moral consideration as rights bearers, though they may still be entitled to special ethical consideration. Where the UDHR does recognize entities other than humans it includes both nation and family as ethically significant collectivities, whose value is presented as self-evident. The characteristic response of feminist ethicists to human rights discourse has been to suggest that it needs to be rethought in ways which are more sensitive to the specificity of different humans, and to the role of rights not simply as moral entitlements, but as defence mechanisms and political weapons in the hands of the disadvantaged. This can be illustrated by looking at an example of a practice which has been of particular interest to feminists: female circumcision. In this case, rights discourses have been identified by feminists as a crucial resource for ethical judgment and prescription, but in a way which has problematic implications for the ways in which human rights have traditionally been understood.

As with the institution of just war, the first move of a feminist ethics in considering the practice of female circumcision would be to establish how it is ethically meaningful within the context of a particular form of ethical life. This is both a phenomenological exercise, in which the 'geography of responsibilities', in Urban Walker's phrase, is mapped, and a genealogical exercise in which patterns of cost and benefit, empowerment and disempowerment are also traced. Since practices such as female circumcision are invariably linked to accounts of ethical necessity, the second step of a feminist ethics would be to demonstrate that this ethical necessity is not simply given but constructed, and is tied up with a highly complex set of cultural, social, political and economic practices and institutions. The justification of the practice is also the justification of the construction and maintenance of a patriarchal world. Since feminism is defined in opposition to patriarchy, it is inevitable that feminists are going to see female circumcision as wrong. What is interesting to examine is what happens when feminist ethicists turn to the discourse of international human rights, either to demonstrate that female circumcision is wrong or to underpin the demand that it must be stopped.

Although a standard list of human rights invariably includes the right to bodily integrity, the archetypal violations of that integrity have not, traditionally, reflected

---

[29] V. Spike Peterson, 'Whose Rights? A Critique of the "Givens" in Human Rights Discourse', *Alternatives*, XV (1990), pp. 303–44.

the specific vulnerabilities of particular categories of humanity. Torture, rather than female circumcision or domestic violence, tends to be taken as the bedrock example of that which humans have a right not to have to endure. Initially this seems unimportant, surely the point is to establish the principle, which can then be extended across different examples of violation. However, this is to ignore the tension between a right to bodily integrity and practices which are frequently part of the means of preserving patterns of familial and community relations which at other points in the UDHR are taken as having ethical value. The idea of universal human rights does not provide an unambiguous resource for contesting practices which maintain gendered relations of power. This is because the differences in women's position across both liberal and non-liberal states are profoundly tied up with the institutional structure and commonsense of the international community, which either sees women as women, and as such less than men (in need of paternal protection along with the children) or, in incorporating women under the category of humanity, is unable to see women at all.

It has become increasingly recognized that the commonsense of the international community has blocked recognition of the fact that being a woman is (to echo Catherine Mackinnon) a way of being human.[30] In response to this, a great deal of work has been done by feminist campaigners at the international and state level to work for the extension of international human rights protections to women and to point to the gendered relations of power inherent in traditional conceptions of what it means to be a bearer of rights.[31] Nevertheless, as Mackinnon has argued, drawing upon a rights discourse as a feminist ethicist has implications for how rights are to be understood.[32] The idea of international human rights as instantiated in the contemporary world order has its roots in the Christian natural law tradition and the equal value of every human soul. The secularization of this tradition into the natural and imprescriptable rights of man (humanity) emerged in stark opposition to the premodern notion of essential inequities in moral status between human beings. The idea of human rights is premised on the recognition that in crucial respects, human beings are the same. To point to gender differences in the meaning of a human right, such as the right to marriage and family life, is not to point to the fact that this right is not available to both men and women (which would simply imply that we need to apply the right consistently), it is to point to the fact that a fundamental and globally present aspect of ethical life is structured by and through gendered relations of power. Once this is appreciated, the strategic value as well as the ethical significance of drawing on a rights discourse in order to protect women's interests changes. Strategically, this is not a matter of rights remaining the same and their sphere of application being extended; instead, new kinds of rights (protections against rape in marriage, domestic violence, genital mutilation, rights to divorce, to property, to custody over children, and so on) must be formulated in ways which might well eventually revolutionize or even destroy the institutions to which the

[30] C. Mackinnon, 'Crimes of War, Crimes of Peace', in S. Shute and S. Hurley (eds.), *On Human Rights* (New York: Basic Books, 1993).

[31] See G. Ashworth, 'The Silencing of Women', pp. 259–76; J. Steans, *Gender and International Relations*, pp. 122–25.

[32] In what follows I am indebted to insights from Mackinnon's argument in 'Crimes of War, Crimes of Peace'. See also K. Hutchings, 'Ethics, Feminism and International Affairs', in J.-M. Coicaud and D. Warner (eds.), *Ethics and International Affairs* (Geneva: United Nations University Press, forthcoming).

UDHR refers. At the deeper level of ethical significance the strategic necessity of grounding rights on difference can be understood in two ways: first, it can be seen as a dangerous reversion to premodern assertions of essential differences between different categories of humans, and ultimately as undermining the idea of human rights as such; secondly, it can be seen as putting into question the grounding of fundamental human rights in humanity as such—rights become conceptualized always as a strategic weapon in the construction of a form of ethical life which is no more ethically necessary, though for many (including many feminists) it may be preferable, than any other. It seems to me that it is the latter implication which is inherent in the form of feminist ethics for which I am arguing. In such an ethics the notion of human rights cannot act as an ethical trump card. Instead, specific human rights must be interrogated and judged in terms of the ways in which they function in the broader values, structures and institutions of world politics.

One of the key focuses of feminist debate in the context of international politics in recent years has been the organized rape of women in war. I want to end with a brief consideration of this topic because it draws together the implications of a feminist ethics of the kind I am endorsing for thinking about both war and rights. Traditionally, rape is something which soldiers (men) do—regrettable perhaps, a crime perhaps, but not to be seen as a war crime or crime against humanity. In the same way, within the state, rape is a regrettable, criminal thing that men do but this is not understood in the same way as a racist attack; the commonsense assumption is not that men rape or sexually assault women because they are women and therefore they may (or deserve to) be treated in that way. Two features of the rape of women in the Bosnian war shifted this commonplace perspective on rape as something which just happens, particularly in war situations: firstly, rape appeared to be being organized systematically; secondly, rape was linked to enforced pregnancy presented as the victory of the ethnically superior male over the ethnically inferior woman and, by extension, her male compatriots.[33] When the international war crimes tribunal was set up, for the first time an explicit inclusion of rape as a crime against humanity (when committed in armed conflict against a civilian population) was made. In addition, rape and sexual assault could also be identified as crimes against humanity contributing towards genocide if committed with intent to destroy national, ethnic, racial or religious groups. The inclusion of rape and sexual assault amongst crimes against humanity has been greeted as a legal watershed for humanitarian international law and one which, by implication, represents a victory for the interests and rights of women—since the great majority of rape/sexual assault cases (though not all) uncovered by the war crimes tribunal were crimes committed against women.

[33] In her book *Rape Warfare: The Hidden Genocide in Bosnia Herzogovina and Croatia* (Minneapolis: University of Minnesota Press, 1996), Beverley Allen has detailed some of the evidence presented from survivors of rape/death camps. One of the things which is most obvious from Allen's account is the way that the systematic rape and impregnation of women was understood primarily in terms of its effect on the male enemy population. This worked in two main ways. Firstly, women were regarded as the possessions of husbands and fathers, sexual domination of women was a way of humiliating and depriving those husbands and fathers, the women's own humiliation and deprivation, let alone their pain, was instrumental to a broader purpose. Secondly, women were identified as the passive vessels which carried the future generation of the nation. The ethnic/national identity of the next generation was determined by the ethnicity/nationality of the father, therefore by impregnating enemy women, men were ensuring that the enemy people was not being reproduced and more importantly that their own ethnic/national inheritance would be transmitted.

What kind of response would my version of feminist ethics make to this example of the conduct of war and its aftermath? The first response is fairly obvious, even more clearly than in the case of female circumcision; the use of rape as a weapon of war makes sense only in terms of patriarchal assumptions about the meaning of rape as an instrument for hurting and undermining, not the victims themselves as individuals, but their male relations and compatriots who comprise the 'enemy'. Ethical analysis therefore has to go beyond judging the actions of the perpetrators in isolation, to analysing and deconstructing the background values, practices and institutions which give those actions meaning. The focus of feminist ethics is therefore not on retribution but on the possibilities of transformation. The prevention of similar strategic decisions regarding the conduct of war in the future depends on radically changing the patterns of recognition and responsibility which underpin the identification of women as possessions of men or vessels for the propagation of the race. The criteria by which feminist ethics will judge the adequacy of the international community's response to rape as a crime against humanity must be in terms of how much this legislation contributes to the radical change of forms of ethical life which make it possible for rape to be a weapon of war. On these criteria—how does it fare?

Any assessment of the long term implications of the inclusion of systematic rape in wartime as a crime against humanity is bound to be speculative. However, I would argue that there are good grounds for supposing that the impact of the legislation will be limited in relation to the underlying conditions of possibility of mass rape as a weapon of war. This is not to say that the legislation will be wholly ineffective, it may well operate to deter individual perpetrators and it will certainly 'raise consciousness' of the issue and help to put and keep the unacceptability of the strategic use of rape on the international political agenda (along with use of biological warfare or shooting prisoners). What is more doubtful is whether the legislation can help to change things more fundamentally. For the feminist ethicist it is highly significant that the two ways in which rape is defined as a crime against humanity is either in a way which is not specific to sex, or in a way which is specific to a particular collective identity. Why does this matter? In relation to the first way, it is clearly the case that men and boys have been and continue to be victims of rape in wartime. However, by defining the crime against humanity without reference to sex, the relation between the rape of both women and men and patriarchy becomes obscured. Setting aside the sadism or sexual orientation of individuals, women are not systematically and strategically raped in war because they are human but because they are women, equally if men are raped as a matter of strategy this is in order that they be identified with women—the ultimate in hurt and humiliation for the victim and the ultimate assertion of power for the perpetrator. It therefore seems likely that raising consciousness about rape will not necessarily direct attention to the crucial role of the gendered relations of power which make mass rape in war a potentially effective strategy. The second way in which rape is identified as a crime against humanity is even more problematic from a feminist point of view. In this latter case, the definition of rape as a crime against humanity relies on the idea that the forcible impregnation of women by men of different ethnic backgrounds is equivalent to the destruction of a national, ethnic, racial or religious group. Setting aside the problems of essentializing the latter identities as a matter of biological transmission, this comes perilously close to the endorsement of the logic which underlies the possibility of using rape as a strategic weapon in the first place. To define forcible impregnation as genocidal is to accept that the rapist determines the nationality, ethnicity, race or religion of the child and confirms both the potential effectiveness of rape as a weapon and the justifiability of the shame experienced by and attributed to the victims.

Conclusion

In the above argument, I have tried to spell out the kind of ethical theorizing which I consider will make the most fruitful contribution to a feminist international ethics, both in general and by indicating specific differences it may make to particular instances of ethical deliberation. At the level of ethical theory, the most profound difference introduced by my version of feminist ethics is the decisive shift away from the idea that ethical critique depends on some account of ethical necessity, whether understood foundationally or teleologically. This is not to say, however, that ethical judgment and action are not always both grounded and goal-directed. The point emerging from the critical engagement with care ethics of the work of scholars such as Robinson and Urban Walker is that those grounds and goals are inherently contingent and inevitably political. Ethics is always about both the world we inhabit and the world we want to construct. But that 'we' in any given instance does not emerge outside of the highly complex structures, institutions and practices which make a 'we', its viability and potential for inclusiveness, possible. Feminist ethicists are explicit about the political agenda inherent in their ethical judgments and more broadly about the politically contestable nature of what a 'feminist' ethical judgment means. For feminists, any ethicist who disclaims the interwoven nature of politics and ethics is misunderstanding both the world as it is, and as it might be, and risking the possibility of concrete change through reliance on idealized assumptions about the ground and goals of normative judgment and action. What this feminist ethical realism implies is that the focus of ethical theory and of normative judgment and action must be on how the transformation of existing actuality can be concretely accomplished and not remain a matter of wishful thinking. The nature of that transformation is an ongoing subject of political debate within feminism, but nevertheless it is clear that any feminist international ethics will be focused primarily on pointing out how gendered relations of power are supported by existing norms, practices and institutions in international ethical life and on looking for ways of chipping away at those supports, which may sometimes be obvious and intentional manifestations of patriarchy, and sometimes much more subtle, unintended effects of assumptions about universal humanity or justice.

Contested globalization: the changing context and normative challenges

RICHARD HIGGOTT

Introduction

Even leading globalizers—that is, proponents of the continued liberalization of the global economic order occupying positions of influence in either the public or private domain—now concede that in its failure to deliver a more just global economic order, globalization may hold within it the seeds of its own demise. As James Wolfenson, President of the World Bank, noted in an address to the Board of Governors of the Bank in October 1998, '… [i]f we do not have greater equity and social justice, there will be no political stability and without political stability no amount of money put together in financial packages will give us financial stability'. An economic system widely viewed as unjust, as Ethan Kapstein recently argued, will not long endure. These views, of course, are not new. Adam Smith himself acknowledged in *Wealth of Nations* that no society could survive or flourish if great numbers lived in poverty.[1]

If globalization in some instances exacerbates, and in other instances gives rise to, new forms of injustice, then the meaning and scope of justice is no longer self-evident. Nor indeed are the means by which it is to be achieved. We are thus forced to consider again the nature of justice. But it must be a conception of justice that relinquishes the Westphalian co-ordinates. If the territorial boundaries of politics are coming unbundled, to use Ruggie's evocative phrase,[2] then it is inevitable that our conceptual images of politics will become similarly unbundled.

Conventional accounts of justice have failed to address the changing nature of the social bond. Rather they have supposed the presence of a stable political society, community or state as the site where justice can be instituted or realized. Indeed, it is often assumed that a stable political order is a condition of justice and justice requires a clear site of authority and a clearly demarcated society. In short, conventional accounts of justice have tended to assume a Westphalian cartography of clear lines and stable identities; they have assumed a settled, stable social bond as a necessary condition of justice. In so doing conventional theories of justice— essentially liberal individualist theory (and indeed liberal democratic theory more generally)—have to date limited our ability to think about political action beyond the territorial state.

---

[1] Ethan Kapstein, 'Winners and Loses in the Global Economy', *International Organization*, 54:2 (2000), pp. 359–84.

[2] John G. Ruggie, 'Territoriality and Beyond: Problematizing Modernity in International Relations', *International Organization*, 47:1 (1993), pp. 139–74.

But what if a stable bond should no longer exist?[3] If under conditions of globalization the very fabric of the social bond is constantly being rewoven, then can these givens of justice still pertain? Do the forces and pressures of modernity and globalization, as time and space compress, render the idea of a stable social bond improbable and, if so, how are we to think about justice? What happens to justice when social, economic and political conditions destabilize the social bond? When the social bond is undergoing change or modification as a consequence of globalizing pressures, how can justice be conceptualized, let alone realized? Can there be justice in a world where that bond is constantly being disrupted, renegotiated and transformed by globalization? What are the distributive responsibilities, if any, of states under conditions of globalization? What should be the role, again if any, of the international institutions in influencing the redistribution of wealth and resources on a global scale?

These are serious normative questions with which the modern political philosopher—with few exceptions—has yet to engage in a global, as opposed to bounded sovereign, context.[4] They are thus not questions to which this article, authored by someone untrained in political philosophy, can make a major contribution. But we can take another tack, one located more in contemporary political practice, that can offer some insight into the prospects for greater global justice. We can do so by arguing that these questions, by default and in the absence of settled ethical positions, are also 'governance questions'. By starting with governance, rather than first principles grounded in ethical philosophy, we may be proceeding in the reverse order of logical procedure. But, in the absence of institutions of governance capable of addressing these questions, justice (no matter how loosely defined) is unlikely to prevail.

In short, we lack a basic structure at the global level that can make provision for some kind of elemental distributive justice. In this context, therefore, the general aim of this article is to ask a series of questions about the nature of contemporary global governance that assumes a need for greater distributive justice at the global level for the world's poor, but without elaborating the details of what that greater justice (other than advances in poverty alleviation) might look like. The article will examine the current policy debate on global governance issues to see what change, if any, is in train and what impact any such change is likely to have on advancement in the direction of greater global justice. In this regard the article offers a narrative account of some recent changes in the agenda of global governance. In addition, the article tries to capture the flavour of change in intellectual thinking about these issues. Specifically, it argues that we are seeing a 'mood swing' in both the theory and the practice of international political economy, indeed international relations in general, at the dawn of a new century.

The outcome of this mood swing is a greater concentration in the international policy community on the 'governance' or 'management' of globalization than was

---

[3] This supposition is discussed in Richard Devetak and Richard Higgott, 'Justice Unbound? Globalization, States and the Transformation of the Social Bond', *International Affairs*, 75:3 (1999), pp. 483–98.

[4] For some exceptions see Andrew Linklater, 'The Evolving Spheres of International Justice', Charles Beitz, 'Social and Cosmopolitan Liberalism' and Henry Shue, 'Global Environment and International Inequality', all three of which appeared in a special 75th anniversary edition of *International Affairs*, 75:3 (1999).

apparent in the more fundamentalist free-market days of the last two decades of the twentieth century. But it is the specific argument of the article that there is a difference between governance and politics. The principal limitation of the global governance agenda at the beginning of the twenty-first century is shown to be the underdeveloped nature, if indeed not suppressed nature, of its understanding of the salience of politics. Politics, in the context of the emerging global conversation about governance, needs to be understood as not only the pursuit of effective and efficient government, but also as a normative, indeed explicitly ethical, approach to the advancement of a more just agenda of global economic management.

In the 1980s and 1990s free market liberalism (what Ulrich Beck calls 'globalism'[5]), as practice and process, was largely left to private sector corporate actors. The scholarly agenda on globalism was almost exclusively set by the economist. But following a series of striking 'trigger' events in the late 1990s—notably the financial volatility that beset the global economy in general and the states of East Asia, Latin America and Russia in particular—a new view is emerging. For its advocates and detractors alike, globalization as the grand narrative of the contemporary age (which I take to include not only the ideology of globalism, but also an understanding of the phenomenon of shrinking economic and political space) is now too important to be left to the private sector and the economist. More polemically, globalization cannot simply be driven by the neoliberal economic agenda. This is not merely the (often long-held) view of politically marginal analysts residing in departments of international relations, political science, sociology and cultural studies. It is now recognized across the political spectrum, and indeed within the mainstream economic discourse, that globalization has to be *politically* legitimized, democratized and socialized if the gains of the *economic* liberalization process are not to be lost to its major beneficiaries.[6]

There are a range of ways to explain this changing climate of opinion in the domain of both practitioner and analyst. They are discussed in the first section. But the central aim of the article is to ask where this mood swing is taking us. Specifically, where does the relationship between globalization and governance (this time defined as a more ethical politics) head over the next decade? The argument presented here is that it must transgress the divide between the simple profit-maximizing approaches of the 'real world' of corporate capitalism that dominated the policy world in the late twentieth century and the more reflective, but largely ignored, normative interest that prevailed in the academy. The time for a serious marriage of normative and applied policy work in international political economy (indeed international relations in general) is at hand.

In specific terms the interests of the theorist and practitioner of the market must meet seriously the interests of the normative theorist of international politics in a manner that has not occurred since the heyday of Keynesianism. If we take the signals of growing resistance to globalization of the late 1990s to be salient, markets must start to deliver what citizens want or continue on a fraught road to increasing delegitimation and contest. In the past, interest in the question of legitimation has

[5] Ulrich Beck, *Was ist Globalisierung?* (Frankfurt: Suhrkamp, 1997).
[6] See for example, Daniel Rodrik, *Has Globalization Gone Too Far?* (Washington, DC: Institute for International Economics), and Paul Krugman, *The Return of Depression Economics* (London: The Allen Lane Press, 1999).

been largely the domain of the normative political theorist of the bounded sovereign state. This bifurcation cannot be sustained under conditions of globalization. With no utopian teleology implied, it is perhaps time to start thinking about how we conceptualize a 'global polity', or at least an international system with 'polity-like' characteristics.[7]

If the liberalization of the international economy is to continue, or indeed not be rolled back, then metaphorically, Hayek will have to concede more ground to Polanyi and Keynes than practitioners, indeed scholars too, would have imagined just a few years before the end of the twentieth century. That this must happen is less to do with any substantial ideological rejection of the market rather than a re-recognition by some, and an initial learning by many, that markets are social constructs that need to be governed. But, and this is the key point, governed in a way that goes beyond the simple understanding of governance as the effective and efficient management of the modern state. Global governance must find a way to take account of the need to legitimize and democratize those policy processes that occur beyond the boundaries of the state.

The article unfolds in three stages. In Part 1 the characteristics of the 'mood swing'—from the Washington Consensus to the Post Washington Consensus—are outlined. This change in mood is predicated on a narrow definition of globalization as the process of *economic liberalization* and the emergence of an agenda for global governance as a response to this process. Globalization is, of course, more complex than simply economic liberalization plus global governance and the article does not suggest that the Post Washington Consensus and a global governance agenda are synonymous. Global governance has a much wider intellectual history and policy agenda than merely the management of the international economy at the close of the twentieth century. Throughout the twentieth century, notwithstanding failed attempts to build institutions like the League of Nations, the growth of multilateral and regional institutions reflects what one scholar has called an evolving 'constitutionalization' of world order.[8]

But enveloped in the language of a Post Washington Consensus, the new global governance agenda is clearly a response to the backlash that followed the financial crises that has hit the emerging markets of Asia, Latin America and Russia since 1997 and other subsequent forms of resistance to globalization. The Consensus–post-Consensus metaphor attempts to capture the flavour of these changes. In the former market-dominated consensus, no conception of governance was present. In the latter, it is argued that a limited understanding of governance is emerging. In Part 2 of the article the limits of the Post Washington Consensus to questions of governance are subjected to scrutiny. The essence of the critique is that the Post Washington Consensus represents an exercise in 'governance without politics'. Prescriptively, this will not do. We need to bring politics back in to the management of the global economic order, thus Part 3 of the article is a plea for an invigorated normative scholarship of international political economy.

[7] This theme is developed in Morten Ougaard, 'Approaching the Global Polity', Working Paper 42/99, (University of Warwick: Centre for the Study of Globalization and Regionalization, October 1999) and in more detail in a collection of forthcoming essays in Morten Ougaard and Richard Higgott (eds.) *The Global Polity* (London: Routledge, 2001).
[8] See Daniel Elazar, *Constitutionalizing Globalization* (Boston, MA: Rowman & Littlefield, 1998).

1. In the mood: the end of the Washington Consensus and the emergence of 'contested globalization'

The resistance to globalization that has developed over the last 4–5 years can be identified in a number of different ways and in a large body of secondary committed quasi-academic and analytical literature that identifies a range of limitations in, and objections to, globalization as a neoliberal project.[9] Influential in the development of the mood of resistance to globalization has been a range of events in the world of international political economy and international politics as practiced in the closing stages of the twentieth century. Four events are illustrative of this mood swing.

Firstly, the failure of the OECD to establish the Multilateral Agreement on Investment. Rightly or wrongly (and the analysis is contested) this was thought to represent a signal victory for NGO mobilization of opposition to a major neoliberal international initiative *via* the use of the modern technology of the internet.[10] The second factor was the financial crises that hit Asia in the second half of 1997 and then spread to Latin America and Russia in early 1998. The Asian crises were seen initially in some parts of the international policy community, as former IMF President Michel Camdessus described it, as 'a window of opportunity' to consolidate the Anglo-American model of economic development at the expense of the Asian developmental state. However, the longer term reading is one that identifies these crises as significant sources of backlash against the unfettered nature of the globalization project and the spur to a rethink about the role of regulation, re-regulation and the capacity of the state in the political economy of globalization.[11]

The third event was what is now commonly known as 'the battle of Seattle' that aborted attempts at the third Ministerial Meeting of the WTO to set in train the new multilateral (Millennium) round of trade negotiations. Again the significance that one attaches to this event is contested in a range of quarters. For some, such as Mary Kaldor, it was a victory for political globalization from below.[12] In more restrained fashion, the significance of Seattle was that it brought together that range of non-state actors who, in their many different ways over the previous decade, had

[9]   Good secondary discussions of debates about the emergence of globalization and the different ways of analysing this phenomenon are now numerous and need not be reviewed here. The literature is now too voluminous to review here. Perhaps the most comprehensive text on the subject is David Held et al., *Global Transformation* (Cambridge: Polity Press, 1998). But the best single authored text is without doubt Jan Aart Scholte, *Globalization: A Critical Introduction* (Basingstoke, UK: Macmillan, 2000). For a flavour of the *range* of literature on offer see the essays in Richard Higgott and Tony Payne (eds.), *The New Political Economy of Globalization*, 2 vols. (Aldershot, UK: Edward Elgar, 2000). For a flavour of the critiques, see Gerry Mander and Edward Goldsmith (eds.), *The Case Against the Global Economy: And For A Turn Toward the Local* (San Francisco: Sierra Club Books, 1997); Richard Falk, *Predatory Globalization* (Cambridge: Polity Press, 1999); and the essays in Don Kalb et al., *The Ends of Globalization* (Oxford: Rowman and Littlefield, 2000).

[10] See Stephen J. Kobrin, The MAI and the Clash of Globalizations', *Foreign Policy*, 112 (Fall, 1998); Elizabeth Smythe, 'State Authority and Investment Security: Non State Actors and the Negotiation of a Multilateral Agreement on Investment at the OECD', in Richard Higgott, Geoffrey Underhill and Andreas Bieler (eds.), *Non State Actors and Authority in the Global System* (London, Routledge, 2000).

[11] See Martin Rhodes and Richard Higgott, 'Asian Crises and the Myth of Capitalist Convergence', *The Pacific Review*, 13:1 (2000), pp. 1–19.

[12] See Mary Kaldor's 'Civilising Globalization: The Implications of the Battle of Seattle', *Millennium: A Journal of International Studies*, 29:4 (2000), pp. 105–14.

commenced the discussion about what the nature of an opposition to the most rapacious aspects of globalization might look like. In contrast to the activities of NGOs throughout the 1990s,[13] the debate at Seattle was not just issue-specific (gender, environment, social exclusion, development) but also more generally it reflected on the wider question of the very nature of the kind of global polity that might/ should/could emerge out of the mitigation or reform of globalization.

It behoves us, however, to recognize the more cautionary tale told by other observers of Seattle. Jan Aart Scholte offers several sobering observations on Seattle. While noting that events did in fact reflect one of the most sophisticated and in-depth reflections of civil society opposition to globalization to date, Scholte also notes that '… halting a new round of trade liberalization is not the same thing as building a better world'.[14] The policy change that will emanate from Seattle is yet to be determined and until we can say otherwise, its impact should not be over-estimated. In addition it would be a mistake to overestimate, 'romanticise' says Scholte, either the innately progressive nature of, or functionality of, civil society as an agent of policy change. The most appropriate way to see Seattle—and the regular demonstrations at the joint annual spring meetings of the World Bank and the IMF, the failure of the MAI and the overflow from the financial crises of the late twentieth century—is as a series of trigger points on the road to a changing international intellectual and policy agenda, the detailed parameters of which are yet to be fully discerned.

The fourth factor in bringing a change in mood to wider attitudes towards globalization is less an event and more the development of a perception that global liberalization brings with it increased inequality. There is much empirical data (not always consistent it should be added) on this issue. The best sources do, however, identify a rapid post-World War II growth in global income gaps. The income gap ratio between the 20 per cent of the world's population in the richest countries and the 20 per cent in the poorest grew from 30:1 in 1960 to 60:1 in 1990 and 74:1 in 1995. The poorest 20 per cent of the world's population account for only 1 per cent of total global GDP and 40 per cent of the world's population live in absolute poverty.[15] Whether the relationship between increased inequality and globalization is causally related or merely a correlation is theoretically very important, and there is emerging evidence to suggest that there is indeed a causal relationship.[16] But the correlation alone is sufficient to make it a political issue of the utmost importance. It is the identification of the correlation that causes the dispossessed to believe that globalization is a source of their plight.

While the increase in the relative gap at the top and bottom of the scales is hard to dispute, other data can provide evidence of increased aggregate welfare generation overall from which more people in absolute terms have benefited from globalization. The strongest economic point that can be made is that across the

---

[13] For a discussion of the role of NGOs as sites of opposition to the globalization discourse, see Cecilia Lynch, 'Social Movements and the Problem of Globalization', *Alternatives,* 23:2 (1998), pp. 149–73.

[14] Jan Aart Scholte, 'Cautionary Reflections on Seattle', *Millennium: A Journal of International Studies,* 29:4 (2000) p. 116.

[15] Data from United Nations, *Human Development Report* (New York, Oxford University Press, 1999). For a good discussion of the complexity of the relationship between inequality and globalization, see the essays in Andrew Hurrell and Ngaire Woods (eds.), *Inequality, Globalization and World Politics* (Oxford: Oxford University Press, 1999).

[16] The literature is reviewed in Kapstein, 'Winners and Losers in the Global Economy', pp. 359–84.

twentieth century a 'massive divergence in income levels and growth performance' has been conclusively demonstrated.[17] As important as these data are, they are invariably silent on the politics of these numbers.

The important factor in the politics of globalization is the degree to which it is perceived to exacerbate inequality and the degree to which the existing institutions are thought by those who claim to speak for the dispossessed, to underwrite the *status quo* rather than work for its eradication. The point for this essay is that correlation between globalization and poverty is sufficient for the relationship to generate the kinds of combative politics that we have witnessed over the last few years as the gap between beneficiaries and victims of globalization has become more apparent. Any emerging normative agenda must address it full on. It is in this empirical and changing intellectual context that the central elements of the international economic institutional architecture that developed in the post-World War II era have been found to be increasingly wanting at the end of the twentieth century.

The existing architecture is insufficiently flexible to respond to what we might call the 'new politics of contested globalization'. It has led to the end of that orthodoxy (the Washington Consensus) that dominated the 1980s and 1990s and the emergence of a Post Washington Consensus.[18] The principal element of this change is the development of an understanding, amongst leading policymakers of the international institutional policy community, of the importance of the need for a stronger 'governance dimension' to the international economic order. 'Governance' here, as the next section will demonstrate, is to be distinguished from 'politics'. At the present historical juncture, global economic managers are attempting to develop a global governance system, what others such as Stephen Gill might call a 'constitution for global capitalism',[19] but absent some of the more basic polity-like characteristics that accompany governance systems within the jurisdictions of sovereign states. I characterize this process as the emergence of a 'Post Washington Consensus'.[20]

The basic argument is not that these events reflect a fundamentally new aspect of the process of 'global politicization'. Rather, they should be seen as the minimum

---

[17] See the excellent discussion of the available data on these issues in Nicholas Crafts 'Globalization and Growth in the Twentieth Century', IMF Working Paper 00/44, Washington DC.

[18] This is not the place to develop a full exposition of the Washington Consensus save only to note that the term was originated by John Williamson to reflect shared opinion on the key parameters of global economic managament, and specifically policy prescriptions for financial adjustment in developing countries, within the Washington international financial community that included not only the US administration, but also the major international financial institutions and 'think-tanks' such as the IIE. To be fair to Williamson, he merely called it 'the Washington Consensus.' He cannot be held accountable for the expansion of its use and the pejorative connotations that have been attached to the epithet by other observers of these processes. See John Williamson, 'What Washington Means by Policy Reform', in John Williamson (ed.), *Latin American Adjustment, How Much Has Changed?* (Washington: Institute for International Economics, 1990). For discussions see Paul Krugman, 'Dutch Tulips and Emerging Markets', *Foreign Affairs*, 14:1 (1995), pp. 28–9; Robin Broad and John Cavanagh, 'The Death of the Washington Consensus', *World Policy Journal*, 16:3 (1999), pp. 79–88 and Moises Naim 'Washington Consensus or Washington Confusion, *Foreign Policy*, 118 (Spring 2000), p. 103.

[19] Stephen Gill, '*The Constitution of Global Capitalism*'. Paper presented to the British International Studies Association, Manchester, 20–22 December, 1999.

[20] For a detailed elaboration of this argument see Richard Higgott, 'Economic Globalization and Global Governance: The Emergence of a Post Washington Consensus', in Volker Rittberger and Albrecht Schnabel (eds.), *The UN Global Governance System in the Twenty-First Century* (Tokyo: UNU Press, 2001 forthcoming).

response from the international policy community to manage the increasing hostility towards the liberalization and deregulation processes that have been at the heart of globalization. But they may well consolidate a growing trend towards the emergence of rudimentary 'polity-like' qualities to the international system. The Post Washington Consensus is discussed in the next section. Its limitations are addressed in Part 3.

2. The Post Washington Consensus: global governance without politics

The global market place of the 1980s and the first 6–7 years of the 1990s was an 'ethics-free zone'. This was the case whether one was observing practice (both public and private sector) in the international political economy or whether one was reading the scholar on the global economy. In the domain of practice, processes of trade liberalization, financial deregulation and asset privatization were increasing the tempo of the globalization of the world economy. Free enterprise and the market culture had triumphed. Proof of this was to be found, as the economists would say, 'in the numbers'. These numbers reflected massive increases in aggregate welfare overall and not only in the developed world, but also in the rapid processes of industrialization that were taking place in the newly industrializing economies, especially those to be found in East Asia.

In the academic political economy (as opposed to the economics discipline) scholars interested in the global economy were either engaged in refining rational choice method (if they worked, or aspired to work, in the US) or in 'clubby' debates over which mode of structuralist analysis best described the dominant structures of US hegemony.[21] Few of those engaged in either the theory or practice of the inter-national political economy in this period seemed to be much interested in the relationship between the stuff of the (international) political theorist; that is, norma-tive questions of justice and fairness. The goddess of growth was on the throne and for all who agreed to worship her such normative issues were simply not relevant. In the academic domain of the economist, liberal economic theory had triumphed; again as in the policy world, the proof of the pudding was in the numbers. The rest of the social sciences were merely the indulgence of rich universities in developed countries. The Cold War was over and the North–South Divide that had led to demands for a New International Economic Order in the 1970s (if the noise that was emanating from the marginalized South, as opposed to the booming South, was any guide) had become a distant memory.

But the end of one century and the beginning of a new one, following the events identified above, has seen something of a transition in this pattern of practice and thinking. The ethical dimension has found its way into the theory of globalization.[22] In the policy world too, the Post Washington Consensus is not merely driven by the

---

[21] I have developed this point in Richard Higgott, 'Taming Economics, Emboldening International Relations: A New Normative Agenda for International Political Economy', in Stephanie Lawson (ed.), *Ten Years After the Wall: A New Agenda for International Relations* (Cambridge: Polity, 2001).

[22] Of all the *fin de siècle* literature, amongst the most influential is likely to be Nobel prize winner Amartya Sen's attempts to humanize economics in *Development as Freedom* (New York: Basic Books, 1999).

desire to contain the incipient revolt against globalization. There is also in some quarters a genuine recognition of the importance of tackling ethical questions of justice, fairness and inequality.[23] It is in this dual context, and following from the emergence of the new politics of contested globalization, that we can identify the key aspects of the new governance. At this stage there is a disjunction between the new politics and the new governance. The new governance clearly lags the new politics. There are at least three reasons for this.

Firstly, the flagging of the importance of 'governance issues' by the international financial institutions emerged in part to help them dig themselves out of the intellectual hole into which their adherence to unfettered free market ideals throughout the 1980s and first half of the 1990s had forced them. The financial crises since 1997 have provided a way out of the 'economism' that dominated policymaking throughout the 1980s and 1990s.[24]

Secondly, if governance is about the conditions for ordered rule and collective action it differs little from *government* in terms of output. The crucial differences become those of process, structure, style and actors. In the recent public policy literature, governance refers to '... the development of governing styles in which boundaries between and within public and private sectors have become blurred'.[25] But this definition neither notes the way globalization has blurred the domestic–international divide as material fact, nor the longer term historical development of systems of emerging international norms and regimes (both public and private) that represent the elements of a framework of 'governance without government' under globalization.[26]

Thirdly, given the impact of globalization, 'governance' becomes an essential term for understanding not only transnational processes that require institutional responses but also for identifying those non traditional actors (third and voluntary sector non-state actors such as NGOs, GSMs and networks) that participate in the governance of a globalized economy beyond the traditional confines of government. Thus the concept of 'global governance' becomes a mobilizing agent for broadening and deepening policy understanding beyond the traditional international activities of states.

It is in this evolving theoretical context that the initial Washington Consensus (WC) which governed international economic thinking throughout the 1980s and 1990s became a moving feast as the major financial institutions, at odds with each other over the appropriate policy responses to the 1997 financial crises, sought a new approach—paradigm even. The original well known buzzwords of the WC were liberalization, deregulation and privatization. To these the Post Washington Consensus (PWC) has added civil society, social capital, capacity building,

---

[23] Of the policy literature under written by a recognition of the importance of the normative agenda, see Michael Edwards, *Future Positive: International Cooperation in the 21st Century* (London: Earthscan, 1999).

[24] For an elaboration, see Higgott, 'Taming Economics, Emboldening International Relations'.

[25] Gerry Stoker, 'Governance as Theory: Five Propositions', *International Social Science Journal*, no. 155 (1999), p. 17.

[26] See the pioneering essays in Ernst Otto Czempiel and James N. Rosenau, *Governance without Government: Order and Change in World Politics* (Cambridge: Cambridge University Press, 1992). See also Volker Rittberger (ed.), *Regime Theory and International Relations* (Oxford: Clarendon Press, 1993).

governance, transparency, a new international economic architecture, institution building and safety nets.

These themes had, of course, been emerging in the World Bank for some time[27] where influential figures such as then chief economist Joseph Stiglitz, and President James Wolfensen, helped to move the Bank beyond the initial consensus.[28] From the time of the Asian crisis even the WTO has begun to take these issues more seriously.[29] The IMF too has responded, albeit somewhat more slowly. Add to the PWC the UNDP initiatives on 'governance' and 'global public goods'[30] and the UN's 'Global Compact'[31] with the private sector to promote human rights and raise labour and environmental standards, and we had, as we entered the new millennium, a new rhetoric of globalism to accompany globalization as process.

Amongst these activities, potentially most interesting for this article is the attempt by the UN to develop the Global Compact. It may become of significance throughout the first decade of the twenty-first century. While it fits firmly within a neoliberal discourse for developing an interaction between the international institutions and the corporate world, it is an important recognition of the need to globalize some important common values. In this regard, it has strong constructivist overtones too. This should perhaps not be a surprise when one considers its intellectual driving force. That the 'global compact' reads like an attempt to globalize embedded liberalism is perhaps to be expected. The intellectual architect of this agenda was John Ruggie in his capacity as Chief Adviser for Strategic Planning to UN Secretary General Kofi Annan (1997–2000). Not all judgements are positive. For some in the NGO world it 'casts serious doubt on the UN's willingness to challenge the dominance of the institutions wholly owned and operated by the G7'.[32]

The PWC's understanding of governance is underwritten by: (1) a managerialist ideology of effectiveness and efficiency of governmental institutions and (2) an understanding of civil society based on the mobilization and management of social capital rather than one of representation and accountability. In the context of the PWC, civil society is not, in contrast to Robert Cox's recent reformulation, a site of

---

[27] See Cynthia Hewit de Alcantara, 'Uses and Abuses of the Concept of Governance', *International Social Science Journal*, 155 (1998), pp. 105–113.

[28] See Joseph Stiglitz, Towards a New Paradigm for Development: Strategies, Policies and Processes', *The 1998 Prebisch Lecture*, Geneva, UNCTAD, 19 October, 1998. To be found at http://www.worldbank.org/html/etme/jssp101998.htm and 'Towards a New Paradigm for Development'; see also his 'More Instruments and Broader Goals: Moving Towards a Post-Washington Consensus', *The 1998 WIDER Lecture*; Helsinki, 7 January, 1999.

[29] See Jan Aart Scholte, Robert O'Brien and Marc Williams, 'The WTO and Civil Society', Working Paper no. 14 (Warwick University: ESRC Centre for the Study of Globalization and Regionalization, July 1998).

[30] See UNDP, *Governance for Sustainability and Growth* (New York, July 1997) and Inge Kaul, Isabelle Grunberg and Marc A. Stern (eds.), *Global Public Goods: International Cooperation in the 21st Century* (New York: Oxford University Press for the UNDP, 1999).

[31] *The Global Compact: Shared Values for the Global Market* (New York: UN, n.d.); *Business Leaders Advocate Stronger UN and Take Up Secretary General's Global Compact* (New York, UN Press Release, 5 July, 1999) and *The Global Compact: Shared Values for a Global Market* (New York: UN Department of Public Information, DP1/2075, October 1999); Mark Zacher, *The United Nations and Global Commerce* (New York: UN Department of Public Information, 1999). See also John Ruggie and Georg Kell, 'Global Markets and Social Legitimacy: The Case of the "Global Compact"', paper presented to an International Workshop entitled *Governing the Public Domain: Redrawing the Line Between the State and the Market* (York University, Ontario: Robarts Centre for Canadian Studies, November 1999).

[32] Nicola Bullard, 'The United Nations Shows its True Colours', *Focus on Trade* (Bangkok: Focus on the Global South), http//:www.focusweb.org

resistance.[33] But the PWC understanding of governance does represent a departure from the narrowly economistic and technocratic decision-making models of the WC. The PWC does not reject the WC emphasis on open markets. Rather, the PWC is an attempt to institutionally embed, and even maybe, as the UNDP would have it, 'humanize', globalization and the earlier technocratic, prescriptive elements of the WC.[34]

Given that the PWC holds a sanitized view of the sociopolitical dimensions of the development process, why is it an important break with the past? Because it is at least a recognition that governance, if not necessarily politics, matters. This is not historically trivial. Such a recognition was noticeably absent from the economistic analyses of the impact of globalization over the last two decades. Along with the works of a few economists (Stiglitz, Rodrik and Krugman) it demonstrates a growing sensitivity to some of the political complexities inherent in the reform processes. As yet, it has to be said, the PWC and the economic literature show little understanding of *politics*. But conceptual understandings of power and interest, while underdeveloped in the PWC, must offer a starting point for thinking about justice under conditions of globalization that did not exist until the end of the twentieth century.

Theorists are still groping for a universally acceptable definition of 'social and economic justice'. But given the strong perception that globalization, in its unadulterated form, results in unequal treatment for some states and, more importantly, exacerbates poverty for the weakest members of international society, then globalization is seen to deny justice. In the current debate, poverty alleviation seems to have a stronger claim than equality in prevailing definitions of justice.[35] Thus the important normative question is: what is the relevant community or society to which 'social justice' pertains and in what domains should the question of justice be addressed?

This question has traditionally been understood in the contexts of the values that actors attach to their behaviour within market structures. But markets are not the only sites of action. The domain issue is at the core of 'the global governance' question. And, as is now widely understood in the international relations literature, governments are no longer the only actors. NGOs, global social movements, networks, epistemic communities and international organizations all play significant roles in the wider global governance agenda; albeit that, in both in theory and practice, the political process invariably trails the integrated and globalizing tendencies in the world economy. As a consequence, the prevailing anarchical order of the state system is inadequate to the task of managing most of the agenda of globalization. While this may be well understood, the prospects of heterarchy remain more aspirational than real at this time.

Since global governance is an imprecise term, one normative question for students of international relations over the next few years must be to determine how much

[33] Robert Cox, 'Civil Society at the Turn of the Millennium: Prospects for an Alternative World Order', *Review of International Studies*, 25:1 (1999), pp. 3–28.
[34] *Globalization with a Human Face: The UN Human Development Report* (New York: Oxford University Press for the UNDP).
[35] See the excellent paper by Ngaire Woods, 'Order, Globalization and Inequality', in Hurrell and Woods (eds.), *Inequality, Globalization and World Politics*.

authority we should invest in the concept, given the wide-ranging way in which it is used. Currently, understandings of global governance can range along a continuum from basic, informal processes, to enhanced transparency in interstate policy coordination, through to the somewhat grander, although still essentially liberal, visions of a rejuvenated system exhibited in the Commission on Global Governance's *Our Global Neighbourhood.*[36]

But if we accept the argument that the transnationalization of market forces is exacerbating inequality, then the avenue for mitigating this gap lies with a reformist agenda for the global rules and norms that underwrite the current international institutional architecture. Currently driven by 'northern' agendas, it is those states most disadvantaged by globalization that are 'rule-takers'.[37] As a result such rules lack legitimacy even where states actually possess the necessary governmental effectiveness to enforce them should they so wish. Either way, these processes have negative implications for a consensual evolution of global governmental norms.

A starting assumption for the development of a PWC-style global governance is that it, and the continuance of a state system, are not inimical. But to recognize that state power will not go away is not to cling to some Westphalian legend. Rather it is to recognize that states, and interstate relations, remain the principal sites of politics. As a result, the research agenda on global governance is complex. It may therefore help to identify two interconnected understandings of it that are in one way or another coming together in the era of the Post Washington Consensus.

(1) *Global governance as the enhancement of effectiveness and efficiency in the delivery of public goods.* This is a fashionable policy concept, especially in the international institutions which see their role as consolidating or institutionalizing the 'gains' made by the processes of global economic integration. But it fails to recognize that the successful internationalization of governance can, at the same time, exacerbate the 'democratic deficit.' This approach forgets that states are not only problem-solvers, their policy elites are also strategic actors with interests of, and for, themselves. Thus much collective action problem-solving in international relations is couched in terms of effective governance. It is rarely posed as a question of justice, responsible or accountable government, or democracy. These latter questions are the stuff of political theory; but it is the political theory of the bounded sovereign state. Thus we need to think beyond these confines. It is central to the understanding of the relationship between the Post Washington Consensus and global governance, but it also leads to a wider, second understanding of the concept of global governance.

(2) *Global governance as a normative enterprise to enhance democracy.* Paradoxically, the language of democracy and justice takes on a more important rhetorical role in a global context at the same time as globalization attenuates the hold of democratic communities within the confines of the territorial state. Indeed, as the role of the nation state as a vehicle for democratic engagement becomes more problematic, the clamour for democratic engagement at the global level becomes stronger. But these are not stable processes. Understanding of, and attention to, the importance of normative questions of governance and state practice as exercises in accountability and democratic enhancement must catch up with our understanding

---

[36] London: Oxford University Press, 1995.
[37] Hurrell and Woods, *Inequality, Globalization and World Politics*, Introduction.

of governance as exercises in effectiveness and efficiency. The debate is largely divided between theorists and practitioners.

The current theoretical debate over the prospects for transnational democracy mirrors many of the wider debates in contemporary political theory over the nature of democracy in the twenty-first century.[38] Unsurprisingly, the debate within the policy community is narrowly focused. There is still a reluctance in the economic policy community to recognize the manner in which markets are sociopolitical constructions whose functioning (and legitimacy) depends on their possessing wide and deep support within civil society. But one key approach of late has been an increasing effort by the international institutions to identify those agents who can advance the cause of greater accountability and transparency in the management of the international institutions while not undermining the overriding goal of effectiveness and efficiency. In this context the greater incorporation of selected non-state actors into the deliberative process of these organizations is a principal goal of contemporary policy reform. While the incorporation of civil society actors into the policy process is seen as a necessary condition for the legitimation of the liberalizing agenda, most international institutions still see non-state actors as both boon and bane.[39]

The 'post-politics' of the Post Washington Consensus

These two interpretations of global governance (it is hard to call them definitions) stand respectively in relationship to the Washington and Post Washington Consensuses. The initial Consensus was an attempt by an international managerial-*cum*-policy elite to create a set of global *economic* norms to be accepted by entrants to the global economy under the guidance of the existing international institutions. Can the Post Washington Consensus be seen as an attempt to induce support for a new set of *sociopolitical* norms to legitimate globalization by mitigating its worst excesses? If captured by the existing international institutions (claiming that they are the only available sites of global governance) then, reflecting the ideology of globalism in its neoliberal guise, definition (1): effectiveness and efficiency, may well become the dominant mode of understanding global governance. Critical analysts can be forgiven, therefore, for not seeing the growing interest in global governance as an automatically 'progressive' force.

Democratic accountability, definition (2), is currently *at best* a secondary component. Globalization might have rapidly generated a set of technological and economic connections; but it has yet to generate an equivalent set of shared values and sense of community, even amongst those agents actively involved in discussions about greater global participation. Indeed, much of the policy prescriptive work on governance currently being undertaken in or around the international institutions treats governance as a neutral concept in which rational decision-making and efficiency in outcomes, not democratic participation, is privileged.

[38] See the excellent review by Antony McGrew, 'From Global Governance to Good Governance: Theories and Prospects of Democratising the Global Polity', in Ougaard and Higgott, *The Global Polity*, forthcoming.

[39] See P. J. Simmons, 'Learning to Live with NGOS', *Foreign Policy*, 111 (1998).

In this regard, the debate on global governance within the international institutions (UN, World Bank, IMF and WTO) remains firmly within a dominant liberal institutionalist tradition; ethically normative discussions about democracy and justice beyond the borders of the territorial state are still largely technocratic ones about how to enhance transparency and, in limited contexts, accountability. They fail, or in some instances still refuse, to address the assymmetries of power over decision-making that characterize the activities of these organizations. The essence of the liberal institutionalist view remains avowedly state-centric and pluralist and is, not surprisingly, captured nicely by American institutionalist Robert Keohane's definition of global democracy as 'voluntary pluralism under conditions of maximum transparency'.[40]

The liberal institutionalist view is also essentially the reformist view held for the international institutional leaders by senior global decision-makers from US Treasury Secretary Lawrence Summers to UN Secretary-General Kofi Annan. Annan called for better accountability to improve global governance after the abortive MTN Ministerial Meeting in Seattle in November 1999 and Summers called for greater transparency and accountability for the IMF at its Spring 2000 meeting.[41] As previously argued, Annan's Global Compact also approximates the liberal institutionalist genre of thinking, albeit (given its implicit belief that the global corporate sector can be socialized) on the progressivist constructive end of the spectrum.

The preferred term in international policy circles is 'global public policy',[42] not global governance. The aim is to make provision for the collective delivery of global public goods.[43] 'Public policy' has none of the ideological and confrontational baggage present in the notion of 'politics'. Institutional analysis, with its concerns for understanding the mechanisms of collective choice in situations of strategic interaction, is similarly 'de-politicized'. This is not to deny that recent rationalist theorizing of cooperation has not been a major advance on earlier realist understandings.[44] But the problem with rationalist and strategic choice approaches is not what they do, but what they omit. They make little attempt to understand governance as issues of *politics* and *power*. This has implications for the operational capability and intellectual standing of the international institutions.

In essence, the governance agenda as constructed by the international institutions in the Post Washington Consensus era has largely stripped questions of power, domination, resistance and accountability from the debate. To the extent that the international institutions recognize that political resistance is a legitimate part of the governance equation, it is a problem to be solved. It is not seen as a *perpetual* part of the process. In this regard, for many key players, global governance is not about

[40] Robert Keohane, 'International Institutions: Can Interdependence Work? *Foreign Policy* (Spring, 1998), cited in McGrew, 'From Global Governance to Good Governance: Theories and Prospects of Democratising the Global Polity'.

[41] See Kofi Annan, *Renewing the UN* (New York: United Nations, 1999) and Lawrence Summers, *Statement to the International Monetary Fund Financial Committee*, Washington, 16 April 2000.

[42] See Wolfgang H. Reinecke, *Global Public Policy: Governing without Government* (Washington, DC: Brookings, 1998).

[43] See Kaul et al., *Global Public Goods*.

[44] See Robert O. Keohane, *After Hegemony: Collaboration and Discord in the World Economy* (Princeton, NJ: Princeton University Press, 1984); Helen V. Milner, *Interests, Institutions and Information: Domestic Politics and International Relations* (Princeton, NJ: Princeton University Press, 1997).

politics. There are no problems that cannot be 'governed away'. Governance, *pace* definition (1) as effectiveness and efficiency, is 'post-political'. Agendas are set and implementation becomes the name of the game. Notwithstanding the fragmented and dissaggregated nature of political community in a global era, there is no place outside of the rubric of the existing governance structures for non-state political action on global policy issues.

The PWC view of good governance implies the universalization of an understanding of governance based on efficiency and effectiveness, in which democracy is a secondary component. Indeed, much of the prescriptive work on governance currently being undertaken in or around the international institutions treats governance as a neutral concept in which rationality in decision-making and efficiency in outcomes is uppermost. Nowhere is this better illustrated than in the efforts of those around the World Bank and the UNDP to develop public-private partnerships and global public policy networks for the collective provision of public goods.[45] Such work is innovative, certainly by the standards of the international institutions, but it is also limited by the political implications of its 'top down' intellectual origins. Notwithstanding stronger rhetorical efforts to bridge the participatory gap, these recent attempts to develop strategies to advance the collective provision of global public goods still minimize the essence of 'the political' in these processes.

Moreover, this agenda has only a limited notion of public good, largely consistent with a liberal individualist ideology. Any notion of serious redistribution of wealth in the direction of the world's poorest is not considered a public good. Indeed, such support for the world's poor as there is, understood as development aid, is seen by some to be on the brink of collapsing.[46] The global public goods literature, indeed the global governance agenda more generally, does not address this issue. Given the ideological underpinnings of neoliberalism, it is not intellectually, let alone politically, capable of doing so.

Yet as is apparent from activities within the various international institutions— such as the World Bank's 'Global Development Network Initiative (GDNI)[47] and other efforts (and some notable failures to engage civil society in the global policy debates too)—that this blindness to the inevitability of 'politics' cannot long prevail. Civil society in this sense is becoming to global governance what international markets are to economic globalization. But, for a range of reasons, closing the 'participation gap'[48] by incorporating non-state agencies into this process is not without its own problems. Nor does it corrode the importance of sovereign states. With their resources and rule-making capacities, they remain at the base of any strategy to develop the provision of a public goods agenda. This is for at least three reasons.

The first is that, despite their visibility, NGOs and other non-state actors cannot approximate the legitimacy of the national state as the repository of sovereignty and policymaking authority, nor its monopoly over the allegiance of the society(ies) it is

---

[45] See Wolfgang Reinecke and Francis Deng, *Critical Choices: The United Nations, Networks and the Future of Global Governance* (Ottawa: International Development Research Centre, 2000).

[46] See Jean Claude Therien and Carolyn Lloyd, 'Development Assistance on the Brink', *Third World Quarterly*, 21:1 (2000), pp. 21–38.

[47] On the GDN, see the essays in Diane Stone (ed.), *Banking on Knowledge: The World Bank's Global Development Network* (London: Routledge, 2000).

[48] Kaul et al., 'Introduction'.

supposed to represent. Second and related, despite the appeal of expanding the parameters of participation to include these important actors, it is widely recognized that they are often less democratically accountable than the states and inter-state organizations they act to counter and invariably less democratic in their internal organization than their outward participatory activities would suggest.[49] Third, the implementation of resolutions taken in 'global' negotiations, or often by international organizations, remains primarily the function of national states, or at the very least depends on their compliance and complementary activity at the national level for their implementation.

These observations point to significant anomalies in the system. The expansion of participation to non-state actors such as NGOs and GSMs does not solve the problem of the under-representation of developing country states, nor their agendas for greater fairness and redistribution, in the more formalized policy processes. 'Global' governance issues are dominated by the powerful states and alliance constructions and interest representations which feature in the structures of international organizations and groupings such as the G7. Various calls for the expansion of the G7 into the G16, G20 or similar, recognize that in order to be effective, global economic leadership needs diversification, and that collaboration in the provision of public goods depends on an extended participation. There is a widespread recognition that the institutional constructions of key global policy forums are insufficient for the generation of meaningful 'global' collaboration on a range of policy issues. Most importantly, the provision of those public goods identified as crucial to the construction of a fairer global order is complicated by the unequal nature of the negotiation processes and, as seen in Seattle, by the marginalization of developing states within these processes.

As a consequence a case can be made that the PWC is likely to be as challenged in the long run as the WC. It cannot constitute a template for an emerging 'global governance' agenda, nor even an emerging policy agenda. It suffers from the same failings as its predecessor. The PWC is no less universalizing, and attempts to be no less homogenizing, than the WC itself. Global policy debates, in this way, remain reliant on a set of 'generalizable', but essentially Western liberal, principles and policy prescriptions. Even while they offer a more subtle understanding of market dynamics than in the early years of global neoliberalism, these prescriptions still demonstrate a penchant for universalizing notions of a 'one-size-fits-all convergence' on issues of policy reform under conditions of globalization. Such prescriptions may well be resisted in the developing world as but a new form of Western hegemony.[50]

If we accept that states continue to engage in (at least) two-level games,[51] then effectively a conception of governance built on interaction with non-state actors and the development of issue-specific global public policy networks is likely to marginalize the international bargaining role of developing states (through the privileging of civil society and the structures of international organizations). Yet they do this while attempting to enhance the position of states as mediators between

[49] See Leon Gordenker and Thomas G. Weiss, 'NGO Participation in the Global Policy Process', *Third World Quarterly*, 16:3 (1995), pp. 543–55.

[50] For an elaboration on this point see Richard Higgott and Nicola Phillips, 'After Triumphalism: The Limits of Liberalization in Asia and Latin America', *Review of International Studies*, 26:4 (2000).

[51] Robert Putnam, 'Diplomacy and Two Level Games', *International Organisation*, 42:2 (1988), pp. 427–60.

the forces of global change and the societies they are supposed to represent. Thus, and perhaps not surprisingly, for many policy elites in the developing world (representative of their populations or otherwise) attempts to introduce a dialogue with non-state actors represents an alternative to giving them a larger voice in the global policy debates and is therefore something to be resisted.

Thus the international institutions may find themselves on some sort of waste-ground between market economics (in which the state is inactive) and a raging debate about the significance and appropriate functions of state institutions. For example, in the 'good governance' and the social capital–state debates, the World Bank seeks, on the one hand, to plug the 'developmental gaps' and close the 'participation gaps' by engaging civil society. On the other hand, it seeks to dictate what states do and how they do it, as it attempts to both down-play the centrality of the state in global bargaining and offset societal opposition to the state's continued pursuit of neoliberal economic coherence. A similar disjuncture can be seen in attempts by the WTO to secure greater NGO input into the deliberations on the continued reform of the trading system while at the same time fearing the potentially disruptive effect that any such widening of the deliberative process might have on the traditional highly structured nature of trade negotiations.

These fears were realized at Seattle where not only American workers, but Asian and Latin American policy elites were not in accord with their counterparts in the developed world as to what are mutually agreed public goods. To give but one example, the widely held view amongst the economic policy and corporate elites of the developed world that the extension of the remit of the WTO is a public good is not equally shared in the developing world at the end of the twentieth century. Many developing countries do not have the technical ability to keep pace with the current WTO 'Built-in Agenda' from the Uruguay Round, let alone the desire and political conviction to take on board a range of new agenda items (in the areas of investment, competition policy, labour standards, transparency) currently being pushed by the developed countries in general and the US in particular. This antipathy towards further liberal reform of the global economy was exacerbated by the crises at the close of the twentieth century.

Finally, civil society critics of globalization, with their focus on the inter-state bodies such as the IMF, WTO and the World Bank as the instruments of global governance, miss the influence emanating from networks and institutions of private authority and transnational interests. But recent literature demonstrates the increasing influence of networks and sources of private authority ranging over the semi-private regulation of global environmental and labour standards, the regulation of borrowing *via* bond rating agencies, through *ad hoc* regulatory processes for telecommunications and the internet and even the increasingly integrated nature of syndicated criminal activity.[52]

This mix and match of emerging and increasingly well organized egalitarian social movements, and similarly well organized structures of vested economic interest, prevent us painting a simple picture of how global governance is emerging.

---

[52] See John Braithwaite and Peter Drahos, *Global Business Regulation* (Cambridge: Cambridge University Press, 2000); A Claire Cutler, Virginia Haufleur, and Tony Porter (eds.), *Private Authority and International Affairs* (Albany, NY: SUNY Press, 1999) and H. Richard Friman and Peter Andreas (eds.), *The Illicit Global Economy and State Power* (Boulder, CO: Rowman and Littlefield, 2000).

It is for this reason that we should think rather of the global system taking on complex, cross cutting, polity-like features not dissimilar to those that developed within states in the eighteenth and nineteenth century. The system exhibits a preponderant but contested ideology (currently of the neoliberal market variety); a wide range of institutions and organizations (of an intergovernmental and trans-national nature) conducting public service functions (with all the strengths and weaknesses of public service delivery we have come to expect within sovereign com-munities) and the interplay of public and private sector actors attempting to influence the direction of public policy. What is lacking of course are representative and democratic structures of global political space that allow for processes of ordered change.

Despite the seepage of power from states down to local communities and up to supranational organizations, the state remains the principal repository of sovereign authority. Moreover, it is within the most powerful of states and the international institutions they control that a robust methodologically individualist neoliberalism remains the driving ideology. It is here that the polity-like characteristics of the global system break down. The vast majority of the world's population (and the states within which they live) remain rule-takers. The rules that they are forced to take, underwritten by this neoliberal ideology, do not, indeed cannot, address the ethical issues surrounding the task of alleviating the lot of the poor and the dispossessed. Consequently, there is a need to think beyond the Post Washington Consensus.

3. Beyond the Post Washington Consensus—scholarly, normative, political and ethical challenges

It has been argued that the shift from a Washington Consensus to a Post Washington Consensus represents a 'mood swing' in world politics that has raised the salience of the 'global governance' dimension of international relations. It is also argued that the principal limitation of an attempt to create a new consensus around the need for governance, seen as effective and efficient management of global prob-lems by the provision of global public goods by global policy networks, is its lack of an understanding of politics and a wider normative commitment to the creation of a global ethic of poverty alleviation *via* a commitment to redistribution.

The obvious defence of this position by those who advocate modest issue-specific definitions of global governance as the provision of public goods, is that there has to be a reality check on what is feasible and what is practical. This response is not without value, but it misses the larger political point. Largely liberal institutionalist in inspiration and driven by rational actor models, these approaches emanating from the international policy community frequently exhibit a deficient understanding of the way in which politics derails the best-laid schemes. In effect, governance, defined as effectiveness and efficiency, operates with a very old-fashioned understanding of the distinction between policy (administration) and politics. It aspires to 'governance without politics' and as such appears doomed to failure. To attempt to 'depoliticize' globalization—that is to place at one step removed the effects of globalization on much of the world's citizenry—is to misunderstand the manner in which it is both the theory and practice of politics that creates the structures of communities.[53]

For sure, our understanding of 'citizen attitudes' and changes in 'societal values' resulting from perceptions of globalization is as tentative as our understanding of the relationship between inequality and globalization discussed earlier. But, to the degree that globalization registers on the mental maps of the citizenry of a given state, then it would appear to be every bit as salient a factor as the impact of the material dimensions of the processes of liberalization and deregulation.[54] Moreover, there will inevitably be, indeed is, a large variation in the way that citizens of different countries, indeed citizens within countries, perceive the effects of globalization. We can say, however, that there is a large category of actors, groups and individuals who look increasingly negatively at globalization and who firmly believe that it leads to increases in inequality.

This growing concern with inequality is perceived to occur on at least two planes. Firstly, within states, between those sectors of the economy that are the beneficiaries of current innovation and liberalization (especially in services and information technology) on the one hand and the 'losers' in those sectors of the economy that have become less relevant in this historical juncture (especially agriculture and manufacturing) on the other. On a second plane, an increased global inequality between states, and the capacity of states to withstand global economic pressures, is also demonstrable. The conclusion from these perceptions is that a world that sustains major magnitudes of inequality is likely to be unstable. But this is not simply the view of the dispossessed and the 'losers' in the globalization race.

It is also a view that is increasingly to be found amongst established and respected mainstream scholars[55] and, most interestingly, within the mainstream of the economics profession where there is now, as was much less so the case until the late 1990s, acknowledgement of the importance of welfare safety nets of the kind developed under the Post-World War II embedded liberal compromise.[56] Most significantly, as indicated at the outset of this article, an increasing number of senior

[53] Bernard Crick, *In Defence of Politics* (London: Penguin, 1962), p. 24.

[54] For a good discussion of the pitfalls involved in assuming an understanding of the impact of globalization on societal values, see Jean Blondel, 'Globalization, Citizens and the State: Towards an Analysis of the Impact of Globalization in Contemporary Society', mimeo, n.d., p. 11–10. For a discussion of attitudes of elements of US society towards globalization, see Gary Burtless, Robert Z. Lawrence, Robert E. Litan and Robert J. Shapiro, *Globaphobia: Confronting Fears About Open Trade* (Washington, DC: Brookings, 1998), p. 6.

[55] See for example, Fouad Ajami, 'On the New Faith', *Foreign Policy*, 119 (Summer) 2000, pp. 30–34; and Ethan Kapstein, 'Distributive Justice and International Trade', *Ethics and International Affairs*, 13 (1999), pp. 175–204.

[56] On the embedded liberal compromise and the challenge presented to it by globalization, see John G. Ruggie, 'International Regimes, Transactions and Change: Embedded Liberalism in the Post War Economic Order', *International Organization*, 36:2 (1982) and 'At Home Abroad, Abroad at Home: International Liberalization and Domestic Stability in the New World Economy,' *Millennium: Journal of International Studies*, 24:3 (1995), pp. 507–26. Of recent significant supporting statements in favour of the mitigation of the market by the underwriting of this compromise, see Rodrik, *Has Globalization Gone Too Far?* and Krugman, *The Return of Depression Economics*; but see also Jagdish Bhagwati, 'The Capital Myth: The Difference Between Trade in Widgets and Trade in Dollars', *Foreign Affairs*, 77:3 (June 1988); Joseph Stiglitz, Towards a New Paradigm for Development: Strategies, Policies and Processes', *The 1998 Prebisch Lecture*, Geneva, UNCTAD, 19 October, 1998. To be found at http://www.worldbank.org/html/etme/jssp 101998.htm; and 'More Instruments and Broader Goals: Moving Towards a Post Washington Consensus', *The 1998 WIDER Lecture*: Helsinki, 7 January, 1999.

office holders of the major international financial institutions have recognized the destabilizing effects of unfettered liberalization and the growing perception that it exacerbates inequality, and as Paul Krugman intimated, it may be necessary to save liberalism from itself. We could also add it might be necessary to save economists from themselves. In order to do so, what is needed is a revitalized multidisciplinary 'international political economy'.

This new international political economy would go 'beyond economics'. It would combine the breadth of vision of the classical political economy of the mid-nineteenth century with the analytical advances of twentieth-century social science. Driven by a need to address the complex and often all-embracing nature of the globalizing urge, the methodology of the new international political economy would reject old dichotomies—between agency and structure, and states and markets—which fragmented classical political economy into separate disciplines in the wake of the marginalist revolution in economic thought.[57] Rather, the new international political economy would aspire to a hard-headed materialist (that is, real world) political economy that recognized the limits of methodologically individualist, choice-based economic theory.[58] Instead, it would explain how choice is affected by the social meanings of objects and actions. Indeed, if there is one thing that the emerging processes of globalization teach us, it is that monocausal explanations of economic phenomena lack sufficient explanatory power. Such a view now holds increasing sway at the dawn of a new century. Moreover, it holds sway not just among Third World economic nationalists and radical academic critiques of a global neoliberal agenda but also within sections of the mainstream economics community.

This reformist position also reflects a long overdue resistance to the often over-stated virtues of parsimony. In this regard the current era should offer no easy location for specialist parsimonious theorizing.[59] The new international political economy would operate from an assumption that what the marginalist revolution separated, globalization is bringing together. We are in a period of complex contest between the desire for grand totalizing narratives and theories of globalization on the one hand, and the need to produce specific histories of various actors and sites of resistance (be they states, classes, regions, or other localist forms of organization) to the grander projects on the other. The new international political economy must eschew this dichotomy. It should seek to be multi-disciplinary and theoretical in intellectual spirit, and empirically grounded in history, at the same time as it aspires to a normatively progressive research programme.

At the core of these concerns must be the changing institutional patterns which characterize alternative models of capitalism and the mechanisms by which a global economy and a global culture are constructed. Its normative agenda should be

---

[57] See James Caporaso and David Levine, *Theories of Political Economy* (New York: Cambridge University Press, 1992).

[58] For a discussion of these limits see Amartya Sen, 'Rational Fools: A Critique of the Behavioral Foundations of Economic Theory' *Philosophy and Public Affairs*, 6:4 (1977), pp. 713–44, and Ben Fine, 'The Triumph of Economics: Or, "Rationality Can be Dangerous to Your Reasoning"', in James G. Carrier and Daniel Miller (eds.), *Virtualism: A New Political Economy* (New York: Berg, 1998).

[59] Albert Hirschmann, 'Against Parsimony: Three Easy Ways of Complicating Some Categories of Economic Discourse', in Hirschmann (ed.), *Rival Views of Market Society and Other Recent Essays* (New York: Viking Books).

underwritten by a strong policy impetus towards the issues of enhancing justice and fairness under conditions of globalization—especially in the developing world's relationship with the developed.[60] Above all the new international political economy would foreground power in its *structural* as well as its *relational* form and recognize the need to ask the important Lasswellian questions about power of the 'who gets what, when and how' variety.[61]

The new international political economy has major implications for how we understand the current governance agenda emanating from the international policy community. Largely because it is driven by members of a deterritorialized trans-national policy elite, the current policy agenda has no conception of the residual strength of identity politics, the importance of social bonds within communities, the manner in which globalization appears to be picking many traditional social bonds apart without creating new sources of solidarity and, by implicit extension, no ethical agenda for addressing these questions.[62]

In this context, legitimate global governance, without a sense of community, would appear a remote prospect. This is sham governance. Real governance is about political contest over issues such as distribution and justice. In the promotion of the public good, politics is concerned with the empowerment of communities from the bottom up rather than just the top down. Both issues, in other than rhetorical fashion, still fall into the too-hard box for many in the international policy community. They are either ignored, or assumed away as 'policy questions' in which the global distribution of wealth and poverty, as currently constituted, is not part of the agenda for consideration. But governance is about making choices, while most specialists at the international institutions advancing a governance agenda have a conception of international relations that sees the global economy in decontextualized fashion and their tasks as depoliticized and technical.

This is not an argument against the importance that liberal institutionalism places on international institutional reform rather than a normative recognition of the need to move beyond; to recognize the need to start thinking about a 'global polity' and create a global public domain in which a deliberative dialogue between rule-makers and rule-takers, of the kind envisaged by cosmopolitan theorists, can take place.[63] Politics within states would not function if the same rules and styles of operation applied in the domestic public sphere that institutional actors are trying to put in place in an emerging global public sphere. But, the up-scaling of a democratic system from the national to the global level is not going to be easy. It is difficult enough for citizens to contest governmental decision-making within states. With a finely honed facility for stating the obvious, the leading theorist of (pluralist) democracy has recently argued that it is always going to be harder beyond territorial borders.[64]

[60] Anthony Payne, 'The Political Economy of Area Studies?' *Millennium: A Journal of International Studies*, 1999.

[61] See Susan Strange, *States and Markets* (London: Frances Pinter, 1998).

[62] See again, Devetak and Higgott, 'Justice Unbound? Globalization, States and the Transformation of the Social Bond'.

[63] See for example, David Held, *Democracy and the Global Order: From the Modern State to Cosmopolitan Governance* (Cambridge: Polity Press, 1995) and Andrew Linklater, *The Transformation of Political Community* (Cambridge: Polity Press, 1998).

[64] Robert Dahl, 'Can International Organisations be Democratic?', in I. Shapiro and C. Hacker Gordon (eds.), *Democracy's Edges* (Cambridge: Cambridge University Press, 1999).

There is a final way in which the drive for effectiveness and efficiency is a politically inadequate strategy. It is driven by a facile understanding of politics as 'anti-politics'; the prevailing assumption of which appears to be that resistance and opposition will be 'managed away' by incorporation. This, I have suggested, is an untenable reading of the emerging relationship between civil society and the international policy communities. It also, as has again been suggested, makes assumptions about both the benign and progressive nature of NGOs that are not always sustainable. While the policy communities located within the various international institutions have clearly had no choice but to engage with NGOs in current times, they have unleashed a series of tigers that will not remain easily within their control. The increasingly articulate and forceful critiques of globalization that emanate from these non-state actors are changing the nature of negotiating processes and the agendas of multilateral bodies such as the WTO, the World Bank and regional bodies such as APEC. It is too early in the life of these interactions to tell how they will ultimately develop.

The scenarios range across those of the development of positive and eventually fruitful engagement that legitimizes and advances the global policy agenda of the international institutions, on the one end of the spectrum, through to a scenario where the international policy process finishes up with the worst of both worlds—paralysis and an absence of legitimacy—on the other. As even some influential economists now note, it may well be necessary to constrain the free market to save it. Scholars of international politics with a feel for issues of governance, questions of accountability, legitimacy and sovereignty have understood the importance of these sentiments for a long while. The development of a Post Washington Consensus represents but one step on the learning curve for the international policy community, but it does not address the justice and poverty questions on the international agenda. The absence of a wide-scale acceptance of the 'legitimacy' of any top-down agenda in the developing world remains, for quite appropriate reasons, a major challenge for the international policy community under conditions of globalization. These are issues of ethics and politics, not just governance.

Conclusion

This article has made the argument that the development of a global political theory of governance (seen as the apolitical, effective and efficient provision of a limited range global public good—the Post Washington Consensus) represents an advance beyond a simple liberal economic theory of globalization (the Washington Consensus). It has also been argued that, as a 'containing strategy' to address the rising tide of resistance to key aspects of the globalization process, it is likely to prove as ineffective as the initial consensus. This is the case for two reasons. Firstly, the Post Washington Consensus has little or no theory of politics as a vehicle for ordered change. Secondly, it has no ethical theory of justice underpinning it. The global public domain as currently constructed is still seen by the international policy community primarily as an arena for management, not for change *via* legitimate political contest.

The explanation for this remains both practical and intellectual. In practical terms, the key difference between the domestic and international levels is that at the domestic level, important background norms and private arrangements allow difficult issues and questions to be confronted. These norms and private arrangements and political deals, the stuff of domestic politics, do not exist and cannot be implemented in the same way at the international level. Difficult issues—such as redistributive issues that are difficult to avoid at the domestic level—get placed in the 'too-hard box' at the international level. Under the current global governance agenda the Lasswellian questions have been subsumed in the international politics of the global economy. And this at the very time when the dissaggregation of the state and the geographical expansion of the economy is creating new intersecting relationships between local and global actors that will make these issues and questions the stuff of international politics in this new century. In denying them, or at least failing to address them seriously, the international institutions, as significant sites for policymaking, are merely staving off the day when they will have to confront them in other than token fashion. The key contemporary issue is not how simply to manage claims (or repress them even) by containing them within the private or national domain. Rather it is how might we engage them internationally.[65]

This is not to say that there has been no change. Ethical and moral considerations have taken hold in aspects of the global governance agenda in recent years. Notable is the greater sensitivity to questions of gender empowerment and the promotion of democracy. But, not surprisingly given the dominance of the market ideology, less success has been achieved in tackling the ethical and moral consequences of the limits of markets as agents of redistribution. The unequal distribution of wealth has now been an issue of discussion on the contemporary international agenda for more than a decade, but it is still not the primary one.

Moreover, it is still only conducted in international policy circles as but a sub-question in the context of theories of growth, which remain the preserve of the economist. With a few notable exceptions, this discussion is seen as technical rather than ethical and without standing as an autonomous agenda item in its own right. To the extent that it is a normative 'justice question' it is subsumed within the debates of the political theorist and scholar of international relations (along with issues of the democratic deficit, human rights and other so-called 'non-economic issues' such as whether the emerging relationship between global civil society and the extant state system will result in a new form of cosmopolitanism).

This continued bifurcation between the economic and the political, between the technical and the ethical (that is political) cannot be, or should not be, long sustained. The global governance agenda has to be widened to address the 'justice agenda' in a more overtly political way than has been the case to date. Failure to do so will ensure that global governance will remain inadequate to the task of redirecting resources from the winners of globalization towards the direction of the world's poorest citizens, and globalization will become more, rather than less, contested.

---

[65] This is well discussed in David Kennedy, 'Background Noise: The Underlying Politics of Global Governance', *Harvard International Review*, 21:3 (1999), p. 57.

Universalism and difference in discourses of race

KENAN MALIK[1]

A few weeks after the riot that shook Los Angeles in May 1992, I gave a lecture on racism in America to a group of students at a north London college. The audience was largely young and black. In the discussion that followed, there was a lively debate over my view that the fragmentation of American society into competing ethnic groups—African-Americans, Hispanic-Americans, Korean-Americans, and so on—was a fatal blow to the struggle for black rights. Almost the entire audience disagreed. 'African-Americans', one student explained, 'are different. Our problems are different, our experiences are different, our history is different and our culture is different. We have to gain respect ourselves before we can unite with other people.'

Here was summed up the core ideas that underpin much of current radical thinking on race: first, that social groups define themselves by their history and identity; second, that the particular history and identity of each group sets them apart from other social groups; third, that it is important to recognize this plurality of differences as a positive aspect of society today; and finally, that the struggle for racial equality takes the form of a struggle for group identity.

The 'assertion of difference' has become, for many radicals, the principal dynamic in society today. 'The emergence of new subjects, new genders, new ethnicities, new regions, new communities', claims sociologist Stuart Hall, has given hitherto invisible groups 'the means to speak for themselves for the first time'.[2] Radicals such as Hall have welcomed the contemporary flowering of ethnic differences as an expression, not of social discord, but of a new form of democracy through which sections of society previously silenced have been given voice. In Britain for example, the 'new ethnicities', Hall writes, posit a 'non-coercive and a more diverse conception of ethnicity, to set against the embattled, hegemonic conception of "Englishness" which ... stabilises so much of the dominant political and cultural discourses'.[3]

During the eighties, the so-called 'politics of difference' emerged to provide an intellectual and philosophical rationale for the kind of arguments expressed by my north London students. The advocates of the politics of difference argue that we are living in a form of society radically different from that of half a century ago—a post-industrial or, more fashionably, postmodern society. Though postmodernism is an ambiguous term and few have tried to define it with any great clarity, for most of

[1] This essay is adapted from Kenan Malik, *The Meaning of Race: Race, History and Culture in Western Society* (London: Macmillan, 1996).

[2] Stuart Hall, 'The Local and the Global', in Anthony D. King (ed.), *Culture, Globalization and the World-System: Contemporary Conditions for the Representation of Identity* (Basingstoke, UK: Macmillan, 1991), p. 34.

[3] Stuart Hall, 'New Ethnicities', in James Donald and Ali Rattansi (eds.), *'Race', Culture and Difference* (London: Sage Open University, 1992), p. 258.

its theorists the postmodern society is characterized by its very heterogeneity and diversity.

For postmodernists, the Enlightenment project of pursuing a rational, scientific understanding of the natural and social world, and of creating a universal outlook from fragmented experience, has failed. They wish instead to celebrate plurality and fragmentation. Social fragmentation, they argue, is a way of giving voice to those who have been previously excluded from the political arena. The advocates of plurality argue that the assertion of difference helps undermine the grip of the dominant groups over political and social discourse. Traditional politics, they say, serves to silence the voices of the weak and the oppressed, to consign their histories and experiences to the margins and to subsume all experience to the dominant outlook. Because British history is written by those who want to create a singular national identity it denies the experiences and histories of, for example, black people who are not part of that singular identity. By 'decentring' discourse and giving hitherto marginalized groups centre-stage, it is possible to create a more democratic form of social dialogue.

I want to argue here that this pursuit of difference, far from creating a more democratic form of social dialogue, is deeply problematic. The idea of difference has always been central, not to the anti-racist agenda, but to that of racial thought. The politics of difference is profoundly anti-humanist, and provides no resources for the emancipation of the powerless or the oppressed. Indeed, on the contrary, it is an acceptance of powerlessness and marginality, recognition of political failure and defeat.

West and the Rest

'The world begins to be decolonised', Stuart Hall writes, at 'that moment when the unspoken discovered that they had a history which they could speak' and that they had 'languages other than the languages of the master'.[4] The central argument in contemporary theories of difference is the idea that Enlightenment discourse, by establishing universal norms and by equating such norms with European societies and cultures, has ensured the silence of non-European peoples and cultures. According to critics like Edward Said,[5] Western science and philosophy have established a form of knowledge whereby non-Western societies and cultures are represented solely in terms of the categories of Western thought, and in which Western society acts as a standard against which all other societies are judged. This inevitably leads to the silencing of other voices. At the same time the differences between Western and non-Western cultures are rationalized through non-Western peoples being defined as the 'Others', distinguished solely through their antagonism to the dominant image of the 'self', and against whose peculiarities the self-image of the West is created. The result has been the acquisition of an aura of superiority for Western cultures and an imposition of a sense of inferiority upon non-Western ones.

[4] Stuart Hall, 'The Local and the Global', in King (ed.), *Culture, Globalization and the World-System*, p. 35.
[5] Edward W. Said, *Culture and Imperialism* (London: Chatto & Windus, 1993), p. 58.

From the Renaissance onwards, Stuart Hall explains, Europe began to define itself in relation to a new idea—'the existence of many new "worlds" profoundly different from itself'.[6] This gave rise to the discourse of the Other, which 'represents what are in fact very differentiated (the different European cultures) as homogeneous (the West)'. Further 'it asserts that these different cultures are united by one thing: the fact that they are all different from the Rest'. At the same time the 'Other' (or the 'Rest' in Hall's terminology) 'though different among themselves, are represented as the same in the sense that they are all different from the West'.[7]

The sense of 'otherness' that Western discourse imposes on non-Western peoples and cultures is seen as the source of the modern ideas of race. 'The figure of the "Other"', writes Hall, was 'constructed as the absolute opposite, the negation of everything the West stood for'.[8] Through the representation of an absolute difference between the West and its Others, the idea of difference took on a racial form. '[R]ace emerged with and has served to define modernity by insinuating itself in various fashions into modernity's prevailing conceptions of moral personhood and subjectivity', David Goldberg believes. 'By working itself into the threads of liberalism's cloths just as that cloth was being woven, race and the various exclusions it licensed became naturalised in the Eurocentric visions of itself and its self-defined others, in its sense of Reason and rational direction.'[9]

Since the framework of 'the West and its Others' is so central to contemporary theories of the meaning of race, I want to examine in this essay some of its assumptions. The concept of the Other was developed in the phenomenological tradition, particularly by Edmund Husserl, as a constitutive factor in the subject's self-image. The Other was conceived as the perceiving, conscious, meaning-conferring other person who helps, or forces, the conscious subject to define its own world picture and its view of its place in it. Through the work of writers such as Jean-Paul Sartre, Claude Lévi-Strauss, Jacques Lacan and Michel Foucault, the concept of the Other entered post-structuralist discourse.[10]

In post-structuralist discourse the Other is a social object, the difference against which the Self is measured. In Michel Foucault's seminal work, *Folie et Deraison*, lepers were the Others of medieval society, a prime source of contamination, whose exclusion from everyday life helped provide society with a sense of its normality. As leprosy became less common, so it was less able to play its previous symbolic role.

---

[6] Stuart Hall, 'The West and the Rest: Discourse and Power', in Stuart Hall and Bram Gieben (eds.), *Formations of Modernity: Understanding Modern Societies* (Cambridge: Polity Press/Open University, 1992), p. 289.

[7] Ibid., p. 280.

[8] Ibid., p. 314.

[9] D.T. Goldberg, *Racist Culture: Philosophy and the Politics of Meaning* (Oxford: Blackwell, 1993), p. 10.

[10] Claude Lévi Strauss, *Structural Anthropology*, vol.1, trans by Claire Jacobson and Brooke Grundfest Schoepf (Harmondsworth: Penguin, 1972 [orig. pub. 1963]); Claude Lévi Strauss, *Structural Anthropology*, vol.2, trans. by Monique, London (Harmondsworth: Penguin, 1978 [1971]); Claude Lévi Strauss, *The Savage Mind* (London: Weidenfeld & Nicolson, 1966 [1962]); Jean-Paul Sartre, *Being and Nothingness* (London: Methuen 1957); Jacques Lacan, *Écrits: A Selection* (London: Tavistock, 1977); Jacques Derrida, *Speech and Phenomena and Other Essays on Husserl's Theory of Signs* (Evanston: Northwestern University Press, 1973 [1967]); Jacques Derrida, *Of Gramatology* (Baltimore, MD: Johns Hopkins Press, 1976 [1967]); Jacques Derrida, *Writing and Difference* (London: Routledge & Kegan Paul, 1978 [1967]); Michel Foucault, *Madness and Civilisation* (London: Tavistock, 1967); Michel Foucault, *The Order of Things* (London: Tavistock, 1970); Michel Foucault, *The Archaeology of Knowledge* (London: Tavistock, 1972).

Instead, argues Foucault, a new Other was born: those who were non-productive—the criminal, the homeless and, especially, the mad. 'A new leper is born', writes Foucault, 'who takes the place of the first.'[11]

The Other, then, is that which lies outside a particular culture or society's epistemological boundaries. Not only is everything beyond the boundary treated as the Other, but society requires an Other without which there can be no sense of Self. A single category that can encapsulate the idea of an object of study, an object of exclusion and an object through the perception of whose difference self-identity can be affirmed has proved very attractive in the study of race. Most contemporary studies define racial difference in terms of the Other.

The distinction between the West and its Other is, for many contemporary theorists, implicit in the categories of Enlightenment universalism. Stuart Hall has pointed out how the establishment of the Other was fundamental to the development of Enlightenment thought:

> This 'West and the Rest' discourse greatly influenced Enlightenment thinking . . . In Enlightenment discourse, the West was the model, the prototype and the measure of social progress. It was western progress, civilisation, rationality and development that were celebrated. And yet . . . without the Rest (or its own internal 'others') the West would not have been able to recognise and represent itself as the summit of human history. The figure of 'the Other', banished to the edge of the conceptual world and constructed as the absolute opposite, the negation, of everything which the West stood for, reappeared at the very centre of the discourse of civilisation, refinement, modernity and development in the West. 'The Other' was the 'dark' side—forgotten, repressed and denied; the reverse image of enlightenment and modernity.[12]

According to such critics, through the discourse of universalism the characteristics of the West and its Others were eternalized and the differences established as absolute. Thus Peter Hulme observes that Western understanding of non-Western cultures creates a distinction between 'self' and 'other' by 'establishing character-istics as eternal verities immune from the irrelevances of the historical moment: "ferocious", "hostile" "truculent and vindictive"—these are present as innate charac-teristics irrespective of circumstances'.[13]

Many of these ideas are central to my book *The Meaning of Race*.[14] Here I argued that the discourse of race helped recast social differences as natural ones, eternal-izing what were historically contingent features. I argued, too, that in certain circumstances the notion of the 'other' has helped establish a sense of self-identity. Despite this I want to argue that the framework of 'the West and its Others' is unhelpful in understanding the concept of race. The category of the Other is ahistorical and takes little account of the specificities of time and place in the creation of the discourse of race. Instead it steamrollers historical, social and geographical differences into a single discourse of 'the West and its Others'.

---

[11] Michel Foucault, *Folie et deraison: Histoire de la folie à lâge classique*, 2nd edn. (Paris: Galimard, 1972), p. 17; an abridged English version can be found in Madness and Civilisation, trans. Richard Howard (London: Tavistock, 1967).

[12] Hall, 'The West and the Rest', in King (ed.), *Culture, Globalization, and the World System*, pp. 312–14.

[13] Peter Hume, *Colonial Encounters: European and the Native Caribbean, 1492–1797* (London: Methuen, 1986), p. 49.

[14] Kenan Malik, *The Meaning of Race: Race, History and Culture in Western Society* (London: Macmillan, 1996).

In *Culture and Imperialism* Edward Said posits the existence of 'a fundamental ontological distinction between the West and the rest of the world' whose boundary we may consider 'absolute':

Throughout the exchange between Europeans and their 'others' that began systematically half a millennium ago, the one idea that has scarcely varied is that there is an 'us' and a 'them', each quite settled, clear, unassailably self-evident. As I discuss it in *Orientalism*, the division goes back to Greek thought about barbarians, but, whoever originated this kind of 'identity' thought, by the nineteenth century it had become the hallmark of imperialist cultures as well as those cultures trying to resist the encroachments of Europe.[15]

Having established a transhistorical, ontological distinction that collapses the subtleties of two millennia of history, Said subsequently reads history backwards, conceiving of the past in terms specific to the present so that all encounters between Europeans and their Others, whatever their form, comprise part of 'the distinction between the West and the rest of the world'. For instance, the acquisition of Ireland by England's Henry II in the twelfth century is deemed to be an imperialist conquest and the English nobility's attitudes towards the Irish is assumed to be racial in form:

The high age of imperialism is said to have begun in the late 1870s, but in English-speaking realms it began well over seven hundred years before . . . Ireland was ceded by the Pope to Henry II of England in the 1150s; he himself came to Ireland in 1171. From that time on an amazingly persistent cultural attitude existed towards Ireland as a place whose inhabitants were a barbarian and degenerate race.[16]

Said does not tell us what it is about the Pope's award of Ireland to Henry II that is of the same moment as the European powers' scramble for Africa from the 1870s onwards. Nor does he explain in what way twelfth-century perceptions of the Irish show a continuity with nineteenth-century perceptions of Africans. That continuity is simply assumed. Such assumptions are rarely valid. Human consciousness is not static or innate but is constantly recreated through changing social and historical circumstances. Without investigating social phenomena in their specificity, we fall into the trap of projecting specifically contemporary values and judgements on to past epochs.

In Herman Melville's *Moby Dick* the narrator Ishmael observes sourly that 'a purse is but a rag unless you have something in it'. The outward appearance of something tells us little. Only through understanding an object or phenomenon in its context can we appreciate its content or meaning. This is particularly so with social phenomena, such as 'race'. 'A Negro is a Negro', wrote Marx. 'He only becomes a slave in certain circumstances'.[17] Possessing a black skin does not mean that one is a slave, nor indeed that one is an object of racism. However, we have a tendency to assume this because we mistakenly assume that the contemporary signification of blackness has always been so.

Take, for instance, the contemporary reading of Shakespeare's *Othello*. Today the play is generally taken to be an example of the racist outlook of the Elizabethan period.[18] Yet as C. L. R. James has pointed out, this interpretation is simply the

---

[15] Said, *Culture and Imperialism*, p. 28.
[16] Ibid., p. 266.
[17] K. Marx and F. Engels, *Selected Works* (London: Lawrence & Whishart, 1968), p. 79.
[18] See, for example, Ruth Cowing, 'Blacks in Renaissance Drama and the Role of Shakespeare's Othello', in David Dabydeen (ed.), *The Black Presence in English Literature* (Manchester University Press, 1985).

product of our own 'race-ridden consciousness'. For Elizabethan audiences, what was important was not Othello's 'race' but the fact that he was a stranger:

[Y]ou could strike out every single reference to his black skin and the play would be essentially the same. Othello's trouble is that he is an outsider. He is not a Venetian. He is a military bureaucrat, a technician hired to fight for Venice, a foreign country. The senate has no consciousness whatever of his colour. That is a startling fact but true. They haven't to make allowances for it. It simply has no place in their minds.[19]

The meaning of a black skin has not always been the same. Nor have the concepts of self and of difference. In the past people perceived of themselves and of others in very different fashion, indeed in ways that would strike us as irrational and incomprehensible. Given the complexity of the development of the discourse of race, it is simply not possible to understand it within a single framework of the 'West and its Others'.

There might appear to be a contradiction in this critique of the framework of the 'West and its Others'. On the one hand I am claiming that contemporary theorists of difference regard the idea of the Other as a product of Enlightenment universalism—in other words, as a specifically modern development. On the other hand, I am also arguing that theirs is an ahistoric understanding of the relationship between Self and Other in that they view the dichotomy as an epistemological constant. There is indeed a contradiction here, but it arises out of the very use of the idea of the Other. Post-structuralist and postmodernist discourse tend to regard the Other as both a product of post-Enlightenment philosophy and as a constant in human perception. The conflation of these two ideas in fact plays a major part in the confusion about the relationship between Enlightenment discourse and the discourse of race.

We can understand better both the ahistoricity of the concept of the Other, and the contradictions it embodies, by looking in some depth at a text that was key to developing the framework of the 'West and its Others'—Edward Said's *Orientalism*. Published in 1978, the book became very influential in its discussion of the way in which Western understanding of the Orient—by which Said meant the Middle East—imposed upon it a reality created in the West. The confusions and contradictions in *Orientalism* reflect the broader problems with post-structuralist theories of difference.

Orientalism and Historicism

In *Orientalism* Said argues that Western historians, philologists and philosophers have fabricated a complex set of representations about the Orient which for the West have effectively become the Orient. Said suggests that the creation of the Orient in literary, historical and scholarly accounts established a discourse through which the West could assert political and military control over the Orient:

My contention is that, without examining Orientalism as a discourse, one cannot possibly understand the enormously systematic discipline by which European culture was able to manage—and even produce—the Orient politically, sociologically, militarily, ideologically,

---

[19] C. L. R. James, *Spheres of Existence: Selected Writings* (London: Allison & Busby, 1980), p. 141.

scientifically and imaginatively during the post-Enlightenment period. Moreover, so authoritative a position did Orientalism have that I believe that no one writing, thinking, or acting on the Orient could do so without taking account of the limitations on thought and action imposed by Orientalism. In brief, because of Orientalism, the Orient was not (and is not) a free subject of thought and action . . . [T]his book . . . also tries to show that European culture gained in strength and identity by setting itself off against the Orient as a sort of surrogate and even underground self.[20]

For Said, then, Orientalism constitutes a body of thought which both limits how those in the West are able to think about the Orient and allows the West to establish physical power over it. The discourse of Orientalism establishes a dualism between the West and the Orient which strengthens Western cultures and imprisons those of the Orient. This dualism shapes the reality of the Orient for the peoples of both the West and the Orient itself.

Despite such major claims there is, however, a total lack of precision in Said's work as to what he means by 'Orientalism' and what are the historic and epistemic boundaries that delimit it as a discourse. Said himself observes in his Introduction that 'by Orientalism I mean several things'. But these 'several things' are often so contradictory, and sometimes mutually exclusive, that the term 'Orientalism' is rendered meaningless.

Central to Said's argument would seem to be the idea that Orientalism is a post-Enlightenment discourse, the product of the Enlightenment's universalizing categories and one which allowed the West to establish colonial power over the Orient:

Taking the late eighteenth century as a very roughly defined starting point Orientalism can be discussed and analysed as the corporate institution for dealing with the Orient—dealing with it by making statements about it, authorizing views of it, describing it, by teaching it, settling it, ruling over it: in short, Orientalism as a Western style for dominating, restructuring and having authority over the Orient.[21]

But Said also argues that 'the demarcation between the Orient and the West. . . already seems bold by the time of the *Iliad.*' In Aeschylus's *The Persians* and Euripides's *The Bacchae*, 'Asia speaks through and by virtue of the European imagination, which is depicted as victorious over Asia, that hostile "other" world beyond the seas'. The two plays, writes Said, distil the distinctions between Europe and the Orient which 'will remain essential motifs of European imaginative geography'.[22] Orientalism now no longer seems to be the specific product of Enlightenment categories but originates at the very dawn of what Said conceives of as European civilization. Within the earliest of Athenian plays appear the concepts that were to be articulated later by the Enlightenment *philosophes*. This allows Said to suggest that Orientalism 'can accommodate Aeschylus, say, and Victor Hugo, Dante and Karl Marx'.[23]

Any concept of a discourse that can accommodate four writers as historically, politically and philosophically diverse as Aeschylus, Hugo, Dante and Marx can but be profoundly ahistoric. The specificities of Aeschylus's understanding of the

[20] Edward W. Said, *Orientalism: Western Concepts of the Orient* (Harmondsworth: Penguin, 1985 [1978], p. 3.
[21] Ibid., p. 3.
[22] Ibid., pp. 56–7.
[23] Ibid., p. 3.

barbarian, Dante's view of Islam and Marx's analysis of India disappear beneath the swamp of an all-encompassing 'Orientalism'. And if the concept of the non-Western world as the 'Other' derives from the universalizing impulse of the Enlightenment, yet is premised on 'a line . . . drawn between two continents' by Ancient Greek playwrights and philosophers, in what way is Enlightenment discourse specific to the Enlightenment? Said seems here to posit a view of 'Western thought' essentially untouched since its creation.

The ahistoricism of *Orientalism* leads Said to mimic the very discursive structures against which he polemicizes. Said creates a 'Western tradition' which runs in an unbroken line from the Ancient Greeks through the Renaissance, the Enlightenment to modernism. It is a tradition which defines a coherent Western identity through a specific set of beliefs and values which remain in their essence unchanged through two millennia of European and Western history. This of course is the myth of 'Western civilisation' propagated by many an advocate of Western superiority, from Gobineau to Goebbels and beyond.

In reality there is no such continuous tradition. The idea that modern Western culture has its roots in Greek learning is, as Martin Bernal has shown, the product of post-Enlightenment Romantic thought.[24] Nineteenth-century racial discourse expunged from history the roots of Greek learning in Afro-Asiatic cultures and the Enlightenment's debt to Arab learning, and fabricated instead the myth of an organic 'Western' tradition from ancient Greece to modern Europe.

Said not only accepts the reality of such a tradition, but he also erases, as Aijaz Ahmad observes, the fractures, conflicts and divisions within European societies and treats Europe as a homogenous maker of history:

> It is rather remarkable how constantly and comfortably Said speaks . . . of *a* Europe, or the West, as a self-identical, fixed being which has always had an essence and a project, an imagination and a will; and of the 'Orient' as its object—textually, militarily, and so on. He speaks of the West, or Europe, as the one that produces that knowledge, the East as the object of that knowledge. In other words, he seems to posit stable subject-object identities, as well as ontological and epistemological distinctions between the two. In what sense, then, is Said himself not an Orientalist—or at least as Sadek el-Azm puts it, an 'Orientalist-in-reverse'? Said quite justifiably accuses the 'Orientalist' of essentialising the Orient, but his own essentialising of the 'West' is equally remarkable. In the process Said of course gives us the same 'Europe'—unified, self-identical, transhistorical, textual—which is always rehearsed for us in the sort of literary criticism which traces its own pedigree from Aristotle to T. S. Eliot.[25]

For Said a European, by virtue of being European, must necessarily be racist. '[E]very European', he writes, 'in what he could say about the Orient, was consequently a racist, an imperialist, and almost totally ethnocentric.'[26] Every European? Surely even Count Gobineau would have been somewhat more circumspect about making such sweeping statements. As Ahmad observes, 'These ways of dismissing entire civilisations as diseased formations are unfortunately far too familiar to us, who live on the other side of the colonial divide, from the history of imperialism itself'.[27]

---

[24] Martin Bernal, *Black Athena: The Afroasiatic Roots of Classical Civilisation* (London: Free Association Books, 1987).
[25] Aijaz Ahmad, *In Theory: Classes, Nations, Literatures* (London: Verso, 1992), p. 183.
[26] Said, *Orientalism*, p. 204.
[27] Ahmad, *In Theory*, p. 182.

Elsewhere, Said himself has argued cogently against such ahistoric attitudes:

If you know in advance that the African or Iranian or Chinese or Jewish or German experience is fundamentally integral, coherent, separate, and therefore comprehensible only to Africans, Iranians, Chinese, Jews or Germans you first of all posit as essential something which, I believe, is both historically created and the result of interpretation—namely the existence of Africanness, Jewishness, of Germanness, or for that matter Orientalism or Occidentalism.[28]

Yet such cautionary reminders of the dangers of an unhistorical approach are all too often lost amidst the rush to establish that the categories of Western thought are in and of themselves imbricated with racial thought. A few chapters on from his warning against thinking of cultures as 'fundamentally integral, coherent, separate', Said argues that there exists a 'fundamental ontological distinction between the West and the rest of the world' and that 'we may consider' 'the geographical and cultural boundaries between the West and its non-Western peripheries' as 'absolute'.[29]

Discourse, power and knowledge

The filiation between the discourse of difference and that of race that is suggested by the ahistoricism of both is strengthened by the idealism which permeates contemporary radical thinking about race. Rather than being rooted in the real world, discourse often appears, as Salman Rushdie writes of the migrant imagination in *Shame*, to have 'floated up from history, from memory, from Time'. We can see this quite clearly in Said's work, in which the relationship between the discourse of Orientalism and the reality of the West's domination of the Orient is often obscure.

At first sight it might seem strange to accuse Said of ignoring the social and material realities which gave rise to the discourse of Orientalism. After all, one of the significant features of *Orientalism* is its insistence that literary and scholarly criticism must take into account the context of imperialism which has shaped their objects of study. Yet such are the contradictions within Said's work that one sometimes wishes he himself would take heed of his strictures on the need for contextual reading.

On the one hand Said holds that Orientalism is a representation, a fabrication by Western writers and travellers of an Orient that has no real existence. On the other hand he argues that knowledge contained within the discourse of Orientalism played a key part in allowing Europe to subjugate the non-Western world. But if the discourse of Orientalism was effective in allowing Western politicians and generals to take actual control over the Orient, then it must have been more than simply a 'representation'. As Robert Young has asked, 'How can Said argue that the "Orient" is just a representation, if he also wants to claim that "Orientalism" provided the necessary knowledge for actual colonial conquest?'[30]

Said attempts to circumvent this problem by arguing that the texts of Orientalism 'can create not only knowledge but the reality they appear to describe'.[31] What does

[28] Said, *Culture and Imperialism*, p. 35.
[29] Ibid., p. 129.
[30] Robert Young, *White Mythologies: Writing History and the West* (London: Routledge, 1990), p. 129.
[31] Said, *Orientalism*, p. 94.

Said mean by this? He could be suggesting that the reality of the Orient is contained within the texts of Orientalism. If so, this would seem to be a highly textualized understanding of reality, especially coming from an author who has been critical of Orientalism precisely for its textuality. If indeed the texts contained the reality, there would be no need for contextual reading, for the context would lie in the texts themselves.

Alternatively Said could mean that the texts of Orientalism impose on the Orient its reality. When Orientalists conceive of the Orient in a particular fashion, the Orient succumbs to that vision. David Goldberg clearly reads Said in this way:

> Naming the racial Other, for all intents and purposes, is the Other. There is, as Said makes clear in the case of the Oriental, no Other behind or beyond the invention of the Other in the Other's name. These practices of naming and knowledge construction deny all autonomy to those so named and imagined, extending power, control, authority and domination over them. To extend Said's analysis of the 'Oriental' to the case of race in general, social science of the Other establishes the limits of knowledge about the Other, for the Other is just what the racialised social science knows.[32]

Goldberg transforms European colonialists into the witchdoctors of modernity who, through the invocation of 'names', extend 'power, control, authority and domination' over their subject peoples. A very potent magic indeed. In Salman Rushdie's novel *The Satanic Verses*, one of the central characters, Saladin, finds himself incarcerated in a detention centre for illegal immigrants. Saladin discovers that his fellow inmates have been transformed into beasts—water buffaloes, snakes, manticores. He himself has become a hairy goat. How do they do it, Saladin asks a fellow prisoner. 'They describe us', comes the reply, 'that's all. They have the power of description and we succumb to the pictures they construct.' Similarly Said and Goldberg seem to be suggesting that the only role allotted to the 'Other' is to succumb to the picture constructed by the Western 'self'. It is a picture of the relationship between the West and its Other in which the Other is transformed into simply a passive victim.

Elsewhere Said has claimed that 'Representation itself [keeps] the subordinate subordinate, the inferior inferior'.[33] But in what way is this an understanding of the Orient different from that contained in the discourse of Orientalism itself, an understanding of the Orient as a passive, submissive Other moulded entirely by the history-making West? Said and Goldberg complain that the universalizing discourse of the West silences the voices of the Other. Yet it is Said and Goldberg themselves who silence the Other by conceiving of it as a compliant, inert object constituted solely by Western knowledge. The West produces its image of the Orient as the Other, and the Orient meekly accepts the image that is constructed.

Whichever way we might interpret them, Said's comments also raise, as Ahmad notes, the question of the very relationship between Orientalism and colonialism:

> In a revealing use of the word 'delivered', Said remarks at one point that Orientalism delivered the Orient to colonialism, so that colonialism begins to appear as a product of Orientalism itself indeed, as the realisation of the project already inherent in Europe's perennial project of inferiorising the Orient first in discourse and then in colonisation.[34]

---

[32] Goldberg, *Racist Culture*, p. 150.
[33] Said, *Culture and Imperialism*, p. 95
[34] Ahmad, *In Theory*, p. 181.

For Said, Orientalism seems to be not the product of social developments or material forces but their creator. Just as the West is ontologically incapable of understanding the non-Western world except as its Other, so the West is ontologically driven to impose its power over the rest of the globe. Said's argument that 'psychologically, Orientalism is a form of paranoia',[35] an argument that he repeats frequently, suggests that he views Orientalism as the compulsion of a diseased European psyche. The drive to colonization arises out of a psychological need in the Western mind, a need that is already present at the time of the Greeks with their view of the barbarian Other, and which becomes manifest through post-Enlightenment colonial power. Having detached the discourse of race from real social movement, Said provides us with a theory of race and imperialism which sounds like nothing so much as the Romantic vision of a people's destiny unfolding through history, except that where the Romantics saw this as the positive affirmation of a people's heritage, Said regards it as the destructive consequence of a deranged mind.

There is yet another problem that arises from Said's idealism. 'The real issue' he claims, 'is whether there can be a true representation of anything, or whether any or all representations, because they are representations, are embedded first in the language and then in the culture, institutions and political ambience of the representer'. Said plumps for the second definition and argues that 'a representation is *eo ipso* implicated, intertwined, embedded, interwoven with a great many other things beside "truth", which is itself a representation'. Representations cannot be 'truthful', and 'truth' is but a representation, constituted 'by some common history, tradition, universe of discourse'.[36] Having established that Orientalists' 'objective discoveries . . . are and always have been conditioned by the fact that its truths, like any truths delivered by language, are embodied in language', Said then quotes Nietzsche to the effect that language is but 'a mobile army of metaphors, metonyms and anthropomorphisms' and that 'truths are but illusions about which one has forgotten that this is what they are'.[37]

But if true representations are not possible, and truth itself is but a represent-ation, then in what way can we criticize Orientalism? After all, one representation is as good as another and there is no objective means by which to challenge the picture that Orientalists provide us of the Orient. The relativism of Said's outlook (a relativism with which, as we shall see later, he is not entirely comfortable) denies the possibility of challenging the very discourse he despises.

The problem in comprehending the relationship between the representation and the real arises from the concept of 'discourse' which Said derives from Michel Foucault. I use the term 'discourse' in a relatively loose sense, meaning a coherent body of knowledge which shapes and limits the ways of understanding a particular topic. Central to Foucault's concept of a discourse, however, is the idea that social facts can never be conceived of as being 'true' or 'false'. The very language we use to describe facts imposes truth or falsity upon those facts. Hence it is the discourse itself that creates the truth about a particular topic and competing discourses create competing truths. Truth lies not in the relationship between discourse and social

---

[35] Said, *Orientalism*, p. 72.
[36] Ibid., pp. 272, 273.
[37] Ibid., p. 203.

reality but in the relationship between discourse and power. It is the relationship between discourse and power which decides which one of the many truths is accepted as *the* truth. For Foucault 'power produces knowledge' and 'power and knowledge directly imply one another' because 'there is no power relation without the correlative constitution of a field of knowledge, nor any knowledge that does not presuppose and constitute . . . power relations'.[38]

For Foucault, a discourse is a way of constituting power, and is at the same time verified by that power. The knowledge which a discourse produces constitutes a kind of power, exercised over those who are 'known'. When that knowledge is exercised in practice, those who are known in a particular way will be subject to it. Those who produce the discourse also have the power to make it true, to enforce its validity:

Truth isn't outside power . . . [I]t induces regular effects of power. Each society has its regime of truth, its 'general politics' of truth; that is, the types of discourse which it accepts and makes function as true; the mechanisms and instances which enable one to distinguish between 'true' and 'false' statements; the means by which each is sanctioned; and the techniques and procedures accorded value in the acquisition of truth; the status of those who are charged with saying what counts as true.[39]

But what does Foucault mean by 'power'? He is very vague about this. Power, for Foucault, cannot be conceived of in class or social terms. It is not the property of an individual or a class, nor does it emanate from an identifiable source or institution, such as the state. Power is simply omnipresent. Its threads are every-where and it is only through power that 'reality' is constituted. Given the omnipresence of power, and its role in constituting reality, Foucault is forced to conceive of power relations in arbitrary terms. Power struggles do not emanate from social or historical movement, but simply pit all against all: 'There aren't immediately given subjects of the struggle, one the proletariat the other the bourgeoisie. Who fights against whom? We all fight each other. And there is always within each of us something that fights something else.'[40] I shall return to the consequences of Foucault's understanding of power later. What is important now is to grasp how belief in the arbitrary nature of both power and truth leads to an extreme relativism. If power is simply the constituting element in all social systems, how can we choose between one society and another? And if a discourse makes its own truth, whose validity is given by the strength of an arbitrary power, how are we to distinguish between different representations or discourses? We can neither relate ideas and representations to real social movements, nor can we pass value judgements on different sets of ideas.

The logic of the Foucauldian argument would lead us to suppose that it is the very act of attempting to establish an objective truth that is the problem. And this is indeed the argument that the more extreme proponents of a relativistic outlook use against Enlightenment discourse. The phenomenologist Emmanual Levinas objected to the very idea of knowledge in the traditional Western sense because in the process of understanding, he argued, Western philosophy undermines and devalues whatever societies, cultures or modes of living it comes across: 'Western philosophy coincides with the disclosure of the other where the other, in manifesting itself as a being,

---

[38]   Michel Foucault, *Power/Knowledge* (Brighton: Harvester, 1980), p. 27.
[39]   Ibid., p. 131.
[40]   Ibid., pp. 207–8.

loses its alterity. From its infancy philosophy has been struck with a horror of the other that remains other.'[41]

What Levinas means is that Western thought cannot allow objects of study to remain outside of its epistemological boundaries or to be defined in their own terms. For Levinas conventional knowledge, conceived of as the relationship between subject and object, always involves appropriating one to the other. This he calls 'the imperialism of the same', drawing a parallel between the physical subjugation of the Third World and the intellectual subordination of its ideas, history and values. Just as Western politicians and generals annex foreign lands, so the West's intellectuals and philosophers appropriate all other knowledge. Robert Young similarly argues that Western universalism 'articulates a philosophical structure which uncannily simulates the project of nineteenth-century imperialism; the construction of know-ledges which all operate through forms of expropriation and incorporation of the other mimics at a conceptual level the geographic and economic absorption of the non-European world by the West.'[42]

Since all knowledge and understanding requires the appropriation of the object by the subject, implicit in every act of understanding, says Levinas, is an act of violence. The only solution to this problem for Levinas, and for other theoreticians of difference, such as Robert Young and Gayatri Chakravorty Spivak, is to abjure entirely knowledge in the conventional sense. Instead of 'grasping' the object, says Levinas, we must 'respect' it; in the place of assimilation there should be 'infinite separation'.

At this point difference becomes resolved into *indifference*, an unwillingness to engage with what any one else has to say. It is an outlook described much more succinctly and lucidly than by any postmodern professor by the TV character Archie Bunker in the American sitcom *All in the Family*. In one particular episode, Edith tells Archie to lace his bowling shoes 'over' rather than 'under'. 'What's the difference?' demands Archie. When Edith tries to explain, Archie cuts her short: 'I didn't say—"What's the difference—explain it to me". I said "What's the differ-ence—who the hell cares?".'

In the indifference of postmodernism, Christopher Miller perceptively observes, the politics of difference mirror the arguments of racial thinking. 'The impulse to leave the other alone', he writes, 'rejoins the impulse to obliterate the other on the ground that they have in common: the inability to describe something outside the self, to see in Clifford Geertz's words "ourselves among others, as a local example of the forms human life has locally taken".'[43] In other words, the advocates of racial thinking and the theorists of difference seem equally indifferent to our common humanity. While one posits the notion of a 'Britishness' or 'Frenchness' or 'Americanness' accessible only to those privileged by race or history, the other renounces any possibility of access across the divide of cultural or ethnic difference. Said himself is well-aware of the dangers of such an outlook. He reminds us that the pluralist approach of privileging every voice, far from ensuring a more democratic society, would simply create a modern-day Tower of Babel: '[I]f everyone were to

---

[41] Emmanual Levinas, 'The Trace of the Other', in Mark C. Taylor (ed.), *Deconstructing in Context* (Chicogo University Press, 1986), p. 346.

[42] Young, *White Mythologies*, p. 3.

[43] Christopher Miller, *Theories of Africans: Francophone Literature and Anthropology in Africa* (University of Chicago Press, 1990), p. 10.

insist on the radical purity or priority of one's own voice, all we would have would be the awful din of unending strife, and a bloody political mess'.[44] Social dialogue requires, not that all voices are equal, but a willingness to engage in critical debate and to accept that some views are more valid than others. If all voices are to be heard and all views are equally valid, we may have cacophony but there can be no dialogue. Unfortunately, Said's more reasoned approach has got submerged, both in his work and that of other post-structuralist writers, beneath the inexorable logic of the anti-universalist argument.

Humanism, colonialism and the Holocaust

Associated with the anti-universalist stance of post-structuralist theories has been an unremitting hostility to a humanist approach. Humanism is a philosophy which takes human experiences as the starting point for humankind's knowledge of itself and its relation to nature. This anthropocentric outlook underpinned the scientific and philosophical revolution unleashed by the Renaissance and the Enlightenment.

At the heart of humanism are two key beliefs. First, humanists hold that human beings, while an inherent part of nature and subject to its laws, nevertheless have an exceptional status in nature because of their unique ability, arising out of human sociability, to overcome the constraints placed upon them by nature. Second, humanists believe in the unity of humankind, holding that all humans possess something in common, a something which is often described as a common 'human nature'.

The humanist outlook has expressed itself in a variety of political forms, from liberalism to Marxism. Liberal humanists tend to view human nature as a static, eternal quality given by nature. David Hume, for instance, argued that 'there is a great uniformity among the acts of men, in all nations and ages, and that human nature remains the same in its principles and operations'.[45]

Marx, on the other hand, saw the human essence as a social or historical construction. In his 'Theses on Feuerbach', for example, Marx criticized the German philosopher Ludwig Feuerbach for 'abstract[ing] from the historical process' and assuming that the human essence was an internal dumb generality which naturally unites the many individuals'. But, argued Marx, 'the human essence is no abstraction inherent in each single individual. In its reality it is the ensemble of the social relations.'[46] In other words, 'historical humanism', as Georg Lukács called it, sees 'man' not as naturally given but 'as a product of himself and of his own activity in history'.[47]

Whether liberal or Marxist, underlying all humanistic strands is a belief in human emancipation—the idea that humankind can rationally transform society through the agency of its own efforts. Indeed, no emancipatory philosophy is possible without a humanist perspective, for any anti-humanistic outlook is forced to look outside

[44] Said, *Culture and Imperialism*, p. 22.
[45] D. Hume, *Inquiry Concerning Human Understanding* (Oxford University Press, 1994; [1748]).
[46] Karl Marx, 'Theses on Feuerbach', in Marx and Engels, *Selected Works*, p. 29.
[47] Georg Lukács, *The Historical Novel*, trans. by Hannah and Stanley Mitchell (London: Merlin, 1962), pp. 28–9.

humanity for the agency of salvation. Conversely, no humanist outlook is possible without an accompanying belief in human rationality and capacity for social progress.

Anti-humanistic strands developed from the Enlightenment onwards, largely in opposition to the idea of rational human emancipation. Just as there have been a number of different strands of humanism, so there have been a number of different strands of anti-humanism, ranging from the conservatism of Burke, the Catholic reaction of de Maistre to the nihilism of Nietzsche and the Nazism of Martin Heidegger. All rejected Enlightenment rationalism and the idea of social progress because they despaired of the capacity of humankind for such rational progress. Anti-humanism rejected ideas of equality and human unity, celebrating instead difference and divergence and exalting the particular and the authentic over the universal.

Anti-humanism developed therefore as a central component of élite theories and hence of racial theories. In the postwar era, however, anti-humanism came to represent a very different tradition—the liberal, indeed radical, anti-colonialist and anti-racist outlook. In the hands of such critics of Western society as Frantz Fanon, Jean-Paul Sartre, Michel Foucault, Jacques Derrida and Louis Althusser, among others, anti-humanism became a central thread of structuralist and post-structuralist theories, and a key weapon in the interrogation of racist and imperialist discourses. 'Humanism', Sartre wrote in his famous preface to Fanon's *The Wretched of the Earth*, 'is nothing but an ideology of lies, a perfect justification for pillage; its honeyed words, its affectations of sensibility were only alibis for our aggression'.[48]

How did a philosophical outlook which originated within conservative anti-emancipatory politics, and which was a key component of racial theory, become a central motif of radical anti-racist, anti-imperialist doctrines? And how did philosophers such as Nietzsche and Heidegger, whose work had previously been seen as paving the way for twentieth-century racist and fascist ideologies, become icons of anti-racist discourse? Understanding this puzzle will take us a long way towards explaining the relationship between theories of race and the contemporary discourse of difference.

There were two main strands to postwar radical anti humanism. One developed out of anti-colonial struggles, the other through Western (and in particular French) academic philosophy and was subsequently elaborated by the 'new social movements' such as feminism and environmentalism which emerged in the late sixties and seventies.

In *The Wretched of the Earth*, Martinique-born Algerian nationalist Frantz Fanon gave voice to the rage of colonial peoples against their inhuman treatment at the hands of the imperialist powers. The humanist idea of 'Man', wrote Fanon, which lay at the heart of the Western post-Enlightenment tradition, was achieved through the dehumanizing of the non-Western Other:

That same Europe where they were never done talking of Man, and where they never stopped proclaiming that they were only anxious for the welfare of Man: today we know what sufferings humanity has paid for every one of their triumphs of the mind.[49]

---

[48] Jean-Paul Sartre, 'Preface', in Frantz Franon, *The Wretched of the Earth* (Harmondsworth: Penguin, 1967 [1961]), p. 21.
[49] F. Fanon, *The Wretched of the Earth*, p. 251.

Europeans only became human, suggested Fanon, by denying humanity to their colonial Other. As Sartre put it, 'Humanism is the counterpart of racism: it is a practice of exclusion'.[50] According to Sartre, 'There is nothing more consistent than a racist humanism since the European has only been able to become a man through creating slaves and monsters'.[51] To maintain a belief in humanism while treating non-European peoples as animals, Europeans declared that non-Europeans were in fact sub-human. Herein lies the source of racial theory in humanism. At the same time, argued Fanon, humanists salved their consciences, by inviting the sub-human colonial Other to become human by imitating 'European Man':

> Western bourgeois racial prejudice as regards the nigger and the Arab is a racism of contempt; it is a racism which minimises what it hates. Bourgeois ideology, however, which is the proclamation of an essential equality between men, manages to appear logical in its own eyes by inviting the subhuman to become human, to take as their prototype Western humanity as incarcerated in the Western bourgeoisie .[52]

The category 'human' was empty of meaning, such critics asserted, because it was ahistoric. The invocation of a common human nature hid the fact that human nature is socially and historically constructed. When humanists assert the universality of human nature, what they are really talking about are the particular human values expressed in European society. '[T]hose universal features which define the human', argues Robert Young, 'mask over the assimilation of human itself with European values.' The category of the human, he believes, 'however exalted in its conception' is 'too often invoked only in order to put the male before the female, or to classify other "races" as sub-human, and therefore not subject to the ethical pre-scriptions applicable to humanity at large'.[53] Third World critics, however, did not reject humanism in its entirety. Fanon, for instance, recognized that the contradiction lay not so much in humanism itself as in the disjuncture between the ideology of humanism and the practice of colonialism:

> All the elements of a solution to the great problems of humanity have, at different times, existed in European thought. But Europeans have not carried out in practice the mission which fell to them, which consisted of bringing their whole weight to bear violently upon these elements, of modifying their arrangement and their nature, of changing them and, finally, of bringing the problem of mankind to an infinitely higher plane.[54]

Fanon called therefore for a new humanism stripped of its racist, Eurocentric aspects: 'Let us decide not to imitate Europe; let us combine our muscles and our brains in a new direction. Let us try to create the whole man, whom Europe has been incapable of bringing to triumphant birth'.[55]

For Fanon, then, the humanist idea of 'the whole man' was key to emancipation. Despite the critique of Western humanism as a camouflage for the dehumanization of non-Western peoples, humanism remained a central component of the ideology of Third World liberation struggles of the postwar era, virtually all of which drew

---

[50] Jean-Paul Sartre, *Critique of Dialectical Reason*, vol.1: *Theory of Practical Ensembles*, trans. Alan Sheridan-Smith (London: New Left Books, 1976), p. 752.
[51] Sartre, 'Preface', in Fanon, *The Wretched of the Earth*, p. 22.
[52] Fanon, *The Wretched of the Earth*, p. 131.
[53] Young, *White Mythologies*, pp. 122, 123.
[54] Fanon, *The Wretched of the Earth*, p. 253.
[55] Ibid., p. 252.

on the emancipatory logic of universalism. Indeed Western radicals were often shocked by the extent to which anti-colonial struggles adopted what the radicals conceived of as tainted ideas. The concepts of universalism and unilinear evolutionism, Lévi-Strauss observed, found 'unexpected support from peoples who desire nothing more than to share in the benefits of industrialization; peoples who prefer to look on themselves as temporarily backward rather than permanently different'.[56] Elswhere he noted ruefully that the doctrine of cultural relativism 'was challenged by the very people for whose moral benefit the anthropologists had established it in the first place'.[57]

The willingness of Third World radicals to maintain at least a residual support for a humanistic outlook stemmed from their continued engagement in the project of liberation. Postwar radicals in the West, however, increasingly rejected humanism, not simply in its guise as a cover for racism and colonialism, but in its entirety. For postwar European intellectuals the most pressing problem was not that of establishing the ideological foundations of liberation struggles but rather of coming to terms with the demise of such struggles in Western democracies. Western intellectuals had, on the one hand, to excavate the social and intellectual roots of the Nazi experience, an experience which more than any other weighed upon the European intellectual consciousness in the immediate postwar period, and on the other, to explain why the possibilities of revolutionary change, which had seemed so promising in the early part of the century, appeared to have been extinguished. For many the explanation lay in some deep-seated malaise in European culture.

Postwar radicals asked themselves why it was that Germany, a nation with deep philosophical roots in the Enlightenment project and a strong and vibrant working-class movement, should succumb so swiftly and so completely to Nazism. The answer seemed to be that it was the logic of Enlightenment rationalism itself and the nature of democratic politics that had given rise to such barbarism. As Theodor Adorno and Max Horkheimer, members of the 'Frankfurt School' of radical German scholars, put it in their seminal work, *Dialectic of Enlightenment*, 'Enlightenment is totalitarian'.[58] In *Dialectic of Enlightenment* Adorno and Horkheimer developed the two motifs—a critique of Enlightenment rationality and social progress, on the one hand, and of mass society, on the other—which were to become immensely influential in shaping postwar discourse.

The idea that the Holocaust—and indeed all Western barbarism—found its roots in Enlightenment rationalism and humanism became a central tenet of postwar radicalism, as Lévi-Strauss expressed in an interview in *Le Monde*:

All the tragedies we have lived through, first with colonialism, then with fascism, finally the concentration camps, all this has taken shape not in opposition to or in contradiction with so-called humanism in the form in which we have been practising it for several centuries, but I would say almost as its natural continuation.[59]

According to Lévi-Strauss, the Enlightenment ambition of mastering nature, of setting humanity above nature, inevitably had destructive consequences for human-

---

[56] Lévi-Strauss, *Structural Anthropology* vol.2, p. 53.
[57] Claude Lévi-Strauss, *The View from Afar*, trans. Joachim Neugroschel and Phoebe Hoss (Harmondworth: Penguin, 1987 [1983]), p. 28.
[58] Theodor Adorno and Max Horkheimer, *Dialectic of Enlightenment* (London: Verso, 1979 [1944]), p. 6.
[59] Claude Lévi-Strauss, *Le Monde* 21–22 Jan. 1979; cited in Todorov, *On Human Diversity*, p. 67.

ity itself. A humanity which could enslave nature was quite capable of enslaving fellow human beings.

The idea that technological and social progress could be the cause of barbarism has led many critics to find evidence not simply of humanism but of the whole project of 'modernity' behind the Holocaust. Zygmunt Bauman has suggested that the Final Solution was the 'product' not 'failure' of modernity and that 'it was the rational world of modern civilisation that made the Holocaust thinkable':

> The truth is that every ingredient of the Holocaust—all those many things that rendered it possible—was normal . . . in the sense of being fully in keeping with everything we know about our civilisation, its guiding spirit, its priorities, its immanent vision of the world—and of the proper ways to pursue human happiness together with a perfect society.[60]

Bauman's hint that 'civilisation' itself may have been responsible for the barbarism of the Final Solution is made explicit by Richard Rubinstein who (in a phrase approvingly quoted by Bauman) argues that the Holocaust 'bears witness to the *advance of civilisation*':

> The world of death camps and the society it engenders reveals the progressively intensifying night side of Judeo-Christian civilisation. Civilisation means slavery, wars, exploitation, and death camps. It also means medical hygiene, elevated religious ideas, beautiful art, and exquisite music. It is an error to imagine that civilisation and savage cruelties are antitheses . . . Both creation and destruction are inseparable parts of what we call civilisation.[61]

Here again in the debate on the origins of the Holocaust, as in the discussion about the Other, we can see the conflation of arguments about the post-Enlightenment discourse with those about a supposed tradition that has existed from the beginnings of the Western (or Judeo-Christian) history. But what can it mean to suggest that barbarism is an inseparable part of civilization? It is, on the one hand, logically meaningless, since the two concepts are defined in opposition to each other. On the other hand to suggest that 'the advance of civilisation' inevitably leads to 'slavery, wars, exploitation, and death camps' can only mean that barbarism is an eradicable part of human nature. But is this not to posit a concept of human nature that is as ahistoric as that supposedly held by humanists? Condemning civilization as forever imbricated with inhumanity is certainly an argument that sits uneasily with a critique of humanism which claims that an ahistoric notion of 'Man' has been used to deny humanity to the West's Others.

The argument that humanism and rationalism (or 'modernity') are the causes of the Holocaust implies, in the words of Tzvetan Todorov, 'not only that the speaker is disregarding or repressing the ideological origins of fascism in nineteenth century *antihumanism* . . . but also that the speaker is wilfully cultivating a logical paradox, since he is complacently deducing the thesis of the *inequality* of man on the basis of human *equality*'.[62]

The second motif in the Frankfurt School analysis of fascism which came to dominate postwar thought was the critique of mass society. The concept of mass society began to win acceptance among sociologists in the 1950s. For the sociologists

---

[60] Zygmunt Bauman, *Modernity and the Holocaust* (Cambridge: Polity Press, 1989), pp 6, 13, 8.

[61] Richard L. Rubenstein, *The Cunning of History*(London: Harper Row, 1978), pp. 91, 95.

[62] T. Todorov, *On Human Diversity: Nationalism, Racism and Exoticism in French Thought*, trans. C. Porter (Cambridge, MA.: Harvard University Press, 1993), p. 68.

of the mass society, technological progress and mass democracy had combined to debase society, creating a mass of people with little intellectual depth, spiritual involvement or cultural profundity. The creation of such a mass society had taken humanity to the abyss of barbarism. Behind the rise of Nazism lay the willingness of the unthinking masses to follow herd-like behind demagogic leaders such as Adolf Hitler. This idea was first expressed in the Frankfurt School's analysis of the 'authoritarian personality'—a personality type characterized by extreme obedience and unquestioning respect for authority and usually accompanied by rigidity, conventionality, prejudice, and intolerance of weakness or ambiguity.[63] According to the authors of *The Authoritarian Personality*, the potential of fascism lay in the presence of such a personality type within the mass of the people. Given that democratic societies, such as the USA, were also mass societies, the sociologists of the Frankfurt School believed that the potential existed for the rise of fascism there too.

The critique of Enlightenment rationality and the critique of mass society became fused into the 'totalitarian' theory of fascism. Popularized by Hannah Arendt in her book *The Origins of Totalitarianism*, the theory suggested that fascism was a species of totalitarianism, similar to the Soviet Union, Communist China or (a comparison that later totalitarian theorists would make) the Ayatollah Khomeini's Iran and Saddam Hussein's Iraq. The components of a totalitarian state were a herd-like mass, a compelling totalizing ideology that subsumed all under its cold logic and a machine-like society that effaced all individuality in the name of a higher rationality. For Arendt totalitarianism represented the 'madness of the mob', the 'refuse of all classes', falling under the leadership of *déclassé* intellectuals. The members of the mob sought to merge into something larger than themselves, to give up their individualism to belong to the mass.[64] The critique of totalitarianism—and of totality— was to become a defining feature of post-structuralist discourse.

The irony in this is that the critique of totalitarianism is in substance a reworking of the nineteenth-century critique of Enlightenment rationalism and of mass society pursued by philosophers such as Nietzsche and Heidegger, whose work flowed from the hostility of the intelligentsia to equality and mass democracy. Arendt was a student of Heidegger's and her theory of totalitarianism carries over the main themes of Heidegger's thought in its anti-mass character, its incipient anti-rationalism and in particular its hostility to the Enlightenment as the embodiment of both.

Heidegger had been an active member of the Nazi Party until 1943. After the war he attempted to rehabilitate his reputation and in the document *Rectoral Addresses— Facts and Thoughts* he marshalled the arguments which he hoped would distance himself from the Third Reich. The key piece of evidence for the defence was the assertion that Nazism was simply another manifestation of the spirit of modernity. According to Heidegger there existed a 'universal will to power within history, now understood to embrace the planet' and that 'everything stands in this historical reality, no matter whether it is called communism, fascism or world democracy'.[65] It

---

[63] Theodor Adorno, Else Frenke-Brunswik, Daniel J. Levinson and R. Nevitt Sanford, *The Authoritarian Personality* (New York: Norton, 1950).

[64] Hannah Arendt, *The Origins of Totalitarianism* (New York: Harcourt, Brace & Jovanovich, 1973), p. 309.

[65] Cited in Thomas Rockmore, *On Heidegger's Nazism and Philosophy* (Berkeley, CA: University of California Press, 1994), pp. 93–4.

is a telling measure of the degree of confusion in postwar theory that liberal and Nazi explanations of the Holocaust can barely be prised apart. As James Heartfield observes, 'Heidegger's thought, having tried to articulate—or spiritualise—national socialism, went on to a more remarkable achievement. Through Hannah Arendt and the totalitarian thesis, Heidegger's ideas shaped the interpretation and critique of fascism after its defeat.'[66]

Indeed, it did more than that. The anti-humanism of Heidegger, and his fellow thinkers, became a central theme of post-structuralist and postmodernist discourse, of colonial discourse analysis and of the theories of difference and cultural pluralism. As Heartfield remarks, 'how perverse that the rejection of . . . barbarism should preserve the very prejudices that gave rise to it'.

Underlying the commonality of themes in racial and post-structuralist theory is their attempt to come to terms with the same problem—the disjuncture between a belief in equality and progress, and a society that can seem to deliver neither. Read the whole of the passage in which Sartre rails against the hypocrisy of Western humanism and this becomes clear:

> Liberty, equality, fraternity, love, honour, patriotism and what have you. All this did not prevent us from making anti-racial speeches about dirty niggers, dirty Jews and dirty Arabs. High-minded people, liberal or just softhearted, protest that they were shocked by such inconsistency; but they were either mistaken or dishonest, for with us there is nothing more consistent than a racist humanism since the European has only been able to become a man through creating slaves and monsters.[67]

Nineteenth-century thinkers who held fast to Enlightenment principles—whether liberal or revolutionary—argued that the disjuncture could be closed by social transformation. By the end of the century, however, liberals had by and large come to despair of the possibility of any such transformation and were drifting over to the long-held conservative belief that inequalities were both inevitable and necessary. By the midpoint of the twentieth century, the experience of Nazism and the defeat of working-class movements had led radicals to similar pessimistic conclusions. As Stuart Hughes observes in his wonderfully lucid study of postwar intellectual thought, there was within the radical intelligentsia a widespread

> disappointment in the course of recent history, in the strategy of the political parties that laid claim to the inheritance of Marx, and, most particularly, in the proletariat itself. The class which Engels had celebrated as the 'heirs of classical philosophy' had failed to perform in the style expected of it.[68]

Postwar developments entrenched such views. The experience of the failure of the student revolts of May 1968, the collapse of both Stalinist and social democratic parties in the eighties and the demise of Third World liberation movements all added to the belief that social transformation was a chimera.

The very goals of 'modernity' seemed unattainable. As Bauman has put it, 'Postmodernity is modernity coming to terms with its own impossibility: a self-monitoring modernity, one that consciously discards what it was once unconsciously doing'.[69] For postwar theorists the gap between belief and reality could be closed

---

[66] James Heartfield, 'The Heidegger Affair' (unpublished paper).
[67] Sartre, 'Preface' in Fanon, *Wretched of the Earth*, p. 22.
[68] Hughes, *The Sea Change*, pp. 135–6.
[69] Zygmunt Bauman, *Modernity and Ambivalence* (Cambridge: Polity Press, 1991), p. 272.

not by transforming the reality but by relinquishing their beliefs. Despairing of social change, post-structuralist and postmodernist thinkers asserted instead that equality and humanity had no meaning, and that difference and diversity should be our goal.

Despair about social transformation also led postwar theorists to see the barbarism of the twentieth century not as a product of specific social relations, but unspecifically as the consequence of 'modernity'. The claim that the categories of modernity necessarily give rise to a racial division of humanity conflates two different meanings of 'modernity'. On the one hand there is modernity in the sense of an intellectual or philosophical outlook which holds that it is possible to apprehend the world through reason and science—what has come to be called the 'Enlightenment project'—and the technological advance that such an outlook has engendered. On the other hand modernity has also come to mean the particular society in which these ideas found expression—in other words, capitalism.

By conflating the social relations of capitalism with the intellectual and techno-logical progress of 'modernity', the product of the former can be laid at the door of the latter. The specific problems created by capitalist social relations became dehistoricized. In post-structuralist discourse racial theory, colonialism or the Holocaust are not investigated in their specificity, as products of distinctive tendencies within capitalist society, but are all lumped together as the general consequence of 'modernity'. In this way the positive aspects of capitalist society— its invocation of reason, its technological advancements, its ideological commit-ment to equality and universalism—are denigrated while its negative aspects—the inability to overcome social divisions, the propensity to treat large sections of humanity as 'inferior' or 'subhuman', the contrast between technological advance and moral turpitude, the tendencies towards barbarism—are seen as inevitable or natural.

From the 'Right to be Equal' to the 'Right to be Different'

The terrain of anti-racist struggle today is no longer that of social equality but cultural diversity. Indeed, the very meaning of social equality has come into question: for many the concept of equality in the old sense is a form of discredited universalism which does not take into account the differences within society. Equality has come to be redefined from 'the right to be the same' to mean 'the right to be different'.

In the sixties and seventies, the struggle for equal rights meant campaigns against immigration laws or against segregation through which different 'races' were treated differently; today, it means campaigns for separate schools, demands to use different languages, the insistence on maintaining particular cultural practices. The black American critic bell hooks observes that in the past, 'civil rights reform reinforced the idea that black liberation should be defined by the degree to which black people gained equal access to material opportunities and privileges available to whites— jobs, housing, schooling, etc.' This strategy could never bring about liberation, argues hooks, because such 'ideas of "freedom" were informed by efforts to imitate the behaviour, lifestyles, and most importantly the values and consciousness of white colonisers'.[70] In the Alice in Wonderland world of postmodern discourse, the struggle for equality is likened to the racist practices of the 'white colonisers' while the rejection of equal rights is seen as the hallmark of social advancement. 'Equality' has come to mean oppression, 'difference' liberation.

The shift from campaigning for the 'right to be equal' to proclaiming the 'right to be different' is predicated on the antihumanist, anti-essentialist tendencies in post-structuralist discourse. But these tendencies themselves are a product of the dis-illusionment with social change which has become an increasingly prominent feature of contemporary politics. Campaigning for equality requires one to believe that it is possible to effect social change, to transform society through humanity's collective efforts. Conversely proclaiming difference requires us to accept society as it is, to accept as given the divisions and inequalities that characterize our social world. In this sense the philosophy of difference is a rationalization of the demise and defeat of social movements over the past decades which has led radicals to renounce the very idea of social struggle. The ideas of difference seek to accommodate to this new political era.

For all their desire to be different, what postmodern pluralists really want is their particular history, their particular culture, their particular story to be acknowledged. Pluralism is about accepting the common framework of society but arguing about what we want to be included in it.

Unable to transform society, postmodern critics accommodate to, and occasion-ally even celebrate, oppression. bell hooks writes nostalgically of the segregated South of her childhood as a 'marginal space where black people (though contained) exercised power, where we were truly caring and supportive to one another':

I had come from an agrarian world where folks were content to get by on little, where Baba, mama's mother, made soap, dug fishing worms, set traps for rabbits, made butter and wine, sewed quilts and wrung the necks of chickens... The sweet communion we felt (that strong sense of solidarity shrouding and protecting my growing up years was something I thought all black people had known) was rooted in love, relational love, the care we had towards one another.[71]

hooks might have added that this was also a world where poverty was endemic, starvation common and lynching an ever-present threat. hooks goes on to contrast the romanticized black community of her childhood with the 'corrosive' nature of sixties black militancy:

Looking back, it is easy to see that the nationalism of the sixties and seventies was very different from the racial solidarity born of shared circumstance and not theories of black power. Not that an articulation of black power was not important; it was. Only it did not deliver the goods; it was too informed by corrosive power relations, too mythic, to take the place of that concrete relational love that bonded black folks together in communities of hope and struggle.[72]

For hooks, struggle itself becomes the problem. The aspiration to power is necessarily 'corrosive' in contrast to the 'concrete relational love' that characterized black communities in the past. In the face of social movements that failed to 'deliver

---

[70] bell hooks, *Yearning: Race, Gender and Cultural Politics* (London: Turnabout, 1991), p. 15.
[71] hooks, *Yearning*, p. 35.
[72] Ibid., p. 36.

the goods', post-structuralist and postmodernist thinkers are forced to romanticize oppression, decry equality and accept difference and marginality. bell hooks makes this clear when she derives the politics of difference from the defeat of the sixties' black liberation movement:

In the wake of the black power movement, after so many rebels were slaughtered and lost, many of these voices were silenced by a repressive state; others became inarticulate. It has become necessary to find new avenues to transmit the messages of black liberation struggle, new ways to talk about racism and other voices of displaced, marginalised, exploited, and oppressed black people.[73]

The philosophy of difference is the politics of defeat, born out of defeat. It is the product of disillusionment with the possibilities of social change and the acceptance of the inevitability of an unequal, fragmented world. Unable to pursue the goal of equality, postmodernists have simply refashioned its meaning and embraced difference. The consequence has been the celebration of marginality, of parochialism and indeed of oppression. Transcending such an outlook requires not simply intellectual conviction but political aspiration.

[73] Ibid., p. 25.

Does cosmopolitan thinking have a future?

DEREK HEATER[1]

It certainly has a past.[2] And that past, especially in its Stoic foundations, reveals a clear ethical purpose: 'As long as I remember that I am part of such a whole [Universe],' explained Marcus Aurelius, '... I shall ... direct every impulse of mine to the common interest'.[3] Moreover, the word 'cosmopolitan' derives from *kosmopolites*, citizen of the universe, and *polites*, citizen, notably in its Aristotelean definition, has a decided ethical content. Accordingly, if the citizen of a state (*polis*) should be possessed of civic virtue (*arete*), by extension, the citizen of the universe (*kosmopolis*) should live a life of virtue, guided by his perception and understanding of the divine, natural law. True, in non-academic parlance the word 'cosmopolitan' has, from the eighteenth century, acquired the vague and vulgar connotation for an individual of enjoying comfortable familiarity with a variety of geographical and cultural environments. None the less, the more precise, political–ethical sense of a *kosmopolites* is so much more apposite to our present purpose that this essay will be framed in the main by this meaning.

With the question thus interpreted, it follows that we wish to know whether state citizenship, as we currently understand it, might be paralleled by a world citizenship of comparable content; if so, we obviously also wish to know what the implications must be for the individual's moral and political behaviour and the institutional contexts which would be needed to facilitate this cosmopolitan behaviour. Less obviously, perhaps, because the problem has been relatively neglected, we should wish to know how the novice world citizen can be educated into the role. Now, although state citizenship is itself a highly contentious concept and has developed along the separate republican and liberal pathways, there would surely be little dispute that its essential components are: identity, morality/responsibilities, rights and competence. Accepting this list as a rough rule-of-thumb, in order to respond to the question, 'Does cosmopolitan thinking have a future?', we should proceed along the following lines. We must conceive of these four elements as they would be experienced and lived by a putative world citizen. This exercise would provide an agenda for future cosmopolitan thinking. But—only if these lines of investigation

---

[1] I wish to record my gratitude to the reader of the first draft of this article for most helpful suggestions for improvements, which I have striven to incorporate.

[2] For the Greek foundations, see H. C. Baldry, *The Unity of Mankind in Greek Thought* (Cambridge: Cambridge University Press, 1965). An informative recent article focusing on the Roman period (though rather misleading on Alexander the Great's importance in the history of cosmopolitan thinking) is Lisa Hill, 'The Two *Republicae* of the Roman Stoics: Can a Cosmopolite be a Patriot?', *Citizenship Studies*, 4 (2000), pp. 47–63.

[3] Marcus Aurelius Antoninus (trans. C. R. Haines), *The Communings with Himself* (i.e. Meditations) (London:Heinemann and Cambridge, MA: Harvard University Press,1961), X, 6.

are worthwhile at all. For there is a convinced and strong body of academic opinion that denies this, a point of view that we cannot ignore. Accordingly, at the risk of a little repetition between this section and the next, we need to sketch in the main hostile arguments and the ways in which they can be rebutted.

The debate already underway

As interest burgeoned in the cosmopolitan concept in the second half of the 1990s and exposition was buttressed by advocacy, so scholars inimical to the case engaged in vigorous debate with its supporters: the advocates of communitarianism versus the exponents of cosmopolitanism; those who hold to the view that only a bounded citizenship is proper citizenship versus those who believe that world citizenship is a valid variant.[4] Indeed, the very recency and intensity of these exchanges suggest that the debate is likely to continue.

To start, then, with a summary of some of the main points in the antis' academic armoury. At root, they assert, cosmopolitanism is unreal, floating on the air of vague utopianism. Global institutions do not exist for the exercise of a world citizenship; international law is precisely that—inter-national; and the individual is dependent upon his or her state as the fount of justice. Furthermore, the ideas of a world community and world citizenship do not impinge on the thoughts or imaginations of the vast bulk of humanity. Michael Walzer is characteristically trenchant in articulating this view: he asserts: 'I am not a citizen of the world .... I am not even aware that there is a world such that one could be a citizen of it. No one has offered me citizenship ...'.[5] Danilo Zolo takes this absence of a sense of world community one stage further by arguing that democracy is impossible in a heterogeneous population, which the planet's population clearly is.[6] The corollary must therefore be that world citizenship is impossible since in this age only a democratic form of citizenship is conceivable. But, in any case, assert the communitarians, the very essence of citizenship presupposes an exclusive status in a compact community. 'The claim to citizenship,' Rob Walker declares, 'like the claims to individual autonomy and state sovereignty on which the modern concept of citizenship depends, makes no sense except as a way of responding to our celebration of particular patterns of inclusion and exclusion'.[7]

For opponents of world citizenship this is a clinching argument: cosmopolitans are guilty of an abuse of language by having the impertinence to deploy the word 'citizenship' in their discourse; in truth, even the values they seek to promote have little or no meaning outside a state context. Did not Hegel teach us that, 'All the

---

[4] Two notable sets of argument-on-paper are: Martha C. Nussbaum et al., *For Love of Country: Debating the Limits of Patriotism* (Boston, MA: Beacon Press, 1996); and Kimberly Hutchings and Roland Dannreuther (eds.), *Cosmopolitan Citizenship* (Basingstoke: Macmillan and New York: St Martin's, 1999).

[5] Quoted in Andrew Linklater, *The Transformation of Political Community* (Cambridge: Polity Press, 1998), p. 225, n.5.

[6] Danilo Zolo, Cosmopolis: Prospects for World Government (Cambridge: Polity Press, 1997).

[7] R. B. J. Walker, 'Citizenship after the Modern Subject', in Hutchings and Dannreuther, *Cosmopolitan Citizenship*, p. 183. For a combative exposition of the communitarian interpretation of citizenship, see David Miller, 'Bounded Citizenship', in the same work.

value man has, all spiritual reality, he has only through the state'?[8] Gertrude Himmelfarb picks up Martha Nussbaum's list of universal values, which the latter believes provide cosmopolitanism with its moral content and vindication: 'where can we find those substantive, universal, common values? And what are they, specifically, concretely, existentially?' Himmelfarb asks, and replies: 'To answer those questions is to enter the world of reality—which is the world of nations, peoples and polities'.[9]

Two models of identity/loyalty are often used to explain and criticize the notion of world citizenship. Expounding the simple bipolar model, communitarians argue that commitment to the state should be given the clearest priority over commitment to the world community, if any recognition is accorded at all to that latter nebulous idea; furthermore, that patriotism is, as a matter of fact, immeasurably the stronger emotional and moral force. The more complex model conceives a variety of commitments in concentric circles, extending round the individual in ever-increasing distances—family, locality, region, state, subcontinent (for EU members) and the world. According to the communitarian, the world, being most remote in experience and understanding, is bound to be by far and away the feeblest in its attraction of allegiance and rightly so, and definitely not worthy of the title, 'citizenship'.

The purpose of this article is to demonstrate the feasibility and utility of further cosmopolitan thinking, and, by identifying topics for this attention, we shall, at least implicitly, be countering the above arguments of repudiation. Even so, a succinct rejoinder to the components of the negative case will be helpful here.

That cosmopolitanism does not reflect reality is partly false and partly its very point. The proposition is partially false because belief in a Natural Law and its concomitant rights—natural, of man, human, in sequence of nomenclature—have a long tradition: belief in the existence of a morality and an identity above the principles shaped by states has been and still is widely held. And the proposition is partially true because the purpose of the cosmopolitan agenda is to change a reality which it perceives as currently under the strain of obsolescence. Cosmopolitanism is an idea, and it is not necessary to be a Marxist to appreciate his dictum that the point of philosophers is to change the world. If nationhood has a monopoly on citizenship and that monopoly is in practice being shown to be inadequate by such forces as European integration and globalization, then it is the communitarians' attempt to preserve state citizenship as the sole version of the status that is detached from reality. Some current authorities in the field of cosmopolitan thinking have indeed latched on to the word 'transformation' to indicate the depth of change occurring in the contemporary world and the need for an appropriate response.[10] One is reminded of de Tocqueville's designation of the undermining and destruction of the *ancien régime* as 'the great transformation'. Radical change requires radical thinking.

---

[8] G. W. F. Hegel, *Reason in History*, quoted in Adrian Oldfield, *Citizenship and Community* (London: Routledge, 1990), p. 82.

[9] Gertrude Himmelfarb, 'The Illusions of Cosmopolitanism', in Nussbaum, *For Love of Country*, pp. 74–5.

[10] For example, Linklater, *The Transformation of Political Community*; David Held and Anthony McGrew, David Goldblatt and Jonathan Perraton, *Global Transformations: Politics, Economics and Culture* (Cambridge: Polity Press, 1999); David Held and Anthony McGrew (eds.), *The Global Transformations Reader* (Cambridge: Polity Press, 2000).

Moreover, this process of transformation at the turn of the twentieth century is having a direct impact on the meaning of citizenship. The central argument proceeds along the following lines. If, because of globalization, states are decreasingly able to defend or promote their citizens' interests, then those citizens are in effect, at least to some degree, disenfranchized. There is a consequent need to re-enfranchize them at alternative levels, both sub- and supra-national.[11] Such an argument, of course, depends on a more flexible interpretation of the word 'citizenship' than communitarians can accept. But they are working to the Aristotelean/republican version of the concept. The Kantian/liberal version does allow for much less rigidity, and it is therefore not surprising that cosmopolitan thinkers place great reliance on the illustrious work of Kant. Thus, if the likes of Walzer do not believe that they are, or can be considered to be, world citizens, then the proponents of world citizenship aver: so much the worse for the world's legal and political systems, still inhibiting the status of world citizenship from developing beyond its embryonic form; and so much the worse for the constrained civic morality of those suffering such parochial attitudes.

No one, after all, is obliged to swallow Hegel's moral prescription. There is an alternative to hand for cosmopolites in the form of Habermas's discourse ethics. Summarized, he teaches that 'norms cannot be valid unless they can command the consent of everyone whose interests stand to be affected by them. ... One of its central beliefs is that the validity of the principles on which it acts can only be determined through a dialogue which is in principle open to all human beings'.[12]

We come now to the crucial issue of multiple identity. It is easy enough to demolish the caricatures of both positions; because patriotism is not enough, and the destruction of nations by a world state does not bear contemplating. What is at issue is how far world citizenship could and should balance patriotic citizenship on the bipolar model; and whether progressive ethical weakening by distance on the concentric model could and should be reversed, in some measure even if not completely. It is the possibilities for restructuring the concentric model that has been given the more attention for the obvious reasons that such thinking is both more practicable and closer to the needs of cosmopolitanism than the bipolar model. This is a complex field in itself. To oversimplify: some commentatators draw lessons from the classical Stoic thoughts on the matter;[13] some argue that, since all humans are morally equal, any justification for treating those distant from us any differently from those close must be seriously questioned, not automatically accepted;[14] while others hold that balancing competing duties against others in the several circles should be decided on pragmatic grounds.[15] What cosmopolitan thinkers cannot abide, as being ethically disreputable, is the denial or disparagement of a moral responsibility at the outermost, global circle.

From this hasty presentation of the two sides in the cosmopolitan debate it is surely evident that there is sufficient strength in the communitarians' arguments to

---

[11] See, for example, Matthew Horsman and Andrew Marshall, *After the Nation-State: Citizens, Tribalism and the New World Disorder* (London: HarperCollins, 1994), pp. 216–33.

[12] Linklater, *Transformation of Political Community*, p. 91.

[13] For example, Hill, 'The Two *Republicae* of the Roman Stoics'.

[14] Charles R. Beitz, 'Cosmopolitan Liberalism and the States System', in Chris Brown (ed.), *Political Restructuring in Europe: Ethical Perspectives* (London: Routledge, 1994).

[15] Chris Brown, 'The Idea of World Community', in Held and McGrew, *Global Transformations Reader*.

warrant further, consolidating thinking by the cosmopolites, and that there is sufficient validity in the cosmopolites' arguments to justify that further intellectual investment. However, before suggesting the lines along which this thinking might profitably be pursued, it is worthwhile outlining an interpretive historical pattern that adds even greater force to the case for continued work.

The historical pattern

The reader is asked to consider the following thoughts derived from the contemplation of the broad historical pattern of the relationship between state citizenship, nationhood and world citizenship.

The truth that forms the foundation of some contemporary scholars' hostility to cosmopolitan citizenship is that citizenship is a status and form of political identity that connects the individual to the state, the 'state', for all intents and purposes, being synonymous with 'nation'. True this pattern may be, but it has not always been so in the past; it may not, perhaps, remain so in the future—whether that future proves to be some distant time or rather sooner.

Political thinking in fourth-century Athens could accommodate the concepts of citizenship as expounded by Aristotle, pan-Hellenic nationhood as expounded by Isocrates and world citizenship as expounded by Zeno, without linking state citizenship and nationhood or assuming the incompatibility of world citizenship with either. This Greek tolerance of three basic and simultaneous forms of political identity is also evident in Rome and in the classical revivals of the Renaissance and, especially, the Enlightenment.

The key factors in this peaceful coexistence of the three concepts were the relatively weak political contents of the cosmopolitan and national ideas. To illustrate briefly: the Stoic philosophy required its adherents to live a life of civic virtue and participation while yet keeping faith with the cosmopolitan ethic: the biographies of Seneca and Marcus Aurelius are models of this ideal. More significant, however, are the traditional notions of nationhood. A 'nation', even as late as the eighteenth century, was understood as a component of, not coterminous with, a state. In France, for instance, the inhabitants of the country were commonly referred to as 'a people of the French nations'[16], while Montesquieu equated the French nation with the 'lords and bishops',[17] and was by no means alone in asserting an elitist meaning to the word 'nation', as distinct from *patrie*.

Nevertheless, all this was changing even as Montesquieu wrote. 'Nation' was being conflated with 'state'. This semantic shift was encapsulated in the 1789 Declaration of Rights, Article III of which proclaimed that 'the principle of all sovereignty rests essentially in the nation'. The state was the people was the nation. This conflation of state and nation in the new theory of popular national sovereignty gave birth to (or was given birth by?) nationalism, an ideology of such power that cosmopolitan thinking was all but expunged in the nineteenth century.

---

[16] See Guido Zernatto, 'Nation: The History of a Word', *The Review of Politics*, VI (1944), p. 362.
[17] Montesquieu, *L'Esprit des Lois,* XXVIII, p. 9.

This development is crucial for our present purpose. Since cosmopolitan thinking is now being taken seriously, and since, as many would accept, these scholarly investigations and practical proposals are prompted in part by the debilitation of the nation-state, then this historical sketch throws a new light on the current interest. In 1977 Hedley Bull offered us the insight of what he called 'the new medievalism'[18] to describe the increasing diversity of the loci of power, and this image has been recently revived as 'neo-medievalism'.[19] Let us now, however, introduce an alternative historical pattern or analogy, which we may call 'the new classicism'.

To recapitulate and develop, it looks something like this. In classical thinking about sociopolitical identities, from ancient Greece to Enlightenment Europe, citizenship, nationhood and world citizenship were held in mutually compatible, parallel spheres of life. What each portended changed over time: citizenship for Aristotle was not the same as Bodin's concept. What Herodotus meant by nationhood was different from Montesquieu's meaning. Marcus Aurelius had a tighter understanding of world citizenship than Thomas Paine. Yet, over this great span of time, whenever the three identities were thought about, room was found for all. Then, for two hundred years, from *c.* 1800 to *c.* 2000 the nation-state, girded up by the doctrine of nationalism, demanded a single political identity for its people: national-citizenship. Cosmopolitan citizenship, even as an idea, let alone a programme, had, as far as was possible, to be pushed out of human consciousness. This was an aberration—a mere two-century diversion from the more than two-millennia tradition of possible multiple identity. What is now happening, though without any awareness of the classical background, is a separation of citizenship from its fusion with nationhood (by intra- and supra-state trends) and the restoration of cosmopolitan thinking. We are entering a period of classical revival if we did but know it.

Even so, the interpretations, hopes and ambitions of contemporary cosmopolitan scholars and campaigners exceed the mental horizons of the Stoic, neostoic and *philosophe* cosmopolites. Nevertheless, the limitations of these earlier thinkers can be most effectively transcended only if it is possible to model a modern world citizenship on a modern state citizenship. An indication of what this requires must now therefore be attempted.

Components of citizenship

Identity

At the heart of being a citizen is identity. There is not much point in being a citizen, except in the very weakest sense of the term, unless you feel that you are a citizen. The French Revolutionaries understood this: they knew that they had to transform the subjects of Louis XVI into citizens of France, not merely by constitutional draftsmanship, but by nurturing a civic consciousness. True, one's identity as a

[18] Hedley Bull, *The Anarchical Society: A Study of Order in World Politics* (London: Macmillan, 1977), esp. pp. 264–76.
[19] See, for example, Linklater, *The Transformation of Political Community*, pp. 193–5.

citizen has a dual meaning: one's legal status as shown on a passport, for instance, as well as one's feeling of belonging. It is this latter, psychological meaning that we are discussing here. And in that sense citizens have an identity by virtue of recognizing what they share with their fellow-citizens. In the words of W. J. M. Mackenzie, 'Those who share a place share an identity ... whether "the place" is taken to be "space-ship earth"; or a beloved land ...' [20] Can individuals have multiple political identities and can one of these identities be cosmopolitan? (For there is no intention, even among present-day world federalists, of cosmopolitanism subsuming state citizenship and nationhood just as nationalist citizenship submerged cosmopolitanism.)

Of course multiple civic identity is possible: it is a fact of life in all federal states and in the EU. What future cosmopolitan thinking must investigate is how a world citizenship identity can be strengthened and spread in order to counterbalance state citizenship and national identities. This is no easy task. The Stoic tradition is but marginally helpful, in part because it was essentially an elitist philosophy: the cosmopolis and its natural law was comprehensible only to those furnished with a sufficiently developed rational faculty. And the neostoics and the *philosophes* did little more than assert the common origins and homogeneity of mankind without confronting the severe problem of the very strongly held cultural, including religious, differences which overlay the fundamental sameness (a problem of which Samuel Huntington has recently reminded us).[21]

More helpful clues concerning ways of firming-up a cosmopolitan identity may be gleaned from the history of state citizenship. Civic loyalty has often been cemented by means of an uplifting mythology, a patriotic history and the bonding enthusiasm aroused by symbols and ceremonies. Even so, transferring, say, the recommendations of Rousseau or the practices of the French Revolution to a global arena presents difficulties. There are no widely known universal myths or heroes, there are no heart-racing universal ceremonies, and there is no well-used history of the world interpreted as an entity. Or, rather, attempts by anthropologists, historians, UN and UNESCO to provide these supports for an imaginative cosmopolitan identity have enjoyed little success. Even at the subcontinental level of the European Community/Union the symbols recommended by the Adonnino Committee in 1985—postage-stamps, flag and anthem—have had feeble effects. Schools, too, have sometimes been expected to perform a role; but this aspect of the means of consolidating a cosmopolitan identity will be more conveniently dealt with, alongside the element of competence, in a separate subsection on education below.

The root contrast between a consciousness of state citizenship and of world citizenship is, of course, that state citizenship has always been a status marking off the citizen from the non-citizen. Originally this was a distinction internal to the polity as well as a means of distinguishing between citizens of different polities. The inter-state type of distinction has been hardened as a means of self-identity by the impact of nationalism: I am a citizen, you are an alien. But, short of the discovery of aliens in the extra-terrestrial sense, putative world citizens will have no other group in contrast with whom they can consolidate their global identity. That, however, is a cosmological, not a cosmopolitan question.

---

[20] W. J. M. Mackenzie, *Political Identity* (Harmondsworth: Penguin, 1978), p. 130.
[21] Samuel P. Huntington, *The Clash of Civilizations and the Remaking of World Order* (New York: Simon & Schuster, 1996).

Marcus Aurelius was conscious of being 'a part of the whole Universe controlled by Nature';[22] the neostoic Justus Lipsius knew that all men are 'sprung first out of the same stock';[23] and Paine wished to broadcast the truth that 'mankind of whatever nation or profession they may be ... [are] the work of one Creator'.[24] The challenge to today's cosmopolitan thinkers is to give much fuller content to these expressions of cosmopolitan identity and translate them into terms relevant to the present and future world's peoples, who are of diverse religions, or none, and who, for the most part, are limited in their mental horizons to their local and national cultures, sanctified by long generations of loyalty. Moreover, in this process of translation humankind must be brought to understand and care that they are all (in Mackenzie's 1970s parlance) citizens of 'space-ship earth'. If this expression of identities is achievable, it will accelerate the growth of a practicable world citizenship, not least in its ethical dimension.

Morality/responsibilities

Civic identity is a moral identity. Through membership of and by relating to a social group, the individual acquires a moral commitment to that group. The citizen owes loyalty to the state, has an obligation to abide by the laws of the state, has the responsibility of treating fellow-citizens with respect, has the duty to participate in and support the state in its civilian and military needs. This, at any rate, is the prescription of the civic republican style of citizenship. We must then build in the liberal stress on rights, that is, the moral obligation of the state to honour the entitlements of the individual *qua* citizen and the obligation of the citizen to recognize that fellow-citizens have equal rights. We thus arrive at an ethical structure of duties and rights relating citizen to state and citizen to citizen (the so-called 'vertical' and 'horizontal' civic relationships in the current argot).

The act of transferring this moral content of citizenship to the global plane raises two major questions that have, implicitly or explicitly, underlain cosmopolitan thinking throughout its history, and still require further work. One is to define the moral component of world citizenship in the forms of ideals, responsibilities and rights. The matter of rights will be discussed in the subsection below devoted to that aspect of citizenship. The thrust of thinking about ideals and responsibilities will be treated here. The second question has caused a great deal more debate and controversy: this is whether there is any real possibility of individuals adhering at one and the same time to two moral codes: that required of them *qua* state citizens, and that required of them *qua* world citizens.

First, then, what can be identified as cosmopolitan ideals? That a cosmopolitan morality should be seen to have a set of ideals as a kind of collectively-agreed lowest common denominator has been propounded by Janna Thompson, who has written that 'cosmopolitanism is founded on moral ideals. It depends on the notion that

[22] Marcus Aurelius, *The Communings*, X, 6.
[23] Justus Lipsius (ed. R. Kirk; trans. J. Stradling), *Two Bookes of Constancie* (New Brunswick, NJ: Rutgers University Press, 1939), I, ix.
[24] Quoted T. J. Schlereth, *The Cosmopolitan Ideal in Enlightenment Thought* (Notre Dame, IN and London: University of Notre Dame Press, 1977), p. 106.

there are values which everyone in the world ought to accept, whatever their personal interests or community loyalties.' She goes on to list four such ideals, namely, peace and security, self-determination of communities, freedom of individuals and individual well-being.[25] It is permissible, however, to wonder (as additions to a future agenda) whether these ideals are truly acceptable in all cultures, and how they would help to define the individual's sense of moral identity and behaviour as a citizen of the world.

The matter of identifying universal responsibilities has become an interesting political issue at the end of the twentieth century. From 1948 to 1976 there emerged from the UN the Universal Declaration, two International Covenants and an Optional Protocol expounding and committing states to honour fundamental human rights. All very well, but are not human beings, or should they not be, also the bearers of universal responsibilities? If the liberal tradition of citizenship rights has a corresponding notion of universal human rights, surely the civic republican tradition of citizenship duties and responsibilities should also be reflected at the global level. In 1987 the InterAction Council, a group of highly distinguished ex-heads of state and government started meetings in order to draft a set of human ethical standards in the form of a Universal Declaration of Human Responsibilities complementary to the Universal Declaration of Rights; it appeared in due course in 1997. The document deserves far greater publicity and discussion than it has in fact received.

We come now to the second question, that is, whether an individual, even if accepting dual identities—state and cosmopolitan—can comfortably accommodate two sets of moral demands deriving from these separate sources. Aristotle famously showed that, 'it is possible to be a good citizen without possessing the excellence which is the quality of the good man'.[26] Since, however, by his own argument, man can achieve his full potential only through the civic life of the *polis*, one feels that this is the goodness to which Aristotle gives priority. Kant, in contrast, prefers the goodness of man to the goodness of the citizen. 'Kant's political theory,' says Kimberly Hutchings, 'is always cosmopolitan in the sense that it is guided by principles which are derived from the universal law'. Yet the dichotomy is still there, as she explains: 'this universalist orientation is necessarily in tension with the actual nature of political and legal order'.[27] Reason, argues Kant, urges us towards the universal moral law; nature urges us towards the political positive law. However, the contribution of Kant to cosmopolitan moral thinking has attracted considerable attention in recent years and perhaps needs little further work.[28]

Let us, therefore, now focus on three issues which throw into sharp relief the ways individuals may be morally torn between their roles as state and world citizens.

[25] Janna Thompson, 'Community Identity and World Citizenship', in Daniele Archibugi, David Held and Martin Kohler (eds.), *Re-imagining Political Community: Studies in Cosmopolitan Democracy* (Cambridge: Polity Press, 1998), p. 191.

[26] Aristotle (trans. and ed. E. Barker), *The Politics of Aristotle* (Oxford: Clarendon Press, 1948), 1276b; see generally, vol. III, p. iv.

[27] Kimberly Hutchings, 'Political Theory and Cosmopolitan Citizenship', in Hutchings and Dannreuther, *Cosmopolitan Citizenship*, pp. 14–15.

[28] See, for example, Daniele Archibugi, 'Immanuel Kant, Cosmopolitan Law and Peace', *European Journal of International Relations*, 1 (1995), pp. 429–56; Kimberly Hutchings, *Kant, Critique and Politics* (London: Routledge, 1996); Andrew Linklater, *Men and Citizens in The Theory of International Relations*, 2nd edn. (London: Macmillan, 1990).

These ways are: the demand of patriotic loyalty to one's state as a priority before any cosmopolitan moral law; the specific and ultimate temptation to commit crimes against humanity in pursuit of state policy; and the tug of conscience to protect the planet's environment irrespective of the economic policy or interests of one's state.

It is an irony of this field of study that the civic republican style of citizenship, which can be called upon as a model from state-citizenship theory to bolster cosmopolitan responsibility, is in fact used in its modern form of communitarianism to counter the case for world citizenship. The republican-communitarian ideal of civic harmony and commitment depends on the compactness of the community—whether city-state, township or nation-state. A world citizenry of six billion spread over the whole globe is a far cry from Aristotle's view that a *polis* of 'a hundred thousand would exceed its natural proportions' necessary for concord among its citizens.[29] Even so, an attempt might be made to coalesce cosmopolitanism and communitarianism by overt policies to strengthen the understanding and perceived importance of supranational responsibilities. Bellamy and Castiglioni have suggested an approach related to their interest in citizenship of the EU, and boldly call it 'cosmopolitan communitarianism'.[30] They provide an argument that might fruitfully be extended, though admittedly with much greater difficulty, to the global scale. Indeed, a cardinal problem underlying the common use of the EU as a model for moulding a global identity and institutions is the vastly more variegated experiences, traditions, cultures and economies of the world's component states.

That individuals' actions are not circumscribed by the laws and policies of their own states was asserted with unambiguous clarity by the Nuremberg Charter and the Tribunal's judgment. 'The very essence of the Charter', declared the judgment, 'is that individuals have international duties which transcend the national obligations of obedience imposed by the individual State'.[31] We are trespassing now onto the topic of universal rights, the subject of our next subsection; for the duty of an individual to disobey an order to commit a 'crime against humanity' by obeying a higher, moral law is the mirror image of the right of human beings not to suffer such crimes. However, the point to be made here is that the Nuremberg principles are still being widely flouted, so that the question arises: is it possible to sensitize more human consciences to accept that their cosmopolitan duty must override their national duty in circumstances of hideous violence?

Just as the issue of crimes against humanity is usually viewed from the perspective of rights, so the issue of environmental degradation in the context of citizenship is also usually viewed from the perspective of rights—sometimes referred to as 'third generation' rights (after civil/political and social/economic). At their simplest, these rights are intended to protect the individual against the dangers of passive smoking, for example. However, the concept also has temporal and spatial extensions: the right of future generations to inherit as far as possible an environment no less

---

[29] Aristotle (trans. J. A. K. Thomson), *The Ethics of Aristotle* (Harmondsworth: Penguin, 1955), IX, 10.

[30] Richard Bellamy and Dario Castiglione, 'Between Cosmopolis and Community: Three Models of Rights and Democracy within the European Union', in Archibugi, Held and Kohler, *Re-imagining Political Community*, esp. pp. 162–7.

[31] Quoted in Ian Brownlie, *Principles of Public International Law*, 4th edn. (Oxford: Clarendon Press, 1990), p. 562. See also Geoffrey Robertson, *Crimes Against Humanity: The Struggle for Global Justice* (London: Allen Lane, 1999).

degraded than that enjoyed by their forebears, and the stretching of many serious problems, such as pollution, well beyond the confines of the state or its capacity to counteract the damage. These two forms of extension of the principle of environmental rights, of course, overlap. Moreover, the problem is without question a crucial and live element in any definition of world citizens' responsibilities and the balancing of their loyalty to their state and their obligations to the planet.

The urgent need for strengthening institutional control and public accountability in this vital global problem area is well voiced in this brief passage:

> No mechanism exists for forcing recalcitrant states into line. But even if this did exist, the democratic status of these processes and outcomes is debatable.
>
> Policy discussion and negotiations are invariably technical and decision-making largely unaccountable. ... Yet ... there is no issue on which the retention of state autonomy, or even state sovereignty, is so potentially counterproductive and the absence of public accountability so regrettable.[32]

Here, then, is a world-wide problem that cries out for a sense of cosmopolitan responsibility, a consciousness of a world citizenship transcending, indeed at odds with, state citizenship. Active members of such bodies as Greenpeace often find themselves operating against states not their own (for example, Japanese whaling) or multinational companies (for example, Shell). In such instances there is no clash between perceived cosmopolitan responsibility and loyalty to the citizen's own state. This question of choice arises when such individuals campaign on grounds of global ethical consideration and conscience against policies internal to their own state (for example, the nuclear industry). Facing up to choosing between conflicting moral obligations in situations of this kind is assuredly an issue of cosmopolitan thinking that will persist into the future.

Rights

T. H. Marshall firmly embedded into future understanding of citizenship his analysis of the status as consisting of three 'bundles' of rights—civil, political and social.[33] With the addition of 'economic' to 'social', this division will be used in this subsection.

Before examining the cosmopolitan equivalents of these three forms of citizens' rights, however, some preliminary observations are required, observations needed because of the distinction, most notably enshrined in the 1789 French Declaration, between the rights of man and the rights of the citizen. The assumption of the framers of this document was that certain rights (for example, to a say in taxation [Art.XIV]) attach to the individual *qua* citizen, while others (such as freedom of religion [Art.X]) attach to the individual *qua* human being. Marx defined the distinction by characterizing the rights of man as the rights of 'egoistic man, man separated from other men and the community'.[34] Since 1789 it has become common-

---

[32] Held and McGrew, Goldblatt and Perraton, *Global Transformations*, pp. 411–12.

[33] T. H. Marshall, *Citizenship and Social Class and other Essays* (Cambridge: Cambridge University Press, 1950).

[34] Karl Marx, 'On the Jewish Question', in David McLellan (ed.), *Karl Marx: Selected Writings* (Oxford: Oxford University Press, 1977), p. 52.

place to accept that citizens have rights *vis-à-vis* their state, and since 1948 we have also had the Universal Declaration of Human Rights. The distinction appears to persist. Human Rights are pre-political, natural and imprescriptible, cannot be justifiably assaulted by the state; citizens' rights are those positively afforded by the state. Thus it can be suggested that Bills of Rights in state constitutions delineate state citizens' rights, while the International Bill of Rights (the collective term for the four UN documents already referred to) delineate human or world citizens' rights.

But the validity of this neat presentation has been questioned, and will doubtless continue to be an issue of some interest. Four positions need to be taken into consideration, related to the belief that the three basic forms of citizenship rights do or can exist at the global level and be bound together into a holistic theory of human rights as cosmopolitan rights.

The first position is that of Marx, namely, that human rights are those enjoyed by 'egoistic man'. He could not conceive of a man enjoying human rights as a conscious member of a universal community overarching both class and state in a capitalist world. Are we justified in entertaining such a conception? After all, and secondly, the Universal Declaration of Human Rights does not expect individuals to experience these rights except through the agency of the state. For, although, in the words of the Preamble, 'the peoples of the United Nations have ... reaffirmed their faith in human rights', it is 'Member States [who] have pledged themselves to achieve ... the promotion of [their] universal respect and observance'. So, human rights are dependent upon citizens' rights. But, thirdly, do citizens' rights not, contrariwise, in fact flow from human rights? Alan Gewirth has argued that human rights are necessary for human action. Consequently, the primary justification of governments is that they serve to secure these rights.... The civil, political and social rights associated with citizenship will ultimately be derived from these human rights.[35] Any sharp distinction between citizenship rights and human rights is therefore spurious.

The fourth position is based upon observation of practice. It is that a combination of the phenomenon of migrant workers and states' obligations to honour human rights has blurred the traditional exclusivity of citizens' rights. The British authority on Comparative Jurisprudence, J. P. Gardner, has stated:

> The terms 'citizenship' and 'human rights' both describe aspects of the legal relationship between individuals and the state. There is an overlap between these two concepts which is complicated by the inclusion of catalogues of fundamental rights in the constitutions of many states. This seems to link human rights, fundamental rights and citizenship.[36]

Moreover, because an appeal can be made by alien residents and citizens alike for protection and welfare in accordance with the human rights code, he has felt the need to coin the term 'new citizenship' to distinguish this condition from the exclusive 'nationality citizenship'.[37]

Could this 'new citizenship' be thought of as a quasi-world citizenship? If this is not stretching the term too far, it must none the less be acknowledged that the rights

---

[35] Quoted in Geraint Parry, 'Conclusion: Paths to Citizenship', in U. Vogel and M. Moran (eds.), *The Frontiers of Citizenship* (Basingstoke: Macmillan, 1991), pp. 173–4.

[36] J. P. Gardner (ed.), *Hallmarks of Citizenship: A Green Paper* (London: British Institute of International and Comparative Law, n.d.), p. 189.

[37] J. P. Gardner, 'What Lawyers mean by Citizenship', in *Commission on Citizenship, Encouraging Citizenship* (London: HMSO, 1990), esp. p. 66.

enjoyed in this manner are of the civil, social and economic kind, not the political. They include, for example, the right not to be tortured or suffer from discrimination, to have a reasonable standard of living and to own property. Increasingly, the world community is recognizing that intervention in states is necessary to uphold some of these rights by expeditions into parts of the former Yugoslavia, the creation of the Hague and Arusha Tribunals and the proposed International Criminal Court on the one hand, and aid in response to natural disasters including famine on the other. When national citizenship fails to protect people's civil, social and economic rights, their only resort is to hope for better conditions in their alternative capacity as world citizens. But does this linkage between human rights, fundamental rights and citizenship need to be clarified? How can the world citizenship rights—if that is what they are—be more effectively protected?

However one addresses these questions, two basic factors are paramount. One is that abuse of civil rights can be legally defined, and protective and retributive measures can, in principle, be put in train; whereas social and economic rights are relative and qualitative guides, dependent on the availability of resources and the will to distributive justice, legally virtually unenforceable. The second basic factor is the need for better institutional frameworks for the protection of rights, leading on to the issue of universal political rights.

Political rights are the very foundation of citizenship. Even if contemporary state citizenship, let alone world citizenship, cannot precisely live up to Aristotle's formula of 'ruling and being ruled in turn',[38] some form of political involvement is the quintessence of citizenship. At the state level, indeed, Article 21.1 of the Universal Declaration asserts that 'Everyone has the right to take part in the government of his country, directly or through freely chosen representatives'. This political right is the guarantee, insofar as it can be given, of the state upholding the other citizenship rights. And yet, it is precisely this political right that is lacking at the global level.

Much of the cosmopolitan thinking during the first half of the twentieth century, epitomized by some of the fictional work of H. G. Wells, concentrated on plans for a world state. That is no longer, if it ever seriously was, considered to be either feasible or desirable. Opportunities for individuals to act as political world citizens must therefore be sought in more diffused and flexible forms of popular global participation. Hence the importance of the concept of cosmopolitan democracy as worked out by David Held and those of like mind. (Because this is the subject of the separate contribution by Peter Jones to this collection, it requires no elaboration here.) Yet three questions arise: Would governments be willing to facilitate this development? Would individuals be sufficiently motivated to press governments to act? And, even if the institutional structures were to be put in place, would individuals have the necessary competence to operate the systems?

The first and second of these questions prompted the launch in 1999 of Charter 99—A Charter for Global Democracy. Addressing prospective world citizens, the Charter makes the appeal:

We call upon you, therefore, to start the new century by initiating the process of democratic global governance....The first aim is to make already existing processes of world administration and governance accountable.... Finally, if most ambitiously, we want global

---

[38] Aristotle, *Politics*, 1283b.

governance to be compatible with the principles of equality, human rights and justice, including social and economic justice.[39]

At the time of writing the Charter had garnered signatories from 119 countries.

After the Second World War a World Citizens' Registry was created and very quickly boasted over three-quarters of a million signatures. Governments ignored it. Can this new initiative, by presentations to parliamentarians, governments and the UN, exert any greater leverage in order to make some headway towards the realization of even a minimal political world citizenship? And even if progress is made, how many 'world citizens' given this opportunity would be capable of acting the role? Assuredly schools must have a function; they should be able to provide signal help in the complementary processes of learning that one is, in fact or potentiality, a world citizen and developing the skills that are necessary to live a global civic life.

Education

The advocacy and practice of education for citizenship has a fascinating history. It reveals so much about what has been thought to be the proper behaviour—in both attitudes and competence—of the citizen of any given state. What Aristotle advocated in mid-fourth-century BC Greece was very different from what the Board of Education advocated in early twentieth-century England, and the practices of the United States of America have been different from those of Nazi Germany. So much is obvious. But if some states have been eager to shape their embryonic citizens to their social and political purposes, doubts can easily be raised as to whether those same states would happily accept, as they might very well interpret it, the diversion of their younger generation's attention from loyalty to the state for the sake of their mental moulding as citizens of the world.

It has to be said, on the other hand, that the history of education for citizenship in modern democratic polities has been undertaken in a halting and inefficient manner. Recognition of both the unsatisfactory nature of this teaching and its crucial importance for the political health of a democratic state has produced a sudden blossoming of interest in many countries in the closing years of the twentieth century.[40] The question accordingly arises whether this efflorescence of concern to improve citizenship education is likely to cause the decay of any work which schools might be undertaking in World Studies: education for world citizenship could be seen not only as a competitor for space in the curriculum, but also possibly subversive of the state's political purpose in promoting civic education at all.

---

[39] The text of Charter 99 may be obtained from the One World Trust, c/o 18 Northumberland Avenue, London WC2N 5BJ.

[40] See Carole L. Hahn, *Becoming Political: Comparative Perspectives in Citizenship Education* (Albany, NY: State University of New York Press, 1998); Orit Ichilov (ed.), *Citizenship and Citizenship Education in a Changing World* (London and Portland, OR: Woburn Press, 1998); Judith Torney-Purta, John Schwille and Jo-Ann Amadeo (eds.), *Civic Education Across Countries: Twenty-four National Case Studies from the IEA Civic Education Project* (Amsterdam: International Association for the Evaluation of Educational Achievement, 1999).

In any case, education for world citizenship has an even less sure place in schools than education for state citizenship. What tradition there is (to strain the botanical metaphor) has only shallow roots. Little thought was given before the twentieth century about what contributions schools might make.[41]

The terms 'Education in' or 'for World Citizenship' seem to have come into fashion in England in the two decades *c*. 1925–45. The distinguished international historian C. K. Webster published *The Teaching of World Citizenship* in 1926 on behalf of the Education Committee of the League of Nations Union (LNU), which was cultivating this kind of work in schools. When the LNU link became embarrassing for schools because of the controversial stance of the League in the late 1930s, this educational activity was continued by the inauguration of a new semi-autonomous body. This was named the Council for Education in World Citizenship (CEWC), which is still functioning. CEWC played a useful role in the creation of UNESCO, but this organization, rather than using 'World Citizenship', preferred the term 'Education for International Understanding', later expanded to the extraordinarily cumbersome 'Education for International Understanding, Cooperation and Peace and Education relating to Human Rights and Fundamental Freedoms'. By the 1970s and 1980s educationists were talking in terms of 'World Studies' or, particularly in the USA, 'Global Studies'. Meanwhile, distinct units of work were devised in schools: Development Studies, Multicultural Studies, Peace Studies, Environmental Education, Human Rights Education (HRE).

This proliferation of labels and diversification of curriculum content are especially pertinent to our enquiry. Many educationists have been convinced that young people should have their horizons broadened beyond the traditional insular, national, even nationalistic teaching of some civic subjects, notably History. They were not so sure, however, how to focus their teaching; and, at the same time, were nervous about hostile interpretations of their intentions. Together with the problem of time-tabling already alluded to ('the law of the conservation of the curriculum' in Eric James's vivid phrase), an understanding of these past difficulties will help us to assess the chance of this kind of school learning prospering in the future.

Soon after the establishment of CEWC two of its leading lights expressed their unhappiness about the term 'world citizenship'. Gilbert Murray, the distinguished classicist and keen supporter of the League, wrote, 'It seems to profess too much',[42] and Nowell Smith, headmaster of Sherborne, thought 'education for world citizenship [to be] unattractive and even to most people at first sight or hearing repellent'![43] These comments reflected both the uncertainty concerning the educational objectives of 'education for world citizenship' and the political suspicion it is capable of arousing. If the term means favourably presenting in the classroom the case for some kind of world polity, then this could be construed as unacceptable indoctrination. If it means teaching a hotch-potch of Peace Studies, HRE, and so

[41] See, for example, D. G. Scanlon (ed.), *International Education: A Documentary History* (New York: Teachers College, Columbia University, 1960).

[42] Quoted in Derek Heater, *Peace Through Education: The Contribution of the Council for Education in World Citizenship* (Lewes: Falmer Press, 1984), p. 47.

[43] Quoted in Derek Heater, 'Political Education for Global Citizenship', in James Lynch, Celia Modgil and Sohan Modgil (eds.), *Cultural Diversity and the Schools, vol. 4: Human Rights, Education and Global Responsibilities* (London and Washington, DC: Falmer Press, 1992), p. 192.

on, then it could be pedagogically incoherent. And if it means giving global perspectives to traditional subjects, most obviously History, Geography and Religious Education, though more acceptable and manageable, problems still arise in the forms of the absence of a unifying 'world citizenship' framework and the difficulty of reaching agreement to discard established subject-matter in order to provide room in the syllabuses for the new. What is more, replacing 'national' History or Geography with 'world' material can, indeed has been, the cause of some controversy.

In the 1980s the clash between the opponents and supporters of World Studies in Britain became exceedingly acrimonious. Professor Roger Scruton of Birkbeck College attacked:

World Studies masquerades as a 'discipline' whose aim is to produce an open mind towards the differing cultures and varying conditions of humanity. In reality, however ... It is designed to close the child's mind to everything but the narrow passions of the radical.... The World Studies movement ... seeks ... to replace serious knowledge and formal scholarship with political posturing and infantile, manipulative games.[44]

A counter-attack was launched from the University of York:

He conveys a veneer of academic respectability whilst, in fact, reaching conclusions based on selective use of a narrow range of evidence ... and no school or classroom observation.[45]

One of the authors of this counter-assault, Dr Selby, is currently the Director of a flourishing centre of curriculum research and development at the Ontario Institute for Studies in Education (OISE). Nevertheless, despite the vitality of the Canadian-based work, the overall impression, as already suggested, is that education for state citizenship is overshadowing education for world citizenship. In England, citizenship education will become mandatory in state secondary schools (Key Stages 3 and 4) in 2002. The Order specifies that pupils should be taught about 'the world as a global community, and the political, economic, environmental and social implications of this' (Key Stage 3) and 'the wider issues and challenges of global interdependence and responsibility, including sustainable development' (Key Stage 4). And learning about human rights features in the lists for both stages.[46]

Even so, the bulk of the listed subject-content for citizenship education in the English National Curriculum relates to citizenship at the local and national levels— as one would expect, though to the disappointment of the proponents of World Studies. The Order is not, however, prescriptive in detail. Schools will need to devise their own appropriate ways of fulfilling these requirements. There is consequently no reason to believe that further thought is either unnecessary or unlikely in the field of education for world citizenship—in England, certainly, at the secondary level immediately and at the primary level with rather less urgency. The hope must be entertained that the confusion and quarrels of the past will not be repeated.

[44] Roger Scruton, *World Studies: Education or Indoctrination?* (London: Institute for European Defence and Strategic Studies, 1985), pp. 30, 39.
[45] Graham Pike and David Selby, 'Scrutinising Scruton: An Analysis of Roger Scruton's Attack on World Studies', *Westminster Studies in Education*, 9, p. 5.
[46] Department for Education and Employment, *Citizenship: The National Curriculum for England*, KS3–4 (London: HMSO), pp. 14, 15.

A likely future?

Scholars engaging in future cosmopolitan thinking, by pursuing the mutual compatibility of nationhood, state citizenship and cosmopolitan citizenship of 'the new classicism' model, can be assured that they are not trying to achieve the untried and impossible. And by investigating the feasibility of developing a world citizenship whose components reflect the structure of state citizenship, future cosmopolitan thought has a possible agenda. These are the core suggestions of this essay. It remains to ask whether cosmopolitan thinking along these lines, or any other, is likely to be continued in the twenty-first century. Tennyson, as we are so frequently reminded, 'dipt into the future' and saw 'the Parliament of Man, the Federation of the World'.[47] Thankfully, the task here is not to predict institutional developments, but to extrapolate current thinking.

The recent literature published in English indicates not only a great welling-up of interest, but also, in many cases, the engagement of scholars of the first rank in work on the cosmopolitan theme.[48] From *c.* 1914 to *c.* 1970 there was, in truth, a great outpouring of writing on world government and on world citizenship. But for the most part, work in the first category tended to be impractical plans for a federation of the world and, in the second category, assertions of faith rather than scholarly analysis. One has only to compare—to be illustrative and invidious—Streit's relatively practical *Union Now*[49] and Cohen's rare philosophical *The Principles of World Citizenship*[50] (for all their positive qualities at the time) with Held's *Democracy and the Global Order*[51] and Hutchings and Dannreuther's symposium[52] to recognize the progress to greater depth of thought that has been achieved in recent years. Without too much danger of exaggeration, we may judge that the best current cosmopolitan thinking is of a higher calibre than at any time in the past.

Damning with faint praise this might seem to be, in the light of the limitations of past thought (*pace* Kant), and inconsiderate of works by a few scholars (again to be invidious) of the likes of Clark and Sohn[53] and Falk[54] in the recent past. What, however, appears to have been happening in the 1990s is the taking up of some older ideas, the development of new ideas, and the involvement of a growing band of writers in work which reveals a realism of commitment and an intensity of original scholarship at least comparable with work in any other branch of the Social Sciences.

This academic work has also seen penetrating publications emanating from meetings of politicians and people with public-service backgrounds, most signi-

[47] Alfred Tennyson, *Locksley Hall*.
[48] The bibliography in Hutchings and Dannreuther, *Cosmopolitan Citizenship*, provides a useful list.
[49] Clarence K. Streit, *Union Now: A Proposal for a Federal Union of the Democracies of the North Atlantic* (London: Cape, 1939).
[50] L. Jonathan Cohen, *The Principles of World Citizenship* (Oxford: Blackwell, 1954).
[51] David Held, *Democracy and the Global Order: From the Modern State to Cosmopolitan Governance* (Cambridge: Polity Press, 1995).
[52] See fn. 4 above.
[53] Grenville Clark and Louis B. Sohn, *World Peace Through World Law* (Cambridge, MA: Harvard University Press, 1958).
[54] A prolific writer; see, for example, *A Study of Future Worlds* (New York: Free Press, 1975); *On Humane Governance: Toward a New Global Politics* (Cambridge: Polity Press, 1995).

ficantly the Report of the Commission on Global Governance.[55] For example, James Rosenau wrote a paper on 'Changing Capacities of Citizens' for that Commission. Furthermore, the Report accords due weight to ethical considerations, devoting one of its seven chapters to 'Values for the Global Neighbourhood'. At the head of the chapter summarizing the Commission's proposals stands this sentence: 'A global civic ethic to guide action within the global neighbourhood, and leadership infused with that ethic, is vital to the quality of global governance.'[56] The whole book is written on the assumption that further work would be undertaken to assist the process of implementing the recommendations.

But can the momentum of thinking and publishing—of various kinds, by various hands, from both purely intellectual and practical motives—be sustained for any length of time? Several conditions might well be necessary for the continuation of this work. And underlying these conditions is the fact that circumstances in the world outside the scholar's study affect even those whose studies are sited in ivory towers.

This, specifically, is a significant condition for the continuation of cosmopolitan thinking. It is surely unlikely that the burgeoning of this work in the 1990s would have occurred at all had it not been for the coincidence of a number of world developments. These were: the phenomenon of globalization; the belief that the 'billiard-ball' sovereignty of the nation-state was being enfeebled by sub- and trans-national forces; the progressive integration of the EU as a prototype of supra-national citizenship; and the spread of liberal democracy with the collapse of auto-cratic civilian and military regimes in the former Soviet bloc, Latin America and some states of Africa. If these developments are consolidated, the relevance of cosmopolitan thinking will persist.

Whether these developments will continue to be conducive to cosmopolitan thinking is perhaps more nicely balanced than some authorities tend to suggest. Globalization in the form of the spreading availability of rapid electronic communication may continue to enhance the sense that there does exist a global community. Yet globalization in the form of the growing power of multinational companies may exacerbate the global rich-poor divide and enable them to downplay any responsibility for being accountable to a world citizenry.

Globalization is also weakening the state-citizen tie, as are the processes of federalization, devolution and intensification of feelings of regional nationhood. The loosening of that tie increases the acceptability of a cosmopolitan bond. On the other hand, the processes of decolonization and Yugoslav and Soviet disintegration have multiplied the number of states which still cling to the Westphalian states-system. That system, however, is under strain, most noticeably in Europe, where the EU has a magnetic attraction for applicant and would-be applicant states. The Maastricht Treaty created the status of citizen of the Union, a title which will apply to many millions more as the candidate-states become members, and would be firmed up if talk of an EU constitution becomes a reality. Yet the prospects of strengthening 'Euro-citizenship' is not without its opponents, most evidently in England; and, in any case, the translation of the European formula to a global dimension has only too obvious difficulties.

---

[55] Commission on Global Governance, *Our Global Neighbourhood* (Oxford: Oxford University Press, 1995).
[56] *Our Global Neighbourhood*, p. 335.

But, at least the geographical expansion of state-democracy provides a more hopeful platform for the construction of democratic global governance than ever before. After all, such a hope has the most distinguished lineage from Kant's vision of a league of 'republican' states. On the other hand, is democracy in the Western, liberal sense really in such a healthy condition? Vast numbers in Asia and Africa do not enjoy effective democratic conditions; and in countries such as Russia disillusionment is widespread.

If the braking power of the resistant forces succeed in decelerating the developments which provided the mood for positive cosmopolitan thinking in the 1990s, scholars and public figures who have contributed to this thinking could conceivably become dispirited. Furthermore, will-power of a persistent kind may well be called for in confronting academic opposition from those who either deplore, or at least discount the power of, the forces of cosmopolitanism. However, political thinking surely thrives on debate, even contention. And cosmopolitan thinking would show itself to be a more sickly strain of study than its recent robust nature suggests if it waned before the shadow of those political conditions and academic pursuits that remain untransformed.

Individuals, communities and human rights

PETER JONES

The two global norms that are most widely recognized in our world are human rights and the principle of national self-determination. Sometimes these norms are presented as complementary, sometimes as rivals. Of the two, national self-determination seems to have secured more widespread acceptance. No doubt the uncertain meaning of national self-determination has aided its widespread popularity. Quite what sort of entity (or 'self') does the adjective 'national' describe? What sort of arrangements does 'self-determination' demand? Those who apparently share a common commitment to the principle of national self-determination can nevertheless give markedly different answers to these questions. Moreover, whatever meaning we give to national self-determination, its reality has long been questioned and is increasingly challenged by the forces of globalization.

Yet, although the idea of national self-determination is fraught with problems, it is not one that seems to trouble people's consciences in quite the same way as the idea of human rights. People may feel more or less warmly towards the principle of national self-determination, but nowadays they do not generally wring their hands about the global reach of the principle. They do not feel that it constitutes an imposition by one part of the world upon another. By contrast, many people do entertain reservations about the global pretensions that accompany the doctrine of human rights. Even if they themselves are won over by the doctrine, they often hesitate about the propriety of implementing it in a comprehensively global fashion. In this article, I want to track down the thought that seems to underlie this unease and to examine how far that thought should really make us hesitate about giving the idea of human rights a truly universal status.

Relativism, cultures and diversity

The converse of universalism is particularism, and the form of particularism that is most commonly turned against the claims of human rights theorists is cultural relativism. Sometimes, those who play the cultural card are content to observe only that not all cultures recognize the rights that human rights theorists wish everyone to have; hence, they conclude, human rights are not truly universal. 'Not universal' here means only 'not, as a matter of fact, universally accepted'. But, of course, that merely empirical observation is of no force against the moral claim that all human beings have certain rights and that they should be treated accordingly. Those who do not accept that moral claim may be simply adjudged mistaken.

The more relevant form of cultural relativism is one that challenges the morality rather than the ubiquity of human rights thinking. That relativism, like other forms of moral relativism, is commonly associated with moral scepticism, but it does not have to be. It can itself be a four-square moral doctrine. 'Cultural relativism' might describe the position that holds that right conduct for the members of a society is conduct that conforms to the morality evolved by their particular society. Some contemporary communitarians seem to entertain a position of this sort. Clearly this form of cultural relativism, while it rejects moral universalism, does not reject morality altogether since it itself asserts a moral position: the right thing for people to do is to conform to the norms of their particular community. It presents a view of right conduct; it simply denies that there is any substantive form of conduct that is right for all humanity. I shall describe this sort of relativism as ethical cultural relativism.

More commonly, however, cultural relativism is associated with moral scepticism. It holds that, while people may generally suppose that there is a secure non-relative foundation for their moral beliefs, that supposition is mistaken. Each moral belief is embedded within a culture and each culture is the product of chance and circumstance. All cultures are the contingent creations of the historical communities that bear them and there are no foundations for morality external to a culture. This sort of view dismisses human rights thinking by dismissing the credibility of *any* morality that claims to transcend its cultural origins. I describe this form of relativism as sceptical cultural relativism.

Here I do not want to assess the merits of cultural relativism in either its ethical or sceptical forms. Rather, I want to ask whether the allure of cultural relativism explains the sense that there is something wrong about imposing human rights upon a society that does not already accept them. I want to suggest that it does not.

There is a simple and commonly acknowledged reason why sceptical cultural relativism cannot, of itself, account for that sense of wrong: it is ensnared by its own scepticism. Asserting the wrongness of imposing human rights upon a population entails taking a moral stand, and a cultural relativism that delivers moral scepticism removes the foundation upon which that stand might be taken. But there is also another reason. A cultural relativism that questions the foundation of moral judgement is not really an ethical position at all. It is a meta-ethical position. Rather than making moral claims, it makes claims about morality. It can certainly insist that human rights theorists are mistaken in supposing they have any good transcultural or metacultural reason for promoting their doctrine, but it does not have the resources to insist that they are guilty of a moral wrong in promoting their doctrine.[1]

The same cannot be said of ethical cultural relativism. That is a moral doctrine and, since it holds that right conduct for the members of a society is conduct that conforms with the morality of their particular society, it must condemn human rights theorists who endeavour to make people conform to a different code of conduct. Here, then, we do have a morality that vetoes the universalism that is

---

[1] Richard Rorty is a good example of someone who buys into sceptical cultural relativism without giving up a commitment to human rights. See his 'Human Rights, Rationality, and Sentimentality', in Stephen Shute and Susan Hurley (eds.), *On Human Rights: the Oxford Amnesty Lectures 1993* (New York: Basic Books, 1993), pp. 111–34.

essential to human rights thinking. Yet there are two reasons why ethical cultural relativism also fails to provide a fully persuasive explanation of people's hesitancy about human rights.

The first is that its condemnation of moral universalism is almost too strong. What, according to this moral theory, would be the wrong of which we would be guilty were we to impose human rights upon a population? The answer is that we would be making that population behave wrongly. Since, according to ethical cultural relativism, right conduct for the members of a society is conduct that conforms with the norms of their own society, we would be guilty of making them behave wrongly if we persuaded or obliged them to conform to a different, external, set of norms. I suggest that this condemnation is 'too strong' because it claims more than those who condemn human rights thinking usually wish to claim. They are usually content to insist that the members of a society should not have to conform to a doctrine of human rights that they themselves do not accept. They do not usually go on to make the stronger claim that the members of that society would behave wrongly if they embraced and acted on that doctrine.

The other reason why ethical cultural relativism fails convincingly to explain people's reluctance about human rights is the curious nature of that relativism as a moral position. Why should we hold that right conduct for a population consists in compliance with the norms of their particular society, irrespective of what those norms happen to be? Remember that the ethical cultural relativist does not make the banal (and perhaps tautological) observation that the members of a society will generally regard right conduct as conduct that conforms with the norms of their society. Rather he himself asserts that right conduct for the members of a particular society is indeed conduct that conforms with the norms of their society. But why should anyone want to hold such a position? What could be our reason for giving critical moral endorsement to a range of different positive moralities without regard to the content of those positive moralities? There must surely be some answer. An ethical relativism that could provide us with no answer would seem just bizarre. But if it does have an answer to offer, that would seem to be, necessarily, of a non-relativist kind. My aim here is not to engage in the kind of trick that is often used to catch out comprehensive assertions of relativism—the trick of revealing that the relativist must, after all, commit himself to at least one non-relative proposition. There is nothing logically wrong with adopting a thin moral universalism as the foundation for a thick moral relativism. Rather my point is simply that, if we are to find a plausible moral objection to human rights thinking in ethical cultural relativism, we shall discover it in the non-relative principle that undergirds that ethic rather than in ethical relativism itself.

What, then, might that be? One much favoured answer lies in the good of cultural diversity. We certainly have ample reason to value cultures. 'Culture' is a generous if amorphous term and, because it is so all-inclusive, it is hard not to be won over by the richness of a world characterized by many different cultures. Imagine a mono-cultural world characterized by only one literary tradition, one musical form, one diet, one language, one form of life, and so on. Such a world would be infinitely poorer than the diverse world in which we live. There is good reason, therefore, to be alarmed at the prospect of a globalized world in which a single culture progressively displaces all others. I wish to say nothing to challenge the alarming nature of that prospect (however real or unreal a prospect it may be). Once again, however, I do want to question whether it is the good of cultural diversity that explains people's objection to the evangelism of human rights theorists.

Certainly, if we think of enthusiasm for human rights as a creeping disease that will eventually wipe out cultural diversity, we have reason to keep it at bay. But, if the world is made poorer by the disappearance of cultural diversity, for whom is it made poorer? Given a conception of cultural diversity as something that is good for all humanity, the answer must be 'all of us'. Yet, when a population finds its culture suppressed, or is made to live under the tutelage of another's culture, we typically think that it is that specific population, rather than all humanity, that has been wronged. Certainly all humanity may be, in some degree, losers if a particular culture disappears; but our primary sense is that it is the bearers of the culture that are the victims. In other words, the wrong done by destroying, suppressing or devaluing a culture is a wrong perpetrated against those whose culture it is, rather than a wrong suffered equally by all humanity, and we cannot explain the particularity of that wrong by appealing to the general good of cultural diversity.

Self-determination

So if neither cultural relativism nor the good of cultural diversity explains people's reservations about human rights, what does? The answer seems to lie in the thought that, if the human rights theorist imposes values upon a society, he flouts the right of the members of that society to determine for themselves how they shall live. The wrong is a failure to acknowledge and to respect a right of self-determination. That is the relevant objection gestured towards, but not actually delivered by, cultural relativism. What does the moral work in this objection is not the mere fact that a society happens to possess a culture; it is the presumption that the members of the society are wedded to that culture and the consequent presumption that, in obliging them to depart from that culture, we are obliging them to depart from the way they themselves wish to live. In fact, the critical value here has nothing to do with the notion of culture as such. We might characterize the object of people's self-determination in terms of values, rules, traditions, and so on, and avoid all the baggage that comes with the term 'culture'. That would make no difference to the right of self-determination that is at stake here.

It is also worth noticing that cultures themselves have no rights. 'Culture' is a term that describes the beliefs and the form of life that a society has evolved. But we do not ascribe rights to beliefs themselves or to forms of life themselves. Beliefs and forms of life are not entities possessed of moral standing to which we might, as a consequence, owe duties. It is people—the people who hold beliefs and who live forms of life—who possess moral standing and who are therefore capable of holding rights that relate to beliefs and forms of life. Cultures matter only because, and in so far as, they matter to people, so that any moral claim that relates to culture must be a claim rooted in the concerns of those who bear the culture or who are otherwise interested in its existence.

The striking feature of the appeal to the value of self-determination against human rights is that it appeals to a value to which human rights theorists are themselves characteristically committed. Many different (and often incompatible) theoretical foundations have been proffered for human rights and the values that underlie particular human rights may not be all of a piece. But one feature that is common to most versions of human rights theory is the claim that we should accord people a significant degree of control over the shape of their own lives. That is obviously true of liberal thinking about human rights, but it is also true more generally. Human rights thinking has to be grounded in some idea of the moral standing of human persons and of the concern and respect due to human persons, and it is hard to embrace those ideas without also accepting that we should pay some deference to people's own beliefs or wishes about how they should live.

If this principle of respecting people's beliefs and preferences about their own mode of living is so essential to human rights thinking, how can it be turned against the idea of human rights? The most obvious answer is that the doctrine of human rights is an essentially individualist doctrine and its individualism places it in opposition to communities that are committed to non-individualist forms of life. Human rights militate against communal forms of life and therefore compromise the right of people to determine for themselves how they shall live. It is that claim that I shall examine in the remainder of this essay.

Individualism and human rights

Before conducting that examination, I want to distinguish between two sorts of individualism that might be said to inhabit human-rights thinking. The first concerns the 'unit' of moral standing and the bearer of rights. Human-rights thinking recognizes human beings as possessing moral standing as human individuals and it also ascribes rights to them as individuals. It is therefore distinct from those forms of thinking that invest moral standing in groups and that insist that groups can have claims that, morally, are not reducible to the claims of the individuals who make them up. I say that human-rights thinking is 'distinct from' rather than 'opposed to' this group-based moral thinking because the two can be combined coherently. That is, we might ascribe rights to individuals on some matters and to groups on others so that the two sorts of right coexist harmoniously. Human-rights thinking does not, therefore, exclude the possibility that groups might possess moral standing as group-entities. It is simply that human-rights thinking does not itself deliver that possibility.

If this is what we mean by 'individualism', human-rights thinking is unquestionably individualist. The rights it asserts treat human individuals as the ultimate units of standing.[2] I shall argue in due course that that does not rule out the possibility that there are some rights that individuals can possess as groups and *only* as groups. But the right of a group will still be a right grounded in the standing of the individuals who make it up.

'Individualism' may then describe a stance on who or what we should regard as the ultimate unit of moral concern and, in that sense, human rights theorists must own up to being individualist. 'Individualism' is also a term applied to forms of life.

---

[2] That does not rule out the possibility that some non-human individuals might also have moral standing.

Quite what should count as an individualist form of life is not altogether clear. Almost all forms of life that significant numbers of people actually live involve interaction with others and depend upon background social institutions. The notion that people in the West are unlike those in the East in living 'individualist' modes of life is grossly misleading. Nevertheless, I want to give some sense to the distinction between individualist and communal forms of life. Presumably we should regard a form of life as more individualist to the extent that it approximates to a form that a person can live and experience as an independent individual. It may be that this form draws on certain background social institutions, but the life that the person actually lives is individualist in the sense that it is not a life lived jointly or cooperatively with others. So, for example, the life of a lone stamp collector, as opposed to one who belongs to a stamp collecting club, may be said to exhibit this sort of individualism. By the same token, a communal form of life is one that people can live only along with others; the participation of others is essential to the kind of life it is. Communalism in this sense can take in everything from playing in a football team to living in a closely integrated tribal community.

'Individualism' of this sort is also sometimes associated with human rights but the justification for that association is much more questionable. There is a clear distinction between, on the one hand, investing individual persons with the right to determine how they shall live and, on the other, prescribing and promoting a form of life as the best form. Individuals who have the ultimate right to decide upon their form of life can use that right to opt for whatever form of life they judge best, individualist or communal. Limiting people to individualist forms of life is quite simply inconsistent with giving them the freedom to determine how they shall live. Of course it may be that, in a society in which individuals have a significant degree of control over how they shall live, more individualist forms of life will be easier to sustain than more communal forms, simply because more communal forms have to secure a larger measure of willing cooperation among the potential participants. If people could be coerced into collective forms of life, those forms might be easier to achieve (although whether it would be right to describe a collective form of life brought about in this way as 'communal' is certainly moot). But setting restrictions on what may be done to people to secure or promote a form of life is quite different from endorsing one form of life as better than another.

Human rights theorists do not therefore have to plead guilty to imposing a particular form of life upon a population. Of course, that begins to raise the question of the content they give to human rights. But, for the moment, we can simply notice that merely vesting rights in human individuals is not the same as compelling them to live individualist forms of life.

Three conceptions of human rights

In order to explore further the issue of how far human rights constrain the sorts of life that people may live, I want to distinguish three different ways of conceiving these rights. These conceptions represent three possible views of the practical role that we might expect human rights to perform: a 'moral minimum', a 'basic moral structure', and a 'comprehensive morality'.

(1) Human rights as moral minimum

If a human rights theory aims to establish only a 'moral minimum', it will aspire to establish a limited set of fundamental requirements to which every society must conform. Beyond that minimum, it will leave each society free to organize its life as it sees fit. Human rights are very commonly thought of in that way. They are conceived as a set of obligatory but basic standards that leave much of life unprovided for so that societies are left with a significant space within which they can organize themselves according to their own lights. It is perhaps in this form that a commitment to human rights is most commonly combined with an acceptance of the right of national self-determination. If we acknowledge both sorts of right, to which should we give priority? For the human rights theorist, the first must trump the second. States or societies or peoples or nations (whichever term is more to our liking) are entitled to shape their own destinies but only in ways that do not violate the human rights of their members. Nevertheless, that still leaves very considerable scope for societies to assume different forms.

Of course, the moral minimum prescribed by human rights can be more or less minimal, so that those who agree in thinking of human rights on this model may disagree about just how minimal those rights should be. But the general spirit of this conception is to limit the content of human rights to a basic set of moral requirements beyond which societies are left free to shape themselves as they see fit.

This conception of human rights suggests a clear separation between those matters that fall within, and those that fall without, their compass. It presents us with a picture of a moral world in which human rights make uncompromising demands within a limited territory but have little or no implications for people's lives beyond that territory. That simple dichotomous picture may describe with reasonable accuracy the character of some of the rights commonly claimed as human rights. For example, rights such as the right not to be subject to arbitrary arrest or the right to a fair trial, have a high degree of independence from the rest of people's lives and the rest of a society's affairs. They provide safeguards for individuals within the judicial domain but make little or no prescription beyond that domain. (We may believe that those rights stem from underlying principles or values that have implications beyond the judicial domain, but I leave that possibility to one side.) Other human rights, however, fit less easily into this model of an isolated and disconnected minimum.

(2) Human rights as basic moral structure

Rights such as the right to freedom of opinion and expression, or to freedom of conscience and religion, or to freedom of assembly and association have implications for the general ways in which societies are to organize and conduct their affairs. So too do rights that relate to political participation. These are not rights that societies can meet in a once and for all fashion and then set to one side as of no further consequence for the way in which they conduct their affairs. They are rights that intrude into the very way societies are to structure their arrangements. They still have a limited range: rights to freedoms, by their very nature, do not prescribe the use we are to make of those freedoms and rights of political participation do not prescribe the use we are to make of our decision-making power. But they do make prescriptions that relate to the way in which a society should organize and conduct its life.

Perhaps, then, these sorts of human right are a more proper focus for complaint. Perhaps they are more 'impositional' in that they dictate a society's character in fuller, more far-reaching ways than rights, such as the right to be tried fairly or the right not to be tortured, that fit more comfortably into the model of a moral minimum. After all, these are the rights that are most closely associated with Western liberalism and a common complaint against human rights is that they manifest the continued imperialism of the West. Even so, I want to resist the claim that we should see these rights as imposing upon populations a particular form of life. Rather, I want to suggest, they relate to a society's basic structure.

I borrow the term 'basic structure' from the writings of John Rawls.[3] For Rawls the principles and rules that make up the basic structure of a society do not attempt to provide comprehensively for how people should live. Indeed, in a liberal society the basic structure should not be founded upon any 'comprehensive doctrine'—moral, philosophical or religious—prescribing how people should live; nor should it seek to promote any 'conception of the good' grounded in a comprehensive doctrine. That is not its proper role. Its role is to establish the ground-rules within which people are to pursue their conceptions of the good whatever those conceptions happen to be. We might therefore describe the role of the basic structure as 'regulative'. It does not dictate to people what ends they should pursue or what aspirations they should entertain, or what life-shaping beliefs they should hold. It simply lays down the basic framework within which people are to pursue the different, and sometimes competing or conflicting, ends or aspirations or beliefs that they possess.

Some human rights can reasonably be regarded as rights governing the basic structures of societies. Rights relating to basic freedoms and to participation in political structures are the most obvious examples. Socioeconomic rights might also figure in this conception of human rights in that they place a minimum of resources at people's disposal.[4] It may be that virtually all of the rights typically claimed as human rights and recognized in international declarations and covenants can be seen as contributing to the basic structure of societies, in that virtually all have implications for the proper shape and operation of their major institutions. However, my principal focus here is upon rights that are regulative in that they set the institutional and legal terms within which people are to live their lives. Given their limited character, human rights may not provide for all of the basic structure needed by a society, but they can still be important contributors to it.

---

[3] John Rawls, *Political Liberalism* (New York: Columbia University Press, 1993); *Collected Papers*, Samuel Freeman (ed.) (Cambridge, MA: Harvard University Press, 1999).

[4] I do not wish to press this point very hard. Since socioeconomic human rights aim to secure only a basic minimum of goods and services, they are more likely to matter to people for the immediate needs they satisfy than for any larger instrumental purpose. Moreover, if each society, however rich or poor, is expected to provide for these rights only from its own resources, there is an element of bad faith in representing these rights as *human* rights.

Understood in this way, human rights are not predicated upon the goodness of a particular form of life, nor do they aim to promote any particular form of life. They simply invest individuals with rights to decide what sort of lives they shall live and with rights that set the ground-rules for the pursuit of their preferred form.[5] If we consider the closely integrated communities that are supposed to characterize parts of the non-Western world, there is no reason why human rights, understood on this model, should be at odds with these forms of life. Of course, there is often a large element of romanticism and misrepresentation in the way these communities are portrayed, but let us set that to one side and suppose that we confront a community all of whose members are committed to a shared form of life. If this community is genuinely consensual, if it sustains a form of life to which all of its members are fully wedded, respecting the right of each of its members to live the form of life they wish entails respecting the communal form of life to which they are committed.

The riposte this claim is likely to provoke is that what is really on offer here is the liberal ideal of the autonomous life dressed up as an impartial theory of human rights. What pretends to be a merely regulative conception of human rights is really based upon a commitment to the superiority of liberal forms of life. Perhaps it is necessary, then, to insist again upon the distinction between, on the one hand, ascribing moral standing to individual persons and, as a consequence, respecting their own wishes or convictions about how they should live and, on the other, obliging people to live particular forms of life because we deem those the best forms. The conception of human rights that I am presenting here does not require people to invent or to reinvent themselves, which is a barely coherent idea anyway. Nor does it require us to fetishize 'choice' such that we have to insist that forms of life have value only if they have been self-consciously chosen by those who live them. Rather, it requires only that we respect the forms of life to which people are committed, and those will include traditional forms of life which people have inherited and which they have, in no meaningful sense, chosen for themselves. What is significant about a form of life on this conception of human rights is that it is the form that matters to the people who live it, that it is the form of life which they themselves wish to live or believe they should live.

(3) Human rights as comprehensive morality

The openness to different forms of life that characterizes human rights conceived on the models of a moral minimum or a basic structure does depend upon their being conceived on those models. The mere notion that all human beings possess certain rights is too indeterminate to guarantee that openness. Logically, it is possible to invest human rights with a much more comprehensive content and with one that would effectively confine people to a single form of life.[6] For example, we might hold

---

[5] I have attempted to outline a conception of human rights of this sort in 'Human Rights and Diverse Cultures: Continuity or Discontinuity?', *Contemporary Review of International, Social and Political Philosophy*, 3 (2000).

[6] There are, in fact, both logical and moral difficulties in attempting to articulate a morality that is *fully* comprehensive exclusively in terms of rights. See my *Rights* (Basingstoke: Macmillan, 1994), pp. 204–9. Even so, a 'thick' theory of human rights could move a considerable way towards comprehensiveness.

that all human beings have the right to live, and the right to live *only*, lives that accord with the one true faith (whatever we reckon that to be). The more comprehensive a moral content we give a theory of human rights, the less accommodating it can be of diverse modes of life and the more it must conflict with the idea of self-determination, whatever 'self' is at stake. So my claim is not that any version of the idea of human rights will be capable of accommodating a wide range of forms of life, both individualist and communal. Rather it is that the idea of human rights is capable of being understood in a way that makes it hospitable to many different forms of life. It is also fair to add that, for the most part, human rights as these have been formulated in international instruments approximate more closely to the models of a moral minimum or a basic structure than to a comprehensive morality.

Human rights, democracy and self-determination

One important way in which human rights may seem to champion the claims of individualism against those of communalism is by placing constraints upon collective decision-procedures such as democracy. The slogan 'democracy and human rights' has become very common, as if the two exist in a symbiotic relation or stem from the same fundamental values. Indeed, democracy is itself frequently brought within the compass of human rights. Both the UN's Universal Declaration of Human Rights (1948) and the International Covenant on Civil and Political Rights (1966) include rights that seem to require democracy.[7]

Yet individual rights and democracy can also be construed as potential rivals. Immunity rights constrain collective decision-procedures. If I have the right to a fair trial or the right to worship the god of my choice, the *demos* has no power to subject me to an unfair trial or to prevent my worshipping my own god in my own way. To that extent, the domains of individual rights and democratic power are inversely related. The more we enlarge one, the more we diminish the other. That simple picture of rivalry between democracy and individual rights is in some ways too simple; for example, some of the rights that we commonly ascribe to individuals, such as rights to freedom of expression and opinion, are also essential to the functioning of democracy. But there are, nevertheless, well-recognized choices to be made amongst different ways of dividing control over people's lives. At one extreme there are libertarians or anarchists who would assign little or no control to collective decision-procedures; at the other, there are democratic Hobbesians who refuse to compromise the sovereignty of the *demos* in any way. Most people, including most who sign up to the idea of human rights, would locate themselves somewhere between these two extremes, but locating ourselves anywhere entails making a choice.

How far should we regard that choice as one between individuals and communities? In one simple respect the choice clearly is of that sort—it is a choice between decision-making by individuals individually and by individuals collectively. In several other respects, however, it is misleading to represent striking a balance

---

[7] UDHR, article 21; ICCPR, article 25. I say only 'seem to require' because regimes that fall short of democracy have sometimes been thought capable of satisfying these articles. For argument that democratic government is now required by international law, see Thomas M. Franck, 'The Emerging Right to Democratic Governance', *American Journal of International Law*, 86 (1992), pp. 46–91.

between individual rights and democracy as choosing between the claims of individuals and those of communities.

Firstly, a commitment to democracy does not entail giving some sort of independent moral standing to a community as opposed to the individuals who make it up. The individuals who have an interest in being able to exercise democratic political power are the same individuals who have an interest in holding rights that give them immunities against that power. Setting the appropriate balance between the immunities conferred by individual rights and the powers available to the democratic process is a matter of balancing the interests of the same set of individuals. It is not a matter of balancing the interests of individuals against those of a distinct entity called a 'community'.

Secondly, as I have already insisted, individually-held rights that constrain democracy typically include rights that give individuals the freedom to live communal as well as individual modes of life. As constraints upon democracy, these rights are therefore indifferent as between communal and individual forms of life. Democratic power can be used to impose individualist forms of life upon those who are committed to other forms, just as it can be used to impose communal forms of life upon those who wish to have no part in them. The contest between individually-held rights and democracy does not therefore translate into a contest between individual and communal forms of life. It is a contest of a different sort: a contest between different ways of distributing the power to determine how we shall live.

Thirdly, we might encounter the complaint that, since rights are claims of special weight, in according individuals rights that constrain democracy, we are implicitly ranking the individual concerns protected by individual rights above the collective concerns promoted by democracy. One answer to that objection lies in the point I have just made: it is a mistake to suppose that individual rights must always be addressed to individualist concerns or that collective decision-making must always be inspired by communitarian concerns. But there is also another answer. Historically, the principal drive behind asserting human rights (and before that, natural rights) has been a desire to protect the vulnerable, especially those who would otherwise find themselves left to the mercy of political power. In political contexts, therefore, we ascribe immunity rights to those who need their protection and, in the context of democratic political power, that means ascribing rights to individuals severally that will protect them against possible misuses of political power by the same set of individuals collectively. Thus, ascribing rights to individuals that limit the extent to which their lives are at the disposal of political power need not entail some sort of grand calculation that the matters safeguarded by individual rights are of greater moment than those that are subject to collective decision. That ascription of rights is simply a matter of recognizing the roles in which people are vulnerable and of making provision for their vulnerability.[8]

But cannot people be vulnerable as groups and might they not therefore need the protection afforded by group rights? The answer to both questions is 'yes' but before I examine the implications of that answer, I want to turn to another thorny issue concerning democracy and self-determination.

---

[8] The idea of human rights as 'protective' does not mean that those rights can impose only negative obligations upon governments. They might also 'protect' by demanding positive action from governments as in the case of rights to personal security and rights to socioeconomic goods.

Although I have spent the last few paragraphs considering democracy and individual rights as potential rivals, democracy and human rights are, as I remarked earlier, frequently joined together nowadays in a single slogan. Democracy is logically linked to human rights if we include in those rights the right of all adult individuals to participate equally in the government to which they are subject. Consequently, the aspiration to achieve global recognition for human rights has been increasingly accompanied by an aspiration to establish democracy as the only legitimate form of government. The undemocratic forms of government to which that aspiration stands opposed include forms that are sanctioned by traditional cultures and widely accepted by those who are subject to them.[9] It therefore raises the same sort of questions as the general idea of human rights about the legitimacy of wishing arrangements upon societies that run counter to their cultures.

How real an issue is that? It might on reflection appear quite unreal. If we require a society to be democratic, all we are doing is vesting ultimate control of its affairs in the population at large. If we vest political power in a population, how can we be criticized for flouting its wishes since we are enabling it to act on its wishes? But, of course, if it wishes to be governed undemocratically, we do flout its wishes if we insist that it must take charge of its own affairs.

There can therefore be legitimate complaint that visiting democracy upon a society can be an act of imposition rather than an act of liberation. I do not wish to argue against that complaint but I do want to unearth the values upon which it is based and to show that those values have a certain similarity to the democrat's even though they are not quite the same.

I return to a point I made earlier in this article: cultures themselves have no standing. Cultures matter only because they matter to people. So what gives moral purchase to the fact that a non-democratic form of government is embedded in a population's culture is not the mere fact that it is part of their culture. It is the presumption that the population at large embraces that culture and so endorses the non-democratic form of government that forms part of it. In other words, the appeal to a traditional culture against democracy is still an appeal to a form of populism. It is an appeal that takes as authoritative what a population wishes for itself.

That populism does not equate with democracy. It is closer to the doctrine of popular sovereignty. That doctrine holds that the legitimate government of a society is the government endorsed by its population and the form of government a population endorses might be undemocratic. However, the populism implicit in the appeal to a population's culture is akin to democracy in that it vests ultimate authority on political matters in the population whose government is at issue. Contemporary proponents of cultural populism are also likely to accept that, in assessing the will of a people, the voice of each member of the population is to count and to count equally.

This sort of cultural populism might sometimes generate a stance that comes close to paradox. Suppose that a society is governed by a traditional monarch whom its population believe to be their divinely ordained ruler. They believe that monarchy is, uniquely, the form of government approved by God and that the rightful

---

[9] Although there are plenty of undemocratic national governments still in existence, not many can any longer claim the sanction of tradition.

monarch is someone chosen by God rather than by themselves. In that case, they will believe that the legitimacy of their form of government, and the authority of the individual who wields power over them, in no way depend upon their own endorsement. In other words, they themselves reject any notion that political authority is popular in origin. What reason, then, could we as outsiders, who do not share the populations' beliefs and who believe in a different god or in no god, have for respecting their form of government? It is difficult to see how that reason could be other than one that turns upon the deference that we owe to the population and the respect we should show for their beliefs. *We* should respect their form of government because it is the form that they endorse, even though *they* do not themselves believe that the legitimacy of their form of government depends upon their own endorsement.

Ironically, therefore, the cultural populist may find that his reason for respecting and deferring to a population's culture is at odds with the culture itself. That is symptomatic of a general truth that people are sometimes reluctant to concede: how ever 'hands-off' we try to be, we cannot value another's culture without taking a stand on principles that are logically external to (though not necessarily incompatible with) that culture.

Groups and rights

I want now to return to the question of groups and vulnerability. There have been plenty of occasions when individuals, just as individuals, have been the victims of unjust treatment but it has probably been more common for individuals to suffer mistreatment by governments or majorities because of their group affiliations. Ethnic and religious groups, for example, have been common targets for persecution. If individuals are at risk not just as independent individuals but also as bearers of group identities, do we not need to add group rights to individual rights to provide for that risk? The answer depends upon quite what it is that we are trying to protect people from. If, for example, we ascribe to individuals the right not to suffer disadvantage or persecution because of their race, their individually-held rights will provide for cases in which they are vulnerable to disadvantage or persecution because they belong to a particular racial group. It is a mistake to suppose that wrongs directed at groups can be countered only by group rights.

There are, however, cases where, if we use the language of rights at all, we seem obliged to ascribe rights to groups. Take the case of religious affiliation. If we aim to protect people's freedom of worship, we can intelligibly do so by ascribing to each individual person the right of freedom of worship. The fact that acts of worship usually take a collective form and usually take place within more or less institutionalized contexts, does not prevent our conceiving the right to engage in worship as a right possessed by each individual worshipper. But consider now the right of the members of a religious group not to have their sacred sites desecrated. It is difficult to factor that into so many rights held separately by each individual who subscribes to the relevant faith. If we use something like a notion of moral ownership to deal with this case, a sacred site would seem to be the special property of the faithful as a group and, if its desecration violates a right, that would seem to be a right possessed by the faithful as a group. Where the title to a good necessarily has this collective form, it cannot be factored into a number of rights held independently by separate individuals.

Group rights can extend beyond cases of group ownership. Consider the right of those belonging to a linguistic group to conduct their lives using their native language. People's right simply to speak their language is entirely intelligible as a right held by each individual language-user. If a government were to ban comprehensively the use of a minority language, we could quite reasonably regard that ban as violating a right held by each individual member of the linguistic minority rather than a right held by the minority as a group. The fact that language is a group phenomenon does not mean that all rights relating to language use must be group rights. But suppose now that the linguistic issue is of a rather different kind: it concerns the right of a linguistic minority that the public affairs of the larger society should be conducted in its language as well as in the language of the majority. In other words, the issue is one of whether legislative and court proceedings, tax forms, public signage, and the like, should cater for both languages. Acknowledging and providing for this dual language right would involve considerable cost and inconvenience for the society concerned. If we take any individual minority language-user, the benefit gained by that individual from a policy of public bilingualism would not justify the cost the policy would impose upon the rest of the society. If the relevant minority were very small in number, the benefit might again be insufficient to justify the cost. But if the minority were much larger, the benefit to the minority might well outweigh the cost to the society in general, in which case the minority might begin to mount a reasonable claim that its language should be recognized and used in public life. If we formulate that claim as a right, it must be a group right for, as we have seen, the claim of any individual member of the group *qua* individual is not, on its own, enough to ground the right. It is only the combined claim of all of the individuals in the linguistic group that suffices to make the case for the right. Thus the group as whole possesses a right that none of its members possesses individually.[10]

This idea of rights resulting from the accumulation of a number of individual claims, each of which, taken on its own, falls short of a right, goes against the grain of rights thinking. Aggregated claims of this sort are more normally associated with consequentialist theories, such as utilitarianism, that rights theorists generally shun. But, if we do not introduce quantitative considerations of this kind, it is difficult to understand why we should find it acceptable that in multilingual societies some language-users enjoy rights that others do not.

There are, then, some rights which, if they are rights, must be group rights—rights held by groups rather than by individuals separately. To that extent, if we are in the business of protecting the vulnerable, we may need to supplement individually-held human rights with group rights. If we do that, must we make a move from an 'individualist' morality to a different, 'communitarian', morality? In answering that question, I want to distinguish between two way of conceiving group rights. I label these two conceptions 'collective' and 'corporate'.[11]

---

[10] What I say here is guided by the analysis of collective rights given by Joseph Raz, *The Morality of Freedom* (Oxford: Clarendon Press, 1986), pp. 207–9.

[11] I examine the distinction between these two ways of understanding groups rights in 'Group Rights and Group Oppression', *Journal of Political Philosophy*, 7 (1999), pp. 353–77.

Group rights have been controversial in moral and political philosophy because they have been conceived most frequently on a corporate model. The supposition has been that a right-holding group must be closely analogous to a right-holding person. Just as we conceive a right-holding individual as a single unified entity possessed of moral standing as an individual person, so (it has been supposed) we must conceive a right-holding group as a single unified entity possessed of the same sort of moral standing. The parallel between the group and an individual person can be drawn more or less closely. A favourite concern of those who conceive group rights on the corporate model has been to establish quite how many characteristics of persons we can ascribe to groups (for example, consciousness, intentionality, responsibility), and quite which characteristics are crucial to a group's holding rights. But the crucial feature of the corporate conception is that, for whatever reason, the right-holding group is conceived as an entity that possesses moral standing *qua* group and that moral standing is seen as crucial to its capacity to hold rights.

In law, the idea of corporate personhood has been commonplace. In our moral thinking, it has not, and one thing that has made people reluctant to embrace the idea of group rights has been their reluctance to ascribe the qualities and moral status of personhood to groups. Clearly, if we embrace a corporate conception of group rights, we move away from 'moral individualism' of any kind. We might think of the groups that hold rights as 'group-individuals', but we move to a world in which groups now enjoy a moral ultimacy that goes beyond anything that might be encompassed by the morality of human rights.

There is, however, another way of conceiving group rights that does not force upon us this moral dichotomy between groups and individuals. Consider again the case of the linguistic minority that claims a right to use its language in the conduct of public roles and in public life generally, rather than only in matters private to itself as a minority. We saw in that example how the claim of an individual member of the minority would not be of sufficient weight on its own to justify the duties that this right would impose upon the rest of the society. We also saw how the combined claim of very many members of the minority might well suffice to justify the imposition of those duties. If it does, the individuals who make up the minority will possess a right as a group that none of them possesses individually.

Here, then, we have a right that is authentically a group right. Yet this group right does not require that we ascribe moral standing or any other moral quality to the group as an entity distinct from the individuals who make it up. Certainly the right is a right held by the members of the group only as a group, but the right is still a right held by the individuals who constitute the group. It is simply that those individuals hold that right 'collectively' or jointly rather than independently. This idea of rights held collectively or jointly is quite capable of making sense of rights that are commonly claimed as group rights, such as rights of national self-determination or rights relating to a group's culture. But it does not require us to see groups as entities that enjoy a moral status that is somehow separable from the persons make them up. The moral standing that is crucial to right-holding is provided by the several individuals who make up the group, even though the right possessed by these individuals is a right they hold together rather than separately.

We can therefore conceive group rights on this collective, rather than on a corporate, model. In the context of arguments about individualism, the significance of this collective conception is that it shows that we can acknowledge group rights and other sorts of group claim without abandoning the thought that individual persons remain the ultimate units of moral significance. That should not be surprising. All we are acknowledging is that some of what is most important to people relates to identities that they possess and to activities in which they can engage only with others. We do not adequately provide for the lives of people if we fail to recognize and provide for the communal dimensions of their lives. But in recognizing and providing for those communal dimensions, we are still recognizing and providing for the individual persons whose well-being is at stake, rather than for some communal entity whose moral significance is less than wholly reducible to the moral significance of the people who make it up.

Can the idea of human rights accommodate this collective conception of group rights, so that some human rights can be group rights? If some of the things that matter fundamentally to all human beings are collective goods to which they can hold only joint claims, I see no reason why we should not think of these as human rights. But I do not want to address that issue here.[12] Nor perhaps does the terminological question of whether we might describe a group right as a 'human right' matter very much. What does matter is that the fundamental values and concerns that underlie collective rights can be the same as those that underlie individual rights, so that the two sorts of right emanate from the same morality rather than from two rival moralities, one 'individualist', the other 'communitarian'.

Conclusion

The supposition that a doctrine of human rights must ignore or devalue the communal aspects of people's lives, is therefore mistaken. Human rights thinking unquestionably manifests a certain form of moral individualism. It ascribes moral standing to human beings as individual persons and it ascribes that standing to human beings equally, so that the rights it vests in individual persons are rights that those persons possess equally. It therefore stands opposed to beliefs and ideologies that give different sorts of people different degrees of standing, or that deprives some sorts of human being of any standing, or that give no standing at all to individual persons as individuals. It does not exclude the possibility that 'nations' or political communities as corporate entities may also possess moral standing and therefore hold rights, although it does not deliver that possibility itself. However, it cannot allow that corporate entities are the sole possessors of moral standing or that the rights they possess are comprehensive in range, since that would leave no room for individual human beings to hold rights.

If we turn to the right of self-determination, the potential rivalry between individuals and corporate entities as distinct moral claimants translates into a rivalry between two types of 'self' that can claim that right. Once again, however, this potential rivalry does not have to translate into irreconcilable opposition. We can allow that corporate entities have the right to determine some matters while indivi-

---

[12] See further my 'Human Rights, Group Rights, and Peoples' Rights', *Human Rights Quarterly*, 21 (1999), pp. 80–107.

dual persons have the right determine others, so that each self occupies a different moral space. Moreover, if we reinterpret 'societies' or 'nations' or 'peoples' as collective rather than corporate entities, the opposition between an individual self and a group self disappears since the moral claims of groups become no more than the collective claims of individuals.[13] The balance to be struck between political power and individual immunities will be something to be calculated within the same morality rather than a truce to be established between two different, rival, moralities.

Human rights thinking is, then, individualist in that it gives moral significance to human beings as separate individuals and accords them a measure of control over the course of their own lives. But, in doing that, it does not sanction any particular form of life as the uniquely right form. Nor is there any reason why it should seek either to privilege individualist forms of life or to frustrate communal forms. It leaves human beings free to use their rights to live whatever form of life they wish to live or believe they should live.

Human rights certainly place moral constraints upon the use a society may make of political power. The main practical point of human rights, particularly as foundations for international standards, is to limit what political power may do to (or what it may not do for) those who are subject to it. It follows that human rights will constrain collective decision-processes including democracy, even though human rights may also endorse democracy as the form that political power should take. But it is overly simple to represent the constraints that human rights place upon collective decision-procedures as devices that privilege individualist over communitarian concerns. Finally, we have seen how human rights thinking can fully recognize the communal dimensions of people's lives and can provide for those dimensions through collective as well as individual rights. It is simple nonsense—nonsense upon stilts—to suppose that, if we treat individual persons as the ultimate units of moral concern, that must prevent us from taking full account of the communal dimensions of their lives.

---

[13] See Jones, 'Human Rights, Group Rights, and Peoples' Rights', pp. 95–107.

Thinking about civilizations

ROBERT W. COX*

The word 'civilization'—in the singular but also in the plural—has become common of late in the mouths of politicians and in the writings of international relations academics. Samuel Huntington stirred up a storm in political studies by his vision of the future world as a 'clash' of civilizations (in the plural);[1] and the war in Yugoslavia generated an increased frequency in political rhetoric of the word 'civilization' (in the singular). Indeed, as I shall argue later, conflict in the Balkans revealed more clearly than before the meaning of civilizations and of civilization (in both plural and singular) for our time.

Most people do not think of themselves in the course of a normal day's activities as belonging to a civilization. Civilization is for most people pretty far down on the scale of self-conscious identities. And when politicians evoke civilization, it is usually when they want to arouse their constituents against some demonized enemy. The everyday manifestation of civilization is not in a feeling of belonging. It is in the almost unconscious, taken for granted, *common sense* that expresses a people's shared idea of reality. This idea of reality also includes the sense of what is right and proper in ordinary behaviour. Common sense includes a normative guide to action as well as a perception of 'objectivity' (or what is really out there). I would argue that this common sense, which is different for people in different times and places, is shaped by a people's collective practical responses to their material conditions of existence.

Context and meaning

Words have meaning only in their historical context. The word *civilisation* emerged in French in the eighteenth century, as a process generating the *civilité* associated initially with the status norms of the *noblesse de robe* in the court of the monarchy; and later that particular development in French society was expanded into a

* The substance of this chapter was first given as the plenary lecture to the British International Studies Association conference in Manchester, December 1999. I am grateful to BISA and its Chair, Christopher Hill, for the opportunity to put together some thoughts about the place of civilizations in international studies and for comments made by members of the audience on the occasion of the lecture to which I have tried to respond in the present text.
[1] Samuel P. Huntington, 'The Clash of Civilizations?', *Foreign Affairs*, 72:3, 1993; the article was expanded into a book *The Clash of Civilizations and the Remaking of World Order* (New York: Simon & Schuster, 1996).

universalistic concept by the Revolution. In eighteenth century Germany, the corresponding term was *Kultur*, a word associated with the middle class and the universities rather than the courts, and which soon, with the Romantics like Herder, came to be identified with specific peoples, each with its own particular cultural spirit.[2]

During the nineteenth century, as European dominance embraced the world, 'civilization' became, in European thinking, joined to 'imperialism'. The civilizing process had emerged through a European history conceived as Progress, whether in the Hegelian or the Marxian form, which Europe was spreading to the rest of the world. *La mission civilisatrice* was the more sophisticated and universalistic way of expressing this movement; 'the white man's burden', was the more openly racist.

The imperial movement, however, encountered *Others*, human communities constituted very differently from the European by their respective histories. These other communities, during the nineteenth century, were overlaid by and subordinated to European norms and institutions. Their own norms and institutions were not obliterated. They were occulted, obscured from view, awaiting some stimulus that would arouse once again the native energy that remained with them.[3] The encounter obliged Europeans to recognize the existence of other civilizations while maintaining the conviction that these others would ultimately become included within the embrace of the one civilization—their own—which had a universal vocation.

The imperial rivalries among the European powers of the late nineteenth century and the European civil war of 1914–18 displaced the optimism of European expansionism, of what Charles Morazé called the age of *les bourgeois conquérants*.[4] Pessimism gave more credence to the German concept of *Kultur*, an emphasis on the particularity of peoples, detracting from the universality of *civilisation*.

Oswald Spengler's *Der Untergang des Abendlandes*, a work composed during World War I, is open to much criticism. In some respects it resembles a gigantic poem more than an academic treatise. Perhaps for that reason it marks an ontological shift in the European conception of the world, what Spengler called his Copernican discovery: The Faustian West was not the centre of the universe; it was one among a number of Culture/Civilisations and was approaching the end of its historical trajectory.[5] No longer could the triumph of 'the West' remain

[2] On the origins of the concept of civilization in the European tradition, see Fernand Braudel, *A History of Civilizations*, trans. Richard Mayne (New York: Penguin Books, 1994), pp. 3–8; also Norbert Elias, *The Civilizing Process: The History of Manners and State Formation and Civilization* (Oxford: Blackwell, 1995; originally published 1939). On Herder, see Isaiah Berlin, *Vico and Herder* (London: Chatto and Windus, 1980).

[3] Kinhide Mushakoji, 'Multilateralism in a multicultural world: notes for a theory of occultation', in Robert W. Cox (ed.), *The New Realism: Perspectives on Multilateralism and World Order* (London: Macmillan for the United Nations University, 1996).

[4] Charles Morazé, *Les bourgeois conquérants* (Paris: Armand Colin, 1957).

[5] Oswald Spengler, *The Decline of the West* one volume edn. (New York: Knopf, 1939). 'The system that is put forward in this work ... I regard as the *Copernican discovery* in the historical sphere in that it admits no sort of privileged position to the Classical or the Western Culture as against the Cultures of India, Babylon, China, Egypt, the Arabs, Mexico—separate worlds of dynamic being which in point of mass count for just as much in the general picture of history as the Classical, while frequently surpassing it in point of spiritual greatness and soaring power.' (Introduction, p. 18.)

unchallenged in world history. The only universal truth in history, for Spengler, was the process of rise, maturity and decline of all civilizations.[6]

Following World War II, decolonization gave an initial stimulus to a revolt against the West within the hitherto subordinated civilizations,[7] but the Cold War came to dominate politics and economic and social organization. In the Cold War, two universalisms, both rooted in European history, fought for global dominance. The end of the Cold War left one of these contestants dominant in military power, and the source of a globalizing economy and a spreading popular culture. At the same time, the apparent victory of this Western form of universalism with its core in America became a challenge to subordinated cultures and civilizations to affirm their individuality in the face of one hegemonic form of political, economic, and cultural power. The challengers had far fewer resources but Western universalism had its own weaknesses. The issue for the future structure of world order had become universal globalization versus alternative paths of economic, social and cultural development; or one all-absorbing civilization versus a coexistence of several civilizations.

Conceiving 'civilization'

Pointing to the issue of one versus several civilizations does not answer the question of what exactly these entities called civilizations are. How do we know one? What are its boundaries? Are there some common dimensions of civilization which enable us to distinguish one from another and to discern change in particular civilizations?

Archeologists identified early civilizations in material terms—civilizations in Egypt, the Fertile Crescent, and the environs of Mohenjo Daro to the east.[8] These civilizations had in common a bronze age technology, a form of economic organization that involved some central control and a class structure, and hierarchical systems of political authority. Other civilizations with such characteristics have existed in China, Central and South America and parts of Africa. Each of these materially defined civilizations was united intersubjectively by myth, religion, and language through which their members could communicate with each other, interpret and act upon their different worlds. Myth, religion and language were one and the same until the rationalization of language split them apart. Together they constituted the realm of intersubjective meanings which were the *common sense* of these distinct worlds, their distinctive perceptions of reality.

---

6 The American historian William H. McNeill, during the renewed Western euphoria following the defeat of Nazism in World War II, wrote *The Rise of the West* (Chicago: University of Chicago Press, 1963), subtitled *A History of the Human Community*, in self-conscious opposition to Spengler's thesis. Some twenty-five years after this book's publication, McNeill reflected that 'its scope and conception is a form of intellectual imperialism'; and that 'my review of the whole of human history and the temporary world role played by the United States therefore operated, if it operated at all, entirely at a subconscious level for all concerned': '*The Rise of the West* After Twenty-Five Years', *Journal of World History* I (1990). The article is reproduced in the 1991 edition of *The Rise of the West*.

7 Geoffrey Baraclough, *An Introduction to Contemporary History* (Harmondsworth, Middlesex: Penguin Books, 1964) captures this moment well in ch. VI, 'The Revolt against the West. The Reaction of Asia and Africa to European Hegemony'.

8 For example, Gordon Childe, *What Happened in History* (Harmondsworth, Middlesex: Penguin Books, 1957).

From this, I am inclined to propose as an initial definition of 'civilization': a fit between material conditions of existence (in which I include human organization of an economic and political character) and intersubjective meanings. I do not advance this in a 'vulgar Marxist' sense in which the material base would determine the intersubjective superstructure. Rather I am suggesting something more like Max Weber's notion of elective affinity—different sets of intersubjective meanings might fit with similar material circumstances. The important thing is that the relationship conveys a sense of reality to the people concerned. Of course, there is nothing fixed or immutable in this fit. Material conditions change. So do the meanings that people share intersubjectively. Civilizations are thus in slow but continuing development. Change is of their essence.

Change comes about both from internal contradictions and from encounters with other civilizations. Geography has been at the foundation of civilizations—the ground upon which the material structure of civilization was erected and the site of the myth and poetry that gave it meaning. But historical development loosens the determining influence of geography. As civilizations encounter one another and as peoples migrate, meanings mingle and are discordant. Different peoples in the same geographical site come to perceive reality differently. First nations people in Canada do not see the same reality as middle class urban Canadians. The same goes in France for Islamic North African inhabitants of the urban *banlieux* and graduates of the *Grandes Ecoles*. Civilization is something we carry in our heads which guides our understanding of the world; and for different peoples this understanding is different. The common sense of one people is different from that of another and their notions of reality differ. It may even be that a single individual has to reconcile within him or herself the perspectives and the claims of two different civilizations—the Indian or the Japanese executive of a multinational corporation, for example, or the Central American immigrant in Los Angeles. This is what has made the drawing of geographical boundaries around civilizations in our own times an exercise in futility.[9] We need to know more about the modes of thought characteristic of different civilizations, how these modes of thought came about, and how they may be changing.

I can suggest three dimensions of thought that can help distinguish among civilizations: first, the notions they have of time and space and the relative emphasis on the one or the other; second, the tension between individual and community; and thirdly, what one can loosely call spirituality or cosmology, the common notion of the relationship of humanity to nature and the cosmos.

A focus on time imagines a common past and projects a common future—myths of origin that shape a people's character and vocation, and an eschatology of destiny. A time orientation is protected by the continuity of institutions like churches and states. It is nourished by literary traditions and intellectual dialogue. It is expressed in a concern for planning and development, activities that take place in time and require time for fulfilment.

Space privileges the synchronic over the diachronic. The emphasis is on the relationship among components of a system or the links and interactions in a

---

[9] Huntington, in *Clash of Civilizations*, writes of 'fault lines' separating civilizations and he uses the geological metaphor of 'tectonic plates' colliding. For him, civilizations occupy a geographical sphere and they have a 'core state' as their centre. In fact, he represents civilizations as states writ large; and their relationships are conceived very much in line with neorealist international relations theory.

network. The market is a synchronic concept. Administration, military logic, and geopolitics are pre-eminently spatial in their thought forms. The spatial orientation leads to a concern for homeostasis or the restoration of equilibrium among the interconnected components or else for the establishment of a new equilibrium.[10]

Shifts in emphasis between time and space can mark transformations within civilizations. European civilization began with a strong time orientation centred in the Church and its sense of historical progression from the Old Testament rule of God's law to the moment of revelation in time through Christ and an eschatological anticipation of the Kingdom of Heaven; eighteenth century Enlightenment modernity marked a transition point which gave more emphasis to space through a science based upon universal laws; and contemporary postmodernism undervalues both time and space in a sense of the immediacy of events and their proximity in a world in which everyone is involved with everyone else.[11] This is, of course, a very broad generalization, but it suggests that a shift in time and space orientations can be a clue to civilizational change.

Individualism is a product of European civilization, reaching its most extreme development in America. The civilizations of the East are perceived as stressing solidarity and the obligations of individuals to a range of communities, from the family to the clan and the nation as a whole. Furthermore, individualism is not confined to human behaviour. It also arises in forms of thought. Methodological individualism recognizes only discrete entities and ignores collective wholes. It obscures those phenomena that bind societies together, and which merge the individual into the whole. In the extreme form it denies the existence of society. Only individuals exist.

Individual and community are not, however, mutually exclusive categories. The nature of a civilization depends upon the mix; and the mix can change. Individualistic behaviour may increase among people who still maintain a belief in communal norms; and the disintegration of a society beset by excessive individualism may stimulate a reaction to rekindle a sense of common welfare. This shifting mix is another indicator of civilizational change.

---

[10] There is, of course, an enormous bibliography on time and space. I refer here only to a few works that explicitly link concepts of time and space to the nature of civilizations. This was a central concern for Harold A. Innis in *The Bias of Communication* (Toronto: University of Toronto Press, 1991) and *Empire and Communications* (Toronto: Press Porcépic, 1986). David Harvey, *The Condition of Postmodernity: An Enquiry into the Origins of Cultural Change* (Oxford: Blackwell, 1989), also takes this approach. On the related matter of the diachronic and synchronic in perspectives on society, Jean Piaget, *Etudes sociologiques* (1965) translated into English as *Sociological Studies* (London & New York: Routledge, 1995); and Fernand Braudel, 'History and the Social Sciences: The *longue durée*', in Braudel, *On History*, trans. Sarah Matthews (Chicago: University of Chicago Press, 1980). Braudel's use of the term *durée* recalls Henri Bergson, *Essai sur les données immédiates de la conscience* (translated into English as *Time and Free Will*).

[11] Harvey, in *The Condition of Postmodernity*, writes: 'Spatial and temporal practices are never neutral in social affairs. They always express some kind of class or other social content, and are more often than not the focus of intense social struggle ... During phases of maximal change, the spatial and temporal bases for reproduction of the social order are subject to the severest disruption.' (p. 239). He adds: 'As space appears to shrink to a 'global village' of telecommunications and a 'spaceship earth' of economic and ecological interdependencies—to use just two familiar and everyday images—and as time horizons shorten to the point where the present is all there is (the world of the schizophrenic), so we have to cope with an overwhelming sense of *compression* of our spatial and temporal worlds'. (p. 240.)

The spirituality dimension touches people's sense of the fundamental nature of the world and of humanity's place in it. Monotheism, polytheism and pantheism are three distinctive modes of perception. I am not considering these as forms of religious belief, although the words are theological. I am considering the implications for thought in general of these cosmological postulates. Monotheism posits absolute truths; and it separates humanity from nature. Nature exists to satisfy humanity's needs. Polytheism knows a multiplicity of truths and is non-exclusive when it comes to deities and values. Pantheism perceives humanity as one with nature.

Much human conflict is overtly justified as defence of absolute truth, even when covertly less lofty motivations are at work. The absolutist residue of monotheism remains resilient despite the decline of formal religion. No one preaches polytheism as such to the world today but an openness to a plurality of values and to recognition of difference challenges absolutism in public discourse.[12] Pantheism is an emerging force in public concern for maintenance of the biosphere in which humanity shares the fate of other forms of life. In pantheism the cosmologies of aboriginal peoples meet with a new cosmology derived from deep ecology.[13]

These different and conflicting forms of spirituality are also shaping changes in civilizations. They find expression in conflicts concerning material life—in the connection of race, gender, ethnicity and religion with economic oppression, and in the common fate of humanity in a fragile biosphere.

Beyond these internal dimensions of civilizations is the sense of relationship to other civilizations. Awareness of the Other may be the catalyst for arousing a self consciousness of one's own civilizational identity. For the European Middle Ages, Islam was the significant Other. At that time, Islam was the higher of the two in terms of philosophy, medicine, trade and urban development; and it aroused in Christendom a fanaticism manifested in the Crusades. In twentieth century Europe, Islam reappears as Europe's Other but now, as a consequence of the imperial expansion of Europe during the nineteenth century and the technological and economic supremacy of Europe and America, in a relationship of subordination and resentment which is perceived as a latent threat to a dominant Euro-American civilization.

The material foundations of this dominance and subordination have been echoed in modes of thought among both dominant and subordinate civilizations. Euro-

---

[12] See, for example, David L. Miller, *The New Polytheism: Rebirth of the Gods and Goddesses* (New York: Harper and Row, 1974), who writes: '... monotheistic thinking ... fails a people in a time when experience becomes self-consciously pluralistic ...'(p. 7); and '... polytheism is not a matter of some new theology, sociology, or psychology. It is rather a matter of many potencies, many structures of meaning and being, all given to us in the reality of our everyday lives.' (p. 65.)

[13] Fritjof Kapra, *The Web of Life: A New Scientific Understanding of Living Systems* (New York: Doubleday, 1996), writes: 'Shallow ecology is anthropocentric, or human-centered. It views humans as above or outside of nature, as the source of all value, and ascribes only instrumental, or "use", value to nature. Deep ecology does not separate humans—or anything else—from the natural environment. It sees the world not as a collection of isolated objects, but as a network of phenomena that are fundamentally interconnected and interdependent. Deep ecology recognizes the intrinsic value of all living beings and views humans as just one particular strand in the web of life.

'...the emerging new vision of reality based on deep ecological awareness is consistent with the so-called perennial philosophy of spiritual traditions, whether we talk about the spirituality of Christian mystics, that of Buddhists, or the philosophy and cosmology underlying the Native American traditions.' (p.7.)

American dominance in scholarship and media have defined the identity of subordinate civilizations in what Edward Said called 'orientalism'.[14] The elites of subordinate civilizations confront the choice of imitating the dominant civilization while trying to preserve something of their own or of reviving their myths of origin in order to reject the dominant civilization and to claim the intellectual space to create something different.

Culture and identity

Two terms that are very current in contemporary discourse appear to have a link to the concept of civilization. These are culture and identity. I do not want to propose any dogmatic definitions of these words but just to say how I would distinguish them from my use of 'civilization'.

'Culture' is sometimes used as an equivalent to 'civilization' but more usually refers to norms and behaviour patterns of a more limited group. 'Multicultural' refers to a society composed of a number of such groups of different ethnic or religious backgrounds, all of which may belong to the same civilization. Culture and civilization are not isomorphic concepts. Culture is an anthropologist's word, and civilization is an historian's. In the anthropological connotation, a culture is a composite of practices and norms that are mutually coherent. It evokes the notion of homeostasis as a natural restorer of equilibrium. The idea of equilibrium is alien to the notion of 'civilization'. Thinking about civilizations leads rather to considerations of development and change through encounters and transformations.

Another sense of 'culture' derives from the German, and this is closer to the meaning of 'civilization'. In this particular meaning, 'culture' is the creative force of civilization. Spengler, for example, uses 'culture' to refer to the early stages of the civilizing process, and 'civilization' he uses to refer to the stages of maturity and decline.[15] However, because of the common usages of 'culture' in English it is probably best to avoid confusing it with 'civilization'.

Postmodernism has given wide currency to the notion of 'identity' as the self-consciousness of collective subjects of history, especially those whose existence has hitherto been obscured in the dominant discourses. Feminism and post-colonial literature have given particular emphasis to such identities. One might think of a civilization as a very large realm of identity, and often it seems to be so in the rhetoric of appeals to defend the principles of Western civilization, or some other definition of civilization. I prefer to leave the notion of identity to refer to self-consciousness. Insofar as it may relate to civilization it refers only to a conscious affirmation of belonging to a civilization. It does not refer to the 'common sense' or perceptions of 'reality' that characterize particular civilizations and which are to be

---

[14] Edward Said, *Orientalism* (New York: Random House, 1978).

[15] Spengler, *Decline of the West*, Introduction, esp. p. 31: '... every Culture has *its own* Civilization. In this work, for the first time, the two words, hitherto used to express an indefinite, more or less ethical, distinction, are used in a *periodic* sense, to express a strict and necessary *organic succession*. The Civilization is the inevitable *destiny* of the Culture ... Civilizations are the most external and artificial states of which a species of developed humanity is capable. They are the conclusion, the thing-become succeeding the thing-becoming ... They are an end, irrevocable, yet by inward necessity reached again and again.'

found at a deeper level of consciousness—a level at which something that has been shaped by the historical development of a people comes to be understood by them as universal and natural. It is only through deep critical reflection that the formation of such 'common sense' through time and the perception of 'reality' that corresponds to it can be revealed.

Present day issues in the development of civilizations

Development and change in civilizations today has to be approached from two aspects: first, the contradictions within civilizations that pose choices among visions of the future; and second, the external influences coming from coexisting civilizations that have an impact on those choices. This puts the emphasis upon the dynamics of civilizational development. It differs from attempts to draw the boundaries of civilizations which is the more usual approach. To attempt to define the essence of a civilization reifies it in a non-historical way and reinforces exclusionary defensive tendencies. I would aim rather for a global perspective on the processes of change in a full range of contemporary civilizations, avoiding so far as possible a perspective rooted in any one of them.

Taking as a guideline the definition of a civilization as a fit between material conditions of existence and intersubjective meanings, political economy or *social economy* is, I suggest, the most promising field in which to seek the potential for change and development. Social economy is precisely the area in which different forms of human organization, including the language and the concepts that make human organization intelligible, mesh with technologies and material resources to create viable human communities.[16]

One form of civilization, which Susan Strange called the 'business civilization',[17] is clearly pre-eminent in discourse about world affairs. It is the vehicle for economic globalization. Its ideology is nourished in business schools around the world and in economic journalism and political rhetoric in the economically powerful countries. The business civilization has no formal organization. It is informally ordered by a *nébuleuse* of interrelated bodies which generate policy—international agencies like the World Trade Organization, the IMF, the Bank for International Settlements, the World Bank and the OECD and unofficial bodies like the annual World Economic Forum at Davos.[18] This civilization cuts across pre-existing historical civilizations in different parts of the world, although it is an offshoot and transformation of Euro-American civilization rooted mainly in the United States. Members of the business civilization who are drawn from other civilizations—Indian, Japanese, Islamic, African, for example—must confront the personal dilemma of dual civilizationship.

---

[16] Ronald J. Deibert, *Parchment, Printing, and Hypermedia: Communication in World Order Transformation* (New York: Columbia University Press, 1997) argues compellingly for a non-reductionist theory of communication and civilizational change, developing the work of Harold Innis (see n. 10).

[17] Susan Strange, 'The Name of the Game', in Nicholas X. Rizopoulos (ed.), *Sea-Changes: American Foreign Policy in a World Transformed* (New York: Council on Foreign Relations Press, 1990), pp. 260–73.

[18] Robert W. Cox, 'A Perspective on Globalization', in James H. Mittelman (ed.), *Globalization: Critical Reflections* (Boulder, CO: Lynne Rienner, 1996), p. 27.

The transformation of the Euro-American tradition into the business civilization privileges space over time. The 'end of history' idea[19] springs from it: the notion that with globalization the ultimate in human society has been achieved and nothing further is possible except more of the same. The spatial orientation is implicit in the synchronic concept of the market. The absolutism of monotheism is rendered into a universalistic economic theory with its social correlates—what in French is called *la pensée unique*. Individualism and competitiveness are its basic assumptions regarding human conduct; and society, the real existence of which is moot, is just their by-product, an illusion created by the invisible hand.

The business civilization is, however, something of an abstraction or ideal type—a projection into the future of some powerful tendencies in the present. There are other forces at work which are rooted in the gradual transformation of the social organization and practices of coexisting civilizations. The interaction of these forces shape social economies which are the different ways in which people are organized to satisfy their material needs. Karl Polanyi called these 'substantive economies' by contrast to the formal economics of theory.[20] There is a growing literature on comparative capitalism which demonstrates the substantive variety of forms of social economy that constitute the different realities of peoples who all experience in some measure the impact of globalization.[21]

These different social economies are all beset by issues, contradictions, and open or potential conflicts the resolution of which will orient their future course. Globalization says: There is no alternative. In the thinking of globalization, societies will inevitably be shaped to conform to the requirements of economic competition which means they will become more and more alike. Those who contest globalization affirm the possibility of alternatives that embody values both derived from their past and imagined as more desirable futures.

In America, which is the model for globalization, a thriving economy has in recent years generated both a high level of employment, much of it in low-paid and precarious jobs, and a growing polarization of incomes. There are signs that rampant individualism may have passed the point at which it serves as a dynamic of economic competition to become a threat to social cohesion.[22] The vitality of civil

---

[19] Most notably expounded in Francis Fukuyama, *The End of History and the Last Man* (New York: The Free Press, 1993).

[20] Karl Polanyi, *The Great Transformation* (Boston, MA: Beacon Press, 1957).

[21] E.g. Suzanne Berger and Ronald Dore (eds.), *National Diversity and Global Capitalism* (Ithaca, NY: Cornell University Press, 1996); John Zysman, 'The Myth of a 'Global Economy': Enduring National Foundations and Emerging Regional Realities', *New Political Economy*, 1:2 (July 1996), pp. 157–84; Mitchell Bernard, 'East Asia's Tumbling Dominoes: Financial Crisis and the Truth About the Regional Miracle', in Leo Panitch and Colin Leys (eds.), *The Socialist Register, 1999: Globalization and Democracy* (London: Merlin Press).

[22] The American sociologist Robert D. Putnam has suggested that civil society in the United States has lost much of the spirit of association once noted by de Tocqueville as its salient characteristic. He sees this as being replaced by a privatizing and individualizing of leisure time with non-participation in group activities. He calls this a decline of 'social capital' which refers to networks, norms, and social trust that facilitate coordination and cooperation for mutual benefit. See Putnam, 'Bowling Alone: America's Declining Social Capital', *Journal of Democracy*, 6:1 (January 1995). The same author has made a study in collaboration with others about social capital in Italy: Putnam with Robert Leonardi and Raffaella Y. Nanetti, *Making Democracy Work: Civic Traditions in Modern Italy* (Princeton, NJ: Princeton University Press, 1993). The Italian study contrasted with the American in finding stability in a northern Italy with a higher propensity for cooperative social interaction and a south where this was lacking—characteristics both of which had a long historical legacy. It may be

society—those voluntary associations which de Tocqueville once saw as the strength of the American polity—is reportedly in decline. But so anchored in public consciousness is the 'American way' that there, in America, it becomes hard to imagine an alternative future.

In Europe, the emulators of America hold the preponderance of economic power and political influence; but popular opinion, reflected in recent elections which have returned social democratic parties, is more sceptical regarding the social consequences of economic globalization.[23] This critical response has become divided as some social democratic leaders, won over by neoliberal arguments of the need to strive for global market competitiveness, now propose to moderate its social consequences by policies to enhance the competitive opportunity of individuals, and to strengthen a form of 'competitive corporatism' that would offer more security to established workers.[24] At the same time, those who remain suspicious of this social liberalism have so far failed to present a compelling alternative. European societies show signs of following the American course—with growing income gaps, and culturally and ethnically distinct pockets of urban squalor and violence. The difference from America is the residual survival of a stronger social base for an imagined alternative.

The conflict in Europe, which is social and economic at bottom, opposes two modes of thought, two sets of intersubjective meanings—one is spatially oriented towards competition in the world market, individualist in its ontology, absolutist in certainty as to the principles on which it is founded, and dominant in its relationship with 'backward' and less efficient societies; the other is time-oriented towards building a future which embodies social as well as economic goals, with more emphasis on community as a basis for human security, and open to the acceptance of difference without domination among peoples.

Asia has been the site of a variety of forms of capitalism, much influenced by that in Japan. Japanese capitalism grew within the framework of a continuous social tradition which gave loyalty to institutions—state and corporation—precedence over

recalled that Giambattista Vico in the early eighteenth century envisaged as a possible end stage in the cyclical evolution of civilizations a 'barbarism of reflection' more inhuman than the primitive 'barbarism of sense' among peoples who 'have fallen into the custom of each man thinking only of his own private interests'. *The New Science of Giambattista Vico* translated from the third edition (1744) by Thomas Goddard Bergin and Max Harold Fisch (Ithaca, NY: Cornell University Press, 1970), paras. 1102–6. Robert Putnam, Susan Pharr and Russell Dalton in a forthcoming book, *What is Troubling the Trilateral Democracies?* (Princeton, NJ: Princeton University Press, 2000), use opinion surveys to show a general decline in people's confidence in their political institutions, most marked in the United States but noticeable in all of the rich countries (except for Iceland and Denmark). *The Economist* in its issue of 17 July 1999 began a series 'Is there a crisis?' enquiring why citizens of the mature democracies are losing confidence in their institutions.

23 Michel Albert, *Capitalisme contre capitalisme* (Paris: Seuil, 1991) presented the case for a 'Rhineland model' of capitalism confronting the Anglo-Saxon model, the former characterized by consensus, corporatism, long-term planning and a stabilizing relationship between banks and industry, the latter by a focus on short-term profits, shareholder dividends and stock markets facilitating predatory behaviour such as hostile take-overs.

24 Hans-Jürgen Bieling, 'European Integration and Industrial Relations—A Critique of the Concept and Strategy of "Competitive Corporatism", (unpublished draft); also M. Rhodes, 'Globalization, labour markets and welfare states: a future of "competitive corporatism"?', in M. Rhodes and Y. Mény (eds.), *The Future of European Welfare: A New Social Contract?* (London, 1998); also Ignacio Ramonet, 'Social-conformisme', *Le Monde diplomatique*, avril 1999, and José Vidal-Beneyto, 'La social-démocratie privatisée', *Le Monde diplomatique*, juillet 1999.

individualism.[25] However, many of the features considered characteristic of Japanese society have been strained in the decades since World War II by the nature and rapidity of economic growth and the impact of American-inspired popular culture. The identity of state and corporation, symbolized by the notion of Japan Incorporated, has weakened as corporations have gained more operational autonomy; and the formerly strong cohesion of family and community may be dissolving, leading to more emphasis on consumerism and individualism and to a lesser commitment to work and organizational loyalties.[26] A by-product of these disruptive tendencies has been an outbreak of radical forms of alienation.[27] Contending social forces in Japan which might foreshadow a transformation of the 'common sense' of Japanese people, and which are rooted in the economic and social changes of recent decades, are reflected in the choice Japan faces between remaining within the American security blanket and asserting its independence as a geopolitical entity; and the option of independence opposes those who would revive an imagined imperial past to those who would pursue the postwar hopes for a new form of non-aggressive democratic and internationalist future. The factors of individualism versus community and of dominance versus sharing are inherent in this predicament.

Other societies in southeast Asia, so recently devastated by global finance, must either succumb to external direction in their economic development or else devise means of regulating international financial flows so as to gain room for pursuit of internally determined social and economic goals. Recovery could take the form of state-directed capitalism evoking traditions of community and authority; but a more radical alternative could emerge from the development of a civil society able to mobilize people in a common social project and to gain acceptance of sacrifice with equity in its pursuit.[28]

Russia and China are both old civilizations that have in different degrees been subordinated to concepts of civilization derived from Europe—in the form both of socialism and capitalism. Russia has experienced three successive waves of Westernization: under Peter the Great, the Bolsheviks, and the attempt through 'shock therapy' to introduce Western capitalism. The last has produced a predatory, corrupt, mafia dominated, version of capitalism. The weakness of civil society has

---

[25] See Shigeto Tsuru, *Japan's Capitalism* (Cambridge: Cambridge University Press, 1993); Chalmers Johnson, *MITI and the Japanese Miracle* (Stanford, CA: Stanford University Press, 1982); James Fallows, *Looking at the Sun: The Rise of the New East Asian Economic and Political System* (New York: Pantheon, 1994); and Chie Nakane, *Japanese Society* (Harmondsworth, Middlesex: Penguin, 1973).

[26] Professor Tamotsu Aoki, a cultural anthropologist, Research Center for Advanced Science and Technology, University of Tokyo, at a symposium convened jointly by the International House of Japan and the Friedrich-Ebert-Stiftung, Tokyo, 26 September 1996.

[27] Yumiko Iida, 'Virtual Kingdom and Dreams of Apocalypse: Contemporary Japan Mirrored in *Aum Shinrikyo*', paper presented at the 10th annual conference, Japan Studies Association of Canada, Toronto, 3–4 October 1997. Aum Shinryiko, a doomsday cult, attracted a large number of highly educated Japanese.

[28] Mitchell Bernard, 'East Asia's Tumbling Dominoes', analyses the 'Asian crisis' in terms of the different forms of social class relations of production evolving in different Asian countries interacting with global finance. He argues that an alternative to foreign capital acquiring control of Asian economies, such as is likely to continue under IMF 'structural adjustment', could be popular support for an alternative conception of locally-controlled and socially and ecologically-oriented development based on a coalition of worker and peasant social forces, and with some middle-class support for something like a Tobin tax to curb speculative financial movements.

left people passively vulnerable to the kleptocracy, and has left government without a secure base in the people. It has also, together with the preponderance of foreign financial and political influences, obstructed the emergence of an alternative social and political project.[29] Yet a sense of the uniqueness of Russian history remains latent as rejection of the West and as an alternative vision of society. The 'Russian idea' appeals to an imagined past of communal values and the hope of a future good society guided by belief in the absolute truth inherent in the Russian soul.[30]

In China, elements of the old Confucian tradition survived into the Communist era and remain a stabilizing force in society. The Confucian inheritance combines sentiments of social responsibility with an open attitude towards truth. Capitalist processes have been introduced under Party-state control with less sense of cleavage than in Russia. The regime's effort to retain socialism within capitalism has combined economic decentralization and high growth with movement towards integration into the global economy. Chinese capitalism, like neoliberalism elsewhere, has produced a polarization of rich and poor, massive unemployment, and the decline of public services for health and welfare, moderated only slightly by socialist ethics. The Party has monopolized the functions of civil society and remains suspicious of any autonomous grouping of people which inhibits the articulation of any alternative social project.[31]

Up to now, international studies have been concerned primarily with states, the inter-state system, and markets. The tendencies I have been discussing suggest that civilizations and civil societies be brought into the picture in order to explain the historical transformations of the late twentieth century. Civilizations explain the potential of societies to espouse new directions of development. Civil societies shape common sense and collective purposes. A strong civil society can be the inner strength of a civilization and the creative force for its development; its absence, the explanation of subordination to an expansive Other.

---

[29] There is much recent reporting on the criminalization of Russian capitalism. See *Le Monde*, 21 August 1999; and *The Economist*, 28 August–3 September 1999. Grigory Yavlinski, an advocate of economic liberalism, excoriated 'Russia's phony capitalism' in *Foreign Affairs*, May–June 1998, citing George Soros as saying that in the process of privatization, first 'the assets of the state were stolen, and then when the state itself became valuable as a source of legitimacy, it too was stolen' (p. 69). The problem has been evident also in other countries of the former Soviet bloc which have too readily accepted the notion that state control of the economy was the evil. Sabina Neumann and Michelle Egan in 'Between German and Anglo-Saxon Capitalism: The Czech Financial Markets in Transition', *New Political Economy*, 4:2 (July 1999), argue that 'the deliberate failure to establish a system of rules and enforcement over financial markets was the result of the belief that overregulation would cramp the natural growth of capitalism' (p. 190.)

[30] Nicholas Berdyaev, *The Russian Idea* (London: Geoffrey Bles, 1947), is the classic statement. Tim McDaniel, *The Agony of the Russian Idea* (Princeton, NJ: Princeton University Press, 1996) traces its history and its influence from Tsarist times, through the Soviet period, to Yeltsin's 'reforms'. McDaniel argues that the vision of the West held by Russian reformers was a mythical West defined as the opposite of the Soviet system, so that the idea of capitalism conceived by the reformers was both unlike real Western capitalism and totally divorced from traditional Russian morality and culture. It is notable that the evocation of the 'Russian idea' has parallels with a nationalist current in Japanese politics that appeals to an imagined past. See Yumiko Iida, 'Fleeing the West, making Asia home: transpositions of otherness in Japanese pan-Asianism', *Alternatives*, 22 (1997).

[31] George T. Crane, 'Imagining the Economic Nation: Globalization in China', *New Political Economy*, 4:2 (July 1999); Lily Ling, 'Hegemony and the Internationalizing State: A Post-Colonial Analysis of China's Integration into Asian Corporatism', *Review of International Political Economy*, 3:1 (1996); and Gregory T. Chin, 'Beneath the "Miracle": Explaining China's Economic Growth', paper prepared for the Annual Conference of the Canadian Political Science Association, Sherbrooke, Québec, June 1999 (unpublished).

If the challenge to established ways of understanding the world is everywhere rather weak compared to the form of 'common sense' propagated by global media, it is nevertheless true that popular movements stimulated by material inequities and grievances have articulated alternative projects of society. These latent new directions are very diverse: some appeal to alternative absolute values while others are more open to recognition of a diversity of truths; some are grounded in a sense of time and continuity in contrast to the space orientation of modernism; most emphasize community over individualism; and the pantheist notion of humanity in union with nature is now more prominent in reactions to the hegemony of globalization. The 'battle in Seattle' gave some evidence of this diversity of protest.[32]

Civilizations and world order

Civilizations, I have argued, are to be thought of as processes or tendencies rather than as fixed and bounded essences. The historical dialectic moves ever onward. Each apparent culmination engenders the contradictions that lead to a further movement. The problem for political analysis is to spot these contradictions and to assess the possible directions of change.

The bias implicit in enquiring into the development of civilizations is an acknowledgment that there *is* collective choice about the future of societies. By 'collective choice' I mean the gradual emergence through civil society of a common understanding of the nature of the world and a vision of the future of society. It is conceivable but unlikely that one single vision could emerge common to all people. More likely there will be several collective visions.

The war in Yugoslavia has been a catalyst of issues in the contemporary development of civilizations. The war solved nothing, but it did illustrate options and potential directions of change. Broadly, for the world as a whole and not just the NATO countries, it underlined the choice between a single concept of civilization and recognition of a plurality of civilizations. NATO military force, which was primarily a projection of American air power, represented and was perceived both by its proponents and by its opponents to be an expression of the one-civilization option. NATO power became a potentially global force foreshadowing possible similar interventions in other conflicts. It demonstrated a mode of warfare that is lethal for enemy populations and economies while minimizing loss to its perpetrators. As such, it was a warning to forces resisting the one-civilization vision of the future. American and NATO military-political power are a support for economic globalization, which is the material basis for the one-civilization perspective; and a doctrine of human rights derived from Euro-American historical experience and grounded in individualism has been universalized as the one-civilization's core value.

The apparent dominance achieved by NATO force and the one-civilization implications that can be drawn from it could, however, prove to be ephemeral. Public opinion in the United States and in the Congress was almost evenly divided on the

---

[32] The 'battle in Seattle' refers to the anti-globalization, anti-multinational corporation demonstrations from a variety of groups that paralyzed the World Trade Organization conference in Seattle, 30 November–3 December 1999.

war, suggesting that a future United States government would be reluctant to engage in other such interventions unless American geopolitical interests were directly involved. Public opinion and elite opinion in the European allies was also divided and there was open opposition within some EU governments. The increasing fragility in the alliance, together with differences within the military over the conduct of the war, hastened the conclusion of an accommodation with the Serbian forces. NATO's apparent success could mask its inner weakness.

The air campaign against Serbia also mobilized public opposition as well as government opposition to NATO in Russia and China, while opinion in other countries of Asia and in Africa was apprehensive about Euro-American global dominance. A prospect of global hegemony that had hitherto moved with stealth in economic globalization and cultural penetration now appeared as an overt military-political challenge. Non-European civilizations were challenged by the attack on Serbia to affirmations of self-conscious difference and rejection of the universal claims of NATO-backed Euro-American power.

A major factor in the apparent dominance of globalization ideology and the one-civilization perspective has been the weakness of civil society in both West and non-West. Indicators are a weakening of public support for political institutions as shown by low voting turnouts at elections and a sense of the futility of party politics; the erosion of public services held hostage to budgetary constraints imposed by global finance; the progression of organized crime and its corrupting influence on politics and economy; and the atrophy of social solidarity with the progress of individualistic consumerism. The weakness of civil society is the greatest factor of uncertainty in the development of social forces that could sustain the development of civilizations.

There are, however, signs of a renaissance of civil society out of people's alienation from formal politics and economic power. The component elements of a multi-civilization world are perceptible in the negative reactions to globalization among states and within civil societies; but these reactions are fragmented and lack a coherent doctrine and institutional support such as NATO and the *nébuleuse* of economic governance provide for the one-civilization project.

The United Nations might be thought of as the obvious institutional framework for a multi-civilizational world were it not for the fact that the United Nations has become a hostage to American power—either used as an instrument of American policy where this is possible or, where this seems impractical, substantially set aside as in the case of the war against Yugoslavia.[33]

In a multi-civilizational world order, the role of a world organization would be to seek out principles acceptable in the 'common sense' or intersubjectivity of each of the different civilizations—to distill a kind of supra-intersubjectivity from the distinct intersubjectivities of its component parts. This could only come about through a lengthy learning process from experience in reconciling conflicts. Two conditions would be indispensable:

---

[33] Brian Urquhart, a former Under Secretary-General of the United Nations, described in his article 'The Making of a Scapegoat', in *The New York Review of Books* (12 August 1999) how the United States manipulated the appointment process to the Secretary-Generalship of the United Nations in December 1996 so as to eliminate the reappointment of Boutros Boutros-Ghali, which had the support of all members of the Security Council except for the United States, and to secure the appointment of Kofi Annan. This article was a review of Boutros Boutros-Ghali's book *Unvanquished: A US–UN Saga* (New York: Random House, 1999).

- First, the emergence of a core body of people who would cultivate an empathetic understanding of forms of common sense other than their own—who could bridge intersubjectivities; and
- Second, the development of civil societies capable of articulating the basic sentiments and goals of the people who compose them.

Civil society is the force that develops the intersubjective content of civilizations; and the core group which assumes the task of reconciliation of differences would have to keep abreast of these developments in the dynamics of civilizations.

This concept of a structure for world order is far from being an institutionalized form of global governance. It envisages a weak centre embodying certain accepted common principles in a world fragmented among peoples guided by different sets of social practices and goals. Such a pluralistic framework of weak centre in a fragmented whole has precedence in world history—in the European medieval Papacy, and in periods of Chinese history, for example. Such a structure would not displace the nation-state system or the international economy. It would provide the framework of principles within which the state system and economic relations could be regulated.

Struggle among social forces is the principal dynamic of change in societies. In the European tradition, this was understood by Giambattista Vico at the beginning of the eighteenth century[34] and by Karl Marx in the nineteenth. This perception remains just as valid at the beginning of the twenty-first century. The nature of class conflict is, however, changing, no longer tied so closely to property in the means of production as Marx saw it, but expanding to include other forms of dominance and subordination and of particular interests versus the general welfare. The arena of social struggle lies in civil society which is why developments in civil society are the key to understanding civilizational changes.

Certain common principles can be affirmed as starting points for thinking about an inter-civilizational world:

- Mutual recognition of difference;
- Maintenance of the biosphere upon which all forms of life depend;
- Avoidance of violence in dealing with conflict and especially in the use of weapons of mass destruction;
- Mutual support in promoting social equity, reversing the current trend towards social polarization;
- Suppression of organized criminal activity that becomes an occult political and economic power; and
- Consensual understanding of basic human rights.

Human rights is a particularly problematic case in the search for common understanding among coexisting civilizations. The conflict over Kosovo brought it to the fore and underlined the difficulties. Despite political rhetoric, there are no pure cases free of ambiguity and inconsistencies. Why is human rights a justification for intervention in one instance while similar instances are ignored—for example, the

---

[34] *The New Science of Giambattista Vico* translated from the third edition (1744) by Thomas Goddard Bergin and Max Harold Frisch (Ithaca, NY: Cornell University Press, 1970).

war in Chechnya, the oppression of Kurds, the genocide in Rwanda, or the dis-possession of Palestinians? How can we justify intervention that results in dramatic-ally increasing the intensity of the oppression it was intended to stop? Max Weber alerted us to the distinction between an absolute ethic which brooks no exception and an ethic of responsibility which contemplates the consequences of an action before undertaking it.[35] The ambiguities and inconsistencies of external intervention also lend substance to suspicions that other motives, geopolitical and economic, are at work under the cover of human rights.

In the European Enlightenment tradition rights are represented as innate in the human being and universal to a common human nature. This is the basis for much Western political rhetoric. In an historical mode of thinking, rights are not innate, they are the product of people's historical struggles which become enshrined in their common sense; and human nature is not uniform and universal but is formed differently by different histories. This historical mode of thinking is more attuned to understanding a multi-civilizational world.[36] From it we may derive the proposition that somewhat different concepts of human rights will be formed by the histories of different civilizations, arising in each case out of the conflicts that have shaped those civilizations, and that they will reflect the cosmologies, the relationship of humanity to nature, and the balance between individual and community characteristic of those civilizations.

The challenge in a multi-civilizational order is to find means of encouraging popular forces struggling for an entrenchment of human rights in *their* society without appearing to impose one civilization's norms upon another. An externally imposed order would remain fragile, vulnerable to the charge of imperialism.

To evoke the idea of a multi-civilizational world order is to affirm that an alterna-tive, even more than one alternative, to the one and final civilization of globalization is possible. This can be a rallying force—a myth if you like, and myth is a powerful social force—for those who resist the claims of a one civilization world and of the *pensée unique*. Greens, cultural nationalists, anti-imperialists, those who are dis-advantaged and marginalized by economic globalization and other forms of domination including feminists and native peoples, all can find reason to support this view of the world which allows for the expression of diversity and the exploration of alternative possibilities for social and economic development.

---

[35] Max Weber, 'Politics as a Vocation', in H. H. Gerth and C. Wright Mills (eds.), *From Max Weber. Essays in Sociology* (London: Routledge & Kegan Paul, 1948), pp. 120–28.

[36] This view of history is, I think, consistent with that of R. G. Collingwood, *The Idea of History* (Oxford: Clarendon Press, 1946). In *The New Leviathan* (Oxford: Cumberlege, 1942), Collingwood wrote: 'Civilization is a thing of the mind …; an enquiry into its nature, therefore, belongs to the sciences of the mind, and must be pursued by the method proper to those sciences'. (p. 280.) I believe Collingwood rejected the term 'idealism' applied to his own work. My own thinking about historical materialism includes relating 'things of the mind' to the material context of thought, which I think is not inconsistent with Collingwood although not explicit in his work. Collingwood regards civilization as a process leading towards civility and away from barbarism. Writing during World War II, Collingwood was addressing 'German barbarism' which he saw as a recent growth, specifically Nazism; but the more general conception of tendencies towards civility or barbarity stands apart from the German question. He is quite clear as an historian that this process does not imply a 'one civilization' outcome because 'the civilizing process … leads in different places and at different times to different results'. And: '… as men who create a particular society aim at creating a universal society but, owing to facts over which they have no control, find it turning under their hands into a particular society'. (p. 288.)

At this moment in world history it is not sufficient either to celebrate or to deplore the dominant tendencies as they may be perceived by a dispassionate external observer. This would leave an impression of inevitability. A critical approach will seek out the contradictions in those tendencies which would open the possibility of action towards alternative futures. It would also try to think through what desirable alternatives might look like and anticipate reconciliation among differing visions of the future rooted in the aspirations of particular groups and peoples.

Existing institutions can play a role in this process—states, international institutions, universities, churches, non-governmental organizations, and diplomacy—but in and of themselves these are not the forces to build a world climate for coexistence among civilizations. They can be agencies used to this end but a broader force must be present to activate and orient them. Behind these institutions is the climate of human purposes and attitudes that would be necessary to make these institutions work to that end. In the past, critical moments like the end of a great war have generated surges of collective motivation that pushed institutions in new directions. At present, one may well ask where such a movement could come from. Possibly the motive force could arise from deeper awareness across civilizations of their common fragility in the face of threats to the biosphere, from the dangers to all from increasing social polarization, and from the existence of uncontrolled weapons of mass destruction; and at the same time from awareness of the possibility of transcending these impending disasters through consensual action taken in mutual recognition of and respect for differences.

The two critical factors in arousing this awareness—the strengthening of civil societies as the substrata of civilizations and the existence of a core body of people capable of linking civilizations in mutual understanding—cannot be reduced to institutional formulas. They can come about only through a conscious shaping of minds towards those ends. The European medieval monastic movement or the formation of the mandarin class in China are suggestive historical precedents but differ from the present world situation insofar as each of those past movements led to a single civilizational perspective. The present challenge is to encourage the formation of *organic intellectuals* (to use Gramsci's term) who can *both* articulate the visions of possible future societies drawing upon the experience of different existing social formations *and* become links among these different visions and movements.

In today's world more and more people have acquired experience that lends itself to this task and many of them may be prepared to assume the responsibility of participating in a collective endeavour. Among teachers, aid workers, journalists, peace activists, environmentalists, diplomats and international civil servants, as examples, some individuals see the world not only through the perceptual lens they grew up with but can also, by reflecting upon their own uniqueness, imagine how other people of whom they have experience perceive the world. Such individuals are capable of thinking and acting in terms of a coexistence of different forms of common sense. The network linking them together in a global movement might arise quite informally out of the contacts inherent in their daily work. Institutionalization might follow.

Academic educators may be inspired to study comparatively the different forms of 'common sense' that coexist and to trace their origins and developmental patterns. Activists may use this knowledge to show how diversity need not mean conflict.

Journalists may in their reporting analyse the different senses of 'reality' that constitute situations of conflict while avoiding lending themselves to making propaganda for one 'true' position. Diplomats may focus on genuine reconciliation which takes account of differing perspectives rather than scoring a win for the institution they work for.

Such a movement could both work through existing institutions and generate new institutional forms. Will the impetus for it come from aversion to the dogmas and effects of globalization? Perhaps in part. Or would some more dramatic catalyst, some global catastrophe, be ultimately required to bring together the forces that could activate the movement?

Index